Python Graphics

A Reference for Creating 2D
and 3D Images

Second Edition

Bernard Korites

Apress®

Python Graphics: A Reference for Creating 2D and 3D Images, Second Edition

Bernard Korites
Duxbury, MA, USA

ISBN-13 (pbk): 978-1-4842-9659-2
https://doi.org/10.1007/978-1-4842-9660-8

ISBN-13 (electronic): 978-1-4842-9660-8

Managing Director, Apress Media LLC: Welmoed Spahr
Acquisitions Editor: Celestin Suresh John
Development Editor: James Markham
Coordinating Editor: Gryffin Winkler
Copy Editor: Mary Behr

Cover designed by eStudioCalamar

Cover image by THeBid Djimbalinux on Pixabay (www.pixabay.com)

Distributed to the book trade worldwide by Apress Media, LLC, 1 New York Plaza, New York, NY 10004, U.S.A. Phone 1-800-SPRINGER, fax (201) 348-4505, e-mail orders-ny@springer-sbm.com, or visit www.springeronline.com. Apress Media, LLC is a California LLC and the sole member (owner) is Springer Science + Business Media Finance Inc (SSBM Finance Inc). SSBM Finance Inc is a **Delaware** corporation.

For information on translations, please e-mail booktranslations@springernature.com; for reprint, paperback, or audio rights, please e-mail bookpermissions@springernature.com.

Apress titles may be purchased in bulk for academic, corporate, or promotional use. eBook versions and licenses are also available for most titles. For more information, reference our Print and eBook Bulk Sales web page at www.apress.com/bulk-sales.

Any source code or other supplementary material referenced by the author in this book is available to readers on GitHub (https://github.com/Apress). For more detailed information, please visit https://www.apress.com/gp/services/source-code.

Paper in this product is recyclable

For Sam, Oscar, Ava, Max, Margot, Alex, and Cole

Table of Contents

About the Author

Bernard Korites holds degrees from Tufts and Yale. He has been involved in engineering and scientific applications of computers for his entire career. He has been an educator, consultant, and author of more than ten books on geometric modeling, computer graphics, simulation of physical processes, and the application of computers in science and engineering.

He has been employed by Northrop Aviation, the Woods Hole Oceanographic Institute, Arthur D. Little, and Itek. He has consulted for the US Navy, Aberdeen Proving Grounds, and others. He was Chief Engineer on an expedition to take the longest sediment core sample in the North Atlantic aboard the Canadian Icebreaker John Cabot. He has explored the benthic environment aboard the submersible Alvin and has spent time aboard the USBCF Albatross. Early in his Career, he developed software to find physical interference between systems of solid objects. This found wide application in the design of power plants, submarines, and other systems with densely packed spaces.

He appreciates comments, advice, or suggestions regarding this book or any related subject. His website, `www.korites.com`, has his contact information.

About the Technical Reviewer

Andrea Gavana has been programming in Python for more than 20 years and dabbling with other languages since the late 1990s. He graduated from university with a master's degree in Chemical Engineering, and he is now a Master Development Planning Architect working for TotalEnergies in Copenhagen, Denmark.

Andrea enjoys programming at work and for fun, and he has been involved in multiple open source projects, all Python-based. One of his favorite hobbies is Python coding, but he is also fond of cycling, swimming, and cozy dinners with family and friends. This is his third book as a technical reviewer.

Acknowledgments

I would like to thank Shonmirin P. A. at Apress for her excellent help and support throughout the process of writing this book and Mark Powers, also at Apress, for his encouraging comments that came at just the right time.

Introduction

This book shows how to use Python's built-in graphics primitives (points, lines, and arrows) to create simple or complex graphics for the visualization of two- and three-dimensional objects, data sets, and technical illustrations. It is intended for Python developers who want to build their own graphic images rather than be limited by functions available in existing Python libraries.

This book shows how to create virtually any 2D or 3D object or illustration. It also shows how to display images; use color; translate, rotate, shade, and add shadows that are cast on other objects; remove hidden lines; plot 2D and 3D data; fit lines, curves, and functions to data sets; display points of intersection between 2D and 3D objects; and create digital art.

It also includes applications in a variety of sciences including astronomy, physics, population dynamics, climate change, and resource management. These applications are intended to illustrate graphics programming techniques by example, which is the best way to learn a language.

Python source code is included and explained for all illustrations in the book.

Armed with Python's primitive graphics elements and the techniques described in this book plus core math skills, especially geometry, you will be ready to create and customize detailed illustrations and data visualizations.

CHAPTER 1

Python Essential Commands and Functions

In this chapter, you will learn the essential Python commands and functions you will need to produce the illustrations shown in this book. You will learn how to use Python's basic plotting functions, set up a plotting area, create a set of two-dimensional coordinate axes, and use basic plotting primitives (the dot, the line, and the arrow), which are the building blocks you will use to construct images throughout this book. In Chapter 2, you will learn how to use these primitives to build two-dimensional images and then translate and rotate them. In Chapter 3, you will extend these concepts to three dimensions. You will also learn about colors, how to apply text to your plots, including the use of Latex commands, and the use of lists and arrays. By the last chapter, you will be able to create images such as those of Saturn in Figures 1-1a and 1-1b. These were created by Program SATURN in Chapter 10 using different input angles that describe the orientation of Saturn relative to the Sun.

Figure 1-1a. *Saturn*

B. Korites, *Python Graphics*, https://doi.org/10.1007/978-1-4842-9660-8_1

Figure 1-1b. *Saturn*

Programming Style

First, a note on the programming style used in this book. We all have preferences when it comes to style. I favor a clear, top-down, open style. Many programmers try to reduce their code to as few lines as possible. That may be fine in practice but in an instructional text, such as we have here, I believe it is better to proceed slowly in small, simple steps. The intention is to keep everything open, clear, and understandable. This also makes it easier to find errors in the Python code during development of a new program. Since I do not know the skill level of the readers, and since I want to make this book accessible to as wide an audience as possible, I generally start each topic from an elementary level, although I do assume some familiarity with the Python language. If you are just learning Python, you will benefit from the material in this first chapter. As you move through this book, you will learn more about Python's features. They will be explained as they are used. Some Python developers advocate using long descriptive names for variables such as `temperature` rather than T. I find excessively long variable names make the code difficult to read. It's a matter of preference. With relatively short programs such as we have in this book, there's no need for complex programming. Try to adopt a style that is robust rather than elegant but fragile.

As you will see throughout this book, my programs usually have a similar structure. The following shows the layout of Program DOTART, which is typical:

```
1    " " "
2    DOTART
3    " " "
```

```
4
5  import matplotlib.pyplot as plt
6  import numpy as np
7  import random
8
'

'  program statements
'

52 plt.show()
```

The statement `import matplotlib.pyplot as plt` brings into the program a library of functions that are useful in plotting. Samples can be seen in Program DOTART in lines 9-17 and elsewhere in the program. Note that each function in the body of the program is preceded by `plt` which we have defined in line 5 above as shorthand for matplotlib as in line 11 `plt.axis()` and line 22 `plt.scatter()`. The `axis()` and `scatter()` functions are included in the `matplotlib` library.

The contents of the matplotlib library can be found at `https://matplotlib.org/3.5.3/api/_as_gen/matplotlib.pyplot.html`. There are over 130 functions in the library. It is worthwhile browsing through them to see what is available for you to use in your programs.

Similarly, `import numpy as np` brings in a library of math functions. Each function from numpy must be preceded by `np.` as in line 25 `for x in np.arange ()`. The numpy library can be found at `https://numpy.org/doc/stable/`.

`random` is a library of random functions. When one of these functions is used in the program, it must be preceded by `random.` as in Program DOTART, lines 42, 43, and 44. A description of the Python random module can be found at `www.geeksforgeeks.org/python-random-module/`.

To avoid using a prefix (i.e., `plt.`, `np.`, `random.`) in front of functions, you can import functions directly. For example, looking at Program 4BOXES, line 7 `from math import sin(), cos, radians` imports `sin`, `cos`, and `radians`. When functions are imported directly in this way, it is not necessary to use a prefix when using them in the program. I will often import explicitly from the `math` library with a statement, for example, `from math import sin, cos, radians, sqrt`. Then I can use these functions in the program without a prefix.

After importing needed functions, I most often define the plotting area with `plt.axis([0,150,100,0])`. As explained in Section 1.2, these values [0,150,100,0], where the x axis (150) is 50% wider than the y axis (100), produce a round circle and a square

square without reducing the size of the plotting area, at least they do on my computer and monitor with a mathematically correct description of a circle or a square. Computer systems often differ in the spacing of horizontal and vertical rasters so you may have to fiddle with these values on your setup. You will see plenty of examples of circles and squares later. At this point, axes can be labeled and the plot titled if desired. Next, I usually define parameters (such as diameters, time constants, and so on) and lists. Lists will be discussed in Section 1.19.5. Then I define custom functions (functions you define on your own), if any. This may not be necessary at this point since custom functions can be defined at any time from within the program using the `def` function as shown in Program LTP, lines 28, 31, 34, 38, 56, 156, and 174. Another example is in Program PERSPECTIVE, lines 32-47, which create a function named `plothouse()` that plots a house. There are 15 edges to be plotted, each of which requires one line of code. Since the house requires plotting before and after rotation and perspective transformations, the use of the `plothouse()` function saves typing 15 lines of code whereas it takes only one line to invoke the `plothouse()` function once it has been defined.

Finally, in lengthy programs that employ optional inputs, I may at the bottom put a control section that invokes the options. See Program KEYBOARDDATAENTRY, lines 115-127.

Regarding axes, these are essential as a reference for plotting. `plt.axis('on')` plots the axes; `plt.grid(True)` plots a grid. They are very convenient options when developing graphics. However, if I do not want the axes or grid to show in the final output, I replace these commands with `plt.axis('off')` and `plt.grid(False)`. The syntax must be as shown here including the quotes, or lack thereof, and the capitalization of `True` and `False`. See Section 1.10 to learn how to create your own grid lines if you are not satisfied with Python's defaults.

I often begin development of a graphic by using the `scatter()` function, which produces what I call *scatter dots*. `scatter()` must be imported directly, as explained above, or used with a prefix, as explained earlier. Scatter dots are fast and easy to use and are very useful in the development stage. If kept small enough and spaced closely together, dots can produce acceptable lines and curves, although they can sometimes appear a bit fuzzy. So, after I have everything working right, I will often go back and replace the dots with short line segments using either arrows via `plt.arrow()` or lines via `plt.plot()`. As explained in Section 1.19.3, an arrow can be converted to a line by eliminating the parameters that define the size of the arrowhead.

There is another aspect to the choice of dots or lines: which overplots which? You don't want to create something with dots and then find lines covering it up. This is discussed in Section 1.14.

Some variants of Python require the `plt.show()` statement at the end of the program to plot graphics. My setup, Anaconda with Spyder and Python 3.5 (see Appendix A for installation instructions), does not require this but I include it anyway since it serves as a convenient marker for the end of the program. Finally, press the F5 key or click on the Run button at the top to see what you have created. After you are satisfied, you can save the plot by hovering your cursor over it and right-clicking. Then specify where you want it saved.

Regarding the use of lists, tuples, and arrays, they can be a great help, particularly when doing graphics programming that involves a lot of data points. They are explained in Section 1.19.5. An understanding of them, together with a few basic graphics commands and techniques covered in this chapter, are all you need to create the illustrations and images you see in this book.

The Plotting Area

A computer display with a two-dimensional coordinate system is shown in Figure 1-2. In this example, the origin of the x,y coordinate axes, (x=0, y=0), is located in the center of the screen. The positive x axis runs from the origin to the right; the y axis runs from the origin vertically downward. As you will see shortly, the location of the origin can be changed in your program as can the directions of the x and y axes. Also shown is a point p at coordinates (x,y), which are in relation to the x and y axes.

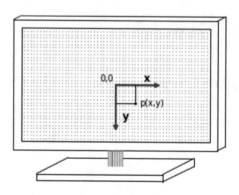

Figure 1-2. *A two-dimensional x,y coordinate system with its origin (0,0) centered in the screen. Point p is shown at coordinates (x,y) relative to x,y*

The direction of the y axis pointing down in Figure 1-2 may seem a bit unusual. When plotting data or functions such as y=cos(x) or y=exp(x), we usually think of y as pointing up. But when doing technical graphics, especially in three dimensions, as you will see later, it is more intuitive to have the y axis point down. This is also consistent with older variants of BASIC where the x axis ran along the top of the screen from left to right and the y axis ran down the left side. As you will see, you can still define y to point up or down, whichever best suits what you are plotting.

Establishing the Size of the Plotting Area

The plotting area contains the graphic image. It always appears the same *physical* size when displayed in the Spyder output pane. Spyder is the programming environment (see Appendix A). However, the *numerical* size of the plotting area, and of the values defining the point (scatter dot), line, and arrow definitions within the plotting area, can be specified to be anything. Before doing any plotting, you must first establish the area's *numerical* size. This is different from the physical size on your monitor. For example, your monitor may be 20 inches across but your graphic's dimensions may be thousands of miles. You must also specify the location of the coordinate system's origin and the directions of the coordinate axes. As an illustration, Listing 1-1 shows Program PLOTTING_AREA, which uses the plt.axis([x1,x2,y1,y2]) function in line 8 to set up an area running from x=-10 to +10; y=−10 to +10. The rest of the script will be explained shortly.

Incidentally, all images in this book, such as the monitor above, have been created using Python.

Listing 1-1. Program PLOTTING_AREA

```
1  import numpy as np
2  import matplotlib.pyplot as plt
3
4  x1=-10
5  x2=10
6  y1=-10
7  y2=10
8  plt.axis([x1,x2,y1,y2])
9
```

```
10 plt.axis('on')
11 plt.grid(True)
12
13 plt.show()
```

Listing 1-1 produces the plotting area shown in Figure 1-3. It has a horizontal width of 20 and a vertical height of 20. I could have made these numbers 200 and 200, and the area would appear in an output pane as the same physical size but with different numerical values on the axes. Line 13 contains the command `plt.show()`. The purpose of this command is to display the program's results in the output pane. With modern versions of Python, it isn't required since the plots are automatically displayed when the program is run. With older versions, it may or may not be displayed. `plt.show()` can also be placed within a program in order to show plots created during execution. Even though it may not be necessary, it's a good idea to include this command at the end of your script since it can serve as a convenient marker for the end of your program. Lines 1, 2, 10, and 11 in Listing 1-1 have been discussed earlier but will be explained further in the following sections. These commands, or variations of them, will appear in all of our programs that create graphics.

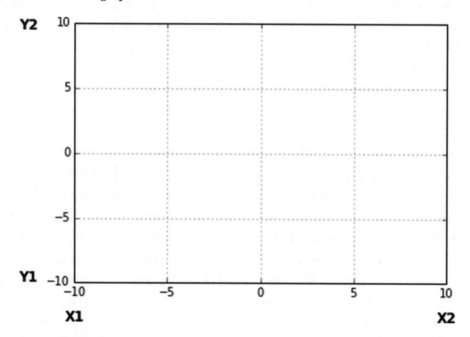

Figure 1-3. *Plotting area produced by Listing 1-1 with (0,0) located in the center of the area*

Importing Plotting Commands

To review what you learned above, while Python has many built-in commands and functions available, some math and graphics commands must be imported. Lines 1 and 2 in Listing 1-1 do this. The `import numpy as np` statement in line 1 imports math functions such as $\sin(\phi)$, $\exp()$, and so on. The `np` in this statement is an abbreviation that may be used when referring to a `numpy` function. When used in a program, these functions must be identified as coming from `numpy`. For example, if you want to code $v=e^{\alpha}$, the program statement is `v=np.exp($\alpha$)` where α was previously defined. You don't have to write out the full length `numpy.exp($\alpha$)` since you defined the shorthand `np` for `numpy` in line 1. `Np.numpy` will do. Graphics commands are handled similarly. The statement `import matplotlib.pyplot as plt` imports the library `pyplot,` which contains graphics commands. `plt` is an abbreviation for `pyplot`. For example, if you want to plot a dot at x,y you write `plt.scatter(x,y)`. I will talk more about `plt.scatter()` shortly.

Functions may also be imported directly from `numpy`. The statement `from numpy import sin, cos, radians` imports the `sin()`, `cos()`, and `radians()` functions. When imported explicitly in this manner they may be used without the `np` prefix as in `x=sin(alpha)`. There is also a `math` library that operates in a similar way. For example, `from math import sin, cos, radians` is equivalent to importing from `numpy`. You will be using all these variations in the coming programs.

There is also a graphics library called `glib` that contains graphics commands. `glib` uses a different syntax than `pyplot`. Since `pyplot` is used more widely, you will use it in your work here.

Line 8 in Listing 1-1, `plt.axis([x1,x2,y1,y2])`, is the standard form of the command that sets up the plotting area. This is from the `pyplot` library and so it is preceded by the `plt.` prefix. There are attributes to this command and there are other ways of defining a plotting area, notably the `linspace()` command, but the form in line 8 is sufficient for most purposes and is the one you will use. x1 and x2 define the values of the left and right sides, respectively, of the plotting area; y1 and y2 define the bottom and top, respectively. With the numeric values in lines 8-11 you get the plotting area shown in Figure 1-3. x1, x2, y1, and y2 always have the locations shown in Figure 1-3 when defined with the `plt.axis(x1,x2,y1,y2)` function as in line 8. That is, x1 and y1 always refer to the lower left corner, y2 to the other end of the y axis, and x2 to the other end of the x axis. Their values can change, but they always refer to these locations. They may be negative, as shown in Figure 1-4.

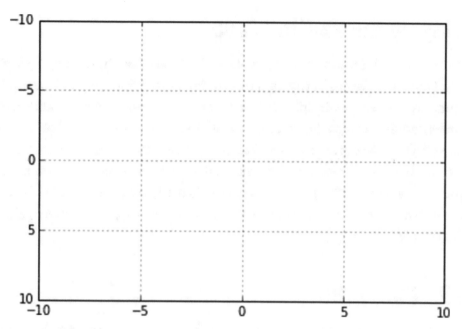

Figure 1-4. *Plotting area with (0,0) located in the center, positive y direction pointing down*

Because the x and y values specified in lines 4-7 are symmetric in both the x and y directions (i.e., −10, +10), this plotting area has the (x=0, y=0) point halfway between. In this case, the center of the area will be the origin used as reference for plotting coordinates. Since x1 < x2, the positive direction of the x axis will run horizontally from left to right. Similarly, since y1 < y2, the positive direction of the y axis will go vertically up. But earlier I said we want the positive y direction to go vertically down. You can do that by reversing the y values to y1=10, y2=−10. In this case, you get the area shown in Figure 1-4 where the positive x axis still goes from left to right but the positive y axis now points down. The center is still in the middle of the plotting area.

You could move the origin of the coordinate system off center by manipulating x1, x2, y1, and y2. For example, to move the x=0 point all the way to the left side, you could specify x1=0, x2=20. To move the (x=0, y=0) point to the lower left corner, you could specify x1=0, x2=20, y1=0, y2=20. But that would make the positive y direction point up; you want it to point down, which you can do by making y2=0, y1=20. This will make the origin appear in the *upper* left corner. You are free to position the (0,0) point anywhere, and change the direction of positive x and y, and scale the numerical values of the coordinate axes to suit the image you will be trying to create. The numerical values you are using here could be anything. The physical size of the plot produced by Python will be the same; only the values of the image coordinates will change.

Displaying the Plotting Area

In line 10 of Listing 1-1 the statement `plt.axis('on')` displays the plotting area with its frame and numerical values. If you omit this command, the frame will still be displayed with numerical values. So why include this command? Because, when creating a plot it is sometimes desirable to turn the frame off. To do that, replace `plt.axis('on')` with `plt.axis('off')`. Having the command there ahead of time makes it easy to type `'off'` over `'on'` and vice versa to switch between the frame showing and not showing. Also, after you have finished with a plot, you may wish to use it in a document, in which case you may not want the frame. Note that `'on'` and `'off'` must appear in quotes, <u>either single or double</u>.

The Plotting Grid

Line 11 of Listing 1-1, `plt.grid(True)`, turns on the dotted grid lines, which can be an aid when constructing a plot, especially when it comes time to position textual information. If you do not include this command, the grid lines will not be shown. To turn off the grid lines, change the `True` to `False`. Note the first letter in `True` and `False` is capitalized. `True` and `False` do *not* appear in quotations marks. As with `plt.axis()`, having the `plt.grid(True)` and `plt.grid(False)` commands there makes it easy to switch back and forth. Again, note that both `True` and `False` must have the first letter capitalized and do *not* appear in quotes.

Saving a Plot

The easiest way to save a plot that appears in the output pane is to put your cursor over it and right-click. A window will appear, allowing you to give it a name and specify where it is to be saved. It will be saved in the .png format (**P**ortable **N**etwork **G**raphics), which is a form of raster image file. If you are planning to use it in a program such as Photoshop, the .png format works. Some word processing and document programs may require the .eps (**E**ncapsulated **P**ost**S**cript) file. If so, save it in the .png format, open it in a program that is able to convert file formats such as Photoshop, and resave it in the .eps format. You can also convert to a .jpg (**J**oint **P**hotographic **E**xperts **G**roup), a raster image type of file. You may see this type of file referred to in different places as a .jpg or a .jpeg file.

The only reason .jpg is three characters long as opposed to four is that early versions of Windows required a three-letter extension for file names. To be safe, use .jpeg since this form seems to now be most widely used.

Grid Color

There are some options to the `plt.grid()` command. You can change the color of the grid lines with the `color='color'` attribute. For example, `plt.grid(True, color='b')` plots a blue grid. More color options will be defined shortly.

Tick Marks

The `plt.grid(True)` command will create a grid with Python's own choice of spacing, which may not be convenient. You can alter the spacings with the `plt.xticks(xmin, xmax, dx)` and `plt.yticks(ymin, ymax, dy)` commands. min and max are the range of the ticks; dx and dy are the spacing. While normally you want the tick marks to appear over the full range of x and y, you can have them appear over a smaller range if you wish. These commands appear in lines 23 and 24 of Listing 1-2.

Listing 1-2. Program TICK_MARKS

```
1  import numpy as np
2  import matplotlib.pyplot as plt
3
4  #——————————plotting area
5  x1=-10
6  x2=140
7  y1=90
8  y2=-10
9  plt.axis([x1,x2,y1,y2])
10 plt.axis('on')
11
12 #——————————grid
13 plt.grid(True,color='b')
14 plt.title('Tick Mark Sample')
```

```
15
16 #————————————tick marks
17 xmin=x1
18 xmax=x2
19 dx=10
20 ymin=y1
21 ymax=y2
22 dy=-5
23 plt.xticks(np.arange(xmin, xmax, dx))
24 plt.yticks(np.arange(ymin, ymax, dy))
25
26 plt.show()
```

The output is shown in Figure 1-5. In line 23, xmin and xmax are the beginning and end of the range of ticks along the x axis; similarly for line 24, which controls the y axis ticks. dx in line 19 spaces the marks 10 units apart from x1=-10 (line 5) to x2=140 (line 6). dy in line 22 is -5. It is negative because y2=−10 (line 8) while y1=+90 (line 7). Thus, as the program proceeds from y1 to y2, y decreases in value; hence dy must be negative.

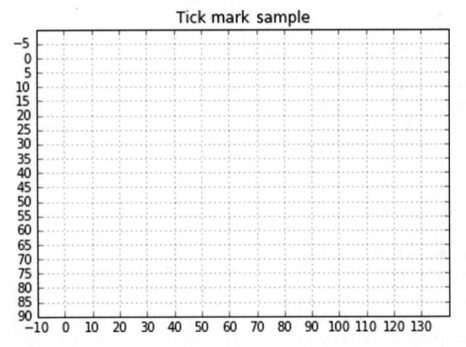

Figure 1-5. *User-defined tick marks*

Custom Grid Lines

The automatically generated grid that is produced by the plt.grid(True) command is not always satisfactory, especially if you want to include text in your plot. It is often not fine enough to accurately place text elements. But if the xtick() and ytick() commands are used to reduce the spacing, the numbers along the axes can become cluttered. The numbers can be eliminated but then you do not have the benefit of using them to position textual information such as when labeling items on a plot. The grid shown in Figure 1-3 would be more helpful if the increments were smaller. You can produce your own grid lines and control them any way you want. The code in Listing 1-3 produces Figure 1-6, a plotting area with finer spacing between grid lines.

Listing 1-3. Program CUSTOM_GRID

```
1   import numpy as np
2   import matplotlib.pyplot as plt
3
4   x1=-5
5   x2=15
6   y1=-15
7   y2=5
8   plt.axis([x1,x2,y1,y2])
9
10  plt.axis('on')
11
12  dx=.5                             #x spacing
13  dy=.5                             #y spacing
14  for x in np.arange(x1,x2,dx):     #x locations
15      for y in np.arange(y1,y2,dy): #y locations
16      plt.scatter(x,y,s=1,color='grey')   #plot a grey point at x,y
17
18  plt.show()
```

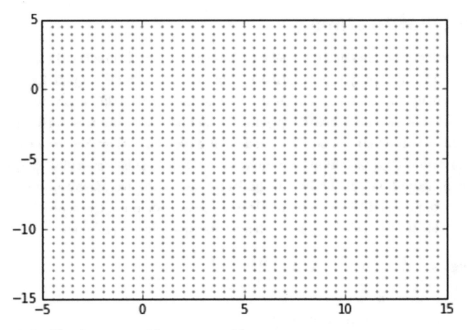

Figure 1-6. *Plotting area with custom grid*

The `scatter()` function in line 16 of Listing 1-3 plots a grey dot at every x,y location. I will discuss `scatter()` in more depth later. Note that `plt.grid(True)` is not used in this program. Lines 1-10 produce the plotting area with axes as before. This time, instead of using the `plt.grid(True)` command, you produce your own custom grid in lines 12-16. Lines 12 and 13 specify the spacing. The loop beginning at line 14 advances horizontally from left to right in steps dx. The loop beginning at line 15 does the same in the vertical direction. The size of the dot is specified as 1 by the `s=1` attribute in line 16. This could be changed: `s=.5` will give a smaller dot and `s=5` will give a larger one. The `color='grey'` attribute sets the dot color to grey. You can experiment with different size dots, colors, and spacings. Sometimes it can be beneficial to use the grid produced by `Grid(True)` along with a custom grid.

Labelling the Axes

Axes can be labeled with the `plt.xlabel('label')` and `plt.ylabel('label')` functions. As an example, the lines,

```
plt.xlabel('this is the x axis')
plt.ylabel('this is the y axis')
```

when added to Listing 1-3 after line 10 produce Figure 1-7 where the custom grid dots have been changed to a lighter grey by using the attribute color='lightgrey' in the plt.scatter() function.

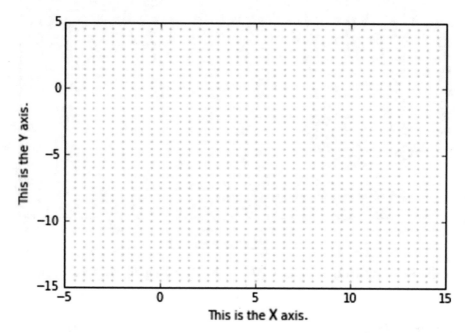

Figure 1-7. *Plotting area with axis labels and custom grid*

In Figure 1-8, you can see the matplotlib grid. This combination of Python's grid plus a custom grid makes a convenient working surface for locating elements.

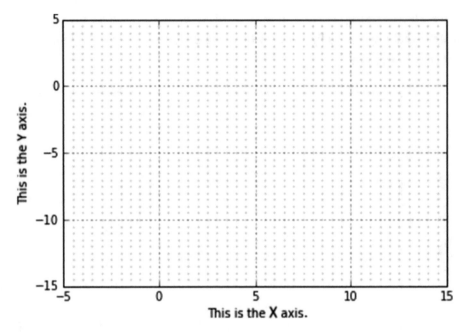

Figure 1-8. *Plotting area with axis labels, the Python grid, and a custom grid*

The Plot Title

Your plot can be titled easily with the `plt.title('title')` statement. Inserting the following line produces Figure 1-9:

```
plt.title('this is my plot')
```

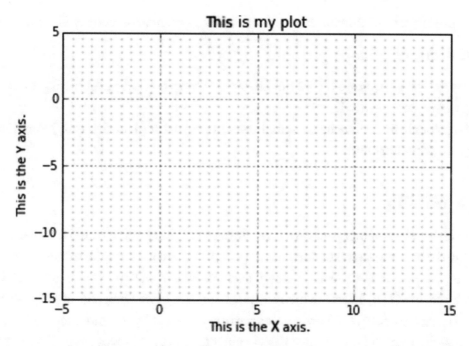

Figure 1-9. *Plotting area with axis labels, Python grid, custom grid, and title*

Colors

As you move along in this book, you will make good use of Python's ability to plot in color. Some of the colors available are

> 'k' for black
>
> 'b' for blue
>
> 'c' for cyan
>
> 'g' for green
>
> 'm' for magenta
>
> 'r' for red
>
> 'y' for yellow
>
> 'gray' or 'grey'
>
> 'lightgray' or 'lightgrey'

For example, the following statement will plot a green dot at coordinates x,y:

```
plt.scatter(x,y,color='g')
```

A swatch of many more colors can be found at `https://matplotlib.org/examples/ color/named_colors.html`.

The color attribute may be used in the `scatter()`, `plot()`, and `arrow()` functions along with other attributes.

Color Mixing

Like an artist, you can mix your own hues from the primary colors of red (r), green (g), and blue (b) with the specification `color=(r,g,b)` where r,g,b are the values of red, green, and blue in the mix, with values of each ranging from 0 to 1 (none to 100%). For example, `color=(1,0,0)` gives pure red; `color=(1,0,1)` gives magenta, a purplish mix of red and blue; `color=(0,1,0)` gives green; `color(.5,0.,.1)` gives more red and less blue in the magenta; `color(0,0,0)` gives black; and `color(1,1,1)` gives white. Keeping the r,g,b values the same gives a grey progressing from black to white as the values increase. That is, `color=(.1,.1,.1)` produces a dark grey, `color(.7,.7,.7)` gives a lighter grey, and `color(.5,.9,.5)` gives a greenish grey. Note that when specifying `'grey'` it can also be spelled `'gray'`.

In Listing 1-4, the Program COLORS shows how to mix colors in a program. Lines 7-9 establish the fraction of each color ranging from 0-1. In this example, the red component in line 7 depends on x, which ranges from 1-100. The x/100 factor gives a value of red of .01 at x=1 and 1 at x=100. The green and blue components each have a value of 0 in this mix. Line 10 draws a vertical line at x from top to bottom having the color mix specified by the attribute `color=(r,g,b)`. This vertical line sweeps across the plotting area producing Figure 1-10. The hue on the left side is almost black. This is because the amount of each color in the mix is 0 or close to it (r=.01,g=0,b=0). The hue on the right is pure red since on that side r=1,g=0,b=0; that is, the red is full strength (r=1) and is not contaminated by green or blue. In between are brightening shades of red.

Listing 1-4. Program COLORS

```
1  import numpy as np
2  import matplotlib.pyplot as plt
3
```

```
4  plt.axis([0,100,0,10])
5
6  for x in np.arange(1,100,1):
7        r=x/100
8        g=0
9        b=0
10       plt.plot([x,x],[0,10],linewidth=5,color=(r,g,b))
11
12 plt.show()
```

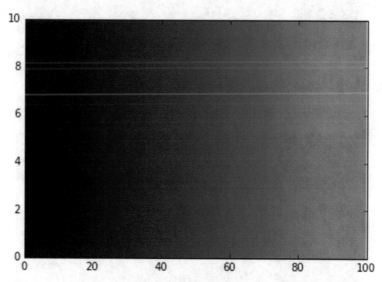

Figure 1-10. *Red color band produced by Listing 1-4 with r=x/100, g=0, b=0*

Figure 1-11 shows the result of adding blue to the mix. Figure 1-12 shows the result of adding green to the red. Mixing all three primary colors equally gives shades of grey ranging from black to white, as shown in Figure 1-13.

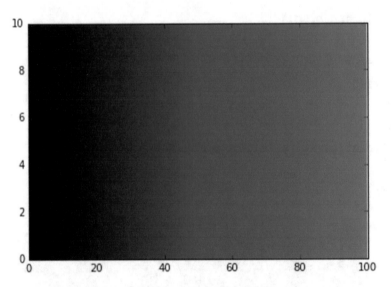

Figure 1-11. *Purple color band with r=x/100, g=0, b=x/100*

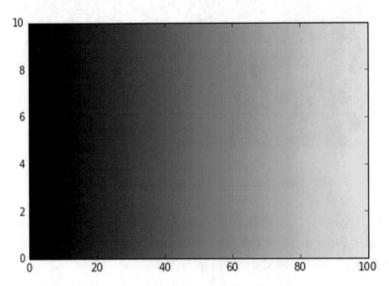

Figure 1-12. *Yellow color band with r=x/100, g=x/100, b=0*

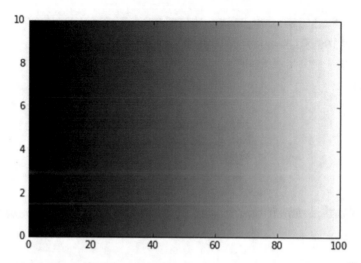

Figure 1-13. *Grey color band with r=x/100, g=x/100, b=x/100*

There are 256 values of each primary color available. Mixing them, as I did here, gives 256^3 which is almost 17 million different hues.

The way an artist tones down a color, like bright red, is to add a bit of red's complementary color, which is green. To tone down green, add a bit of red. Similarly, blue and yellow or orange are complements; they tone down one another. If you look closely at the works of a painting master, you will see the shadows on an orange face are often a tone of greenish blue. Like a painter, you are free to experiment; it's fun.

Color Intensity

The intensity of a color can be controlled with the alpha attribute, as shown in lines 6-8 in Listing 1-5, which produced Figure 1-14. alpha can vary from 0 to 1, with 1 producing the strongest hue and 0 the weakest.

Listing 1-5. Program COLOR_INTENSITY

```
1  import numpy as np
2  import matplotlib.pyplot as plt
3
4  plt.axis([0,100,0,10])
5
6  plt.scatter(60,50,s=1000,color='b',alpha=1)
```

```
7  plt.scatter(80,50,s=1000,color='b',alpha=.5)
8  plt.scatter(100,50,s=1000,color='b',alpha=.1)
9
10 plt.show()
```

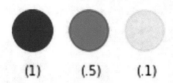

(1)   (.5)   (.1)

Figure 1-14. *Color intensity controlled by the attribute alpha shown in Listing 1-5*

Overplotting

You will normally create your graphics using the functions plt.scatter() for dots, plt.plot() for lines, and plt.arrow() for arrows and lines (arrows without heads). It is important to know which will overplot which. You don't want to create an elaborate image just to find it gets overplotted by something else. Also, it is necessary to know about overplotting if you want a colored or dark background for your graphic, as you have seen with the images of Saturn.

Figure 1-15 shows some examples of overplotting. In (A), a red line (1) goes first and then a green one (2). Notice that the second line overplots the first. In (B), a blue dot (1) is plotted first and then a red line (2). The line overplots the dot. Then another blue dot (3) is plotted. It does not overplot the line. In (C), a red dot (1) is first plotted, then a blue one (2), and then a yellow one (3). They overplot one another. In summary,

- New lines overplot old ones.

- Lines overplot dots.

- New dots overplot old ones.

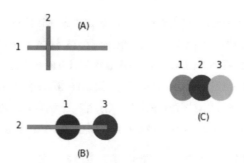

Figure 1-15. *Overplotting with lines and dots*

These examples were created by the following code:

```
#————————————(A)
plt.text(45,10,'(A)')
plt.plot([20,60],[20,20],linewidth=5,color='r')
plt.text(13,21,'1')
plt.plot([30,30],[10,30],linewidth=5,color='g')
plt.text(28,6,'2')
#————————————(B)
plt.text(45,75,'(B)')
plt.scatter(40,60,s=800,color='midnightblue')
plt.text(38,50,'1')
plt.plot([20,60],[60,60],linewidth=5,color='r')
plt.text(13,61,'2')
plt.scatter(60,60,s=800,color='b')
plt.text(58,50,'3')
#————————————(C)
plt.text(108,56,'(C)')
plt.scatter(100,40,s=800,color='r')
plt.text(98,30,'1')
plt.scatter(110,40,s=800,color='b')
plt.text(108,30,'2')
plt.scatter(120,40,s=800,color='y')
plt.text(118,30,'3')
```

Figure 1-16 shows arrows. In (A), a red line is put down first and then a green arrow. The line overplots the arrow. Then a blue arrow is drawn. The red line still takes precedence and covers the blue arrow. In (B), a dark blue dot is plotted first and then a red arrow. The arrow covers the dark blue dot. Then a blue dot is drawn. The arrow still takes precedence and covers the blue dot. In (C), a red arrow is drawn first and then a blue one. The new blue arrow covers the old red one. As a result, we can conclude that

- Lines cover arrows even if plotted after the arrow.

- Arrows cover dots.

- New arrows cover old ones.

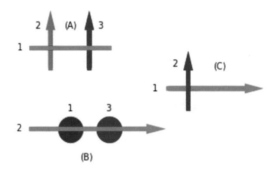

Figure 1-16. *Overplotting with lines, arrows, and dots*

In general, we can say that lines overplot everything, even older lines; dots don't overplot anything except older dots; and arrows overplot dots and older arrows but not lines.

The code that produced Figure 1-16 is

```
#──────────────────────(A)
plt.plot([20,60],[20,20],linewidth=5,color='r')
plt.text(13,21,'1')
plt.arrow(30,30,0,-20,linewidth=5,head_length=4,head_width=2,color='g')
plt.text(22,10,'2')
plt.arrow(50,30,0,-20,linewidth=5,head_length=4,head_width=2,color='b')
plt.text(54,10,'3')
#──────────────────────(B)
plt.scatter(40,60,s=800,color='midnightblue')
plt.text(39,51,'1')
plt.arrow(20,60,60,0,linewidth=5,head_length=4,head_width=2,color='r')
```

```
plt.text(12,61,'2')
plt.scatter(60,60,s=800,color='b') plt.text(58,51,'3')
#————————————————(C)
plt.arrow(90,40,40,0,linewidth=5,head_length=4,head_width=2,color='r')
plt.text(82,41,'1')
plt.arrow(100,50,0,-20,linewidth=5,head_length=4,head_width=2,color='b')
plt.text(92,29,'2')
```

Background Color

The preceding section offers implications for painting a background. Normally, images are drawn on the computer screen in a color against a white background. It can sometimes be useful to plot against a dark background, such as black or midnight blue. Figure 1-17 shows an example taken from Chapter 6. The black background is obtained by first covering the plotting area with black lines. The sphere is then drawn with green lines, which overplot the black background ones. You could also have painted the background with scatter() dots but lines take less computer processing time. If you had chosen to draw the sphere with dots, the background lines would have covered them up. If you did draw the sphere with dots, you could have painted the background with dots first and the newer sphere dots would have overplotted them.

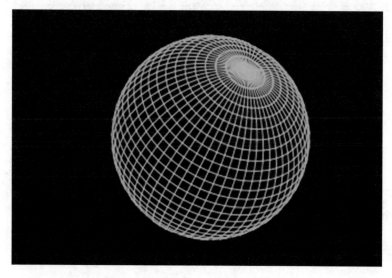

Figure 1-17. Sphere plotted against a black background

The Plotting Area Shape

When using the plt.axis() command to set up a plotting area, it will normally appear in the output pane as rectangular rather than square, even though the x and y axes dimensions, as specified by the program, indicate it should be square. This is shown in Figure 1-18, which was created by Listing 1-6 where the values in Line 7 indicate the area should be square. This distortion may be problematic at times since it can distort objects. For example, a mathematically correct circle may appear as an oval or a mathematically correct square may appear as a rectangle, as shown in Figure 1-18.

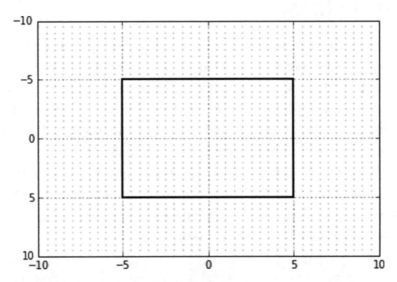

Figure 1-18. *Distortion of a mathematically correct square*

Listing 1-6. Program SQUARE

```
1   import numpy as np
2   import matplotlib.pyplot as plt
3
4   plt.grid(True)
5   plt.axis('on')
6
7   plt.axis([-10,10,10,-10])
8
9   #———————————custom grid
```

```
10 x1=-10
11 x2=10
12 y1=10
13 y2=-10
14
15 dx=.5
16 dy=-.5
17 for x in np.arange(x1,x2,dx):
18       for y in np.arange(y1,y2,dy):
19              plt.scatter(x,y,s=1,color='lightgray')
20
21 #————————————square box
22 plt.plot([-5,5],[-5,-5],linewidth=2,color='k')
23 plt.plot([5,5],[-5,5],linewidth=2,color='k')
24 plt.plot([5,-5],[5,5],linewidth=2,color='k')
25 plt.plot([-5,-5],[5,-5],linewidth=2,color='k')
26
27 plt.show()
```

As shown in Figure 1-19, you can correct this distortion by including the command

```
plt.axes().set_aspect('equal')
```

in Listing 1-6 after line 7. This squares the box by squaring the plotting area. Unfortunately, it also shrinks the plotting area's width. This may not be convenient for certain images where you may want the full width of the plotting area without the accompanying distortions.

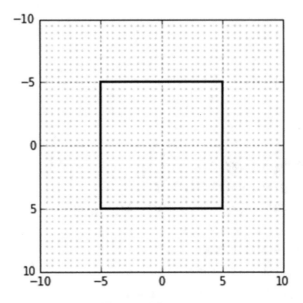

Figure 1-19. *Distortion corrected by equalizing axes*

How to Correct Shape Distortions

Figure 1-20 again illustrates the problem, this time when you try to plot a circle. You have a plotting area with numerically equal x and y dimensions, each of which is 100 units in extent. When you plot a mathematically correct circle, you get Figure 1-20, an ellipse. Listing 1-7 produced Figure 1-20.

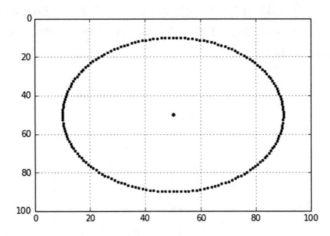

Figure 1-20. *Distortions of a mathematically correct circle*

Listing 1-7. Program DISTORTED_CIRCLE

```
1  plt.axis([0,100,100,0])
2
3  r=40
4  alpha1=radians(0)
5  alpha2=radians(360)
6  dalpha=radians(2)
7  xc=50
8  yc=50
9  plt.scatter(xc,yc,s=10,color='k')
10 for alpha in np.arange(alpha1,alpha2,dalpha):
11       x=xc+r*cos(alpha)
12       y=yc+r*sin(alpha)
13       plt.scatter(x,y,s=5,color='k')
```

Obviously, this is not going to work. You must find a way to get a true circle, not an ellipse.

Applying a Scale Factor When Plotting

The circle in Figure 1-20 is constructed with scatter() dots. You could try to apply a correction factor, a scale factor of sfx, to the x coordinate of each dot as it is plotted. How do you get sfx? Using a ruler (not very elegant I admit, but it works, if you can find one), measure on the screen of your monitor Δx and Δy, which are the x and y displayed spans of the elliptical circle. You use a ruler for this since monitors can differ in horizontal and vertical pixel spacing. What counts is what you see. Suppose these come out to be Δx=7.5cm, Δy = 5cm. The scale factor to be applied to the x coordinate of each point would be sfx=$\Delta y/\Delta x$=5/7.5 $\approx$ .67. Replacing line 11 in Listing 1-6 with

$$x=xc+\textbf{sfx}*r*cos(alpha)$$

where sfx=.67, you get Figure 1-21. The problem with this method is that every x coordinate that is to be plotted must be multiplied by sfx.

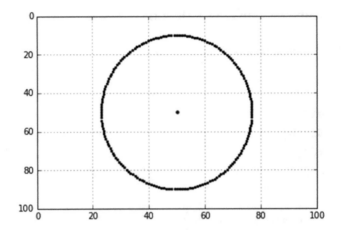

Figure 1-21. *Distortion corrected by applying a scale factor to each point as it is plotted*

The Best Way: Scaling the Axes in plt.axis( )

The best way to correct the distortion is to apply a scale factor to the x axis through the plt.axis() function. Using the circle above as an example, the scale factor to be applied to the x-axis is $\Delta x/\Delta y = 7.5/5 = 1.5$. Using this in the plt.axis() function it becomes

```
plt.axis([0,150,100,0])
```

The circle code, which produced Figure 1-22, now becomes Listing 1-8.

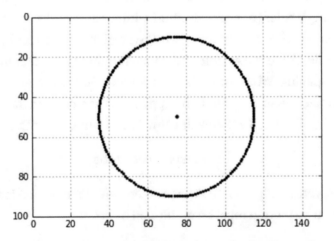

Figure 1-22. *Distortion corrected by applying a scale factor to the x axis*

Listing 1-8. THE_BEST_WAY_TO_CORRECT_DISTORTIONS

```
1  plt.axis([0,150,100,0])
2
3   r=40
4   alpha1=radians(0)
5   alpha2=radians(360)
6   dalpha=radians(2)
7   xc=75
8   yc=50
9   plt.scatter(xc,yc,s=10,color='k')
10  for alpha in np.arange(alpha1,alpha2,dalpha):
11        x=xc+r*cos(alpha)
12        y=yc+r*sin(alpha)
13        plt.scatter(x,y,s=5,color='k')
14
15  plt.show()
```

This gives you Figure 1-22, a visually true circle. Line 1 in Listing 1-8 makes sure the x axis is 1.5 times the y axis in numerical length (i.e., 150/100). The y axis could have any numerical length. You will still get a true circle or a square square as long as the x axis is 1.5 times the y axis as defined by the plt.axis() function in line 1. For example, plt.axis([0,1800,1200,0]) will work. Most of the sample programs in the book use a standard plotting area defined by plt.axis([0,150,100,0]). The 1.5 scaling factor may have to be fine-tuned for your display, if you can find a ruler :)

As you will see in Chapter 12, by adjusting the arguments in the plt.axis() function, you can shrink or magnify an image while keeping the same plotting area.

Coordinating Axes

As you have seen, to construct graphic images, points, lines, and arrows are placed on the plotting area at coordinates that have numerical values relative to an origin at x=0,y=0. While it is not necessary to show either the coordinate axes or their origin, they are often an aid when creating images since they indicate the location of the (0,0) point and the directions of positive x and y values. Figure 1-23 shows axes that are drawn using the plt.arrow() function in Listing 1-9, lines 23 and 24. If you prefer lines instead of arrows, just use lines or take the heads off the arrows by making the head dimensions equal to zero.

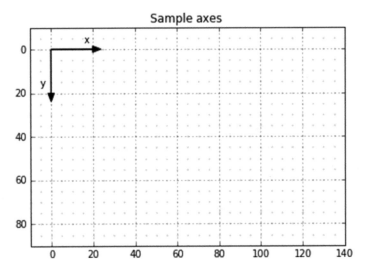

Figure 1-23. *A convenient working surface: 150x100 plotting area, Python grid, custom grid, frame out of the way*

Listing 1-9. Program COORDINATE_AXES

```
1  import numpy as np
2  import matplotlib.pyplot as plt
3
4  x1=-10 #—Δx=150    this should be Δx
5  x2=140
6  y1=90 #--⊗y=100    this should be Δy
7  y2=-10
8  plt.axis([x1,x2,y1,y2])
9
10 plt.axis('on')
11 plt.grid(True)
12
13 plt.title('Sample Axes')
14
```

```
15 #————————————grid
16 dx=5
17 dy=-5
18 for x in np.arange(x1,x2,dx):
19      for y in np.arange(y1,y2,dy):
20            plt.scatter(x,y,s=1,color='lightgray')
21
22 #————————————-coordinate axes
23 plt.arrow(0,0,20,0,head_length=4,head_width=3,color='k')
24 plt.arrow(0,0,0,20,head_length=4,head_width=3,color='k')
25
26 plt.show()
```

Commonly Used Plotting Commands and Functions

You saw the use of several plotting commands and functions in the previous sections. In the following sections, you will look at those commands, and others, in more depth. You will also learn some optional attributes for those functions. Note that I won't list all attributes available since most of them are often not used; I only include here the most important attributes that are required to create the illustrations in this book.

Points and Dots Using scatter( )

plt.scatter(x,y,s=*size*,color='*color* ')

scatter() plots a solid dot, not a circle, at coordinates x,y. size is the size of the dot: s=.5 makes a small dot and s=10 makes a bigger one. We often use the term *point* to describe a small dot. The dot's physical size in relation to your plot will depend on the plotting area's scale. The best way to determine the most appropriate size of a dot is to experiment by making it larger or smaller until you get what you want. color is the dot's color. There are other attributes available for scatter() but we won't use them in this book.

I discussed colors earlier in the section on colors; for most normal applications, those colors should be satisfactory. For example, color='r' gives a red dot and color='k' gives a black one. You can also mix RGB colors, as explained earlier, with the statement color=(r,g,b) where r=red, g=green, and b=blue.

The values of each of these three parameters can range from 0 to 1. While colors can sometimes be useful, much can be done with 'k' (black), 'grey', and 'lightgrey'. As in photography, a simple black and white image can often project more impact whereas color can be distracting. However, as a general rule, the addition of color to a plot can be a great aid in conveying information. But too much color can create confusion. For an example of scatter(),

plt.scatter(40,20,s=2,color='g')

plots a green dot of size 2 at x=40,y=20, as shown in Figure 1-24. Note that these x,y coordinates are relative to the origin of the coordinate axes.

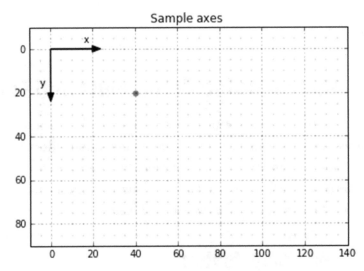

Figure 1-24. *Green scatter() dot at x=40,y=20*

Lines Using plot( )

plt.plot([x1,x2],[y1,y2],linewidth=*linewidth*,
                    color='*color* ',linestyle='*linestyle*')

This command draws a line from x1,y1 to x2,y2. It has a width specified by linewidth, a color by color, and a style by linestyle. Regarding linewidth, the appearance of a line's width will depend on the plot's scale so it can best be determined by experiment. Regarding linestyle, the ones shown in Figure 1-25 are usually sufficient.

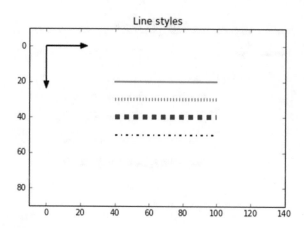

Figure 1-25. *Line styles*

The lines in Figure 1-25 were created by the following code:

```
plt.plot([40,100],[20,20],linewidth=2,color='r')
plt.plot([40,100],[30,30],linewidth=4,color='g',linestyle=':')
plt.plot([40,100],[40,40],linewidth=6,color='b',linestyle='-')
plt.plot([40,100],[50,50],linewidth=2,color='k',linestyle='-.')
```

There are other line styles available, which can be found with an Internet search.

Arrows

```
plt.arrow(x,y,Δx,Δy,line_width='linewidth',
                 head_length='headlength',
                 head_width='headwidth',
                 color='color ')
```

The arrows shown in Figure 1-26 were drawn with the following commands:

```
plt.arrow(40,20,60,0,linewidth=1,color='r',head_length=5,
    head_width=3)
plt.arrow(40,30,60,0,linewidth=1,color='g',linestyle=':',
    head_length=10,head_width=5)
plt.arrow(40,40,60,0,linewidth=1,color='b',linestyle='-',
    head_length=8,head_width=4)
plt.arrow(40,50,60,0,linewidth=4,color='k',linestyle='-',
    head_length=8,head_width=3)
```

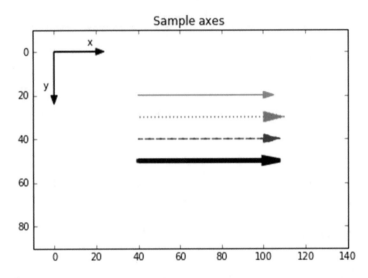

Figure 1-26. *Arrows*

Δx and Δy are the changes in x and y from beginning to end of the arrow's shaft, <u>not</u> including the head length. The linewidth establishes the thickness of the arrow's shaft. The head_width specifies the width of the head; the head_length specifies its length. The arrow's head length adds to the overall length of the arrow. Adding the shaft length to the head length to get the total arrow length is not much of a problem with vertical and horizontal arrows. For example, to draw a horizontal arrow with an overall length of 10, you can specify, for example, a Δx of 7, a head_length=3 or a Δx of 8, a head_length=2. But it can be tricky when constructing oblique arrows that must fit within a specific length. The best thing to do in that case is to use a trial and error approach adjusting Δx, Δy, and head_length until it comes out right. Usually you will want head_length and head_width to remain fixed so it is Δx, Δy that usually get changed.

Arrows can also be used to draw lines. The form of data entry is sometimes more convenient than the plt.plot([x1,x2],[y1,y2]) function. To get a line without the arrowhead, just omit the head_length and head_width attributes. That is, write the following:

plt.arrow(x,y,Δx,Δy,line_width='linewidth',color='color')

where x,y are the coordinates of the arrow's starting point; Δx,Δy are the projections of the arrow's shaft on the x,y directions.

Text

Python considers text to be a graphic element. The way to place text on a Python plot is to use the plt.text() function. The text samples displayed in Figure 1-27 were produced by the code in Listing 1-10, the Program TEXT_SAMPLES. Lines 30 and 31 show how to rotate text:

```
plt.text(x,y,'text',color='color ',size='size',fontweight='fontweight ',
     fontstyle='fontstyle',rotation=degrees)
```

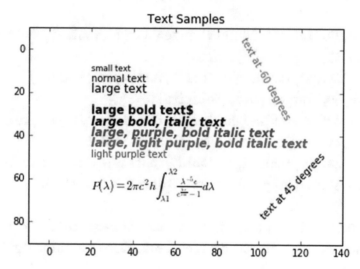

Figure 1-27. *Text samples*

Listing 1-10. Program TEXT_SAMPLES

```
1  import numpy as np
2  import matplotlib.pyplot as plt
3
4  x1=-10
5  x2=140
6  y1=90
7  y2=-10
8  plt.axis([x1,x2,y1,y2])
9
10 plt.axis('on')
```

```
11 plt.grid(False)
12
13 plt.title('Text Samples')
14
15
16 #————————————text samples
17 plt.text(20,10,'small text',size='small')
18 plt.text(20,15,'normal text')
19 plt.text(20,20,'large text',size='large')
20
21 plt.text(20,30,'large bold text',size='large',fontweight='bold')
22 plt.text(20,35,'large bold,italic
23 text',size='large',fontweight='bold',fontstyle='italic')
24 plt.text(20,40,'large, pure, bold italic
25 text',size='large',fontweight='bold',fontstyle='italic',color=(.5,0,.5))
26 plt.text(20,45,'large, light purple, bold italic
27 text',size='large',fontweight='bold',fontstyle='italic',color=(.8,0,.8))
28 plt.text(20,50,'light purple text',color=(.8,0,.8))
29
30 plt.text(100,50,'text at 45 degrees',rotation=45,color='k')
31 plt.text(90,-3,'text at -60 degrees',rotation=-60,color='g')
32
33 plt.text(20,65,r'$P(\lambda)=2 \pi c^{2} h
       \int_{\lambda1}^{\lambda2}\frac{\lambda^{-5}\epsilon}
       {e^{\frac{hc}{\lambda k t}}-1}d\lambda$',size='large')
34
35 plt.show()
```

The equation at the bottom of Figure 1-27 is Max Planck's black body radiation equation, which gives the power radiated by a black body for wavelengths from $\lambda1 \rightarrow \lambda2$. The text for this equation is plotted by line 33 in Listing 1-10. The ability of Python to display this equation illustrates some of Python's graphical power. Python can plot as text much of what can be accomplished with Latex. Notice in line 33 that the Latex text between the single quotes is preceded by the lower case **r**. The **r** in front tells Python to treat the string as a raw string, thus keeping the backward slashes needed by Latex. It is matplotlib that knows it is Latex because of the dollar sign. The Latex code is put between dollar signs. Obviously, there is more Latex text that could be displayed. In fact, this entire book was originally written and formatted in Latex. All the illustrations in it have been created with Python.

Lists, Tuples, and Arrays

To draw an object such as a box with individual lines can often require a lot of typing. For example, to draw a square box you could define each edge with

```
plt.plot([-20,20],[-20,-20],linewidth=2,linestyle='-',color='r')
plt.plot([20,20],[-20,20],linewidth=2,linestyle='-',color='r')
plt.plot([20,-20],[20,20],linewidth=2,linestyle='-',color='r')
plt.plot([-20,-20],[20,-20],linewidth=2,linestyle='-',color='r')
```

A more efficient way is to use lists:

```
x=[-20,20,20,-20,-20]
y=[-20,-20,20,20,-20]
plt.plot(x,y,linewidth=2,linestyle='-',color='g')
```

Each x[i],y[i] pair in these lists represents the coordinates of a point. The `plt.plot(x,y...)` function automatically connects point x[i],y[i] with x[i+1], y[i+1]. The fifth element in these two lists has the same coordinates as element 0. This closes the box.

Finite sequences of numbers enclosed in square brackets such as x=[x1,x2,x3,x4,x5] and y=[y1,y2,y3,y4,y5] are called **lists**. Lists are very useful, especially in computer graphics. The x,y pairs (x1,y1),(x2,y2),(x3,y3).... in these lists substitute for the syntax ([x1,x2],[y1,y2]) in individual `plt.plot` functions. You can draw virtually any shape with them; the lines will be connected in sequence.

List elements can be defined individually as above, or they can be specified as in the following structure:

```
1  x=[ ]
2  for i in range(10):
3          x.append(i*i)
4
5  print(x)
6
7  [0,1,4,9,16,25,36,49,64,81]
```

Line 1 defines an empty list x, which contains no elements. The length of the list is not specified. The loop starting at line 2 increments i from 0 to 9 (10 elements). Line 3 adds i*i to the list as an additional element every cycle through the loop starting with element 0. Line 7 shows the results.

Another way to do this is to predefine the list elements, as in line 1 below. The numbers in the list could be anything; they just serve to define the length of the list. Line 4 changes the value of each element to i*i in the loop starting at line 3.

```
1   x=[0,1,2,3,4,5,6,7,8,9]
2
3   for i in range(10):
4        x[i]=(i*i)
5
6   print(x)
7
8   [0,1,4,9,16,25,36,49,64,81]
```

A list's length can also be defined by

```
g=[0]*10
```

where the list g is defined as having 10 elements each having a value 0. To get the length of a list, use the function

```
len(x)
```

which returns the length of list x, the length being the number of elements in the list. For example, in the following script, the loop will process all elements of list x from element 0 to the last element of x, adding 3 to each element:

```
x=[4,0,7,1]
for i in range(len(x)):
     x[i]=x[i]+3
print(x)
[7,3,10,4]
```

You will use all these methods in the programs that follow so it is wise to understand them now.

A **tuple**, which is a sequence of numbers such as **x=(x0,x1,x2,x3,x4)**, is similar to a list. The difference is, aside from the style of brackets, the elements inside a tuple are immutable, meaning they cannot be changed (mutated). The elements in a list, on the other hand, can be changed. Tuples can be used without the parentheses. For example, v=7,12 is equivalent to v=(7,12), which defines a tuple having two elements, the first having a value of 7 and the second of 12.

The use of lists and tuples is certainly a more efficient method of coding, as opposed to doing it the long way; that is, by using separate np.plot() lines for each leg of a figure. On the other hand, they can sometimes be problematic. For example, if you have long x and y lists or tuples, and your plot is not coming out right, it can be a tedious process to find the offending element. The long way can be speeded up by using copy and paste. Copy the first line and paste it into the code as the second, and then change the x and y coordinate values to produce the second line segment and so on for the remaining lines. Obviously, if you have a lot of points to deal with, you won't want to copy and paste the plt.plot() function over and over again, in which case a list or tuple may become a more viable option. Whether to use lists and tuples, or do it the long way, is a personal preference.

If you want to draw just one line segment, you can use the syntax

```
x=[x1,x2]
y=[y1,y2]
plt.plot(x,y)
```

or

```
plt.plot([x1,x2],[y1,y2])
```

To draw two line segments, you can use

```
x=[x1,x2,x3]
y=[y1,y2,y3]
plt.plot(x,y)
```

or

```
plt.plot([x1,x2],[y1,y2])
plt.plot([x2,x3],[y2,y3])
```

and so on. Each method has its advantages. You will use both in this text.

In fact, Listing 1-11 uses both methods. It first plots a red square using individual np.plot commands for each side and then a green one using lists. The output is shown in Figure 1-28.

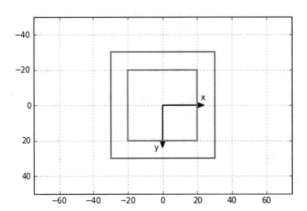

Figure 1-28. *Green box plotted using lists; red box plotted without lists*

Listing 1-11. Program LISTS

```
1   import numpy as np
2   import matplotlib.pyplot as plt
3
4   plt.axis([-75,75,50,-50])
5
6   plt.axis('on')
7   plt.grid(True)
8
9   plt.arrow(0,0,20,0,head_length=4,head_width=3,color='k')
10  plt.arrow(0,0,0,20,head_length=4,head_width=3,color='k')
11
12  plt.text(22,-3,'x')
13  plt.text(-5,25,'y')
14
15  #———————————red box (long way)
16  plt.plot([-20,20],[-20,-20],linewidth=2,color='r')
17  plt.plot([20,20],[-20,20],linewidth=2,color='r')
18  plt.plot([20,-20],[20,20],linewidth=2,color='r')
```

```
19 plt.plot([-20,-20],[-20,20],linewidth=2,color='r')
20
21 #———————————green box (list way)
22 x=[-30,30,30,-30,-30]
23 y=[-30,-30,30,30,-30]
24 plt.plot(x,y,linewidth=2,color='g')
25
26 plt.show()
```

Doing it the long way (lines 16-19) obviously requires a lot more typing than using lists (lines 22-24).

While lists and tuples have some time-saving features, they can be tricky to use. A common trap is to forget that in both lists and tuples the first element is not element 1, it is element 0. For example, with a list

$$x = [1, 2, 3, 4, 5]$$

if you were to include it in a program with the statement print('x[4])=',x[4]), you would get 5 for an answer. If you asked for x[1], you would get 2. To get a 1 for an answer, ask for x[0]. Tuples have the same idiosyncrasy. This peculiar feature is highly error-prone and must always be kept in mind when using lists and tuples. Incidentally, when asking for the value of an element in either a list *or* tuple you must use square brackets, not round ones. For example, to get the third element in x above, which is 3, you ask for x[2].

The following is a typical **array**:

```
A=np.array([ [x0,y0,z0],[x1,y1,z1],[x2,y2,z2],............[xn,yn,zn] ])
```

array() is a numpy function and must be preceded by the np prefix unless imported explicitly, as explained earlier. As you see, the array A above has n+1 elements, each of which is a list containing three items. Each element could represent the x,y,z coordinates of a point in three-dimensional space. Suppose you have an array holding the x,y,z coordinates of three points as in

```
A=np.array([ [7,3,9],[34,21,65],[19,21,3] ])
```

where each element of A represents a point. To print the x,y,z coordinates of the second point (point 1) for example,

```
print(A[1])
34,21,65
```

the result isn't 7,3,9, of course, since that is point 0. To print the z coordinate of point 1,

```
print(A[1,2])
65
```

the 1 is point 1 (0,**1**,2) and the 2 is the z coordinate (x,y,**z**). Other operations on arrays are similar to those used with lists. Arrays are very convenient to use when doing three-dimensional graphics. You will be using them in later chapters.

arange( )

arange() is a numpy function. It is useful for incrementing a floating point variable between limits. It must be used with the `np.` prefix unless it is imported explicitly with `from Numpy import arange`. The syntax is

```
for x in np.arange(start,stop,step):
```

This will produce values of x from `start` to `stop` in increments of `step`. All values are floats. The colon must be included at the end. As an example,

```
for x in np.arange(1,5,2):
    print(x)
1
3
```

What happened to the 5? Shouldn't you be getting 1, 1+2=3, 3+2=5? The 5 is lost to small roundoff errors within the computer. That is, when your computer adds 3+2, it may get something very slightly larger or smaller than 5, which means you may or may not get the 5. This illustrates one of the faults with `arange()`. The cure is to make the `stop` value slightly larger than what you want (or slightly smaller if going in the negative direction).

```
for x in np.arange(1,5.1,2):
    print(x)
1
3
5
```

If you are plotting a circle by incrementing an angle from 0 to 360 degrees and you find the circle isn't closing but is leaving a small gap, the round-off error in the np. arange function could be the problem.

start, stop, and step may have negative as well as positive values. If stop is less than start, step should be negative.

range( )

range() is useful, especially in loops, for incrementing an <u>integer</u> variable through a range. It is a standard Python function and does not need a prefix. The syntax is

```
for x in range(start,stop,step):
```

where all values are integers. As an example,

```
for x in range(1,5,1):
    print(x)
1
2
3
4
```

Again, what happened to the 5? Perversely, <u>Python chooses to have range() return values only up to **one step less than** stop.</u> To get the 5, you have to extend stop by one step.

```
for x in range(1,6,1):
    print(x)
1
2
3
4
5
```

As with arange(), start, stop, and step may have negative values. If stop is less than start, step should be negative.

Summary

In this chapter, you reviewed basic Python commands, those fundamental to Python as well as those specialized to graphics programming. You now have all the programming tools you will need to understand the following chapters and produce the illustrations shown in this book. All the graphics were created by the proper use of three fundamental building blocks: the **dot**, the **line**, and the **arrow**. Once you understand how to use them in a Python program, the main difficulties become the use of two and three-dimensional vector math and geometry, which will be ubiquitous in the work that follows.

CHAPTER 2

Graphics in Two Dimensions

In this chapter, you will learn how to construct two-dimensional images using points and lines. You learned the basic tools for creating images with Python in Chapter 1. In this chapter, you will expand on that and learn methods to create, translate, and rotate shapes in two dimensions. You will also learn about the concept of relative coordinates, which will be used extensively throughout the remainder of this book. As usual, you will explore these concepts through sample programs.

Lines from Dots

You saw how to create a line with the command

```
plt.plot([x1,x2],[y1,y2],attributes)
```

This draws a line from (x1,y1) to (x2,y2) with *attributes* specifying the line's width, color, and style. At times it may be desirable to construct a line using dots instead of using the above line function. Figures 2-1 and 2-2 show the geometry: an inclined line beginning at point 1 and ending at point 2. Its length is Q. Shown on the line in Figure 2-2 is point p at coordinates x,y. To draw the line, you start at 1 and advance toward point 2 in steps, calculating coordinates of p at each step and plotting a dot using the scatter() function at each step as you go. This analysis utilizes vectors, which will be used extensively later.

Note that you do not have coordinate axes in these models. This analysis is generic; it is applicable to any two-dimensional orthogonal coordinate directions.

© Bernard Korites 2023
B. Korites, *Python Graphics*, https://doi.org/10.1007/978-1-4842-9660-8_2

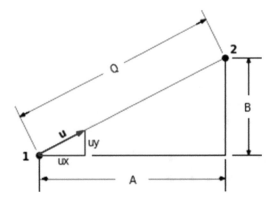

Figure 2-1. *Geometry for creating a line from dots (a)*

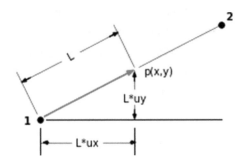

Figure 2-2. *Geometry for creating a line from dots (b)*

To advance from point 1 toward point 2, you must first determine the direction from 1 to 2. This will be expressed as a unit vector $\hat{\mathbf{u}}$ (unit vectors will be shown in bold with a hat; full vectors in bold), as in

$$\hat{\mathbf{u}} = ux\hat{\mathbf{i}} + uy\hat{\mathbf{j}} \tag{2-1}$$

where $\hat{\mathbf{i}}$ and $\hat{\mathbf{j}}$ are unit vectors in the x and y directions, and ux and uy are the *scalar* components of $\hat{\mathbf{u}}$ in the x and y directions.

ux is the cosine of the angle between $\hat{\mathbf{u}}$ and the x axis; uy is the cosine of the angle between $\hat{\mathbf{u}}$ and the y axis. ux and uy are often referred to as direction cosines. It is easy to show they are cosines: the cosine of the angle between $\hat{\mathbf{u}}$ and the x axis is ux/$|\hat{\mathbf{u}}|$, where $|\hat{\mathbf{u}}|$ is the scalar magnitude of $\hat{\mathbf{u}}$. Since $\hat{\mathbf{u}}$ is a unit vector, $|\hat{\mathbf{u}}|$=1;, the cosine of the angle is then ux/(1)=ux. This is similar for uy.

It is important to remember that

$$|\hat{\mathbf{u}}| = 1 \qquad \qquad (2\text{-}2)$$

since this feature enables you to multiply $\hat{\mathbf{u}}$ by a magnitude to get a position vector. For example, as shown in Figures 2-1 and 2-2 you can create a vector from point 1 to p, **v1p**, by multiplying $\hat{\mathbf{u}}$ by L where L is the distance from 1 to p. L gives the vector its magnitude and $\hat{\mathbf{u}}$ gives its direction. A vector from point 1 to p is then

$$\mathbf{v1p} = L\left(ux\hat{\mathbf{i}} + uy\hat{\mathbf{j}}\right) \qquad \qquad (2\text{-}3)$$

You can calculate ux and uy from coordinate values as

$$ux = A/Q = (x2 - x1)/Q \qquad \qquad (2\text{-}4)$$

$$uy = B/Q = (y2 - y1)/Q \qquad \qquad (2\text{-}5)$$

where (x1,y1) and (x2,y2) are the coordinates of points 1 and 2, and

$$Q = \sqrt{(x2 - x1)^2 + (y2 - y1)^2} \qquad \qquad (2\text{-}6)$$

Listing 2-1 gives two examples of lines drawn with dots. The results are shown in Figure 2-3. Smaller dots and closer spacing will produce a finer line (green), which is almost as good as the line obtained by using the `plt.plot([x1,x2],[y1,y2])` function.

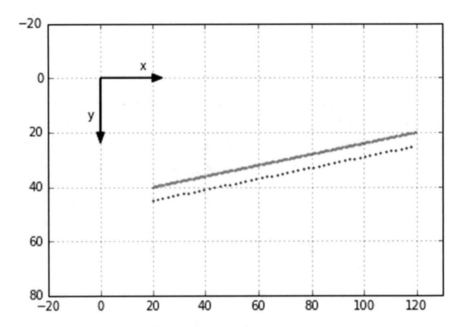

Figure 2-3. *Dot lines created by Listing 2-1*

Listing 2-1. Program DOTLINE

```
1    """
2    DOTLINE
3    """
4
5    import matplotlib.pyplot as plt
6    import numpy as np
7
8    plt.axis([-20,130,80,-20])
9
10   plt.axis('on')
11   plt.grid(True)
12
13   plt.arrow(0,0,20,0,head_length=4,head_width=3,color='k')
14   plt.arrow(0,0,0,20,head_length=4,head_width=3,color='k')
15   plt.text(15,-3,'x')
16   plt.text(-5,15,'y')
17
```

```
18  #———————————————green line
19  x1=20
20  x2=120
21  y1=40
22  y2=20
23
24  q=np.sqrt((x2-x1)**2+(y2-y1)**2)
25  ux=(x2-x1)/q
26  uy=(y2-y1)/q
27
28  for l in np.arange(0,q,.5):
29        px=x1+l*ux
30        py=y1+l*uy
31        plt.scatter(px,py,s=1,color='g')
32
33  #————————————————————————blue line
34  x1=20
35  x2=120
36  y1=45
37  y2=25
38
39  q=np.sqrt((x2-x1)**2+(y2-y1)**2)
40  ux=(x2-x1)/q
41  uy=(y2-y1)/q
42
43  for l in np.arange(0,q,2):
44        px=x1+l*ux
45        py=y1+l*uy
46        plt.scatter(px,py,s=1,color='b')
47
48  plt.show()
```

This program should be self-explanatory since the definitions are consistent with the prior analysis.

Dot Art

Interesting patterns can be created by arranging dots in a geometric pattern. Figure 2-4 shows some examples. In all three cases, the dots are arranged in a two-dimensional x,y matrix. You can vary the size of the dots, colors, and the x and y limits of the matrix. Each matrix is created with nested for loops, as shown in Listing 2-2, lines 20-22, 25-35, and 40-45. These nested loops sweep in the x direction then, at each x, in the y direction, thus filling out a rectangular area. Mondrian is composed of three separate dot rectangles plus a large red dot.

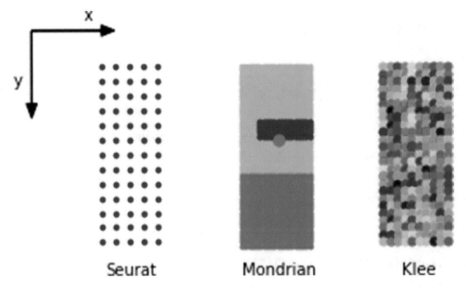

Seurat   Mondrian   Klee

Figure 2-4. *Dot art created by Listing 2-2*

In line 7, you import random. This is a library of random functions that you use in lines 42, 43, and 44 to produce random primary r,g,b color components. They are mixed in line 45. You use random's random.randrange(a,b,c) function to obtain the random values. You could also use the random functions that are included in numpy, although the syntax is a bit different. The random library is being used here to illustrate that there are other math libraries besides numpy.

random.randrange(a,b,c) returns a random number between a and b in increments c. Note that a, b, and c must be integers. To obtain a wide selection of random numbers, let a=1, b=100, and c=1 in lines 42-44. But rr in line 42 must be between 0 and 1.0 so you divide by 100 in line 42. This provides a random value for rr, the red component of the color mix, between 0 and 1.0. This is similar for rg and rb, the green and blue components, in lines 43 and 44. As you can see, the results in Klee are quite interesting.

Listing 2-2. Program DOTART

```
1    """
2    DOTART
3    """
4
5    import matplotlib.pyplot as plt
6    import numpy as np
7    import random
8
9    plt.axis([10,140,90,-10])
10
11   plt.axis('off')
12   plt.grid(False)
13
14   plt.arrow(0,0,20,0,head_length=4,head_width=3,color='k')
15   plt.arrow(0,0,0,20,head_length=4,head_width=3,color='k')
16   plt.text(15,-3,'x')
17   plt.text(-5,15,'y')
18
19   #———————————————————————————————-plot Seurat
20   for x in np.arange(20,40,4):
21        for y in np.arange(10,60,4):
22             plt.scatter(x,y,s=8,color='b')
23
24   #——————————————————————————————-plot Mondrian
25   for x in np.arange(60,80,1):
26        for y in np.arange(10,40,1):
27             plt.scatter(x,y,s=8,color='y')
28
29   for x in np.arange(60,80,1):
30        for y in np.arange(40,60):
31             plt.scatter(x,y,s=8,color='g')
```

```
32
33  for x in np.arange(65,80,1):
34        for y in np.arange(25,30,1):
35              plt.scatter(x,y,s=8,color='b')
36
37  plt.scatter(70,30,s=50,color='r')
38
39  #─────────────────────────────────────plot Klee
40  for x in np.arange(100,120,2):
41        for y in np.arange(10,60,2):
42              rr=random.randrange(0,100,1)/100 #-random red 0<=rr<=1
43              rg=random.randrange(0,100,1)/100 #-random green 0<=rg<=1
44              rb=random.randrange(0,100,1)/100 #-random blue 0<=rb<=1
45        plt.scatter(x,y,s=25,color=(rr,rg,rb))
46
47  #─────────────────────────────────────labels
48  plt.text(105,67,'Klee')
49  plt.text(60,67,'Mondrian')
50  plt.text(21,67,'Seurat')
51
52  plt.show()
```

Circular Arcs from Dots

Listing 2-3 draws a circular arc using points. This is your first program dealing with circular coordinates, angles, and trig functions. The geometry used by Listing 2-3 is shown in Figure 2-5. The output is shown in Figure 2-6.

Lines 25-31 in Listing 2-3 plot the arc. The center of curvature is at (xc,yc) as defined in lines 20 and 21. The radius of curvature is r in line 22. The arc starts at point 1, which is at an angle p1 relative to the x axis. It ends at point 2, which is at an angle p2. These angles, 20 and 70 degrees respectively, are set in lines 25 and 26 where they are converted to radians, the units required by np.sin() and np.cos(). In later programs, you will use the radians() function, which converts an argument from degrees to radians. The points on the arc are spaced an angular increment dp apart, as shown in line 27. dp is set to the total angle spanned by the arc, p2-p1, divided by 100. A wider spacing, say (p2-p1)/20, especially when combined with a smaller dot size, will give a coarser arc. The loop running from line 28 to 31 advances the angle of each point by the increment dp using the arange() function. Lines 29 and 30 calculate the coordinates of each point relative to the *global* x,y system, which has its origin at (0,0). The global coordinates are those used for plotting. xp=r*np.cos(p) and yp=r*np.(sin(p) are the coordinates of p along the arc relative to the arc's center of curvature at (xc,yc). These are *local* coordinates. The coordinates of the center of curvature (xc,yc) must be added to the local coordinates to obtain the global coordinates relative to x=0,y=0. This is done in lines 29 and 30. Line 31 plots a green dot of size 1 at each location using the global coordinates. The results are shown in Figure 2-6 and the code is shown in Listing 2-3.

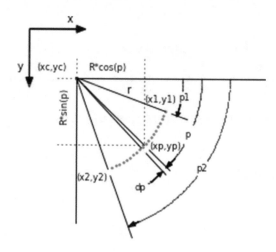

Figure 2-5. *Geometric model used for creating a circular arc with scatter() dots, created by Listing 2-4*

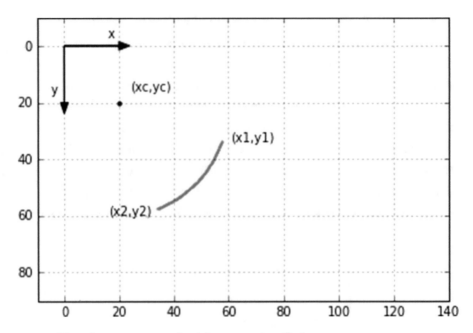

Figure 2-6. *Circular arc created with np.scatter() dots*

Listing 2-3. Program PARC

```
1   """
2   PARC
3   """
4
5   import numpy as np
6   import matplotlib.pyplot as plt
7
8   plt.axis([-10,140,90,-10])
9
10  plt.axis('on')
11  plt.grid(True)
12
13  #————————(shorten line so "axes" is on same line————————axes
14  plt.arrow(0,0,20,0,head_length=4,head_width=3,color='k')
15  plt.arrow(0,0,0,20,head_length=4,head_width=3,color='k')
16
```

```
17   plt.text(16,-3,'x')
18   plt.text(-5,17,'y')
19
20   xc=20
21   yc=20
22   r=40
23
24   #——————————(shorten)——————————————plot arc
25   p1=20*np.pi/180
26   p2=70*np.pi/180
27   dp=(p2-p1)/100
28   for p in np.arange(p1,p2,dp):
29       x=xc+r*np.cos(p)
30       y=yc+r*np.sin(p)
31       plt.scatter(x,y,s=1,color='g')
32
33   #——————————————(shorten)——————————labels
34   plt.text(61,34,'(x1,y1)')
35   plt.text(16,60,'(x2,y2)')
36   plt.scatter(xc,yc,s=10,color='k')
37   plt.text(xc+4,yc-4,'(xc,yc)',color='k')
38
39   plt.show()
```

(Listing 2-4 shows the program that created Figure 2-5.)

Listing 2-4. Program PARCGEOMETRY

```
1    """
2    PARCGEOMETRY
3    """
4
5    import numpy as np
6    import matplotlib.pyplot as plt
7
8    plt.axis([-10,140,90,-10])
9
```

```
10  plt.axis('off')
11  plt.grid(False)
12
13  #————————————————————(shorten)——————————coordinate axes
14  plt.arrow(0,0,20,0,head_length=4,head_width=3,color='k')
15  plt.arrow(0,0,0,20,head_length=4,head_width=3,color='k')
16
17  #————————————————————(sjorten)——————————labels
18  plt.text(16,-3,'x')
19  plt.text(-5,17,'y')
20
21  #————————————————————(shorten)——————————main arc
22  xc=20
23  yc=20
24  r=40
25  plt.scatter(xc,yc,color='b',s=5)
26
27  phi1=20*np.pi/180.
28  phi2=70*np.pi/180.
29  dphi=(phi2-phi1)/20.
30  for phi in np.arange(phi1,phi2,dphi):
31      x=xc+r*np.cos(phi)
32      y=yc+r*np.sin(phi)
33      plt.scatter(x,y,s=2,color='g')
34
35  plt.plot([xc,xc+r*np.cos(phi1)],[yc,yc+r*np.sin(phi1)],color='k')
36
37  x1=xc+(r+3)*np.cos(phi1)
38  x2=xc+(r+10)*np.cos(phi1)
39  y1=yc+(r+3)*np.sin(phi1)
40  y2=yc+(r+10)*np.sin(phi1)
41  plt.plot([x1,x2],[y1,y2],color='k')
42
43  x1=xc+(r+3)*np.cos(phi2)
44  x2=xc+(r+30)*np.cos(phi2)
```

```
45   y1=yc+(r+3)*np.sin(phi2)
46   y2=yc+(r+30)*np.sin(phi2)
47   plt.plot([x1,x2],[y1,y2],color='k')
48
49   plt.plot([xc,xc+r*np.cos(phi2)],[yc,yc+r*np.sin(phi2)],color='k')
50
51   phihalf=(phi1+phi2)*.5
52   phi3=phihalf-dphi/2
53   phi4=phihalf+dphi/2
54
55   plt.plot([xc,xc+r*np.cos(phi3)],[yc,yc+r*np.sin(phi3)],color='k')
56   plt.plot([xc,xc+r*np.cos(phi4)],[yc,yc+r*np.sin(phi4)],color='k')
57
58   x1=xc+(r+3)*np.cos(phi3)
59   x2=xc+(r+15)*np.cos(phi3)
60   y1=yc+(r+3)*np.sin(phi3)
61   y2=yc+(r+15)*np.sin(phi3)
62   plt.plot([x1,x2],[y1,y2],color='k')
63
64   x1=xc+(r+3)*np.cos(phi4)
65   x2=xc+(r+15)*np.cos(phi4)
66   y1=yc+(r+3)*np.sin(phi4)
67   y2=yc+(r+15)*np.sin(phi4)
68   plt.plot([x1,x2],[y1,y2],color='k')
69
70   #————————————————(shorten)————————————P1 arc
71   dphi=(phi3)/100.
72   for phi in np.arange(0,phi1/2-3.2*np.pi/180,dphi):
73       x=xc+(r+5)*np.cos(phi)
74       y=yc+(r+5)*np.sin(phi)
75       plt.scatter(x,y,s=.1,color='k')
76
77   for phi in np.arange(phi1/2+3.3*np.pi/180,phi1,dphi):
78       x=xc+(r+5)*np.cos(phi)
79       y=yc+(r+5)*np.sin(phi)
```

```
80        plt.scatter(x,y,s=.1,color='k')
81
82  #───────────────────────(shorten)────────────P2 arc
83  dphi=(phi3)/100.
84  for phi in np.arange(0,phi2/2-3.2*np.pi/180,dphi):
85        x=xc+(r+25)*np.cos(phi)
86        y=yc+(r+25)*np.sin(phi)
87        plt.scatter(x,y,s=.1,color='k')
88
89  dphi=(phi3)/100.
90  for phi in np.arange(phi2/2+3.2*np.pi/180,phi2,dphi):
91        x=xc+(r+25)*np.cos(phi)
92        y=yc+(r+25)*np.sin(phi)
93        plt.scatter(x,y,s=.1,color='k')
94
95  #───────────────────────(shorten)────────────P arc
96  dphi=(phi3)/100.
97  for phi in np.arange(0,phi3/2-.5*np.pi/180,dphi):
98        x=xc+(r+13)*np.cos(phi)
99        y=yc+(r+13)*np.sin(phi)
100       plt.scatter(x,y,s=.1,color='k')
101
102 dphi=(phi3)/100.
103 for phi in np.arange(phi3/2+9.*np.pi/180,phi3,dphi):
104       x=xc+(r+13)*np.cos(phi)
105       y=yc+(r+13)*np.sin(phi)
106       plt.scatter(x,y,s=.1,color='k')
107
108 #───────────────────────(shorten)────────dp arc
109 dphi=(phi3)/100.
110 for phi in np.arange(phi3+5*dphi,phi3+25*dphi,dphi):
111       x=xc+(r+13)*np.cos(phi)
112       y=yc+(r+13)*np.sin(phi)
113       plt.scatter(x,y,s=.1,color='k')
114
```

```
115 plt.plot([xc,100],[yc,yc],'k')
116 plt.plot([xc,xc],[yc,80],'k')
117
118 #———————————————(shorten)——————————labels
119 plt.text(71,58,'p2',size='small')
120 plt.text(66,44,'p',size='small')
121 plt.text(63,29,'p1',size='small')
122 plt.text(45,66,'dp',size='small')
123 plt.text(41,26,'r')
124 plt.text(3,17,'(xc,yc)',size='small')
125 plt.plot([xc+r*np.cos(phi3),xc+r*np.cos(phi3)],[yc-8,yc+r*np.
    sin(phi3)],'k:')
126 plt.plot([xc,xc],[yc-2,yc-8],'k:')
127 plt.text(25,17,'R*cos(p)',size='small')
128
129 plt.plot([xc-8,xc+r*np.cos(phi3)],[yc+r*np.sin(phi3),yc+r*np.
    sin(phi3)],'k:')
130 plt.plot([xc-2,xc-8],[yc,yc],'k:')
131 plt.text(13,27,'R*sin(p)',size='small',rotation=90)
132
133 plt.text(49,30,'(x1,y1)',size='small')
134 plt.text(20,62,'(x2,y2)',size='small')
135 plt.text(51,49,'(xp,yp)',size='small')
136
137 #———————————————(shorten)——————————arrow heads
138 plt.arrow(47,79,-2,1,head_length=3,head_width=2,color='k')
139 plt.arrow(62,53,-2,2,head_length=2.9,head_width=2,color='k')
140 plt.arrow(64,31,-.9,3,head_length=2,head_width=2,color='k')
141 plt.arrow(52,63,3,-3,head_length=2,head_width=2,color='k')
142
143 plt.show()
```

Circular Arcs from Line Segments

Instead of plotting dots with `np.scatter()` at points along the arc, you can create a finer arc using straight-line segments between points. If you replace the "plot arc" routine in Listing 2-3, beginning at line 24, with

```
24  #————————————————————plot arc
25  p1=20*np.pi/180
26  p2=70*np.pi/180
27  dp=(p2-p1)/100
28  xlast=xc+r*np.cos(p1)
29  ylast=yc+r*np.sin(p1)
30  for p in np.arange(p1+dp,p2,dp):
31          x=xc+r*np.cos(p)
32          y=yc+r*np.sin(p)
33          plt.plot([xlast,x],[ylast,y],color='g')
34          xlast=x
35          ylast=y
```

you get the arc shown in Figure 2-7. In lines 28 and 29 of the code above you define xlast and ylast. These are the last x and y coordinate values plotted at the end of the previous line segment. Since you are just starting to plot the arc before the loop begins, these are initially set equal to the arc's starting point where p=p1. You will need them to plot the first arc segment in line 33. Parameters p, p1, p2, and dp are the same as before. Imagine the loop 30-35 is just starting to run. Lines 31 and 32 calculate the global coordinates of the *end* of the first line segment, which is dp into the arc. Using the previously set values xlast and ylast, which are the coordinates of the beginning of that line segment in 28 and 29, line 33 plots the first line segment. Lines 34 and 35 update the end coordinates of the first segment as xlast, ylast. These will be used as the beginning coordinates of the second line segment. The loop continues to the end of the arc using the end of the preceding segment as the beginning of the next one. Notice in line 30 the loop begins at p1+dp, the end angle of the first line segment. This isn't actually necessary and the beginning of the loop could be set to p1 as before, in which case the first line segment would have zero length. The loop would continue to the end of the arc as before.

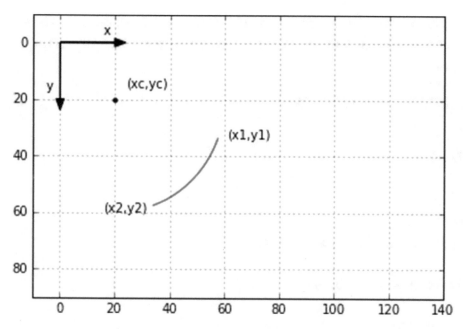

Figure 2-7. *Circular arc created with plt.plot() line segments*

In future work, you will sometimes use curves constructed of dots instead of line segments. Even though dots do not produce as fine results, they avoid complicating the plotting algorithm, which can sometimes obscure the logic of the script. However, line segments do produce superior results so you will use them as well.

Circles

A full circle is just a 360° arc. You can make a full circle by changing the beginning and end angles of the arc in the previous section to p1=0 and p2=360 degrees. This is done in lines 24 and 25 of Listing 2-5. The output is shown in Figure 2-8. Three circles and a solid disc are plotted at different locations. They have different colors and widths. Half the green circle is plotted with solid-line segments, the other half with dashed lines 29-37. The decision to plot a solid or dashed line is made by the if logic between lines 32 and 35. This changes the linestyle attribute in line 33. The blue solid disc is made by plotting concentric circles with radii from r1=0 to the disc's outer radius r2. You could, of course, also make a solid disk with the np.scatter() function. You should be able to follow the logic used here to create the various circles by examining the script in Listing 2-5.

This program could have been shortened by the use of functions. It has been left open for the sake of clarity by using cut and paste to reproduce sections of redundant code.

Listing 2-5. Program CIRCLES

```
1     """
2     CIRCLES
3     """
4
5     import numpy as np
6     import matplotlib.pyplot as plt
7
8     plt.axis([-75,75,50,-50])
9
10    plt.axis('on')
11    plt.grid(True)
12
13    plt.arrow(0,0,20,0,head_length=4,head_width=3,color='k')
14    plt.arrow(0,0,0,20,head_length=4,head_width=3,color='k')
15
16    plt.text(16,-3,'x')
17    plt.text(-5,17,'y')
18
19    #————————————————————————green circle
20    xc=0
21    yc=0
22    r=40
23
24    p1=0*np.pi/180
25    p2=360*np.pi/180
26    dp=(p2-p1)/100
27    xlast=xc+r*np.cos(p1)
28    ylast=yc+r*np.sin(p1)
29    for p in np.arange(p1,p2+dp,dp):
30            x=xc+r*np.cos(p)
```

```
31        y=yc+r*np.sin(p)
32        if p > 90*np.pi/180 and p < 270*np.pi/180:
33            plt.plot([xlast,x],[ylast,y],color='g',linestyle=':')
34        else:
35            plt.plot([xlast,x],[ylast,y],color='g')
36        xlast=x
37        ylast=y
38
39 plt.scatter(xc,yc,s=15,color='g')
40
41 #————————————————————(shorten)————red circle
42 xc=-20
43 yc=-20
44 r=10
45
46 p1=0*np.pi/180
47 p2=360*np.pi/180
48 dp=(p2-p1)/100
49 xlast=xc+r*np.cos(p1)
50 ylast=yc+r*np.sin(p1)
51 for p in np.arange(p1,p2+dp,dp):
52        x=xc+r*np.cos(p)
53        y=yc+r*np.sin(p)
54        plt.plot([xlast,x],[ylast,y],linewidth=4,color='r')
55        xlast=x
56        ylast=y
57
58 plt.scatter(xc,yc,s=15,color='r')
59
60 #————————————————————(shorten)————purple circle
61 xc=20
62 yc=20
63 r=50
64
65 p1=0*np.pi/180
```

```
66   p2=360*np.pi/180
67   dp=(p2-p1)/100
68   xlast=xc+r*np.cos(p1)
69   ylast=yc+r*np.sin(p1)
70   for p in np.arange(p1,p2+dp,dp):
71        x=xc+r*np.cos(p)
72        y=yc+r*np.sin(p)
73        plt.plot([xlast,x],[ylast,y],linewidth=2,color=(.8,0,.8))
74        xlast=x
75        ylast=y
76
77   plt.scatter(xc,yc,color=(.5,0,.5))
78
79   #————————————————(shorten)—————————blue disc
80   xc=-53
81   yc=-30
82   r1=0
83   r2=10
84   dr=1
85
86   p1=0*np.pi/180
87   p2=360*np.pi/180
88   dp=(p2-p1)/100
89   xlast=xc+r1*np.cos(p1)
90   ylast=yc+r1*np.sin(p1)
91   for r in np.arange(r1,r2,dr):
92        for p in np.arange(p1,p2+dp,dp):
93             x=xc+r*np.cos(p)
94             y=yc+r*np.sin(p)
95             plt.plot([xlast,x],[ylast,y],linewidth=2,color=(0,0,.8))
96             xlast=x
97             ylast=y
98
99   plt.show()
```

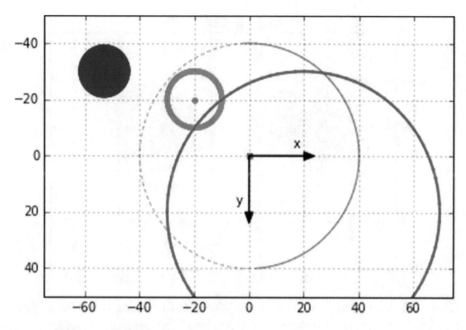

Figure 2-8. *Circles created by Listing 2-5*

Dot Discs

Two discs created with different dot patterns are shown in Figure 2-9. The disc labeled "r,p" is drawn by placing dots in a traditional polar r,p array where r is the radius from the center and p is the angle. The algorithm starts at line 21 in Listing 2-6. The script in Listing 2-6 should be self-explanatory. The only issue with this plot is that the dots are not uniformly spaced but are further apart as the radius increases. This may be undesirable in some situations.

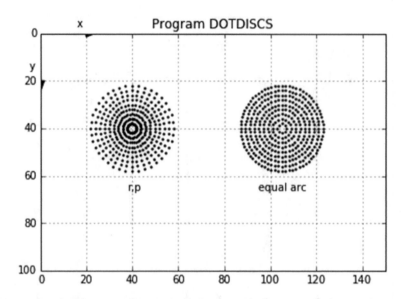

Figure 2-9. *Discs created by different dot patterns in Listing 2-6 where "r,p" contains simple polar coordinates and "equal arc" has modified polar coordinates*

The "equal arc" disc, beginning in line 38, appears better visually. As with the "r,p" disc, the dots are equally spaced in the radial direction. However, in the "equal arc" disc, the number of dots in the circumferential direction at each radial location becomes larger as the radius increases, thus keeping the circumferential arc spacing between dots constant. The model used is shown in Figure 2-10. dc is the circumferential spacing between dots a and b at rmax, the outer edge of the disk. dp is the angular spacing between radii to a and b. To achieve more uniform spacing across the disc, you hold dc constant at all radii. A typical radial location is shown at r=rmax/2. dc at this radius is the same as at rmax and is equal to dc. To accommodate this spacing, the angle between adjacent dots must increase to drp.

In line 44 of Listing 2-6, the disc's outer radius is set to 20. The radial spacing is set to 2 in line 45. Keeping in mind that the circumferential spacing between two points on a circular arc is r×dp where r is the radius and dp is the angle between the points, line 46 calculates dc where you have arbitrarily set the number of dots at rmax to 40 per π radians (80 around the complete circumference). The loop beginning at line 48 starts at r=dr and advances in the radial direction to rmax in steps dr. At each value of r, the angle between dots dpr required to keep the circumferential spacing equal to dc is calculated in line 49. The loop beginning at line 50 then places the dots circumferentially.

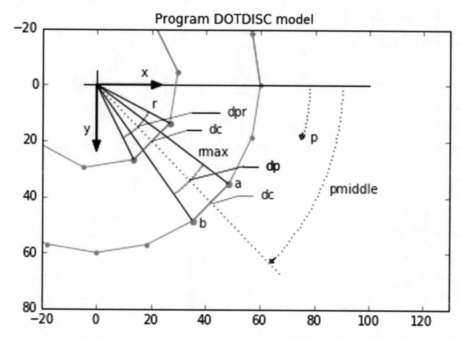

Figure 2-10. *Model for "equal arc" disc used by Listing 2-6*

Listing 2-6. Program DOTDISCS

```
1    """
2    DOTDISCS
3    """
4
5    import matplotlib.pyplot as plt
6    import numpy as np
7    import random as rnd
8
9    plt.axis([0,150,100,0])
10
11   plt.axis('off')
12   plt.grid(False)
13
14   plt.arrow(0,0,20,0,head_length=4,head_width=3,color='k')
15   plt.arrow(0,0,0,20,head_length=4,head_width=3,color='k')
16
```

```
17   plt.text(16,-3,'x')
18   plt.text(-5,17,'y')
19
20   #————————————————(shorten)——————————simple r,p
dot pattern
21   xc=40
22   yc=25
23
24   p1=0
25   p2=2*np.pi
26   dp=np.pi/20
27
28   rmax=20
29   dr=2
30
31   for r in np.arange(dr,rmax,dr):
32        for p in np.arange(p1,p2,dp):
33             x=xc+r*np.cos(p)
34             y=yc+r*np.sin(p)
35             plt.scatter(x,y,s=2,color='k')
36
37   #————————————————————————equal arc length dot pattern
38   xc=40
39   yc=70
40
41   p1=0
42   p2=2*np.pi
43
44   rmax=20
45   dr=2
46   dc=np.pi*rmax/40
47
48   for r in np.arange(dr,rmax,dr):
49        dpr=dc/r
50        for p in np.arange(p1,p2,dpr):
```

```
51              x=xc+r*np.cos(p)
52              y=yc+r*np.sin(p)
53              plt.scatter(x,y,s=2,color='k')
54
55  #─────────────────────(shorten───────────────────────labels
56  plt.text(38,66,'r,p')
57  plt.text(95,66,'equal arc')
58
59  plt.show()
```

Ellipses

Ellipses are shown in Figure 2-12. They were drawn by Listing 2-7. The model used by Listing 2-7 is shown in Figure 2-11. This was drawn by Listing 2-8. The dimension a is called the semi-major since it refers to half the greater width; b is the semi-minor. 2a and 2b are the major and minor dimensions.

The equation of an ellipse, which we are all familiar with, is

$$\frac{x^2}{a^2} + \frac{y^2}{b^2} = 1 \qquad (2\text{-}7)$$

In the special case where a=b=r, this degenerates into a circle, as in

$$x^2 + y^2 = r^2 \qquad (2\text{-}8)$$

where r is the radius.

A possible strategy to use when plotting an ellipse is to start at x=-a and advance in the +x direction using Equation 2-7 to calculate y at each x, and then plot either a dot or a line segment from the last step, as you have done in the past. The y coordinate is easily derived from Equation 2-7 as

$$y = b\sqrt{1 - \frac{x^2}{a^2}} \qquad (2\text{-}9)$$

This seems easy enough. The green ellipse in Figure 2-12 was drawn this way. However, there is a problem. Look at Listing 2-7, lines 48, 49, and 50; the square root in Equation 2-9 and in line 48 gives uncertain results as x approaches +a and line 48 tries to take the square root of a number very close to zero. This is caused by roundoff errors in Python's calculations. The manifestation of this shows up as a gap at the +a side of the ellipse. In the algorithm for the green ellipse, this gap is closed by lines 54 and 55. You can get a decent ellipse this way but you have to be careful.

Another way is to use polar coordinates, as shown in Figure 2-11. You want to determine the coordinates (xp,yp) for a point on the ellipse as a function of the angle p. By varying p, you will have the information you need to plot the ellipse. To determine (xp,yp) vs. p, you note that it lies on the intersection of the ellipse and the radial line. This point is indicated by the red dot. Incidentally, the dot does not appear to lie exactly at the intersection, as can be seen. This is because the scale factor used to adjust the x axis values in line 8 of Listing 2-8 is a bit off. It's from a rough measurement with a ruler and then the results of the calculation were rounded off to determine the scale factor. The resulting slight errors are showing up here. The equation of the line can be determined from the following:

$$xp = r\cos(p) \tag{2-10}$$

$$yp = r\sin(p) \tag{2-11}$$

Combining the above,

$$\frac{yp}{xp} = \frac{r\sin(p)}{r\cos(p)} = \tan(p) \tag{2-12}$$

$$yp = xp\,\tan(p) \tag{2-13}$$

You know that (xp,yp) lies at the intersection of the line and the ellipse. This is where the equations for both the line and the ellipse are satisfied by xp and yp. You can determine the coordinates of this point by substituting Equation 2-13 into Equation 2-7,

$$\frac{xp^2}{a^2} + \frac{xp^2\tan^2 p}{b^2} = 1 \tag{2-14}$$

which works out to

$$xp = ab\left[b^2 + a^2 tan^2\left(p\right)\right]^{-\frac{1}{2}}$$

(2-15)

$$yp = ab\left[a^2 + b^2\,\frac{1}{tan^2\left(p\right)}\right]^{-\frac{1}{2}}$$

(2-16)

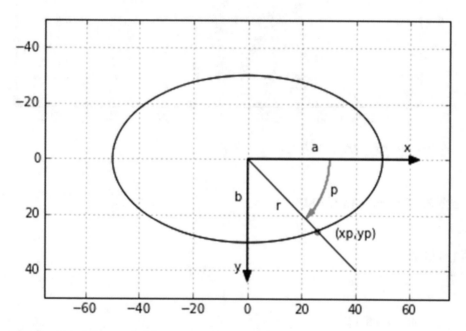

Figure 2-11. *Model created by Listing 2-8 and used by Listing 2-7*

Equations 2-15 and 2-16 are implemented in Listing 2-7 to draw the red ellipse between lines 20 and 36, the green ellipse between lines 39 and 55, and the blue ellipse in lines 58 and 69. The output is shown in Figure 2-12. When drawing the green ellipse, the program loops from -a to +a and uses Equation 2-9 to calculate y values. As mentioned, this can lead to roundoff errors near the extremity of the ellipse at x=+a, which leaves a gap in the ellipse. This is corrected in lines 54 and 55, which draw short lines to close the gap. Note that the blue ellipse is filled in. This is accomplished by line 69, which plots vertical lines from the top to the bottom of the ellipse.

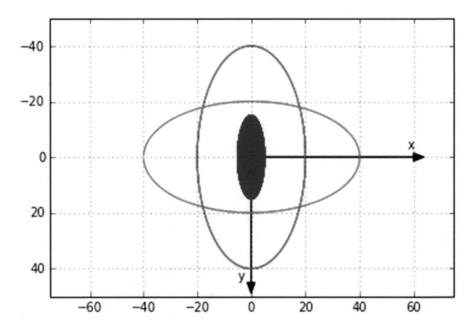

Figure 2-12. *Ellipses created by Listing 2-7*

Listing 2-7. Program ELLIPSES

```
1    """
2    ELLIPSES
3    """
4
5    import numpy as np
6    import matplotlib.pyplot as plt
7
8    plt.axis([-75,75,50,-50])
9
10   plt.axis('on')
11   plt.grid(True)
12
13   plt.arrow(0,0,60,0,head_length=4,head_width=3,color='k')
14   plt.arrow(0,0,0,45,head_length=4,head_width=3,color='k')
15
16   plt.text(58,-3,'x')
```

```
17   plt.text(-5,44,'y')
18
19   #————————(shorten)————————————red ellipse
20   a=40
21   b=20.
22   p1=0
23   p2=180*np.pi/180
24   dp=.2*np.pi/180
25
26   xplast=a
27   yplast=0
28   for p in np.arange(p1,p2,dp):
29           xp=np.abs(a*b*(b*b+a*a*(np.tan(p))**2.)**-.5)
30           yp=np.abs(a*b*(a*a+b*b/(np.tan(p)**2.))**-.5)
31           if p > np.pi/2:
32                   xp=-xp
33           plt.plot([xplast,xp],[yplast,yp],color='r')
34           plt.plot([xplast,xp],[-yplast,-yp],color='r')
35           xplast=xp
36           yplast=yp
37
38   #————————————(shorten)——————————green ellipse
39   a=20.
40   b=40.
41   xp1=-a
42   xp2=a
43   dx=.1
44
45   xplast=-a
46   yplast=0
47   for xp in np.arange(xp1,xp2,dx):
48       yp=b*(1-xp**2./a**2.)**.5
49       plt.plot([xplast,xp],[yplast,yp],linewidth=1,color='g')
50       plt.plot([xplast,xp],[-yplast,-yp],linewidth=1,color='g')
51       xplast=xp
```

```
52        yplast=yp
53
54   plt.plot([xplast,a],[yplast,0],linewidth=1,color='g'
55   plt.plot([xplast,a],[-yplast,0],linewidth=1,color='g'
56
57   #————————————————(shorten)————————blue ellipse
58   a=5.
59   b=15.
60   p1=0
61   p2=180*np.pi/180
62   dp=.2*np.pi/180
63
64   for p in np.arange(p1,p2,dp):
65        xp=np.abs(a*b*(b*b+a*a*(np.tan(p))**2.)**-.5)
66        yp=np.abs(a*b*(a*a+b*b/(np.tan(p)**2.))**-.5)
67        if p > np.pi/2:
68            xp=-xp
69        plt.plot([xp,xp],[yp,-yp],linewidth=1,color='b')
70
71   plt.show()
```

(Listing 2-8 was used to create Figure 2-11.)

Listing 2-8. Program ELLIPSEMODEL

```
1    """
2    ELLIPSEMODEL
3    """
4
5    import numpy as np
6    import matplotlib.pyplot as plt
7
8    plt.axis([-75,75,50,-50])
9
10   plt.axis('on')
11   plt.grid(True)
12
```

```
13  plt.arrow(0,0,60,0,head_length=4,head_width=3,color='k')
14  plt.arrow(0,0,0,40,head_length=4,head_width=3,color='k')
15
16  plt.text(58,-3,'x')
17  plt.text(-5,40,'y')
18
19  #————————————————(shorten)            —————————ellipse
20  a=50.
21  b=30.
22  p1=0.
23  p2=180.*np.pi/180.
24  dp=(p2-p1)/180.
25
26  xplast=a
27  yplast=0
28  for p in np.arange(p1,p2+dp,dp):
29      xp=np.abs(a*b*(b*b+a*a*(np.tan(p))**2.)**-.5)
30      yp=np.abs(a*b*(a*a+b*b/(np.tan(p)**2.))**-.5)
31      if p > np.pi/2:
32          xp=-xp
33      plt.plot([xplast,xp],[yplast,yp],color='k')
34      plt.plot([xplast,xp],[-yplast,-yp],color='k')
35      xplast=xp
36      yplast=yp
37
38  #————————————————(shorten)————————————line
39  plt.plot([0,40],[0,40],color='k')
40
41  #————————————————(shorten————————————point
42  p=45.*np.pi/180.
43  xp=np.abs(a*b*(b*b+a*a*(np.tan(p))**2.)**-.5)
44  yp=np.abs(a*b*(a*a+b*b/(np.tan(p)**2.))**-.5)
45  plt.scatter(xp,yp,s=20,color='r')
46
```

```
47  #————————————————(shorten)————————————labels
48  plt.text(23,-3,'a',color='k')
49  plt.text(-5,15,'b',color='k')
50  plt.text(32,28,'(xp,yp)')
51  plt.text(30,12,'p')
52  plt.text(10,18,'r')
53
54  #————————————————(shorten)————————————p arc
55  p1=0
56  p2=45*np.pi/180
57  dp=(p2-p1)/180
58  r=30
59  for p in np.arange(p1,p2,dp):
60          x=r*np.cos(p)
61          y=r*np.sin(p)
62          plt.scatter(x,y,s=.1,color='r')
63
64  plt.arrow(25,17.5,-1,1,head_length=3,head_width=2,color='r')
65
66  plt.show()
```

2D Translation

In two dimensions, an object has three independent degrees of freedom: it can rotate around one axis direction that is perpendicular to the plane and it can translate in two directions (x and y) within the plane. Pure translation implies the object is moved without rotation; pure rotation implies the object is rotated without translation. The objects in Figure 2-13 are examples of pure translation. The triangle (black) has been translated (moved) to the right (green) without rotation and then down (red). This is a simple thing to accomplish with Python, especially when using lists as in Listing 2-9. For example, to move an object to the right in an amount of dx, just add dx to the x coordinates and replot it. Similarly for the y direction, just add Δy dy to the y coordinates and replot. The small blue boxes were translated across the plotting area by incrementing the x coordinates by 10 units in the loop beginning in line 45.

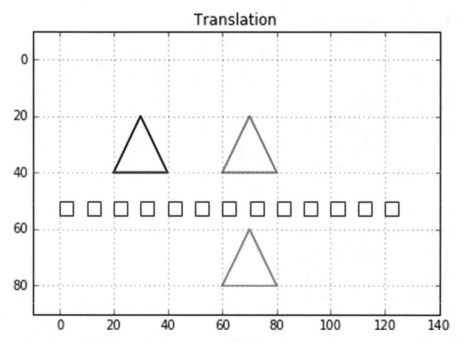

Figure 2-13. *Examples of translation created by Listing 2-9*

Listing 2-9. Program 2DTRANSLATION

```
1   """
2   2DTRANSLATION
3   """
4
5   import numpy as np
6   import matplotlib.pyplot as plt
7
8   x1=-10
9   x2=140
10  y1=90
11  y2=-10
12  plt.axis([x1,x2,y1,y2])
13
14  plt.axis('on')
15  plt.grid(True)
16
```

```
17   plt.title('Translation')
18
19   #—————————————————————————————triangle
20   x=[20,30,40,20]
21   y=[40,20,40,40]
22   plt.plot(x,y,color='k')
23   plt.plot(x,y,color='k')
24   plt.plot(x,y,color='k')
25
26   #—————————————————————translate triangle dx=60
27   x=[60,70,80,60]
28   plt.plot(x,y,color='g')
29   plt.plot(x,y,color='g')
30   plt.plot(x,y,color='g')
31
32   #—————————————————————translate triangle dy=40
33   y=[80,60,80,80]
34   plt.plot(x,y,color='r')
35   plt.plot(x,y,color='r')
36   plt.plot(x,y,color='r')
37
38   #——————————————————————————————————box
39   x=[0,0,5,5,0]
40   y=[55,50,50,55,55]
41   plt.plot(x,y,'b')
42
43   #——————————————————————————translate box
44   y=[55,50,50,55,55]
45   for x in np.arange(0,130,10):
46       x=[x,x,x+5,x+5,x]
47       plt.plot(x,y,'b')
48
49   plt.show()
```

2D Rotation

So far in this chapter, you have seen how to construct images on a two-dimensional plane using points and lines. In this section, you'll learn how to rotate a two-dimensional planar object within its own plane. A 2D object that you might want to rotate could be a rectangle, for example, or something more complicated, which will normally consist of any number of points and lines. Lines, of course, are defined by their end points or a series of points if constructed from dots. As you have seen, curves can also be constructed from line segments or dots. If you can determine how to rotate a point, you will then be able to rotate any planar object defined by points. In Chapter 3, you will extend these concepts to the rotation of three-dimensional objects around three coordinate directions.

Figure 2-14 shows three coordinate systems: the blue xg,yg system is the *global* coordinate system. Its numerical size and the location of the global origin (xg=0, yg=0) are defined by the values in the plt.axis([x1,x2,y1,y2]) statement. This is the system you use when plotting. All plotting coordinates should relate to this system. For example, if writing plt.scatter(xg,yg), xg and yg should be relative to the blue xg,yg system as shown.

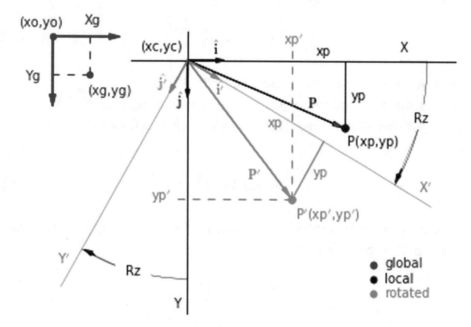

Figure 2-14. *2D rotation model*

The black x,y system is the *local* system. A position (xp,yp) in the local system is equivalent to (xc+xp, yc+yp) in the global system. You use the local system to construct shapes by specifying the coordinates of the points that comprise them. For example, if you want to plot a circle somewhere in the plotting area, you could place (xc,yc) at the circle's center, calculate the points defining the circle around it in reference to the local (black) system, and then relate them back to the xg,yg (blue) system for plotting by translating each point by xc and yc.

Figure 2-14 shows a point P that is rotated through a clockwise angle Rz to a new position at P′. The red coordinate system rotates through the angle Rz. P rotates along with it. The coordinates of P′ in the rotated system, (xp,yp), are the same as they were in the local system. However, in the global system, they are obviously different. Your goal now is to determine the coordinates of P′ in the local system and then in the global system, so you can plot it.

I am using the terminology Rz for the angle because a clockwise rotation in the x,y plane is actually a rotation about the z direction, which points into the plane of the paper. This was illustrated in Chapter 1. It will be explained in more detail in Chapter 3.

Figure 2-14 shows point P in its unrotated position. Its coordinates in relation to the local x,y system (black) are (xp,yp). Its location is defined by the vector **P**,

$$\mathbf{p} = xp\hat{\mathbf{i}} + yp\hat{\mathbf{j}} \tag{2-17}$$

where $\hat{\mathbf{i}}$ and $\hat{\mathbf{j}}$ are unit vectors in the x and y directions.

After **P** is rotated through the angle Rz, it reaches a new position P′ (red) at coordinates (x′,y′) in relation to the x,y (black) system. P′ is defined by the vector **P′** (red) as,

$$\mathbf{p}' = xp'\hat{\mathbf{i}} + yp'\hat{\mathbf{j}} \tag{2-18}$$

The coordinates of P′ in relation to the rotated x′,y′ system are (xp,yp). The position of P′ is thus also defined by the vector

$$\mathbf{p}' = xp\hat{\mathbf{i}}' + yp\hat{\mathbf{j}}' \tag{2-19}$$

where $\hat{\mathbf{i}}'$ and $\hat{\mathbf{j}}'$ are unit vectors in the x′ and y′ directions.

This analysis assumes the x axis points to the right, the y axis points down and the z axis points into the screen. If the y axis point up, z would point out of the screen and a different analysis is required. See Appendix D for clarification.

Your task now is to determine relations for $\hat{\mathbf{i}}'$ and $\hat{\mathbf{j}}'$ in relation to $\hat{\mathbf{i}}$ and $\hat{\mathbf{j}}$ and then substitute them into Equation 2-19. This will give you the coordinates of P′ in relation to the local x,y system. By simply adding xc and yc you get the coordinates of P′ in the global system, which you need for plotting.

Four unit vectors are shown at (xc,yc). $\hat{\mathbf{i}}$ and $\hat{\mathbf{j}}$ point in the x and y directions; $\hat{\mathbf{i}}'$ and $\hat{\mathbf{j}}'$ point in the x′ and y′ directions. By examining Figure 2-14, you can see that the first j′ in Equation 2-21 should have a hat like the î above it.

$$\hat{\mathbf{i}}' = \underbrace{cos(Rz)\ \hat{\mathbf{i}}}_{X\,component} + \underbrace{sin(Rz)\ \hat{\mathbf{j}}}_{Y\,component} \tag{2-20}$$

$$\hat{\mathbf{j}}' = \underbrace{sin(Rz)\ \hat{\mathbf{i}}}_{X\,component} + \underbrace{cos(Rz)\ \hat{\mathbf{j}}}_{Y\,component} \tag{2-21}$$

Plugging these into Equation 2-19, you get

$$\mathbf{p}' = xp\left[cos(Rz)\hat{\mathbf{i}} + sin(Rz)\hat{\mathbf{j}}\right] + yp\left[-sin(Rz)\hat{\mathbf{i}} + cos(Rz)\hat{\mathbf{j}}\right] \tag{2-22}$$

This can be separated into x and y components,

$$\mathbf{p}' = xp'\hat{\mathbf{i}} + yp'\hat{\mathbf{j}} \tag{2-23}$$

where

$$xp' = xp\left[cos(Rz)\right] + yp\left[-sin(Rz)\right] \tag{2-24}$$

$$yp' = xp\left[sin(Rz)\right] + yp\left[cos(Rz)\right] \tag{2-25}$$

These last two equations are all you need to rotate a point from (xp,yp) through the angle Rz to new coordinates (xp′,yp′). Note that both sets of coordinates, (xp,yp) and (xp′,yp′), are in reference to the local x,y axes. They can then be easily translated by xc and yc to get them in the global system for plotting.

In the special case where yp=0, that is when P, before rotation, lies on the x axis at x=xp, Equations 2-24 and 2-25 degenerate to

$$xp' = xp \, cos(Rz)$$ (2-26)

$$yp' = xp \, sin(Rz)$$ (2-27)

which can be easily verified from Figure 2-14. You are, of course, concerned with rotating a generic point that initially is anywhere in the x,y plane so you need the full formulation contained in Equations 2-24 and 2-25. These can be expressed in matrix form as

$$\begin{bmatrix} xp' \\ yp' \end{bmatrix} = \begin{bmatrix} cos(Rz) & sin(Rz) \\ sin(Rz) & cos(Rz) \end{bmatrix} \begin{bmatrix} xp \\ yp \end{bmatrix}$$ (2-28)

which can be abbreviated as

$$[P'] = [Rz][P]$$ (2-29)

The [P'] and [P] matrices are often termed *column vectors* since they contain the components of vectors **P** and **P'**. [Rz] is a transformation matrix; it transforms the **P** vector into the **P'** vector, in this case by rotation through the angle Rz. These vectors are shown in Figure 2-15 where **P** defines the location of the unrotated point P1 (black) and the rotated point P' (red) at P3. You can rewrite [Rz] as

$$[Rz] = \begin{bmatrix} C(1,1) & C(1,2) \\ C(2,1) & C(2,2) \end{bmatrix}$$ (2-30)

$$C(1,1) = cos(Rz)$$ (2-31)

$$C(1,2) = -sin(Rz)$$ (2-32)

$$C(2,1) = sin(Rz)$$ (2-33)

$$C(2,2) = cos(Rz)$$ (2-34)

The definitions in Equations 2-31 through 2-34 will be used in the Python programs that follow. They represent a rotation in the x,y plane in the clockwise direction and use a negative value of Rz to rotate in the counterclockwise direction. Note that [Rz] is purely a function of the angle of rotation, Rz

To convert xp′ and yp′ to xg and yg, you simply add xc to xp′ and yc to yp′, as in

$$xg = xc + xp'$$ (2-35)

$$yg = yc + yp'$$ (2-36)

In matrix form,

$$\begin{bmatrix} xg \\ yg \end{bmatrix} = \begin{bmatrix} xc \\ yc \end{bmatrix} + \begin{bmatrix} cos(Rz) & -sin(Rz) \\ sin(Rz) & cos(Rz) \end{bmatrix} \begin{bmatrix} xp \\ yp \end{bmatrix}$$ (2-37)

which can be abbreviated as

$$\underbrace{[Pg]}_{global} = \underbrace{[C]}_{center} + [Rz]\underbrace{[P]}_{local}$$ (2-38)

or in vector form, as shown in Figure 2-15,

$$\mathbf{P}g = C + \mathbf{P}'$$ (2-39)

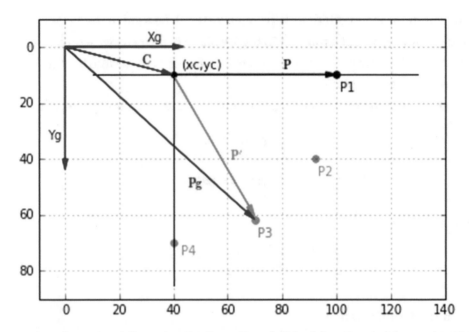

Figure 2-15. *Rotation of a point P1 from Rz=0° (black) to Rz=30° (green), 60° (red), and 90° (grey). Vectors drawn from xg=0, yg=0 to Point 3 at Rz=60° illustrating Equation 2-38. Plotted by Listing 2-10*

As an illustration of the above concepts, Listing 2-10 rotates a point P1 about (xc,yc) from its original unrotated location at (xp,yp)=(60,0) in 30-degree increments. Results are shown in Figure 2-15. The coordinates of the center of rotation, (xc,yc), are set in lines 16 and 17.

Lines 28-37 of Listing 2-10 define a function rotz(xp1,yp1,Rz), which uses the elements of the transformation matrix [Rz] in Equations 2-31 through 2-34 and the angle of rotation Rz to calculate and return the transformed (rotated and translated) coordinates (xg,yg). Lines 35 and 36 in function rotz relate the local coordinates to the xg,yg system for plotting. Note that rotz rotates each point and simultaneously translates it by xc and yc in lines 35 and 36. This puts the coordinates in the *global* system ready for plotting. You rotate the point four times: Rz=0,30,60,90. The use of the function rotz(xp,yp,Rz) enables you to avoid coding the transformation for every point.

Lines 39 and 40 set the original coordinates of P to (60,0). It is important to note that these coordinates are relative to the center of rotation (xc,yc). Line 43 starts the calculation of the first point. This is at Rz=0. Line 44 converts Rz from degrees to radians. Later, I will show how to use the radians() function to do this. Line 45 invokes the function rotz(xp,yp,Rz). xp and yp were set in lines 39 and 40; Rz was set in line 43.

The function returns the coordinates of the rotated point (xg,yg) in line 37. Since Rz was zero in this first transformation, they are the same as the coordinates of the unrotated point P1.

The plotting of point P2 begins in line 50. You set the angle of rotation to 30 degrees in line 50. The routine is the same as before and P2 is plotted as a grey point. Sections P3 and P4 increase Rz to 60 and 90 degrees, plotting the red and final grey point.

Lines 74, 77, 80, and 83 illustrate the use of Latex in printing text on a plot. Looking at line 74, for example,

```
plt.text(28,6,r'$\mathbf{C}$',color='k')
```

the text starts at coordinates xg=28, yg=6. As discussed in Chapter 1, the **r** tells Python to treat the string as raw. This keeps the backward slashes needed by the Latex code between the dollar signs; in this case, $\mathbf{C}$. \mathbf{} makes whatever is between the braces {} bold. In line 80, ^{\prime} places a superscript prime next to P. This won't work if the prefix r is not included.

Listing 2-10. Program 2DROT1

```
1
2    """
3    2DROT1
4    """
5    import matplotlib.pyplot as plt
6    import numpy as np
7
8    plt.axis([-10,140,90,-10])
9    plt.axis('on')
10   plt.grid(True)
11
12   #————————————————————axes
13   plt.arrow(0,0,40,0,head_length=4,head_width=2,color='b')
14   plt.arrow(0,0,0,40,head_length=4,head_width=2,color='b')
15
16   xc=40
17   yc=10
18
```

```
19  plt.plot([xc-30,xc+90],[yc,yc],linewidth=1,color='k') #--X
20  plt.plot([xc,xc],[yc-5,yc+75],linewidth=1,color='k') #--Y
21
22  plt.text(30,-2,'Xg',color='b')
23  plt.text(-7,33,'Yg',color='b')
24  plt.scatter(xc,yc,s=20,color='k')
25  plt.text(xc+3,yc-2,'(xc,yc)')
26
27  #————————————————define rotation matrix rz
28  def rotz(xp,yp,rz): #——xp,yp=un-rotated coordinates relative to xc,yc
29      c11=np.cos(rz)
30      c12=-np.sin(rz)
31      c21=np.sin(rz)
32      c22=np.cos(rz)
33      xpp=xp*c11+yp*c12 #--xpp,ypp=rotated coordinates relative to xc,yc
34      ypp=xp*c21+yp*c22
35      xg=xc+xpp #--xg,yg=rotated coordinates relative to xg,yg
36      yg=yc+ypp
37      return [xg,yg]
38
39  xp=60 #——————————-coordinates of first point P1 relative to xc,yc
40  yp=0
41
42  #——————————————————P1
43  rz=0
44  rz=rz*np.pi/180
45  [xg,yg]=rotz(xp,yp,rz)
46  plt.scatter(xg,yg,s=30,color='k' )
47  plt.text(xg+1,yg+6,'P1',color='k')
48
49  #——————————————————P2
50  rz=30
51  rz=rz*np.pi/180
52  [xg,yg]=rotz(xp,yp,rz)
53  plt.scatter(xg,yg,s=30,color='grey')
```

```
54  plt.text(xg+1,yg+6,'P2',color='grey')
55
56  #————————————————————————P3
57  rz=60
58  rz=rz*np.pi/180
59  [xg,yg]=rotz(xp,yp,rz)
60  plt.scatter(xg,yg,s=30,color='r')
61  plt.text(xg+1,yg+6,'P3',color='r')
62  xpp3=xg #—save for later in line 76
63  ypp3=yg
64
65  #————————————————————————P4
66  rz=90
67  rz=rz*np.pi/180
68  [xg,yg]=rotz(xp1,yp1,rz)
69  plt.scatter(xg,yg,s=30,color='grey')
70  plt.text(xp2+1,yp2+6,'P4',color='grey')
71
72  #————————————————————————————plot vectors
73  plt.arrow(0,0,xc-4,yc-1,head_length=4,head_width=2,color='k')
74  plt.text(28,6,r'$\mathbf{C}$',color='k')
75
76  plt.arrow(0,0,xpp3-3,ypp3-3,head_length=4,head_width=2,color='b')
77  plt.text(45,50,r'$\mathbf{Pg}$',color='b')
78
79  plt.arrow(xc,yc,xpp3-2-xc,ypp3-5-yc,head_length=4,head_
    width=2,color='r')
80  plt.text(61,40,r'$\mathbf{P^{\prime}}$',color='r')
81
82  plt.arrow(xc,yc,xp-4,yp,head_length=4,head_width=2,color='k')
83  plt.text(80,yc-2,r'$\mathbf{P}$',color='k')
84
85  plt.show()
```

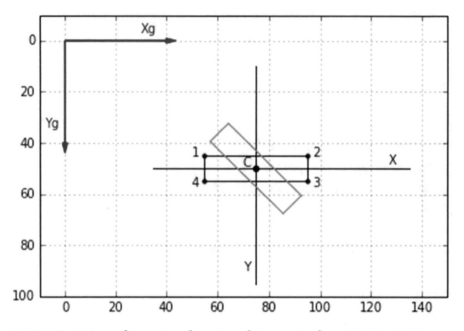

Figure 2-16. *Rotation of a rectangle around its center from Listing 2-11*

Next, you rotate a rectangle around its center, as shown in Figure 2-16. The center of rotation is point c at (xc,yc). The black rectangle shows the rectangle in its unrotated orientation. Its corners are numbered 1-4, as shown. The program plots the unrotated rectangle and then rotates it around point c to the rotated position and displays it in red.

Since the rectangle is defined by its corner points, you can rotate it by rotating the corners around c. The methodology is detailed in Listing 2-11. First, you plot the unrotated rectangle (black). The local coordinates of its four corner points are specified relative to the center of rotation c in lines 42-49. The points are labeled and plotted as dots in lines 51-58 where the local coordinates are converted to global by adding xc and yc in lines 55-58.

Next, you connect the corners by lines. Lines 61-68 translate the local corner coordinates by xc and yc. These points are labeled xg and yg to indicate that they are relative to the global plotting axes. They are set up as lists in lines 70 and 71, and then plotted in line 73, which draws lines between sequential xg,yg pairs.

Note the sequence of coordinate pairs in lines 70 and 71. When line 73 is invoked, it connects (xg1,yg1) to (xg2,yg2), then (xg2,yg2) to (xg3,yg3), and so on. But when it gets to corner 4, it has to connect corner 4 back to corner 1 in order to close the rectangle; hence you have (xg4,yg4) connected to (xg1,yg1) at the end of 70 and 71.

The plotting of the rotated rectangle begins at line 76. Rz is the angle of rotation. It is set to 45 degrees here and then converted from degrees to radians in line 77 (you could have used the `radians()` function to do this).

The function `rotz(xp,yp,Rz)` is defined in lines 29-38. The elements of the rotation transformation matrix shown in Equations 2-31 through 2-34 are evaluated in lines 30-33. xp and yp are the coordinates of an unrotated point. xpp and ypp (xp′ and yp′), coordinates in the rotated system, are evaluated in lines 34 and 35 using Equations 2-24 and 2-25. xg and yg, the coordinates in the global system after rotation and translation, are evaluated in lines 36-37 in accordance with Equations 2-35 and 2-36. Note that these lines rotate the points and simultaneously translate them relative to point c. The transformed coordinates are returned as a list in line 38.

Lines 80-101 transform each of the corner coordinates one by one by invoking function `rotz(xp,yp,Rz)`. For example, lines 80-83 transform corner 1 from local, unrotated coordinates xp1,yp1 to global coordinates xg and yg. The remaining three points are transformed in the same way. The lines connecting the corners are plotted in red in lines 104-107 using lists.

Listing 2-11. Program 2DROTRECTANGLE

```
1    """
2    2DROTRECTANGLE
3    """
4
5    import matplotlib.pyplot as plt
6    import numpy as np
7
8    plt.axis([-10,150,100,-10])
9    plt.axis('on')
10   plt.grid(True)
11
12   #————————————————————————————————————————————axes
13   plt.arrow(0,0,40,0,head_length=4,head_width=2,color='b')
14   plt.arrow(0,0,0,40,head_length=4,head_width=2,color='b')
15   plt.text(30,-3,'Xg',color='b')
16   plt.text(-8,34,'Yg',color='b')
17
```

```
18   xc=75 #——————————center of rotation
19   yc=50
20   plt.plot([xc-40,xc+60],[yc,yc],linewidth=1,color='grey') #--X
21   plt.plot([xc,xc],[yc-40,yc+45],linewidth=1,color='grey') #--Y
22   plt.text(127,48,'X')
23   plt.text(70,90,'Y')
24
25   plt.scatter(xc,yc,s=20,color='k') #--plot center of rotation
26   plt.text(70,49,'c')
27
28   #————————————————————————define function rotz
29   def rotz(xp,yp,rz):
30       c11=np.cos(rz)
31       c12=-np.sin(rz)
32       c21=np.sin(rz)
33       c22=np.cos(rz)
34       xpp=xp*c11+yp*c12 #———-relative to xc,yc
35       ypp=xp*c21+yp*c22
36       xg=xc+xpp #--relative to xg,yg
37       yg=yc+ypp
38       return [xg,yg]
39
40   #————————————————————————plot unrotated rectangle
41   #———————————-rectangle corner coordinates in X,Y system
42   xp1=-20
43   xp2=+20
44   xp3=+20
45   xp4=-20
46   yp1=-5
47   yp2=-5
48   yp3=+5
49   yp4=+5
50
51   plt.text(50,45,'1') #———-label
52   plt.text(97,45,'2')
```

```
53   plt.text(97,57,'3')
54   plt.text(50,57,'4')
55   plt.scatter(xp1+xc,yp1+yc,s=10,color='k')
56   plt.scatter(xp2+xc,yp2+yc,s=10,color='k')
57   plt.scatter(xp3+xc,yp3+yc,s=10,color='k')
58   plt.scatter(xp4+xc,yp4+yc,s=10,color='k')
59
60   #————————————————————plot unrotated rectangle
61   xg1=xc+xp1 #————-corner coordinates in Xg,Yg system
62   yg1=yc+yp1
63   xg2=xc+xp2
64   yg2=yc+yp2
65   xg3=xc+xp3
66   yg3=yc+yp3
67   xg4=xc+xp4
68   yg4=yc+yp4
69
70   xg=[xg1,xg2,xg3,xg4,xg1]
71   yg=[yg1,yg2,yg3,yg4,yg1]
72
73   plt.plot((xg),(yg),color='k')
74
75   #————————————————-rotate rectangle corner coordinates
76   rz=45
77   rz=rz*np.pi/180
78
79   #————————————————————-point 1
80   xp=xp1
81   yp=yp1
82   [xg,yg]=rotz(xp,yp,rz)
83   [xg1,yg1]=[xg,yg]
84
85   #————————————————————-point 2
86   xp=xp2
87   yp=yp2
```

```
88   [xg,yg]=rotz(xp,yp,rz)
89   [xg2,yg2]=[xg,yg]
90
91   #─────────────────────────────────point 3
92   xp=xp3
93   yp=yp3
94   [xg,yg]=rotz(xp,yp,rz)
95   [xg3,yg3]=[xg,yg]
96
97   #─────────────────────────────────point 4
98   xp=xp4
99   yp=yp4
100  [xg,yg]=rotz(xp,yp,rz)
101  [xg4,yg4]=[xg,yg]
102
103  #─────────────────────────────────plot rotated rectangle
104  xg=[xg1,xg2,xg3,xg4,xg1]
105  yg=[yg1,yg2,yg3,yg4,yg1]
106
107  plt.plot(xg,yg,color='r')
108
109  plt.show()
```

To summarize the procedure, you first construct the object, in this case a simple rectangle, using points located at coordinates xp,yp in the local x,y system. This is done by specifying the coordinates relative to the center of rotation at c. Next, you specify Rz, evaluate the elements of the transformation matrix, transform each coordinate by Rz, translate the rotated points by xc,yc to get everything into the global xg,yg system, and then plot. The transformations are carried out by the function rotz(xp,yp,rz), which simultaneously rotates and translates the coordinates into the xg,yg system for plotting. In this case, you transformed all the coordinates first and then plotted at the end using lists. In some programs, you will plot points or lines immediately after transforming.

Next, you rotate a rectangle about its lower left corner. This is shown in Figure 2-17. The program that does this (not listed) is similar to Listing 2-11 except the center of rotation is changed to

$$xc = 55 \qquad\qquad (2\text{-}40)$$

$$yc = 55 \qquad\qquad (2\text{-}41)$$

and the corner coordinates are changed to

$$xp1 = 0 \qquad\qquad (2\text{-}42)$$

$$xp2 = +50 \qquad\qquad (2\text{-}43)$$

$$xp3 = +50 \qquad\qquad (2\text{-}44)$$

$$xp4 = 0 \qquad\qquad (2\text{-}45)$$

$$yp1 = -10 \qquad\qquad (2\text{-}46)$$

$$yp2 = -10 \qquad\qquad (2\text{-}47)$$

$$yp3 = +0 \qquad\qquad (2\text{-}48)$$

$$yp4 = +0 \qquad\qquad (2\text{-}49)$$

These dimensions are relative to the center of rotation, (xc,yc).

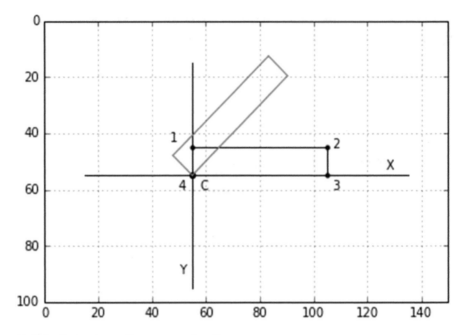

Figure 2-17. *Rotation of a rectangle about a corner*

The center of rotation c does not have to be contiguous with the object; you could put it anywhere as long as the corner coordinates relative to the center of rotation are updated.

Figure 2-18 shows an example of constructing and rotating a circular object. Obviously, without some distinctive feature, you wouldn't be able to see if a circle had been rotated so you make the top half of the starting circle green and the bottom half red. You also add a bar across the diameter with dots at each end. Figure 2-19 shows the model used by Listing 2-12 to generate Figure 2-18.

As shown in Figures 2-19 and 2-18, and referring to Listing 2-12, you construct the starting circle with a center at xcc,ycc in program lines 41 and 42. It has a radius r=10, which is set in line 43. The angle p starts at p1=0 and goes to p2=2π in steps dp in lines 45-47. Note that you are not using the angle definition Rz since p is a local angle about point xcc,ycc (the center of the circle), not xc,yc, the center of rotation. Points along the circle's perimeter are calculated in lines 55 and 56 in local coordinates. When alpha=0, this produces the starting circle.

The use of alpha in the function call in line 57 illustrates that you can use any name for the angle, even though Rz was used in the function definition in line 29. You are passing a number from a function call to a function. It doesn't matter what name it has on either end; the value received by the function will be the same as in the call to that function.

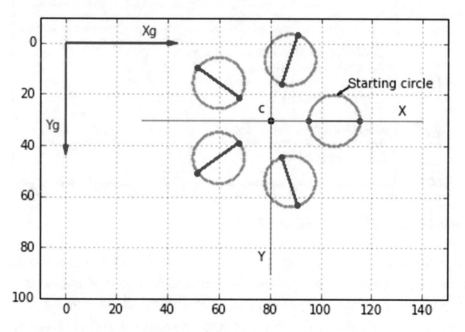

Figure 2-18. *Circles rotated about point c from Listing 2-12*

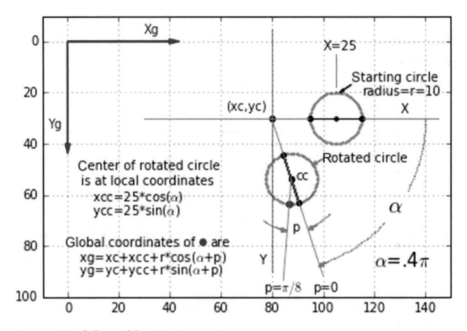

Figure 2-19. *Model used by Listing 2-12*

When alpha>0, the other four circles are drawn. The alpha loop starting at line 53 moves the circle's center (xcc,ycc) clockwise around the center of rotation in steps dalpha, which is set in line 51. The local coordinates are transformed in line 57 by invoking rotz. Alpha's inclusion in the rotz function call has the effect of rotating the circle about its own center (xcc,ycc). Lines 58-61 determine if each circumferential point lies between p=0 and p=π. If so, the point is plotted as red, otherwise as green. Thus, the circle's top half is red, its bottom half is green. Lines 62-70 plot the diametrical bars and points.

An important feature of this approach is that not only is the circle's center rotated around point c in steps dalpha, but each circle itself is rotated about its own center, as can be seen from the reorientation of the red and green sectors and the diametrical bars in the rotated circles. In the next program, you will rotate each circle's center around point c while keeping each circle unrotated about its own center.

Why am I using circles in this demonstration? Primarily to illustrate how to construct circular shapes at any location relative to a center of rotation and rotate them. I am also illustrating the importance of being aware of the location of the center of rotation; it isn't necessarily the same as the center of the circle.

In this case, you are rotating in the plane of the circle, which admittedly isn't very illuminating. But later, these concepts will become useful when I show how to rotate objects, such as a circle, in three dimensions. In the case of a circle, when rotated out of its plane, it produces an oval, which is essential in portraying circular and spherical objects such as cylinders and spheres in three dimensions. Simply rotate a circle out of plane about a coordinate direction and you get an oval.

Listing 2-12. Program 2DROTCIRCLE1

```
1    """
2    2DROTCIRCLE1
3    """
4
5    import matplotlib.pyplot as plt
6    import numpy as np
7
8    plt.axis([-10,150,100,-10])
9    plt.axis('on')
10   plt.grid(True)
11
12   #————————————————————————————————————axes
13   plt.arrow(0,0,40,0,head_length=4,head_width=2,color='b')
14   plt.arrow(0,0,0,40,head_length=4,head_width=2,color='b')
15   plt.text(30,-3,'Xg',color='b')
16   plt.text(-8,34,'Yg',color='b')
17
18   xc=80 #————————————————center of rotation
19   yc=30
20   plt.plot([xc-50,xc+60],[yc,yc],linewidth=1,color='grey') #--X
21   plt.plot([xc,xc],[yc-35,yc+60],linewidth=1,color='grey') #--Y
22   plt.text(xc+50,yc-2,'X')
23   plt.text(xc-5,yc+55,'Y')
24
25   plt.scatter(xc,yc,s=20,color='k') #—plot center of rotation
26   plt.text(xc-5,yc-3,'c')
27
```

```
28   #──────────────────────────────define rotation matrix Rz
29   def rotz(xp,yp,rz):
30         c11=np.cos(rz)
31         c12=-np.sin(rz)
32         c21=np.sin(rz)
33         c22=np.cos(rz)
34         xpp=xp*c11+yp*c12 #--rotated coordinates relative to xc,yc
35         ypp=xp*c21+yp*c22
36         xg=xc+xpp #--rotated coordinates relative to xg,yg
37         yg=yc+ypp
38         return [xg,yg]
39
40   #──────────────────────────────plot circles
41   xcc=25 #-xcc,ycc=center of starting circle in local X,Y system
42   ycc=0
43   r=10 #-radius
44
45   p1=0 #---p1,p2=angles around circle center
46   p2=2*np.pi
47   dp=(p2-p1)/100
48
49   alpha1=0 #--angles around xc,yc
50   alpha2=2*np.pi
51   dalpha=(alpha2-alpha1)/5
52
53   for alpha in np.arange(alpha1,alpha2,dalpha):
54         for p in np.arange(p1,p2,dp):
55               xp=xcc+r*np.cos(p) #—xp,yp=coordinates relative to local
                  X,Y system
56               yp=ycc+r*np.sin(p)
57               [xg,yg]=rotz(xp,yp,alpha)
58               if p < np.pi:
59                     plt.scatter(xg,yg,s=1,color='r') #—plot lower half red
60               else:
61                     plt.scatter(xg,yg,s=1,color='g') #—plot upper
                        half green
```

100

```
62              xp1=xcc+r #—plot diameter bars and bar end points
63              yp1=0
64              [xg1,yg1]=rotz(xp1,yp1,alpha)
65              xp2=xcc-r
66              yp2=0
67              [xg2,yg2]=rotz(xp2,yp2,alpha)
68              plt.plot([xg1,xg2],[yg1,yg2],color='b')
69              plt.scatter(xg1,yg1,s=10,color='b')
70              plt.scatter(xg2,yg2,s=10,color='b')
71
72  plt.text(xc+31,yc-13,'starting circle')
73  plt.arrow(xc+31,yc-13,-3,2,head_length=2,head_width=1)
74
75  plt.show()
```

As shown in Figure 2-20, Listing 2-13 rotates the starting circle through increments of angle dalpha while keeping the orientation of each circle unchanged. The program is similar to the preceding one, with the exception that only the local center of each circle is rotated about point c while the circumferential points, as defined by the starting circle, remain unrotated. The program should be self-explanatory.

Note the difference between Listings 2-12 and 2-13. In Listing 2-12, the rotation takes place in lines 53-70. At each angle alpha, the coordinates of each point around the circle's circumference are determined in lines 55 and 56. These are then transformed in line 57 using the function rotz(xp,yp,alpha). That is, each point around the circumference is rotated by the angle alpha. This has the effect of rotating the entire circle, as shown in Figure 2-18. In Listing 2-13, however, the plotting is done in lines 41-68. Here only the circle's center is rotated in lines 50 and 51. In line 55, rotz(xp,yp,0) uses the angle p=0 in its argument. This has the effect of not rotating the circle itself, only its center, as shown in Figure 2-20.

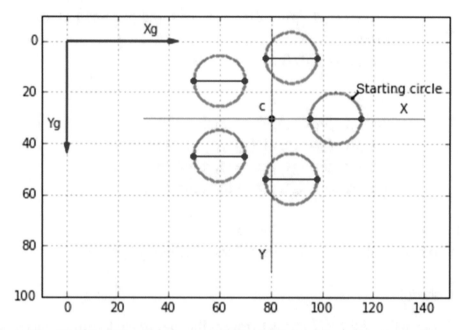

Figure 2-20. *Circles with centers rotated about point c from Listing 2-13*

Which method of rotation should you use: that shown in Figure 2-18 or 2-20? It depends on your application. In one, you may want the entire object, including the points that comprise it, to rotate about a center whereas in another you may want only the center of the object to rotate while the object retains its original orientation. See Figure 2-21.

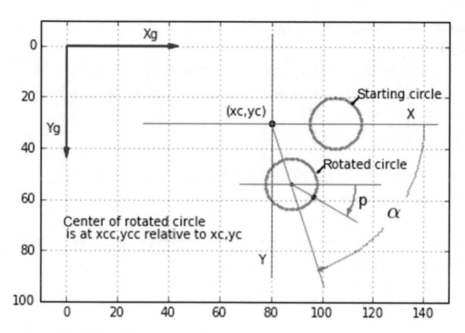

Figure 2-21. *Model used by Listing 2-13*

Listing 2-13. Program 2DROTCIRCLE2

```
1    """
2    2DROTCIRCLE2
3    """
4
5    import matplotlib.pyplot as plt
6    import numpy as np
7
8    plt.axis([-10,150,100,-10])
9    plt.axis('on')
10   plt.grid(True)
11
12   #————————————————(shorten)————————————————-axes
13   plt.arrow(0,0,40,0,head_length=4,head_width=2,color='b')
14   plt.arrow(0,0,0,40,head_length=4,head_width=2,color='b')
15   plt.text(30,-3,'Xg',color='b')
16   plt.text(-8,34,'Yg',color='b')
17
```

```
18   xc=80 #———————————————center of rotation
19   yc=30
20   plt.plot([xc-50,xc+60],[yc,yc],linewidth=1,color='grey') #--X
21   plt.plot([xc,xc],[yc-35,yc+60],linewidth=1,color='grey') #--Y
22   plt.text(xc+50,yc-2,'X')
23   plt.text(xc-5,yc+55,'Y')
24
25   plt.scatter(xc,yc,s=20,color='k') #–plot center of rotation
26   plt.text(xc-5,yc-3,'c')
27
28   #———————————————————————————define rotation matrix Rz
29   def rotz(xp,yp,rz):
30       c11=np.cos(rz)
31       c12=-np.sin(rz)
32       c21=np.sin(rz)
33       c22=np.cos(rz)
34       xpp=xp*c11+yp*c12 #--relative to xc,yc
35       ypp=xp*c21+yp*c22
36       xg=xc+xpp #--relative to xg,yg
37       yg=yc+ypp
38       return [xg,yg]
39
40   #———————————————shorten———————————————plot circles
41   p1=0
42   p2=2*np.pi
43   dp=(p2-p1)/100
44
45   alpha1=0
46   alpha2=2*np.pi
47   dalpha=(alpha2-alpha1)/5
48
49   for alpha in np.arange(alpha1,alpha2,dalpha):
50       xcc=25*np.cos(alpha)
51       ycc=25*np.sin(alpha)
52       for p in np.arange(p1,p2,dp):
```

```
53              xp=xcc+r*np.cos(p)
54              yp=ycc+r*np.sin(p)
55              [xg,yg]=rotz(xp,yp,0)
56              if p < np.pi:
57                      plt.scatter(xg,yg,s=1,color='r')
58              else:
59                      plt.scatter(xg,yg,s=1,color='g')
60              xp1=xcc+r
61              yp1=ycc+0
62              [xg1,yg1]=rotz(xp1,yp1,0)
63              xp2=xcc-r
64              yp2=ycc+0
65              [xg2,yg2]=rotz(xp2,yp2,0)
66              plt.plot([xg1,xg2],[yg1,yg2],color='b')
67              plt.scatter(xg1,yg1,s=10,color='b')
68              plt.scatter(xg2,yg2,s=10,color='b')
69
70  plt.text(xc+34,yc-10,'starting circle')
71  plt.arrow(xc+34,yc-10,-2,2,head_length=1,head_ width=1)
72
73  plt.show()
```

Summary

In this chapter, you saw how to use dots and lines to construct shapes in two dimensions. You learned the concept of relative coordinates, specifically the *local system,* which is used to construct an image with coordinate values relative to a center, which in the case of rotation may be used as the center of rotation, and the *global system* which is used for plotting. You saw how local coordinates must be transformed into the global system for plotting, the origin of the global system being defined through the plt.axes() function. You saw how to construct lines from dots; arrange colored dots in artistic patterns; and draw arcs, discs, circles, and ellipses using dots and line segments. Then you learned about the concepts of translation (easy) and rotation (not so easy). You applied all this to points, rectangles, and circles. In the next chapter, you will extend these ideas to three dimensions.

CHAPTER 3

Graphics in Three Dimensions

In this chapter, you will learn how to create, translate, and rotate three-dimensional objects in a three-dimensional space. You will also learn how to project and display them on the two-dimensional surface of your computer screen. In general, movement of an object implies both translation and rotation. I discussed this in two dimensions in the previous chapter. You saw that translation in two dimensions is trivial. Just add or subtract a quantity from the x coordinates to translate in the x direction, similarly for the y direction. In three dimensions, it is still trivial, although you are able now to translate in the third dimension, the z direction, simply by adding or subtracting an amount to an object's z coordinates. Rotation is another matter, however. The analysis follows the method you used in two dimensions but is complicated by the fact that you now are able to rotate an object around three coordinate directions. In this chapter, I will not discuss 3D translation any further but will concentrate instead on 3D rotation.

The Three-Dimensional Coordinate System

In the previous discussion of two-dimensional rotation, you rotated two-dimensional objects in the two-dimensional x,y plane. You now extend those concepts to three dimensions by introducing a third axis, the z axis, as shown in Figure 3-1. Notice that the z axis points into the screen, not out. This is not an arbitrary choice. We are following the *right-hand rule* convention where the direction of positive z is found by rotating the x axis toward the y axis through the smaller angle between them. The positive z axis will then point in the direction that would be followed by a right-handed screw when turned in this fashion. In this case, the screw would progress into the screen; that is then the direction of the positive z axis. We could construct an entire mathematical theory based on a left-handed system but the convention used most everywhere is that of a

© Bernard Korites 2023
B. Korites, *Python Graphics*, https://doi.org/10.1007/978-1-4842-9660-8_3

right-handed system. Some books and papers label the coordinate axes as x1,x2,x3. Following the right-hand rule, the direction of x3 would be found by rotating x1 into x2, as described above. In this work, we will stay with the x,y,z notation for the directions.

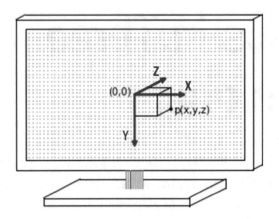

Figure 3-1. *Three-dimensional coordinate axes with point P at coordinates (x,y,z)*

It should be apparent now why I used the nomenclature Rz in the previous discussion of two-dimensional rotation; it refers to rotation about the z axis. This appears as a clockwise rotation in the xy plane when x goes to the right and y goes down. If x went to the right and y were to go up, z would point out of the screen and a positive rotation about the z axis would appear to go counterclockwise.

Following the methods used in this analysis of two-dimensional rotation, in the remainder of this chapter I will discuss separate rotations around the x, y, and z axes and then combined rotations around all three axes. Incidentally, when I say, "rotation around the x axis," for example, I am implying that this is equivalent to "rotation around the x *direction*" and similarly for the y and z directions. While rotation around an imaginary axis that is parallel to the x axis is not precisely the same as rotation around the x axis, the difference is only a matter of translation, as you will see. I will use both terms "about the x axis" and "about the x direction" interchangeably except when confusion may result.

Figure 3-2 shows the right-hand xyz system. Imagine you're standing at the origin, looking out in the direction of the x axis. If you were to turn a right-handed screw clockwise, it would progress in the direction of the positive x axis. The double-headed arrow is the conventional way of indicating the direction of a right hand rotation, Rx; similarly for Ry and Rz.

Why have I chosen to orient the coordinate system as shown in Figure 3-2? Standard `matplotlib` uses a different orientation as shown, for example, in `https://matplotlin. org/mpl_toolkits/mplot3d/tutorial.html#scatter-plots`.

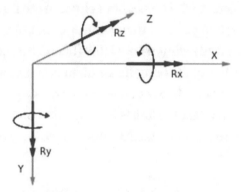

Figure 3-2. *Three-dimensional coordinate axes showing right-hand rotation around each coordinate direction*

As explained, the orientation in Figure 3-2 is somewhat more intuitive. The object being constructed is inside a space defined by the x, y, and z axes. In this situation, the observer is outside the space looking in. The object may be translated and rotated at will to give any view desired. You can look straight in at an object or view it from above or below, as shown in the images of Saturn in Chapter 10. The `matplotlib` orientation, on the other hand, is the one commonly used for data plotting and is the one you'll use for that purpose in Chapter 9; look at Figures 9-1 through 9-5. If you prefer the standard `matplotlib` system, it is easy to change to that orientation; just rotate the axes to any orientation you want, as is done in Chapter 9 where, to get z pointing up, you rotate around the global x direction by -100 degrees (tilts z slightly forward), the global y axis by -135 degrees, and the global z direction by +8 degrees (see lines 191-193 in Listing 9-1). You can fine-tune the orientation by small rotations about the global axes. After you complete this chapter, you should find it easy to shade the background planes, as shown in `matplotlib`, if you want. You can orient the axes any way you want as long as they follow the right-hand rule.

Projections onto the Coordinate Planes

How do we display a three-dimensional object on a two-dimensional computer monitor? We do so by projecting the object onto either of the three two-dimensional coordinate planes (x,y; x,z; and y,z) and then plotting either of those images on the monitor. Figure 3-3 show a three-dimensional line (black) running from A to B. Looking down from above the plotting space onto the x,z plane, you see it as the red line, which is the black line's projection onto the x,z plane. Similarly, the green line shows its projection onto the y,z plane; the blue line is its projection onto the x,y plane. I will use only one of these projections for visualization, normally the x,y projection.

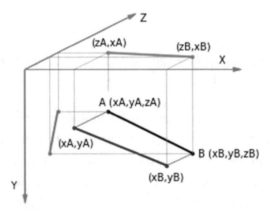

Figure 3-3. *Projection of a three-dimensional line (black) onto the three coordinate planes: red is the x,z projection, green is the y,z projection, and blue is the x,y projection*

The x,y projection is obtained simply by plotting a point's x and y coordinates in the x,y plane; for a line, you plot a line between those coordinates, which are line's endpoints. In the case of the black line, which runs from spatial coordinates (xA,yA,zA) to (xB,yB,zB), you plot a line between xA,yA and xB,yB:

```
plt.plot([xA,xB],[yA,yB],color='b')
```

noting that z=0 in the x,y plane.

This gives you the blue line, which is the projection onto the x,y plane as shown in Figure 3-4. If you want to obtain the top view, you plot the black line's z,x coordinates. If plotting with your normal coordinate axes with x running from left to right and y running down on the left, the y axis replaces the z axis. This is equivalent to a -90 degree rotation about the x axis. You then plot between the line's z and x coordinates of

```
plt.plot([zA,zB],[xA,xB],color='r')
```

to get the red line. To get the green y,z projection, you plot the z and y coordinates using the command

```
plt.plot([zA,zB],[yA,yB],color='g')
```

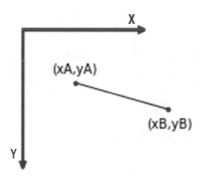

Figure 3-4. *Projection of a three-dimensional line onto the x,y plane*

In this case, you must reorient the screen coordinate axes such that +z runs from left to right across the top of the screen with the y axis running down the right side. This will give a z,y view from *outside* of the x,y,z coordinate system.

Note that in the case of a projection onto the x,y plane, you do not use the object's z coordinates. But you still need them in order to carry out rotations. Similarly for the other projections, one coordinate will not be needed for the projection but will be needed for rotations so it must be included in the analysis.

To simplify everything, you will use the x,y projection in most of the work that follows. As you will see, rotating an object around the three coordinate directions and projecting the object's (x,y) coordinates onto the x,y plane will produce a three-dimensional view.

The projections of three-dimensional objects onto two-dimensional coordinate planes are called *isometric projections*. They are commonly used in engineering and drafting. These images do not appear as they would to the human eye or as they would in a photograph because of the absence of what artists call *foreshortening*, more commonly known as *perspective*. As an example of foreshortening (or perspective), if you look down a line of telephone poles that are running off into the distance alongside railroad tracks, the pole closest to you would look taller than those further away and the rails would appear to merge as they near the horizon. What causes this? It happens simply because there is more area for the eye to cover in the far distance than close up. In the case of telephone poles, it's because there is more vertical space in the distance so the poles, which are all of the same height, occupy a smaller percentage of it; for the railroad tracks, it's the expanding horizontal space that makes the space between tracks appear to vanish to zero. See Figure 3-5. Isometric projections do not take foreshortening into account, but they will in Chapter 4 when I discuss perspective transformations.

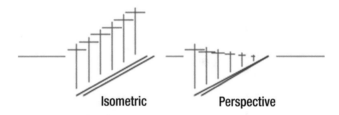

Isometric   Perspective

Figure 3-5. *Isometric vs. perspective views*

While you have seen how to project a simple three-dimensional line and its end points onto the three coordinate planes, you could have worked with a more complicated object consisting of many points and lines. As you have seen, even a circle can be constructed from just points (dots) or lines with any degree of refinement desired and projected onto the coordinate planes.

While a simple example, the three-dimensional line illustrates the method you will use in the following work: define a shape within the three-dimensional x,y,z space in terms of points and lines having coordinates (x,y,z); operate on them by rotating and translating; project them onto the x,y plane; and then plot them using their x and y coordinates. Thus you are able to project a 3D object onto your computer monitor's screen.

To rotate a point in three dimensions implies rotating it around the x, y, and z directions. You saw how to carry out two-dimensional rotation around the z direction, Rz, in the previous chapter. Here, you will derive transformations in three dimensions for rotation around the y, x, and z directions.

Rotation Around the y Direction

Figure 3-6 shows the unit vector geometry for rotation around the y direction, Ry. This is the view that would be seen by looking down onto the top of the x,y,z system. The y axis runs into the plane of the paper.

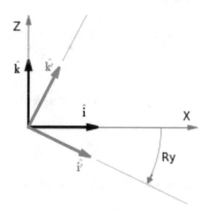

Figure 3-6. *Unit vectors for rotation about the y direction. This is a view looking down on the plotting space. The y axis runs into the plane of the paper*

Following the method used in Chapter 2, a point whose position is initially defined by the vector **P** is rotated to **P′**. Vectors defining the location of P and P′ in the x,y,z (unrotated) and x′,y′,z′ (rotated) systems are

$$\mathbf{P} = xp\hat{\mathbf{i}} + yp\hat{\mathbf{j}} + zp\hat{\mathbf{k}} \tag{3-1}$$

$$\mathbf{P'} = xp'\hat{\mathbf{i}} + yp'\hat{\mathbf{j}} + zp'\hat{\mathbf{k}} \tag{3-2}$$

$$\mathbf{P'} = xp\hat{\mathbf{i}}' + yp\hat{\mathbf{j}}' + zp\hat{\mathbf{k}}' \tag{3-3}$$

where $\hat{\mathbf{i}}$, $\hat{\mathbf{j}}$, and $\hat{\mathbf{k}}$ are unit vectors in the x, y, and z directions and $\hat{\mathbf{i}}'$, $\hat{\mathbf{j}}'$, and $\hat{\mathbf{k}}'$ are unit vectors in the x′, y′, and z′ directions. From Figure 3-6, you can see that

$$\hat{\mathbf{i}}' = cos(Ry)\hat{\mathbf{i}} + (0)\hat{\mathbf{j}} - sin(Ry)\hat{\mathbf{k}} \tag{3-4}$$

$$\hat{\mathbf{j}}' = (0)\hat{\mathbf{i}} + (1)\hat{\mathbf{j}} + (0)\hat{\mathbf{k}} \tag{3-5}$$

$$\hat{\mathbf{k}}' = sin(Ry)\hat{\mathbf{i}} + (0)\hat{\mathbf{j}} + cos(Ry)\hat{\mathbf{k}} \tag{3-6}$$

Plugging them into Equation 3-3 yields

$$\mathbf{P}' = xp\left[\cos(Ry)\hat{\mathbf{i}} - \sin(Ry)\hat{\mathbf{k}}\right] + yp\hat{\mathbf{j}} + zp\left[\sin(Ry)\hat{\mathbf{i}} + \cos(Ry)\hat{\mathbf{k}}\right] \tag{3-7}$$

Separating into **i**, **j**, and **k** components, you get

$$\mathbf{P}' = \underbrace{\left[xp\cos(Ry) + zp\sin(Ry)\right]}_{xp'}\hat{\mathbf{i}} + \underbrace{\left[yp\right]}_{yp'}\hat{\mathbf{j}} + \underbrace{\left[-xp\sin(Ry) + zp\cos(Ry)\right]}_{zp'}\hat{\mathbf{k}} \tag{3-8}$$

$$xp' = xp\cos(Ry) + zp\sin(Ry) \tag{3-9}$$

$$yp' = yp \tag{3-10}$$

$$zp' = -xp\sin(Ry) + zp\cos(Ry) \tag{3-11}$$

Equations 3-9 through 3-11 give the coordinates of the rotated point in the local x,y,z system. Of course, yp'=yp in Equation 3-10 since the y coordinate doesn't change with rotation about the y axis.

Equations 3-9, 3-10, and 3-11 can be expressed in matrix form, as shown in Equation 3-12:

$$\begin{bmatrix} xp' \\ yp' \\ zp' \end{bmatrix} = \begin{bmatrix} \cos(Ry) & 0 & \sin(Ry) \\ 0 & 1 & 0 \\ -\sin(Ry) & 0 & \cos(Ry) \end{bmatrix} \begin{bmatrix} xp \\ yp \\ zp \end{bmatrix} \tag{3-12}$$

This can be abbreviated as

$$[P'] = [Ry][P] \tag{3-13}$$

[Ry], *the transformation matrix* for y axis rotation, is

$$[Ry] = \begin{bmatrix} Cy(1,1) & Cy(1,2) & Cy(1,3) \\ Cy(2,1) & Cy(2,2) & Cy(2,3) \\ Cy(3,1) & Cy(3,2) & Cy(3,3) \end{bmatrix} \tag{3-14}$$

$$Cy(1,1) = cos(Ry) \tag{3-15}$$

$$Cy(1,2) = 0 \tag{3-16}$$

$$Cy(1,3) = sin(Ry) \tag{3-17}$$

$$Cy(2,1) = 0 \tag{3-18}$$

$$Cy(2,2) = 1 \tag{3-19}$$

$$Cy(2,3) = 0 \tag{3-20}$$

$$Cy(3,1) = -sin(Ry) \tag{3-21}$$

$$Cy(3,2) = 0 \tag{3-22}$$

$$Cy(3,3) = cos(Ry) \tag{3-23}$$

These elements will be used in the programs that follow.

Rotation Around the x Direction

Figure 3-7 shows the unit vector geometry for rotation around the x direction.

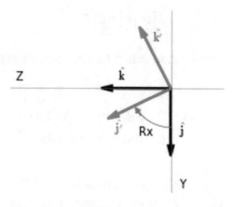

Figure 3-7. *Unit vectors for rotation around the x direction. The x axis runs into the plane of the paper*

You see that

$$\hat{\mathbf{i}}' = (1)\hat{\mathbf{i}} + (0)\hat{\mathbf{j}} + (0)\hat{\mathbf{k}} \tag{3-24}$$

$$\hat{\mathbf{j}}' = (0)\hat{\mathbf{i}} + cos(Rx)\hat{\mathbf{j}} + sin(Rx)\hat{\mathbf{k}} \tag{3-25}$$

$$\hat{\mathbf{k}}' = (0)\hat{\mathbf{i}} - sin(Rx)\hat{\mathbf{j}} + cos(Rx)\hat{\mathbf{k}} \tag{3-26}$$

Following the methods in the previous section,

$$\mathbf{P}' = xp\hat{\mathbf{i}}' + yp\hat{\mathbf{j}}' + zp\hat{\mathbf{k}}' \tag{3-27}$$

$$\mathbf{P}' = xp\hat{\mathbf{i}} + yp\left[cos(Rx)\hat{\mathbf{j}} + sin(Rx)\hat{\mathbf{k}}\right] + zp\left[-sin(Rx)\hat{\mathbf{j}} + cos(Rx)\hat{\mathbf{k}}\right] \tag{3-28}$$

$$= \underbrace{xp}_{xp'}\hat{\mathbf{i}} + \underbrace{\left[yp\,cos(Rx) - zp\,sin(Rx)\right]}_{yp'}\hat{\mathbf{j}} + \underbrace{\left[yp\,sin(Rx) + zp\,cos(Rx)\right]}_{zp'}\hat{\mathbf{k}} \tag{3-29}$$

In matrix form, it's

$$\begin{bmatrix} xp' \\ yp' \\ zp' \end{bmatrix} = \begin{bmatrix} 1 & 0 & 0 \\ 0 & cos(Rx) & -sin(Rx) \\ 0 & sin(Rx) & cos(Rx) \end{bmatrix} \begin{bmatrix} xp \\ yp \\ zp \end{bmatrix} \tag{3-30}$$

which can be abbreviated as

$$[P'] = [Rx][P] \tag{3-31}$$

This leads to the transformation matrix for x direction rotation of

$$[Rx] = \begin{bmatrix} 1 & 0 & 0 \\ 0 & cos(Rx) & -sin(Rx) \\ 0 & sin(Rx) & cos(Rx) \end{bmatrix} \tag{3-32}$$

$$[Rx] = \begin{bmatrix} Cx(1,1) & Cx(1,2) & Cx(1,3) \\ Cx(2,1) & Cx(2,2) & Cx(2,3) \\ Cx(3,1) & Cx(3,2) & Cx(3,3) \end{bmatrix} \tag{3-33}$$

$$Cx(1,1)=1 \tag{3-34}$$

$$Cx(1,2)=0 \tag{3-35}$$

$$Cx(1,3)=0 \tag{3-36}$$

$$Cx(2,1)=0 \tag{3-37}$$

$$Cx(2,2)=cos(Rx) \tag{3-38}$$

$$Cx(2,3)=-sin(Rx) \tag{3-39}$$

$$Cx(3,1)=0 \tag{3-40}$$

$$Cx(3,2)=sin(Rx) \tag{3-41}$$

$$Cx(3,3)=cos(Rx) \tag{3-42}$$

Rotation Around the z Direction

In Chapter 2, you derived the transformation matrix for two-dimensional rotation around the z direction. You will now do it in three dimensions. Repeating the two-dimensional Rz matrix (Equation 3-43) from Chapter 2:

$$\begin{bmatrix} xp' \\ yp' \end{bmatrix} = \begin{bmatrix} cos(Rz) & -sin(Rz) \\ sin(Rz) & cos(Rz) \end{bmatrix} \begin{bmatrix} xp \\ yp \end{bmatrix} \tag{3-43}$$

In three dimensions, you have the following:

$$\begin{bmatrix} xp' \\ yp' \\ zp' \end{bmatrix} = \begin{bmatrix} cos(Rz) & -sin(Rz) & 0 \\ sin(Rz) & cos(Rz) & 0 \\ 0 & 0 & 1 \end{bmatrix} \begin{bmatrix} xp \\ yp \\ zp \end{bmatrix} \tag{3-44}$$

$$[Rz] = \begin{bmatrix} Cz(1,1) & Cz(1,2) & Cz(1,3) \\ Cz(2,1) & Cz(2,2) & Cz(2,3) \\ Cz(3,1) & Cz(3,2) & Cz(3,3) \end{bmatrix} \tag{3-45}$$

$$Cz(1,1) = cos(Rz) \tag{3-46}$$

$$Cz(1,2) = -sin(Rz) \tag{3-47}$$

$$Cz(1,3) = 0 \tag{3-48}$$

$$Cz(2,1) = sin(Rz) \tag{3-49}$$

$$Cz(2,2) = cos(Rz) \tag{3-50}$$

$$Cz(2,3) = 0 \tag{3-51}$$

$$Cz(3,1) = 0 \tag{3-52}$$

$$Cz(3,2) = 0 \tag{3-53}$$

$$Cz(3,3) = 1 \tag{3-54}$$

You can extend the two-dimensional matrix equation to three dimensions in Equation 3-44 by simply observing that in the first row xp′ does not depend on zp, hence C(1,3)=0; in the second row, yp′ also does not depend on zp, hence c(2,3)=0; in the third row, zp′ does not depend on either xp′ or yp′, hence C(3,1) and C(3,2) both equal 0. C(3,3)=1 since the z coordinate remains unchanged after rotation about the z axis.

The three transformations are summarized as follows:

$$[Rx] = \begin{bmatrix} 1 & 0 & 0 \\ 0 & cos(Rx) & -sin(Rx) \\ 0 & sin(Rx) & cos(Rx) \end{bmatrix} \qquad (3\text{-}55)$$

$$[Ry] = \begin{bmatrix} cos(Ry) & 0 & sin(Ry) \\ 0 & 1 & 0 \\ -sin(Ry) & 0 & cos(Ry) \end{bmatrix} \qquad (3\text{-}56)$$

$$[Rz] = \begin{bmatrix} cos(Rz) & -sin(Rz) & 0 \\ sin(Rz) & cos(Rz) & 0 \\ 0 & 0 & 1 \end{bmatrix} \qquad (3\text{-}57)$$

Separate Rotations Around the Coordinate Directions

Figure 3-8 shows *separate* rotations of a box (a) about the x, y, and z directions. The figure was created using Listing 3-1. The rotations are separate, not sequential. That is, box (b) is box (a) rotated by Rx; box (c) is (a) rotated by Ry; and box (d) is (a) rotated by Rz. The rotations are not additive in this case, which means Ry is *not* added to the results of Rx and Rz is not added to the results of Rx and Ry; they are each separate rotations of the original box (a). The rotations take place around the center of the box.

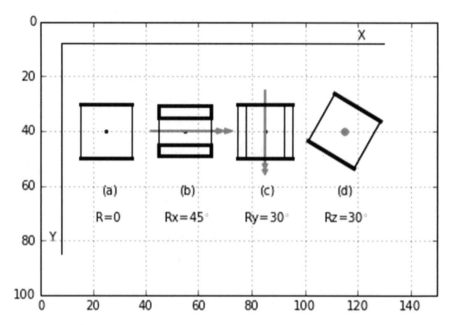

Figure 3-8. *Output from Listing 3-1. Projection (a) of an unrotated box on the x,y plane, (b) rotated around the x direction by Rx=45°, (c) around the y direction by Ry=30°, and (d) around the z direction by Rz=30°. Double-headed red arrows show the direction of rotation using the right-hand rule convention. Heavy lines indicate the top and bottom. The boxes are rotated about their center, which is indicated by a black dot*

Listing 3-1 makes use of functions and lists. Without them, the program would more than double in size. Using them reduces the program size considerably. It could be shortened even further by the use of arrays but the savings would be minimal and tends to obscure the methodology.

Figure 3-9 shows the corner numbering scheme used by Listing 3-1. The corner numbers are in blue. They are Python list numberings and start at 0. Normally we number the corners from 1 to 8. However, in Python, the first element in a list is always 0. We don't have to number the first corner as 0; we could use any number but numbering it 0 serves to remind us that the first element in a list is the 0th element. In the case of an eight-cornered box, the last corner, the eighth, is element 7 in the list. For example, the x coordinate of the first point is x[0], the second is x[1], and so on. It's like numbering the first rung of a ladder as the zeroth rung. Confusing? Yes. Blame it on the C programming language, from which this trap is a carryover. Perhaps the best way to avoid problems is to get in the habit of numbering things from 0 instead of 1, which is what I have done in Figure 3-9. I could have used a different arrangement of numbering in Figure 3-9 but starting with the top left corner and proceeding clockwise seems logical (e.g., I could have started the numbering at the top right-front corner instead of the top upper-left). It doesn't matter as long as the chosen scheme is consistent with the program.

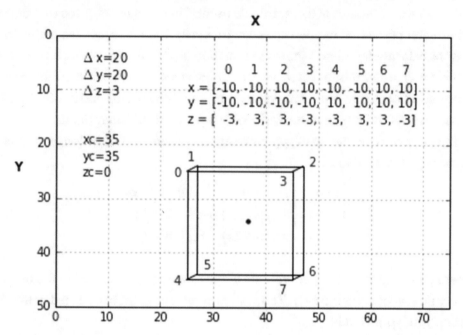

Figure 3-9. *Numbering scheme for the box's corners in Listing 3-1. Lists at the upper right contain the coordinate values. They are the same as the lists in Listing 3-1, lines 14, 15, and 16. The center coordinates xc,yc,zc are not the same as used in Listing 3-1. The z axis is not shown*

The lists shown in the figure define the corner coordinates. There are eight elements in each list because there are eight corners in the box. Corner 2, which is the *third* element in the list, has coordinates x[3]=10, y[3]=-10, z[3]=3. These are *local* coordinates; in other words, they are relative to the box's center, which is the center of rotation.

Listing 3-1 starts off by defining lists for [x], [y], and [z] in lines 14-16. These lines hold the coordinates of the box's corners relative to its center. [xg], [yg], and [zg] in lines 18-20 will hold the global plotting coordinates after rotation transformations have been done. Space is reserved for eight in each list since there are eight corners in the box.

Next are the definitions of the rotation functions rotx, roty, and rotz. They rotate a point's coordinates xp,yp,zp around the x, y, and z directions, respectively. Each function returns a new set of coordinates, xg, yg, and zg, which are the global coordinates of the rotated point. These coordinates will be used for plotting.

121

Looking at the definition of rotx, which begins in line 23, when invoked to do a transformation about the x direction rotx receives the box's center coordinates xc,yc,zc, which, in this case is the center of rotation, plus the point's unrotated coordinates xp,yp,zp and the angle of rotation about the x direction, Rx. The list a=[xp,yp,zp] in line 24 contains the coordinates of the unrotated point. This is, in effect, a vector that points from the center of rotation to point xp,yp,zp. In line 25, b=[1,0,0] is a list of the first row of the Rx transformation matrix shown in Equation 3-55. Line 26, xpp=np.inner(a,b), forms the dot or scalar product of these lists. There is also an np.dot(a,b) function that could be used. For simple non-complex vectors, np.inner(a,b) and np.dot(a,b) give the same results. But for higher dimensional arrays, the results may differ.

To illustrate the calculation of ypp for rotation around the x direction, you have seen that vector $\mathbf{p_{pp'}}$ is related to $\mathbf{p_p}$ by

$$\begin{bmatrix} xpp \\ ypp \\ zpp \end{bmatrix} = \begin{bmatrix} 1 & 0 & 0 \\ 0 & cos(Rx) & -sin(Rx) \\ 0 & sin(Rx) & cos(Rx) \end{bmatrix} \begin{bmatrix} xp \\ yp \\ zp \end{bmatrix} \tag{3-58}$$

where ypp (i.e., yp') is the y coordinate of the rotated point. Line 27 in the program is the second row of Equation 3-57. The scalar product of a and b is formed in line 28 producing ypp (yp'). That is,

$$a = [xp, yp, zp] \tag{3-59}$$

$$b = [0, cos(Rx), -sin(Rx)] \tag{3-60}$$

$$ypp = \text{np.inner}(a,b) \tag{3-61}$$

$$= xp(0) + yp(cos(Rx)) + zp(-sin(Rx)) \tag{3-62}$$

$$= ypcos(Rx) - zpsin(Rx) \tag{3-63}$$

which is line 28. Lines 29 and 30 repeat the process using the third row of Equation 3-57, producing zpp (zp'). Line 31 adds xc,yc,zc, the coordinates of the box's center, to xpp,ypp,zpp, thus translating the rotated points relative to the origin of the global coordinate system producing [xg,yg,zg] which are the global plotting coordinates. roty and rotz follow the same structure using the rows of [Ry] and [Rz] in their b lists.

Next is the function plotbox in line 56. This plots the box using its global corner coordinates xg, yg, and zg. The loop starting in line 57 plots the top by connecting the first three edges (0-1, 1-2, 2-3) with lines. Line 60 closes the top by plotting a line between corners 3 and 0. This has not been included in the loop, which was set up to plot one corner with the next. The problem comes when you try to connect corner 3 with 0; the algorithm in the loop doesn't work. It could be modified to handle it, but it's easier to just add line 60 rather than complicate the loop. The rest of plotbox up to line 68 completes the box. Line 70 plots a dot at its center.

Line 72 starts function plotboxx. This transforms the corner coordinates to get them ready for plotting by plotbox. The loop from line 73 to 74 rotates all eight corners around the x direction by invoking rotx. Line 76 invokes function plotbox, which does the plotting. plotboxy and plotboxz do the same for rotations about the y and z directions.

Up to this point, you have been defining functions. You use functions in this program since many of the operations are repetitive. If you tried to write this program using single statements, it would be at least twice as long.

Control of the program lies between lines 91 and 116. Lines 91-95 plot the first box (a). Since this first box (a) is unrotated, you specify Rx=0 in line 91. You use function plotboxx with the Rx=0 parameter to do the plotting. You could use Ry=0 with plotboxy or Rz=0 with plotboxz. It doesn't matter since the angle of rotation is 0. Lines 92-94 specify the box's center coordinates. Line 95 invokes plotboxx. The result is shown in Figure 3-8 as (a). Lines 98-116 produce the rotated boxes (b), (c), and (d).

To summarize the procedure using box (b) as an example, the angle of rotation is set in line 98; the box's center coordinates in lines 99-101. Then, in line 102, function plotboxx is invoked. The center coordinates and the angle Rx are passed as arguments. plotboxx, which begins in line 72, rotates the eight corners by invoking rotx. plotboxx doesn't use xc, yc, and zc, but it passes them onto rotx, which needs them. rotx rotates and translates the coordinates producing xg,yg,zg. Line 76 invokes function plotbox, which does the plotting.

In lines 91, 98, 105, and 112 you use the function radians(), which was imported from the math library in line 7. (Note that you could have used numpy for this). It converts an argument in degrees to one in radians, which are required by sin() and cos(). In earlier programs, you did the conversion with np.pi/180.

Listing 3-1. Program 4BOXES

```
1     """
2     4BOXES
3     """
4
5     import numpy as np
6     import matplotlib.pyplot as plt
7     from math import sin, cos, radians #-or use numpy
8
9     plt.axis([0,150,100,0])
10    plt.axis('on')
11    plt.grid(True)
12
13    #————————————————————-lists
14    x=[-10,-10,10,10,-10,-10,10,10] #-un-rotated corner coordinates
15    y=[-10,-10,-10,-10,10,10,10,10] #-relative to box's center
16    z=[ -3, 3, 3, -3,-3, 3, 3,-3]
17
18    xg=[0,1,2,3,4,5,6,7] #-define global coordinates
19    yg=[0,1,2,3,4,5,6,7]
20    zg=[0,1,2,3,4,5,6,7]
21
22    #————————————————-function definitions
23    def rotx(xc,yc,zc,xp,yp,zp,Rx):
24        a=[xp,yp,zp]
25        b=[1,0,0] #——————————-[cx11,cx12,cx13]
26        xpp=np.inner(a,b) #---scalar product of
          a,b=xp*cx11+yp*cx12+ zp*cx13
27        b=[0,cos(Rx),-sin(Rx)] #——————[cx21,cx22,cx23]
28        ypp=np.inner(a,b)
29        b=[0,sin(Rx),cos(Rx)] #——————[cx31,cx32,cx33]
30        zpp=np.inner(a,b)
31        [xg,yg,zg]=[xpp+xc,ypp+yc,zpp+zc]
32        return[xg,yg,zg]
33
```

```
34    def roty(xc,yc,zc,xp,yp,zp,Ry):
35        a=[xp,yp,zp]
36        b=[cos(Ry),0,sin(Ry)] #————-[cx11,cx12,cx13]
37        xpp=np.inner(a,  b)
38        b=[0,1,0] #————[cx21,cx22,cx23]
39        ypp=np.inner(a,b) #————-scalar product of a,b
40        b=[-sin(Ry),0,cos(Ry)] #————[cx31,cx32,cx33]
41        zpp=np.inner(a,b)
42        [xg,yg,zg]=[xpp+xc,ypp+yc,zpp+zc]
43        return[xg,yg,zg]
44
45    def rotz(xc,yc,zc,xp,yp,zp,Rz):
46        a=[xp,yp,zp]
47        b=[cos(Rz),-sin(Rz),0] #————-[cx11,cx12,cx13]
48        xpp=np.inner(a,  b)
49        b=[sin(Rz),cos(Rz),0] #————[cx21,cx22,cx23]
50        ypp=np.inner(a,b)
51        b=[0,0,1] #————[cx31,cx32,cx33]
52        zpp=np.inner(a,b) #————scalar product of a,b
53        [xg,yg,zg]=[xpp+xc,ypp+yc,zpp+zc]
54        return[xg,yg,zg]
55
56    def plotbox(xg,yg,zg): # -plots the box using its rotated coordinates
      xg,yg,zg
57        for i in (0,1,2): #————————-plot top
58            plt.plot([xg[i],xg[i+1]],[yg[i],yg[i+1]],linewidth=3,
                 color='k')
59
60        plt.plot([xg[3],xg[0]],[yg[3],yg[0]],linewidth=3,color='k')
          #-close top
61
62        for i in (4,5,6): #————————-plot bottom
63            plt.plot([xg[i],xg[i+1]],[yg[i],yg[i+1]],linewidth=3,
                 color='k')
64
```

```
65        plt.plot([xg[7],xg[4]],[yg[7],yg[4]],linewidth=3,color='k')
          #-close bottom
66
67        for i in (0,1,2,3): #————————plot sides
68            plt.plot([xg[i],xg[i-4]],[yg[i],yg[i-4]],linewidth=1,
              color='k')
69
70        plt.scatter(xc,yc,s=5) #-plot a dot at the center
71
72    def plotboxx(xc,yc,zc,Rx):
73        for i in (0,1,2,3,4,5,6,7): #————————-rotate eight corners
74            [xg[i],yg[i],zg[i]]=rotx(xc,yc,zc,x[i],y[i],z[i],Rx)
75
76        plotbox(xg,yg,zg)
77
78    def plotboxy(xc,yc,zc,Ry):
79        for i in (0,1,2,3,4,5,6,7): #————————-rotate eight corners
80            [xg[i],yg[i],zg[i]]=roty(xc,yc,zc,x[i],y[i],z[i],Ry)
81
82        plotbox(xg,yg,zg)
83
84    def plotboxz(xc,yc,zc,Rz):
85        for i in (0,1,2,3,4,5,6,7): #————————-rotate eight corners
86            [xg[i],yg[i],zg[i]]=rotz(xc,yc,zc,x[i],y[i],z[i],Rz)
87
88        plotbox(xg,yg,zg)
89
90    #————————————-R=0 box(a)
91    Rx=radians(0)
92    xc=25 #————box (a) center coordinates
93    yc=40
94    zc=20
95    plotboxx(xc,yc,zc,Rx) #-since Rx=0 we could use plotboxy or plotboxz
96
97    #————————————Rx box(b)
98    Rx=radians(45)
```

```
99    xc=55
100   yc=40
101   zc=20
102   plotboxx(xc,yc,zc,Rx)
103
104   #————————————————————-Ry box (c)
105   Ry=radians(30)
106   xc=85
107   yc=40
108   zc=20
109   plotboxy(xc,yc,zc,Ry)
110
111   #————————————————————-Rz box (d)
112   Rz=radians(30)
113   xc=115
114   yc=40
115   zc=20
116   plotboxz(xc,yc,zc,Rz)
117
118   #————————————————————-notes
119   plt.text(23,63,'(a)')
120   plt.text(53,63,'(b)')
121   plt.text(83,63,'(c)')
122   plt.text(112,63,'(d)')
123   plt.text(21,73,'R=0')
124   plt.text(47,73,'Rx=45°')
125   plt.text(77,73,'Ry=30°')
126   plt.text(107,73,'Rz=30°')
127   plt.arrow(42,40,25,0,head_width=2,head_length=3,color='r')
      #-red arrows
128   plt.arrow(42,40,28,0,head_width=2,head_length=3,color='r')
129   plt.arrow(85,25,0,27,head_width=2,head_length=2,color='r')
130   plt.arrow(85,25,0,29,head_width=2,head_length=2,color='r')
131   plt.plot([8,130],[8,8],color='k') #-axes
132   plt.plot([8,8],[8,85],color='k')
```

```
133    plt.text(120,6,'X')
134    plt.text(3,80,'Y')
135    plt.scatter(115,40,s=30,color='r') #——-red dot center of box (d)
136
137    plt.show()
```

Sequential Rotations Around the Coordinate Directions

In Listing 3-1, you operated on a box's initial corner coordinates defined by the lists in lines 14, 15, and 16. The program produced *separate* rotations around the x, y, and z coordinate directions. In this section, you begin with the same set of corner coordinates but you rotate *sequentially*. That is, after a rotation Rx about the x direction (b), rotation Ry is *added* to the results of Rx (c). Rz is then *added* to the results of Ry and Rx. The rotations are thus not independent as before but are additive. You do this by replacing the x, y, and z definitions in lines 14, 15, and 16 with a new set of coordinates following each rotation. That is, the box's corner coordinates are updated after each rotation so that the next rotation starts with the updated coordinates. This is accomplished by simply modifying functions plotboxx, plotboxy, and plotboxz between lines 72-88 in Listing 3-1. In Listing 3-2, lines 74b, 80b, and 86b are added. They do the updating by replacing the initial corner coordinates x,y,z with the transformed ones xg,yg,zg after each rotation. The code replaces lines 72-88 in Listing 3-1.

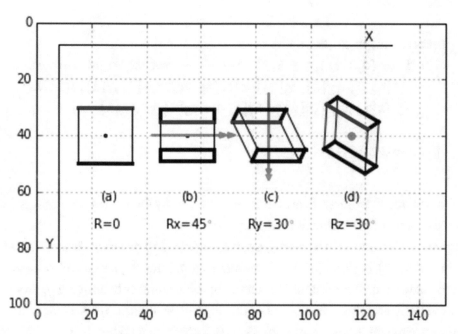

Figure 3-10. *Sequential rotations of a box. Box (a) is rotated by Rx=30° to (b), then by an <u>additional</u> rotation of Ry=30° to (c), and then by an <u>additional</u> rotation of Rz=15° to (d). x and y axes show direction only. Coordinate values are indicated by the grid*

Listing 3-2. Program 4BOXESUPDATE

```
71
72    def plotboxx(xc,yc,zc,Rx):
73            for i in (0,1,2,3,4,5,6,7): #————————rotate eight corners
74                    [xg[i],yg[i],zg[i]]=rotx(xc,yc,zc,x[i],y[i],z[i],Rx)
74b                   [x[i],y[i],z[i]]=[xg[i]-xc,yg[i]-yc,zg[i]-zc]
75
76            plotbox(xg,yg,zg)
77
78    def plotboxy(xc,yc,zc,Ry):
79            for i in (0,1,2,3,4,5,6,7): #————————rotate eight corners
80                    [xg[i],yg[i],zg[i]]=roty(xc,yc,zc,x[i],y[i],z[i],Ry)
80b                   [x[i],y[i],z[i]]=[xg[i]-xc,yg[i]-yc,zg[i]-zc]
81
82            plotbox(xg,yg,zg)
```

```
83
84    def plotboxz(xc,yc,zc,Rz):
85          for i in (0,1,2,3,4,5,6,7): #————————rotate eight corners
86                [xg[i],yg[i],zg[i]]=rotz(xc,yc,zc,x[i],y[i],z[i],Rz)
86b               [x[i],y[i],z[i]]=[xg[i]-xc,yg[i]-yc,zg[i]-zc]
87
88          plotbox(xg,yg,zg)
89
```

The transformation parameters are set in lines 91-116 by the values of rotations Rx, Ry, and Rz and the box center coordinates xc, yc, zc.

The sequence of rotations in this program is hard-wired to produce Figure 3-10 with (a) first, followed by (b), (c), and (d). In a general program, the sequence and values of rotations and center coordinates could be set to anything suitable by moving sections of code around or by entering the sequences through the keyboard. You will do both shortly. But first, you will do sequential rotations of a circle. See Figure 3-11.

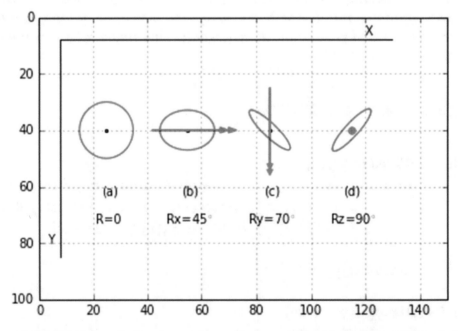

Figure 3-11. *Sequential rotations of a circle created by Listing 3-3. Circle (a) is rotated by Rx=45° to (b), then by an* <u>*additional*</u> *rotation of Ry=70° to (c), and then by an* <u>*additional*</u> *rotation of Rz=90° to (d). Red indicates the upper half of circle. x and y axes show direction only, not coordinate values, which are indicated by the grid*

Listing 3-3 is similar to the preceding modified version of Listings 3-1 and 3-2 where you did sequential rotations of a box. In that program, the box had eight corners, which had to be transformed and updated with every rotation. Here you have a circle, which has many more points, to transform and update.

In lines 23-38, you fill lists between lines 33 and 38 with starting values of local and global coordinates of points around the circumference of the circle. They are spaced dphi=5° apart as shown in line 25. The circle's radius is 10 as shown in line 27. The empty lists were previously defined in lines 14-20. As the loop starting at line 29 advances around the circle with angle phi, lines 30 to 32 calculate the local coordinates of each point. Lines 33-38 add the coordinates to the list using the append() function, which adds elements to a list. For example, with each cycle through the loop, line 33 appends (adds) the local value of xp at the current angle phi to the x list. Since you are just filling the list at this point, you can use xp,yp,zp to also fill the xg, yg, and zg lists in lines 36-38. Note that zp=0 (program line 32) in this initial definition of the circle. That is, the circle starts off flat in the x,y plane.

Lines 41-72 define the transformation functions as before. The circle plotting function extends from line 75-86. Lines are used to plot the circle. The plotting loop runs from 78-82. Line 86 plots a dot at the center.

Rather than counting the number of points around the circle, you use the range(len(x)) function to give the number of elements in the lists. You can use the length of x as a measure since all lists have the same length. Lines 79-82 plot the top half red and the bottom half green. Lines 83-84 update the last xg any yg global coordinates to use when plotting the lines as before. You don't need to include zg here since you use only xg and yg when plotting. Lines 89-108 transform coordinates as was done in Listings 3-1 and 3-2. The difference is here you have to deal with lists len(x) long whereas previously you had only eight corners.

Listing 3-3. Program SEQUENTIALCIRCLES

```
1    """
2    SEQUENTIALCIRCLES
3    """
4
5    import numpy as np
6    import matplotlib.pyplot as plt
7    from math import sin, cos, radians
```

```
 8
 9    plt.axis([0,150,100,0])
10    plt.axis('on')
11    plt.grid(True)
12
13    #————————————————define lists
14    x=[]
15    y=[]
16    z=[]
17
18    xg=[]
19    yg=[]
20    zg=[]
21
22    #——————————fill lists with starting coordinates
23    phi1=radians(0)
24    phi2=radians(360)
25    dphi=radians(5) #-circumferential points spaced 5 degrees
26
27    r=10 #-circle's radius
28
29    for phi in np.arange(phi1,phi2+dphi,dphi): # -establish coordinates
      of circumferential points
30          xp=r*cos(phi)
31          yp=r*sin(phi)
32    zp=0
33    x.append(xp)     #-fill lists
34    y.append(yp)
35    z.append(zp)
36    xg.append(xp)
37    yg.append(yp)
38    zg.append(zp)
39
40    #————————————————-define rotation functions
41    def rotx(xc,yc,zc,xp,yp,zp,Rx):
```

```
42          a=[xp,yp,zp]
43          b=[1,0,0] #——————————-[cx11,cx12,cx13]
44          xpp=np.inner(a,b) #---scalar product of
            a,b=xp*cx11+yp*cx12+ zp*cx13
45          b=[0,cos(Rx),-sin(Rx)] #———[cx21,cx22,cx23]
46          ypp=np.inner(a,b)
47          b=[0,sin(Rx),cos(Rx)] #———[cx31,cx32,cx33]
48          zpp=np.inner(a,b)
49          [xg,yg,zg]=[xpp+xc,ypp+yc,zpp+zc]
50          return[xg,yg,zg]
51
52      def roty(xc,yc,zc,xp,yp,zp,Ry):
53          a=[xp,yp,zp]
54          b=[cos(Ry),0,sin(Ry)] #————-[cx11,cx12,cx13]
55          xpp=np.inner(a, b)
56          b=[0,1,0] #———[cx21,cx22,cx23]
57          ypp=np.inner(a,b) #————-scalar product of a,b
58          b=[-sin(Ry),0,cos(Ry)] #———[cx31,cx32,cx33]
59          zpp=np.inner(a,b)
60          [xg,yg,zg]=[xpp+xc,ypp+yc,zpp+zc]
61          return[xg,yg,zg]
62
63      def rotz(xc,yc,zc,xp,yp,zp,Rz):
64          a=[xp,yp,zp]
65          b=[cos(Rz),-sin(Rz),0] #————-[cx11,cx12,cx13]
66          xpp=np.inner(a, b)
67          b=[sin(Rz),cos(Rz),0] #———[cx21,cx22,cx23]
68          ypp=np.inner(a,b)
69          b=[0,0,1] #———[cx31,cx32,cx33]
70          zpp=np.inner(a,b) #————scalar product of a,b
71          [xg,yg,zg]=[xpp+xc,ypp+yc,zpp+zc]
72          return[xg,yg,zg]
73
74  #————————————define circle plotting function
75  def plotcircle(xg,yg,zg):
```

```
76              lastxg=xg[0]
77              lastyg=yg[0]
78              for i in range(len(x)): #--len(x)=length of all lists
79                      if i < len(x)/2: #--half green
80                              plt.plot([lastxg,xg[i]],[lastyg,yg[i]],
                                linewidth=1,color='g')
81                      else:
82                              plt.plot([lastxg,xg[i]],[lastyg,yg[i]],
                                linewidth=1,color='r')
83              lastxg=xg[i]
84              lastyg=yg[i]
85
86          plt.scatter(xc,yc,s=5) #-plot a dot at the center
87
88      #————————-transform coordinates and plot
89      def plotcirclex(xc,yc,zc,Rx): #————-transform & plot Rx circle
90          for i in range(len(x)): #-for i in range(len(x)): ok too
91                  [xg[i],yg[i],zg[i]]=rotx(xc,yc,zc,x[i],y[i],z[i],Rx)
92                  [x[i],y[i],z[i]]=[xg[i]-xc,yg[i]-yc,zg[i]-zc]
93
94          plotcircle(xg,yg,zg) #————plot
95
96      def plotcircley(xc,yc,zc,Ry):
97          for i in range(len(x)): #————-transform & plot Ry circle
98                  [xg[i],yg[i],zg[i]]=roty(xc,yc,zc,x[i],y[i],z[i],Ry)
99                  [x[i],y[i],z[i]]=[xg[i]-xc,yg[i]-yc,zg[i]-zc]
100
101         plotcircle(xg,yg,zg)
102
103     def plotcirclez(xc,yc,zc,Rz):
104         for i in range(len(x)): #————-transform &  plot Rz circle
105                 [xg[i],yg[i],zg[i]]=rotz(xc,yc,zc,x[i],y[i],z[i],Rz)
106                 [x[i],y[i],z[i]]=[xg[i]-xc,yg[i]-yc,zg[i]-zc]
107
108         plotcircle(xg,yg,zg)
```

```
109
110    #——————————————plot circles
111    Rx=radians(0)
112    xc=25 #——circle (a) center coordinates
113    yc=40
114    zc=20
115    plotcirclex(xc,yc,zc,Rx) #-since R=0 we could use plotcircley or
       plotcirclez
116
117    #——————————————-Rx circle (b)
118    Rx=radians(45)
119    xc=55
120    yc=40
121    zc=20
122    plotcirclex(xc,yc,zc,Rx)
123
124    #——————————————-Ry circle (c)
125    Ry=radians(70)
126    xc=85
127    yc=40
128    zc=20
129    plotcircley(xc,yc,zc,Ry)
130
131    #——————————————-Rz circle (d)
132    Rz=radians(90)
133    xc=115
134    yc=40
135    zc=20
136    plotcirclez(xc,yc,zc,Rz)
137
138    #——————————————-notes
139    plt.text(23,63,'(a)')
140    plt.text(53,63,'(b)')
141    plt.text(83,63,'(c)')
142    plt.text(112,63,'(d)')
```

```
143    plt.text(21,73,'R=0')
144    plt.text(47,73,'Rx=45°')
145    plt.text(77,73,'Ry=70°')
146    plt.text(107,73,'Rz=90°')
147    plt.arrow(42,40,25,0,head_width=2,head_length=3,color='r')
       #-red arrows
148    plt.arrow(42,40,28,0,head_width=2,head_length=3,color='r')
149    plt.arrow(85,25,0,27,head_width=2,head_length=2,color='r')
150    plt.arrow(85,25,0,29,head_width=2,head_length=2,color='r')
151    plt.plot([8,130],[8,8],color='k') #-axes
152    plt.plot([8,8],[8,85],color='k')
153    plt.text(120,6,'X')
154    plt.text(3,80,'Y')
155    plt.scatter(115,40,s=30,color='r') #----red dot center of box (d)
156
157    plt.show()
```

Matrix Concatenation

Comparing Figure 3-12 with 3-11, you can see that, although Rx, Ry, and Rz have the same values in both figures, the resulting orientations of the circle in (c) and (d) are different. This is because the order of the rotation in Figure 3-11 is Rx,Ry,Rz while in Figure 3-12 it is Rx,Rz,Ry. Clearly the order of rotations is important.

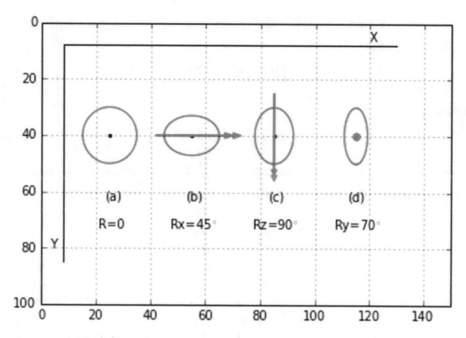

Figure 3-12. *Circle (a) is rotated sequentially by Rx=45° to (b), then by an additional rotation of Rz=90° to (c), followed by an additional rotation of Ry=70 to (d). Red indicates the upper half of circle. x and y axes show direction only, not coordinate values, which are indicated by the grid*

You can demonstrate this yourself. Take a book and place it flat on the edge of your desk front side up, top facing to the right. Imagine the desk's edge is the x direction going from left to right. Next, rotate the book 90 degrees around the x direction, followed by 90 degrees around the z direction. This is RzRx. The book will be upside down with the front facing you. Then lay the book flat again as before, reverse the order by rotating around the z direction first followed by the x direction. This is RxRz. As you can see, you get a different final orientation of the book in the two cases. The RzRx and RxRz may, at first, look like the x and z should be reversed. But the form used here is correct; in the case of RzRx, this indicates Rx operates on the image first, followed by Rz, the reverse for RxRz.

While you have carried out sequential rotations by ordering them and updating rotated coordinates in the program's code, mathematically it amounts to a multiplication of matrices. For example, the following equation produces a rotation Rx of vector [P] followed by a rotation Rz. The two rotations produce the vector [P']. Note, in Equation (3-64), Rx operates on P <u>first</u>.

$$[P'] = [Rz][Rx][P]$$ (3-64)

[Rx] operates on the vector [P], [Rz] then operates on the result of [Rx][P]. To rotate by Rz followed by Rx,

$$[P'] = [Rx][Rz][P] \tag{3-65}$$

In general,

$$[Rx][Rz] \neq [Rz][Rx] \tag{3-66}$$

I used the rotating book example before. I can also show this by a simple example using two-dimensional matrices. Consider two matrices, A and B, where

$$[A] = \begin{bmatrix} a & b \\ c & d \end{bmatrix} \tag{3-67}$$

$$[B] = \begin{bmatrix} e & f \\ g & h \end{bmatrix} \tag{3-68}$$

$$AB = \begin{bmatrix} a & b \\ c & d \end{bmatrix}\begin{bmatrix} e & f \\ g & h \end{bmatrix} = \begin{bmatrix} ae+bg & af+bh \\ ce+dg & cf+dh \end{bmatrix} \tag{3-69}$$

$$BA = \begin{bmatrix} e & f \\ g & h \end{bmatrix}\begin{bmatrix} a & b \\ c & d \end{bmatrix} = \begin{bmatrix} ae+cf & be+df \\ ag+ch & bg+dh \end{bmatrix} \tag{3-70}$$

$$\therefore AB \neq BA \tag{3-71}$$

For only three rotations around three different coordinate directions, there are six combinations of possible transformation sequences:

$$RxRyRz \tag{3-72}$$

$$RxRzRy \tag{3-73}$$

$$RyRxRz \tag{3-74}$$

$$RyRzRx \qquad\qquad\qquad (3\text{-}75)$$

$$RzRxRy \qquad\qquad\qquad (3\text{-}76)$$

$$RzRyRx \qquad\qquad\qquad (3\text{-}77)$$

Each of these combinations involves three separate rotations. You could multiply the three transformation matrices shown in Equations 3-55, 3-56, and 3-57 to get a single transformation matrix for each of these combinations. You could then write a program that would execute each of these combinations: select one combination, input the three angles, and then get the final rotation. But what if you wanted more than three rotations, such as RyRzRxRyRz? That would require a lot of matrix multiplying! Clearly it's much easier to incorporate the sequencing by coding it into the Python program and updating coordinates after each transformation, as you have learned how to do here.

To produce Figure 3-12, lines 110-136 of Listing 3-3 were replaced with the code in Listing 3-4.

Listing 3-4. Program SEQUENTIALCIRCLESUPDATE

```
109
110    #————————————————plot circles
111    Rx=radians(0)
112    xc=25 #————circle (a) center coordinates
113    yc=40
114    zc=20
115    plotcirclex(xc,yc,zc,Rx) #-since R=0 we could use plotcircley or
       plotcirclez
116
117    #————————————————-Rx circle (b)
118    Rx=radians(45)
119    xc=55
120    yc=40
121    zc=20
122    plotcirclex(xc,yc,zc,Rx)
123
124    #————————————————-Rz circle (d)
```

```
125    Rz=radians(90)
126    xc=85
127    yc=40
128    zc=20
129    plotcirclez(xc,yc,zc,Rz)
130
131    #————————————————————-Ry circle (c)
132    Ry=radians(70)
133    xc=115
134    yc=40
135    zc=20
136    plotcircley(xc,yc,zc,Ry)
137
```

Here you have performed the operation RxRzRy, reversing the order of the last two transformations. Circle (a) is plotted as before with Rx=0 in line 111. Also as before, circle (b) is plotted next with Rx=45 degrees in line 118. The difference is in lines 124-136 where the rotations Ry and Rz are reversed and Rz is plotted *before* Ry. The angles have the same values as before. Rearranging the order of plotting is easy; just cut and paste sections of the code. But be sure to update the center coordinates xc, yc, and zc. You could make the program a lot more user-friendly by introducing the input() function, which will give you the ability to input the order of transformations through the keyboard. You could then enter the rotations Rx, Ry, or Rz and the amount and the center coordinates in any order. You will do that next.

Keyboard Data Entry with Functional Program Structure

As you saw in the discussion of matrix concatenation, rearranging the order of rotations in a program can be a useful option. However, as you will see in this section, entering data via the keyboard is much more satisfactory. You will also use a functional programming structure where a few lines of code control various predefined functions that carry out the various operations. This will give you great flexibility in controlling the program.

Listing 3-5 produced the results shown in Figures 3-13 through 3-16. The first figure shows a circle rotated around the x direction by 0°; the second around the y direction by 60°; the third around the x direction by 45°; and the fourth around the z direction by 90°.

All rotations are added to the previous orientation of the circle. The axis of rotation and the amount were entered through the keyboard. The sequence of rotation directions did not matter, nor did the number of rotations.

Referring to Listing 3-5, lines 111-113 specify the circle's center coordinates. All circles have the same center coordinates. The while True: statement in line 115 keeps the data entry loop running so you can do an unlimited number of sequential rotations. Line 116 asks you to specify the axis of rotation in the Spyder output pane. Enter x, y, or z in lowercase letters. To exit the loop, press the Enter key. (**Important**: If you are using the Spyder console, be sure to click the mouse with the cursor in the output pane before entering anything. If you forget and leave it in the program pane, you are liable to get an unwanted x, y, or z imbedded somewhere in the program. If this happens, go to the top of the screen and open a new console. This essentially starts the program over.). If you enter x (lowercase), line 118 asks for the angle of rotation Rx. Enter it as a positive or negative angle in degrees. The input() function returns a string. The float command converts it to a float. Line 119 then invokes function plotcirclex(), which plots the rotated circle. Ry and Rz rotations are carried out in a similar way. Note there is no restriction on the sequence or the number of rotations. Line 126 checks to see if you entered a blank for axis, in which case line 127 exits the program. All circles are rotated around the same center, xc,yc,zc. If you want to be able to move the centers of each circle, just add input() lines for the center coordinates between lines 115 and 116.

Lines 89-108 rotate and update the coordinates of the circle's circumferential points as was done in Listing 3-3. In function plotcircle(), lines 71-86 do the plotting. Each time this function is invoked, the axes and grid are replotted. Line 86 shows the latest plot.

This program is an important illustration of program control. Just the few lines between 115 and 127 control the entire operation of the program and give great flexibility in controlling the sequence of operations and the data used. In other programming languages, such as Basic and Fortran, this is referred to as *top-down programming*. In those languages *subroutines*, which are the equivalents of Python functions, are generally placed at the bottom, while the controlling code is put at the top. In Python, you normally put the functions at the top with the control at the bottom, a style called *bottom-up programming*. Whether control is at the top or the bottom, this program structure is called *functional programming* since the controlling code uses functions to carry out the various operations. Since controlling data is input through the keyboard, it offers considerable flexibility.

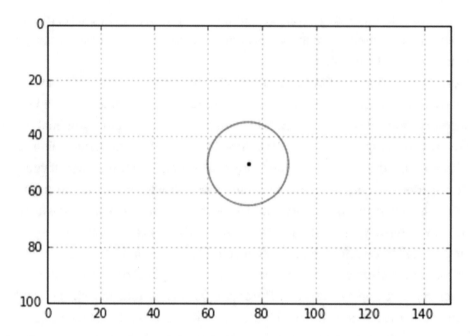

Figure 3-13. *The circle is rotated around the x axis by 0°*

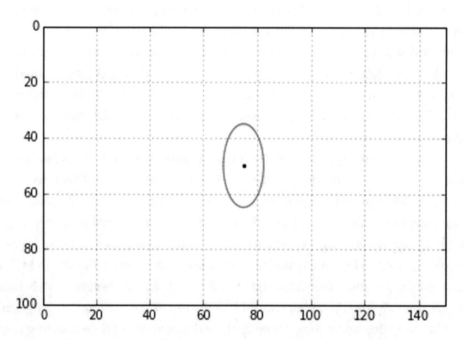

Figure 3-14. *The previous circle is rotated around the x axis by 60°*

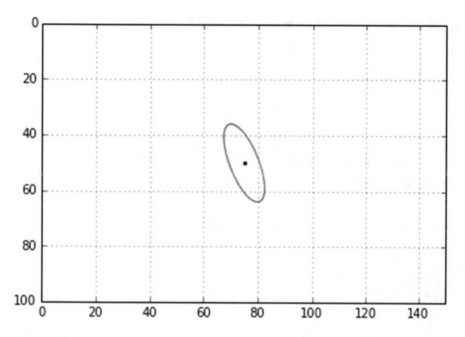

Figure 3-15. *The previous circle is rotated around the y axis by 45°*

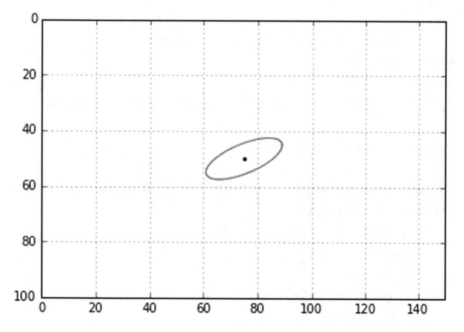

Figure 3-16. *The previous circle is rotated around the z axis by 90⁰*

Listing 3-5. Program KEYBOARDDATAENTRY

```
1    """
2    KEYBOARDDATAENTRY
3    """
4
5    import numpy as np
6    import matplotlib.pyplot as plt
7    from math import sin, cos, radians
8
9    #—————————————————-define  lists
10   x=[]
11   y=[]
12   z=[]
13
14   xg=[]
15   yg=[]
16   zg=[]
17
18   #——————————fill lists with starting coordinates
19   phi1=radians(0)
20   phi2=radians(360)
21   dphi=radians(5) #-circumferential points spaced 5 degrees
22
23   radius=15 #-circle's radius
24
25   for phi in np.arange(phi1,phi2+dphi,dphi): #-establish coordinates of
     circumferential points
26       xp=radius*cos(phi)
27       yp=radius*sin(phi)
28       zp=0
29       x.append(xp) #-fill lists
30       y.append(yp)
31       z.append(zp)
32       xg.append(xp)
33       yg.append(yp)
```

```
34          zg.append(zp)
35
36     #———————————define rotation functions
37     def rotx(xc,yc,zc,xp,yp,zp,Rx):
38          a=[xp,yp,zp]
39          b=[1,0,0] #—————————-[cx11,cx12,cx13]
40          xpp=np.inner(a,b) #--scalar product of
            a,b=xp*cx11+yp*cx12+ zp*cx13
41          b=[0,cos(Rx),-sin(Rx)] #————[cx21,cx22,cx23]
42          ypp=np.inner(a,b)
43          b=[0,sin(Rx),cos(Rx)] #————[cx31,cx32,cx33]
44          zpp=np.inner(a,b)
45          [xg,yg,zg]=[xpp+xc,ypp+yc,zpp+zc]
46          return[xg,yg,zg]
47
48     def roty(xc,yc,zc,xp,yp,zp,Ry):
49          a=[xp,yp,zp]
50          b=[cos(Ry),0,sin(Ry)] #———————-[cx11,cx12,cx13]
51          xpp=np.inner(a, b)
52          b=[0,1,0] #————[cx21,cx22,cx23]
53          ypp=np.inner(a,b) #————————scalar product of a,b
54          b=[-sin(Ry),0,cos(Ry)] #————[cx31,cx32,cx33]
55          zpp=np.inner(a,b)
56          [xg,yg,zg]=[xpp+xc,ypp+yc,zpp+zc]
57          return[xg,yg,zg]
58
59     def rotz(xc,yc,zc,xp,yp,zp,Rz):
60          a=[xp,yp,zp]
61          b=[cos(Rz),-sin(Rz),0] #———————-[cx11,cx12,cx13]
62          xpp=np.inner(a, b)
63          b=[sin(Rz),cos(Rz),0] #————[cx21,cx22,cx23]
64          ypp=np.inner(a,b)
65          b=[0,0,1] #————[cx31,cx32,cx33]
66          zpp=np.inner(a,b) #————————scalar product of a,b
67          [xg,yg,zg]=[xpp+xc,ypp+yc,zpp+zc]
```

```
68          return[xg,yg,zg]
69
70     #————————————define circle plotting function
71     def plotcircle(xg,yg,zg):
72          lastxg=xg[0]
73          lastyg=yg[0]
74          for i in range(len(x)): #-for i in range(len(x)): ok too
75                  if i < len(x)/2: #--half green
76                          plt.plot([lastxg,xg[i]],[lastyg,yg[i]],
                                 linewidth=1  ,color='g')
77                  else:
78                          plt.plot([lastxg,xg[i]],[lastyg,yg[i]],
                                 linewidth=1  ,color='r')
79          lastxg=xg[i]
80          lastyg=yg[i]
81
82          plt.scatter(xc,yc,s=5,color='k') #-plot a dot at the center
83          plt.axis([0,150,100,0]) #-replot axes and grid
84          plt.axis('on')
85          plt.grid(True)
86          plt.show() #-plot latest rotation
87
88     #————————————transform coordinates and plot
89     def plotcirclex(xc,yc,zc,Rx): #————-transform and plot Rx circle
90          for i in range(len(x)):
91                  [xg[i],yg[i],zg[i]]=rotx(xc,yc,zc,x[i],y[i],z[i],Rx)
92                  [x[i],y[i],z[i]]=[xg[i]-xc,yg[i]-yc,zg[i]-zc]
93
94          plotcircle(xg,yg,zg) #————plot
95
96     def plotcircley(xc,yc,zc,Ry):
97           for i in range(len(x)): #————-transform and plot Ry circle
98                  [xg[i],yg[i],zg[i]]=roty(xc,yc,zc,x[i],y[i],z[i],Ry)
99                  [x[i],y[i],z[i]]=[xg[i]-xc,yg[i]-yc,zg[i]-zc]
100
```

```
101        plotcircle(xg,yg,zg)
102
103    def plotcirclez(xc,yc,zc,Rz):
104        for i in range(len(x)): #————transform and plot Rz circle
105            [xg[i],yg[i],zg[i]]=rotz(xc,yc,zc,x[i],y[i],z[i],Rz)
106            [x[i],y[i],z[i]]=[xg[i]-xc,yg[i]-yc,zg[i]-zc]
107
108        plotcircle(xg,yg,zg)
109
110    #————————————plot circles
111    xc=75 #-center coordinates
112    yc=50
113    zc=50
114
115    while True:
116        axis=input('x, y or z?: ') #-input axis of rotation (lower case)
117        if axis == 'x': #-if x axis
118            Rx=radians(float(input('Rx degrees?: ')))
119            plotcirclex(xc,yc,zc,Rx) #-call function plotcirclex
120        if axis == 'y':
121            Ry=radians(float(input('Ry degrees?: ')))
122            plotcircley(xc,yc,zc,Ry)
123        if axis == 'z':
124            Rz=radians(float(input('Rz degrees?: ')))
125            plotcirclez(xc,yc,zc,Rz)
126        if axis == ":
127            break
```

Summary

In this chapter, you learned how to construct three-dimensional coordinate axes and three-dimensional shapes and how to rotate and translate them around the three coordinate directions. This involved derivation of rotation transformations around the three coordinate directions. You saw the difference between rotating an object once from its original orientation and rotating it in sequential steps where each subsequent rotation uses the object's coordinates from the prior rotation as the starting point. You explored the idea that the sequence of rotations is important; Rx,Ry,Rz does not produce the same results as Rx,Rz,Ry. This was shown by a book analogy and by matrix concatenation. You learned how to use the append() function to add elements to a list. You also learned how to use the range(len(x)) function, which returns the number of elements in a lists. Finally, you developed a program where sequential rotations could be entered through the keyboard as opposed to specifying them in the program. All of this work involved the use of lists.

CHAPTER 4

Perspective

I mentioned the difference between isometric and perspective views in the previous chapter. Now you will develop a transformation that will automatically produce a perspective view. It operates much like a camera where rays are traced from the various points that comprise an object onto a plane that you might think of as a film plane. Figure 4-1 shows the geometry. The object is a three-dimensional box in the x,y,z space. The x,y plane represents the *film* plane, so-called because it is analogous to the location of the film in an older camera. There's also a *focal point* that is outside the x,y,z space in front of the x,y plane. Imaginary rays are traced from the box's corners to the focal point. By connecting the points where the rays hit the film plane, which is the same as the xy plane, you can construct a perspective view of the box.

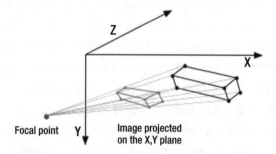

Figure 4-1. *Geometry used to project a perspective image of an object on the x,y plane*

As shown in Figure 4-2, a primitive camera can be constructed by putting a small hole in an opaque sheet. This is called a pinhole camera. Rays from an object passing through this hole will produce a photographic-like perspective image on a film plane. The film captures this image. The perspective transformation you will be producing in this chapter will operate in a somewhat similar manner, except you will be tracing the image on your computer screen instead of on a sheet of film.

© Bernard Korites 2023
B. Korites, *Python Graphics*, https://doi.org/10.1007/978-1-4842-9660-8_4

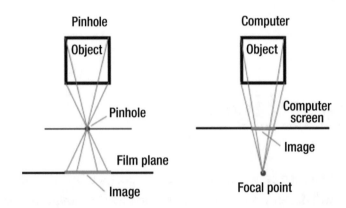

Figure 4-2. *Pinhole camera vs. computer projection geometry*

The *camera obscura* has been used by artists since the time of Vermeer (C 1650). It consisted of a box large enough for the artist to sit in. Its inner walls were painted black and care was taken to ensure no light leaked in from the outside. A small hole was drilled in one wall. This hole faced whatever scene the artist was interested in. Light would come in from the scene, pass through the hole and be projected onto a canvas or sheet of paper attached to the opposite wall, creating a perspective view similar to what we see in Figure 4-1. The image could be easily traced or painted directly on the canvas or paper. The pinhole didn't produce a very good image and was eventually replaced by a lens. A Dutch microbiologist named Antonie van Leeuwenhoek was a contemporary of Vermeer and lived not too far from him in Delft. He did a lot of experimenting with lenses and optics and is reported to have built the first microscope to help him with his studies of microbiology. Some ascribe the first microscope to spectacle maker Zacharias Janssen, born in 1585. It is suspected Vermeer might have availed himself of Leeuwenhoek's and Janssen's work in optics to produce his beautifully detailed works, which show perfect perspective.

The geometry of the camera obscura is similar to our computer model except that the pinhole geometry produces a reversed image. If the focal point is moved far back in the -z direction, the rays from the object become almost parallel and the perspective effect is lost; the image becomes flattened. This phenomenon is well known to photographers when shooting with a long focal length lens. Things get magnified but flattened. The Austrian painter Gustav Klimt liked to paint scenes of distant objects. But his scenes appear flattened. He is thought to have painted while looking through a telescope that probably had a long focal length lens.

Figures 4-3 and 4-4 show the geometry you will use to construct your transformation. Figure 4-3 shows a three-dimensional object inside the x,y,z space. The focal point is outside the space at global coordinates (xfp,yfp,zfp). It can be anywhere in front of (-z direction) the x,y plane. Different locations will produce different views of the object, much as a camera will produce different images when photographing an object from different locations.

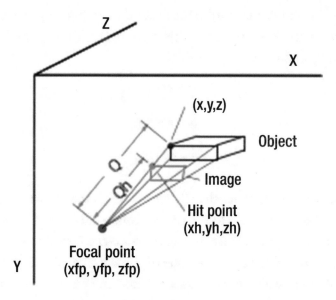

Figure 4-3. *Perspective image projection geometry*

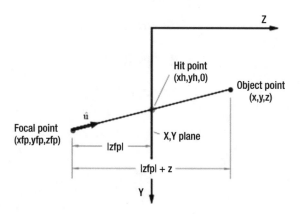

Figure 4-4. *Perspective image projection geometry side view*

Imaginary rays emanating from the corners of the box pass through the x,y plane, which you can imagine is your computer screen. Each ray hits the x,y plane at a *hit point* (xh,yh,zh=0) on its way to the focal point of zh=0 since the x,y plane is at z=0. Connecting the hit points produced by the rays coming from the points comprising the object will produce a perspective image.

A typical point on the object is located at (x,y,z). Referring to Figures 4-3 and 4-4, the distance between the point and the focal point is Q. Qh is the distance from the focal point to the hit point. |zfp|+z is the horizontal distance from the focal point to the object point. |z| is the horizontal distance from the focal point to the hit point. û is a unit vector pointing from the focal point toward the object point. Using this geometry, you can derive the following relations:

$$a = x - xfp \tag{4-1}$$

$$b = y - yfp \tag{4-2}$$

$$c = z + |zfp| \tag{4-3}$$

Since, in Equation 4-3, zfp is negative (it lies in front of the x,y plane), you use its absolute value |zfp| because it adds to z to give the total z-direction distance between the focal point and the object point. You could, of course, write Equation 4-3 as c=z-zfp, which is equivalent, but the use of the absolute value |zfp| makes the following analysis more understandable. Also, it won't matter if you forget and enter a positive z value for zfp.

$$Q = \sqrt{a^2 + b^2 + c^2} \tag{4-4}$$

$$ux = a / Q \tag{4-5}$$

$$uy = b / Q \tag{4-6}$$

$$uz = c / Q \tag{4-7}$$

$$\hat{\mathbf{u}} = ux\hat{\mathbf{i}} + uy\hat{\mathbf{j}} + uz\hat{\mathbf{k}} \tag{4-8}$$

$$Qh = \frac{Q|zfp|}{z + |zfp|} \tag{4-9}$$

$$xh = uxQh + xfp \tag{4-10}$$

$$yh = uyQh + yfp \tag{4-11}$$

$$zh = 0 \tag{4-12}$$

You can show zh=0 (i.e., the hit point lies on the x,y plane, as it should) by the following:

$$|zh = uzQh - |zfp| \tag{4-13}$$

$$= \frac{c}{Q}Qh - |zfp| \tag{4-14}$$

$$= (z + |zfp|)\frac{Qh}{Q} - |zfp| \tag{4-15}$$

$$= \frac{(z + |zfp|)}{Q}\frac{Q|zfp|}{(z + |zfp|)} - |zfp| \tag{4-16}$$

$$= |zfp| - |zfp| \tag{4-17}$$

$$= 0 \tag{4-18}$$

The negative sign in Equation 4-13 is because |zfp| is always positive while you know that the focal point is always in the -z position.

Listing 4-1 illustrates the use of the above model. It enables you to construct an object, rotate it, and then view it in perspective. The object, in this case a house, is defined in lines 14-29. Lines 14-16 establish corner coordinates x,y,z in local coordinates; that is, in relation to a point xc,yc,zc, which is set in lines 18-20. This is at the center of the house and it will be the center of rotation. Lines 22-29 convert x,y,z to global coordinates xg,yg,zg by adding elements to the empty lists set in lines 22-24. Lines 31-47 plot the house by connecting the corner points with lines.

Lines 50-63 define a function that rotates the local coordinates about xc,yc,zc, saving the results as xg,yg,zg. It uses function `roty`, which is defined in lines 54-63. This function was used in prior programs. It is the only rotation function in this program, which means you can only rotate around the y direction. Next is the perspective transformation `perspective(xfp,yfp,zfp)`; it implements Equations 4-1 through 4-12, developed above. The loop beginning in line 67 calculates the coordinates of the hit point for rays that go to the focal point from each of the object's corner points. The hit points, in terms of global coordinates, are saved in lines 79-81.

Control of the program takes place in lines 83-95. Lines 83-85 define the location of the focal point; lines 87-89 define the house's center point. Ry in line 91 specifies the angle of rotation about the y direction. Line 93 then invokes function plothouse(xc,yc,zc,Ry), which rotates the house. Line 94 invokes perspective(xfp,yfp,zfp), which performs the perspective transformation. Line 95 plots the house. This could have been incorporated in the function perspective but it has been placed here to illustrate the sequence of operations.

Listing 4-1. Program PERSPECTIVE

```
1    """
2    PERSPECTIVE
3    """
4
5    import matplotlib.pyplot as plt
6    import numpy as np
7    from math import sin, cos, radians
8
9    plt.axis([0,150,100,0])
10
11   plt.axis('on')
12   plt.grid(True)
13
14
x=[-20,-20,20,20,-20,-20,20,20,-20,20] #---object local corner coordinates
15   y=[-10,-10,-10,-10,10,10,10,10,-20,-20]
16   z=[5,-5,-5,5,5,-5,-5,5,0,0]
17
18   xc=30 #————————————object center coordinates
19   yc=50
20   zc=10
21
22   xg=[ ] #————————————object global coordinates
23   yg=[ ]
24   zg=[ ]
25
```

```
26  for i in np.arange(len(x)):
27          xg.append(x[i]+xc)
28          yg.append(y[i]+yc)
29          zg.append(z[i]+zc)
30
31  #————————plot object
32  def plothouse(xg,yg,zg):
33          plt.plot([xg[0],xg[3]],[yg[0],yg[3]],color='k')
34          plt.plot([xg[1],xg[2]],[yg[1],yg[2]],color='k')
35          plt.plot([xg[4],xg[7]],[yg[4],yg[7]],color='k')
36          plt.plot([xg[5],xg[6]],[yg[5],yg[6]],color='k')
37          plt.plot([xg[8],xg[9]],[yg[8],yg[9]],color='k')
38          plt.plot([xg[4],xg[0]],[yg[4],yg[0]],color='k')
39          plt.plot([xg[5],xg[1]],[yg[5],yg[1]],color='k')
40          plt.plot([xg[6],xg[2]],[yg[6],yg[2]],color='r')
41          plt.plot([xg[7],xg[3]],[yg[7],yg[3]],color='r')
42          plt.plot([xg[0],xg[8]],[yg[0],yg[8]],color='k')
43          plt.plot([xg[1],xg[8]],[yg[1],yg[8]],color='k')
44          plt.plot([xg[2],xg[9]],[yg[2],yg[9]],color='r')
45          plt.plot([xg[3],xg[9]],[yg[3],yg[9]],color='r')
46          plt.plot([xg[4],xg[5]],[yg[4],yg[5]],color='k')
47          plt.plot([xg[6],xg[7]],[yg[6],yg[7]],color='r')
48
49  #————————rotate object about the Y direction
40  def plothousey(xc,yc,zc,Ry):
51          for i in range(len(x)): #————rotate 10 corners
52                  [xg[i],yg[i],zg[i]]=roty(xc,yc,zc,x[i],y[i],z[i],Ry)
53
54  def roty(xc,yc,zc,x,y,z,Ry):
55          a=[x,y,z]
56          b=[cos(Ry),0,sin(Ry)]
57          xpp=np.inner(a,b)
58          b=[0,1,0]
59          ypp=np.inner(a,b)
60          b=[-sin(Ry),0,cos(Ry)]
```

```
61          zpp=np.inner(a,b)
62          [xg,yg,zg]=[xpp+xc,ypp+yc,zpp+zc]
63          return [xg,yg,zg]
64
65   #─────────────────────────────────────perspective transformation
66   def perspective(xfp,yfp,zfp):
67          for i in range(len(x)):
68                  a=xg[i]-xfp
69                  b=yg[i]-yfp
70                  c=zg[i]+abs(zfp)
71                  q=np.sqrt(a*a+b*b+c*c)
72                  ux=a/q
73                  uy=b/q
74                  uz=c/q
75                  qh=q*abs(zfp)/(zg[i]+abs(zfp))
76                  xh=ux*qh+xfp
77                  yh=uy*qh+yfp
78                  zh=0
79                  xg[i]=xh
80                  yg[i]=yh
81                  zg[i]=zh
82
83   xfp=80 #─────────────────────────focal point coordinates
84   yfp=50
85   zfp=-100
86
87   xc=80 #─────────────redefine center coordinates
88   yc=50
89   zc=50
90
91   Ry=radians(45)  #─────────────────────angle of rotation
92
93   plothousey(xc,yc,zc,Ry)                #--rotate
94   perspective(xfp,yfp,zfp)               #--transform
```

```
95  plothouse(xg,yg,zg)                        #--rotate
96
97  plt.show()
```

Figures 4-5 through 4-8 show output from Listing 4-1. Figure 4-5 shows the house in its unrotated (Ry=0) orientation. The right side is red. The focal point is at xc=80,yc=50,-100. This is in line with the house's center but 100 in front of the x,y plane. Figure 4-6 shows the house rotated 45 degrees around the y direction. The perspective effect is apparent. Figure 4-7 shows the house with the same settings but with the focal point moved back from zfp=-100 to zfp=-600. You can see how the image is flattened and the perspective effect is mostly lost. Figure 4-8 shows the house with some random settings. By following the procedure in Listing 4-1, you should be able to create a more elaborate scene quite easily.

Figure 4-5. *Perspective image with Ry=0, zfp=-100*

Figure 4-6. *Perspective image with Ry=45, zfp=-100*

Figure 4-7. *Perspective image with Ry=45, zfp=-600*

Figure 4-8. *Perspective image with Ry=-60, zfp=-100, xc=40, yc=70, xfp=100, zfp=-80*

You will get a more dramatic perspective effect if you put the focal point closer to the xy plane, say z=-70. The question is, where to place the focal point? If you're projecting the image onto the x,y plane, clearly it should be in front of that plane (i.e., i the -z direction). But what about the x,y coordinates of the focal point? The best results, most like what would be seen by the human eye, would be to place it at the same x,y coordinates as the house's center. Of course, if there are many objects in the model, such as more houses and trees, it is not obvious where to place the focal point. All photographers and painters face this dilemma: what gives the most appealing view? The best results will often be obtained by situating it in front of the x,y plane at the coordinates that correspond to the approximate center of the model. This is akin to aiming a camera at the center of a scene to be photographed. Vermeer chose this structure in many of his paintings. In fact, in some of his canvases art historians have found a nail hole in the canvas at the vanishing point where all parallel lines such as room corners and floor tiles converge. The nail hole is in the approximate center of the scene. It is believed he tied a string to a nail hammered into a wood support behind the canvas and used it to trace the converging lines, much as you have used lines in your algorithm. You can see this structure in many of Vermeer's interior paintings.

Summary

In this chapter, you learned how to construct a perspective view. The geometry is based on a simple box camera. You had the perspective image projected onto the x, y plane. You could have used any of the other coordinate planes, for example the x, z plane; the geometry would be similar. You explored the question of where to place the focal point, which corresponds to the observation point of a viewer or a camera. The answer is, unless you are looking for an unusual image, place it at the same, or approximately the same, x, y coordinates as the center of the model. This was the structure used by Vermeer in many of his paintings. It draws your eye into the center of the painting.

CHAPTER 5

Intersections

In this chapter, you will develop algorithms that will tell you where lines and planes intersect a variety of objects. The techniques you will develop will be useful later when you remove hidden lines and trace shadows cast by objects. You will also learn how to show the intersection of lines and planes with a sphere. As you will see, there is no one magic algorithm that will satisfy all situations; each requires its own methodology. While you may never need some of these algorithms, such as a line intersecting a circular sector, the procedures, which rely on vector-based geometry, are interesting and should give you the tools you will need when you encounter different situations.

Instead of using vectors, many of these solutions could be derived analytically. For example, the solution for a line intersecting a sphere can be obtained by combining the equation of a line with that of a sphere. The result is a quadratic equation that, when solved, yields the entrance and exit points. Such an approach can be fast and simple, provided you are dealing with objects that can be represented by simple equations. However, the vector-based procedures, while they may seem more complex, are actually quite simple and intuitive. They can also be much more versatile and adaptable to unusual situations. They are the ones you will use here.

Line Intersecting a Rectangular Plane

Figure 5-1 shows a line intersecting a rectangular plane. You will develop an algorithm and a program to find the point of intersection, called the *hit point*. Here you are stipulating that the plane is finite, but it doesn't have to be. After going through the analysis, you will see there is nothing here that requires the plane be finite. You also start off by assuming the plane is rectangular. It doesn't have to be rectangular but, for now, it is easier to keep it finite and rectangular.

159

© Bernard Korites 2023
B. Korites, *Python Graphics*, https://doi.org/10.1007/978-1-4842-9660-8_5

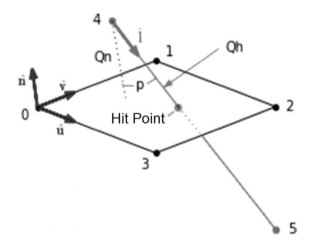

Figure 5-1. *Geometry of a line intersecting a rectangular plane*

The plane has corners at 0, 1, 2, and 3. They have local coordinates of (x0,y0,z0) - (x3,y3,z3) relative to the center of rotation at (xc,yc,zc). The line starts at x[4],y[4],z[4] and ends at x[5],y[5],z[5]. It intersects the plane at the hit point.

There are three unit vectors at corner 0; $\hat{u}$, $\hat{v}$, and $\hat{n}$. Unit vector $\hat{v}$ points from corner 0 to 1; $\hat{u}$ from 0 to 3. $\hat{n}$ is normal to the plane. $\hat{l}$ is a unit vector pointing along the line from 4 to 5. Q_{45} is the distance from 4 to 5. Q_h is the distance from 4 to the hit point. Q_n is the perpendicular distance from 4 to the plane. Your quest is to determine the location of the hit point (xh,yh,zh). Using vector geometry, you can write the following relations:

Distance 4 → 5:

$$a = x[5] - x[4] \tag{5-1}$$

$$b = y[5] - y[4] \tag{5-2}$$

$$c = z[5] - z[4] \tag{5-3}$$

$$Q_{45} = \sqrt{a^2 + b^2 + c^2} \tag{5-4}$$

Unit vector 4 → 5:

$$lx = \frac{a}{Q_{45}}$$

(5-5)

$$ly = \frac{b}{Q_{45}}$$

(5-6)

$$lz = \frac{c}{Q_{45}}$$

(5-7)

$$\hat{\mathbf{l}} = lx\hat{\mathbf{i}} + ly\hat{\mathbf{j}} + lz\hat{\mathbf{k}}$$

(5-8)

Distance 0 → 3:

$$a = x[3] - x[0]$$

(5-9)

$$b = y[3] - y[0]$$

(5-10)

$$c = z[3] - z[0]$$

(5-11)

$$Q_{03} = \sqrt{a^2 + b^2 + c^2}$$

(5-12)

Unit vector 0 → 3:

$$ux = \frac{a}{Q_{03}}$$

(5-13)

$$uy = \frac{b}{Q_{03}}$$

(5-14)

$$uz = \frac{c}{Q_{03}}$$

(5-15)

$$\hat{\mathbf{u}} = ux\hat{\mathbf{i}} + uy\hat{\mathbf{j}} + uz\hat{\mathbf{k}}$$

(5-16)

Distance $0 \rightarrow 1$:

$$a = x[1] - x[0] \tag{5-17}$$

$$b = y[1] - y[0] \tag{5-18}$$

$$c = z[1] - z[0] \tag{5-19}$$

$$Q_{01} = \sqrt{a^2 + b^2 + c^2} \tag{5-20}$$

Unit vector $0 \rightarrow 1$:

$$vx = \frac{a}{Q_{01}} \tag{5-21}$$

$$vy = \frac{b}{Q_{01}} \tag{5-22}$$

$$vz = \frac{c}{Q_{01}} \tag{5-23}$$

$$\hat{\mathbf{v}} = vx\hat{\mathbf{i}} + vy\hat{\mathbf{j}} + vz\hat{\mathbf{k}} \tag{5-24}$$

Unit vector $\hat{\mathbf{n}}$:

$$\hat{\mathbf{n}} = \hat{\mathbf{u}} \times \hat{\mathbf{v}} \tag{5-25}$$

$$= \begin{bmatrix} \hat{\mathbf{i}} & \hat{\mathbf{j}} & \hat{\mathbf{k}} \\ ux & uy & uz \\ vx & vy & vz \end{bmatrix} \tag{5-26}$$

$$\hat{\mathbf{n}} = \hat{\mathbf{i}}\underbrace{(uy \cdot vz - uz \cdot vy)}_{nx} + \hat{\mathbf{j}}\underbrace{(uz \cdot vx - ux \cdot vz)}_{ny} + \hat{\mathbf{k}}\underbrace{(ux \cdot vy - uy \cdot vx)}_{nz} \tag{5-27}$$

$$\hat{\mathbf{n}} = nx\hat{\mathbf{i}} + ny\hat{\mathbf{j}} + nz\hat{\mathbf{k}} \tag{5-28}$$

$$nx = uy \cdot vz - uz \cdot vy \qquad (5\text{-}29)$$

$$ny = uz \cdot vx - ux \cdot vz \qquad (5\text{-}30)$$

$$nz = ux \cdot vy - uy \cdot vx \qquad (5\text{-}31)$$

Vector $0 \rightarrow 4$:

$$V_{04} = vx_{04}\hat{i} + vy_{04}\hat{j} + vz_{04}\hat{k} \qquad (5\text{-}32)$$

$$vx_{04} = x[4] - x[0] \qquad (5\text{-}33)$$

$$vy_{04} = y[4] - y[0] \qquad (5\text{-}34)$$

$$vz_{04} = z[4] - z[0] \qquad (5\text{-}35)$$

Perpendicular distance 4 to plane:

$$Q_n = |V_{04} \cdot \hat{n}| \qquad (5\text{-}36)$$

Hit point:

$$Q_n = Q_h \cos(p) = vx_{04}nx + vy_{04}ny + vz_{04}nz \qquad (5\text{-}37)$$

$$Q_h = \frac{Q_n}{\cos(p)} \qquad (5\text{-}38)$$

$$\cos(p) = \hat{l} \cdot \hat{n} \qquad (5\text{-}39)$$

$$= lx \cdot nx + ly \cdot ny + lz \cdot nz \qquad (5\text{-}40)$$

$$xh = x[4] + Q_h lx \qquad (5\text{-}41)$$

$$yh = y[4] + Q_h ly \qquad (5\text{-}42)$$

$$zh = z[4] + Q_h lz \qquad (5\text{-}43)$$

Equations 5-41, 5-42, and 5-43 give the coordinates of the hit point relative to point 0.

You can test to see if the hit point lies within the boundaries of the plane. Figure 5-2 shows the geometry. Vector **V0h** runs from corner 0 to the hit point h. up and vp are the projections of **V0h** on the 03 and 01 directions, respectively. To test for an in-bound or out-of-bound hit,

if up < 0 or up > Q03   hit is out of bounds

if vp < 0 or vp > Q01   hit is out of bounds

With xh, yh, and zh being the coordinates of the hit point h, you can calculate up and vp as follows:

$$a = xh - x[0] \tag{5-44}$$

$$b = yh - y[0] \tag{5-45}$$

$$c = zh - z[0] \tag{5-46}$$

$$\mathbf{V0h} = a\hat{\mathbf{i}} + b\hat{\mathbf{j}} + c\hat{\mathbf{k}} \tag{5-47}$$

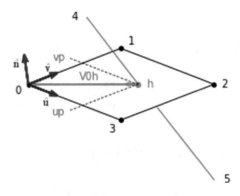

Figure 5-2. *Out-of-bounds geometry*

To find up, you project **V0h** onto the 03 direction. To do that, you take the dot product of **V0h** with û:

$$up = a{\cdot}ux + b{\cdot}uy + c{\cdot}uz \tag{5-48}$$

To find vp, you take the dot product of **V0h** with v̂ :

$$vp = a{\cdot}vx + b{\cdot}vy + c{\cdot}vz \tag{5-49}$$

If you regard the line from 4 to 5 as being finite, you can test to see if it is long enough to reach the plane. From Figure 5-1,

$$a = xh - x[4] \tag{5-50}$$

$$b = yh - y[4] \tag{5-51}$$

$$c = zh - z[4] \tag{5-52}$$

$$Q4h = \sqrt{a^2 + b^2 + c^2} \tag{5-53}$$

if Q45 < Qh LINE TOO SHORT, NO HIT

All of this has been incorporated in Listing 5-1, which has the same structure as Listing 3-5 in Chapter 3, although some of the functions and operations have been altered. As in that program, rotation directions and amounts are entered through the keyboard. Rotations are additive; for example, if the system is rotated first by Rx=40 degrees, followed by Rx=10, the total angle is 50 degrees. Ry and Rz operate similarly.

Some data is hard-wired in Listing 5-1, such as definitions of the rectangular plane and the line intersecting it. They are shown in the lists in lines 18–20. There are six elements in each list numbered [0]-[5]: [0]-[3] are the four corners of the plane while [4] and [5] are the beginning and end of the line. They are coordinated with the diagrams in Figures 5-1 and 5-2. To modify the plane and line, just put new numbers in the lists. For example, item [5] is the end of the line. To drop it down in the +y direction, increase y[5]. The numbers in the lists are in local coordinates relative to the center of rotation (xc,yc,zc), which is at the center of the plane. The values are shown in Lines 14-16.

It takes only three points to define a plane. Here you have a four-corner rectangular plane. If you alter the plane's corner coordinates, be sure they lie in the same plane. The easiest way to do so is to start off with a plane that lies in or is parallel to one of the coordinate planes. It can be rotated out of that coordinate plane later. In line 19, the first four elements of the y list are all zero. That describes a flat plane parallel to the x,z plane at y=0. Also, if altering the [x] or [z] lists, be sure the plane remains rectangular since the calculations of the hit point in this analysis assume that is the case.

Rotation functions `rotx`, `roty`, and `rotz`, which rotate coordinates around the coordinate directions, are included in lines 28-35. They are the same as used in prior programs so they have not been listed.

Line 45 plots a dot at the hit point (xhg,yhg) where the line intersects the plane. If the hit point lies within the plane's boundaries, the color of the dot is red; if it's outside, it is blue. If the line from [4] to [5] is too short and never reaches the plane, the color is changed to green and a dot is placed at [5], the end of the line. This is illustrated in Figure 5-5. The calculation of the hit point is carried out by function `hitpoint(x,y,z)`, which begins in line 53. The program follows the analysis above in Equations 5-1 through 5-49 and should be self-explanatory.

Data input takes place in lines 154-166. This is similar to Listing 3-5. Samples of the output are shown in Figures 5-3, 5-4, and 5-5. Parameters are included in the captions.

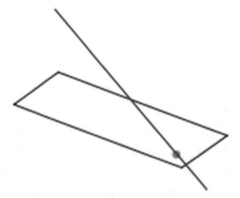

Figure 5-3. *Line intersecting the plane defined by a rectangle. The hit point lies within the plane's boundaries: y[5]=+5, Rx=45°, Ry=45°, Rz°=20*

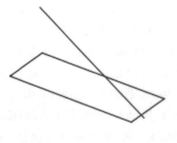

Figure 5-4. *Line intersecting the plane defined by a rectangle. The hit point lies outside the rectangle's boundaries: y[5]=-5, Rx=45°, Ry=45°, Rz°=20*

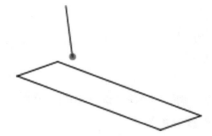

Figure 5-5. *Example of a line too short, in which case a green dot appears at coordinate [5]: x[4]=-40, y[4]=-20, z[4]=15, x[5]=-20, y[5]=-10, z[5]=0, Rx=30°, Ry=45°, Rz°=20*

Listing 5-1. Program LRP

```
1    """
2    LRP
3    """
4
5    import numpy as np
6    import matplotlib.pyplot as plt
7    from math import sin, cos, radians,sqrt
8
9    #———————————fill lists with starting coordinates
10   xg=[ ]
11   yg=[ ]
12   zg=[ ]
13
14   xc=80 #————————center coordinates
15   yc=40
16   zc=40
17
18   x=[-40,-40,40,40,-40,50] #—system (plane and line geometry)
19   y=[0,0,0,0,-20,3]
20   z=[-10,10,10,-10,15,-10]
21
22   for i in range(len(x)):
```

```
23          xg.append(x[i]+xc)
24          yg.append(y[i]+yc)
25          zg.append(z[i]+zc)
26
27  #————————————define  rotation  functions
28  def rotx(xc,yc,zc,xp,yp,zp,Rx):
29          (same as in prior programs)
30
31  def  roty(xc,yc,zc,xp,yp,zp,Ry):
32          (same as in prior programs)
33
34  def rotz(xc,yc,zc,xp,yp,zp,Rz):
35          (same as in prior programs)
36
37  #————————————-plot  plane, line and hit point
38  def plotsystem(xg,yg,zg,xh,yh,xhg,yhg,hitcolor):
39          plt.plot([xg[0],xg[1]],[yg[0],yg[1]],color='k')  #————plot plane
40          plt.plot([xg[1],xg[2]],[yg[1],yg[2]],color='k')
41          plt.plot([xg[2],xg[3]],[yg[2],yg[3]],color='k')
42          plt.plot([xg[3],xg[0]],[yg[3],yg[0]],color='k')
43          plt.plot([xg[4],xg[5]],[yg[4],yg[5]],color='b') #————plot line
44
45          if hitcolor='g': #————plot hit point at [5]
46                plot.scatter(xg[5],yg[5],s=20,color=hitcolor)
47          else: #————plot hit point at h
48                plt.scatter(xhg,yhg,s=20,color=hitcolor)
49
50          plt.axis([0,150,100,0]) #————replot axes and grid
51          plt.axis('on')
52          plt.grid(False)
53          plt.show() #————plot latest rotation
54
55  #————————————find hit point coordinates and color
56  def hitpoint(x,y,z):
57          a=x[5]-x[4]
58          b=y[5]-y[4]
```

```
59      c=z[5]-z[4]
60      Q45=sqrt(a*a+b*b+c*c)  #——distance  point  4  to  5
61
62      lx=a/Q45 #——unit vector components point 4 to 5
63      ly=b/Q45
64      lz=c/Q45
65
66      a=x[3]-x[0]
67      b=y[3]-y[0]
68      c=z[3]-z[0]
69      Q03=sqrt(a*a+b*b+c*c) #——distance 0 to 3
70
71      ux=a/Q03 #——unit vector 0 to 3
72      uy=b/Q03
73      uz=c/Q03
74
75      a=x[1]-x[0]
76      b=y[1]-y[0]
77      c=z[1]-z[0]
78      Q01=sqrt(a*a+b*b+c*c) #——distance 0 to 1
79
80      vx=a/Q01 #——unit vector 0 to 1
81      vy=b/Q01
82      vz=c/Q01
83
84      nx=uy*vz-uz*vy #——normal unit vector
85      ny=uz*vx-ux*vz
86      nz=ux*vy-uy*vx
87
88      vx1b=x[4]-x[0] #——vector components 0 to 4
89      vy1b=y[4]-y[0]
90      vz1b=z[4]-z[0]
91
92      Qn=(vx1b*nx+vy1b*ny+vz1b*nz) #——perpendicular distance 4 to plane
93
```

```
94        cosp=lx*nx+ly*ny+lz*nz #—cos of angle p
95        Qh=abs(Qn/cosp) #——distance 4 to hit point
96
97        xh=x[4]+Qh*lx  #——hit  point  coordinates
98        yh=y[4]+Qh*ly
99        zh=z[4]+Qh*lz
100
101       xhg=xh+xc #——global hit point coordinates
102       yhg=yh+yc
103       zhg=zh+zc
104
105  #———————————————out of bounds check
106       a=xh-x[0] #——components of vector V0h
107       b=yh-y[0]
108       c=zh-z[0]
109
110       up=a*ux+b*uy+c*uz #——dot products
111       vp=a*vx+b*vy+c*vz
112
113       hitcolor='r' #——if inbounds plot red hit point
114       if up<0: #——change color to blue if hit point out of bounds
115           hitcolor='b'
116
117       if up>Q03:
118           hitcolor='b'
119
120       if vp<0:
121           hitcolor='b'
122
123       if vp>Q01:
124           hitcolor='b'
125
126       a=x[5]-x[4]
127       b=y[5]-y[4]
128       c=z[5]-z[4]
129       Q45=sqrt(a*a+b*b+c*c)
```

170

```
130
131      if Q45 < Qh:
132          hitcolor='g'
133
134      return xh,yh,xhg,yhg,hitcolor
135
136 #——————————transform  coordinates  and  plot
137 def  plotx(xc,yc,zc,Rx):    #——transform  &  plot  Rx  system
138      for i in range(len(x)):
139          [xg[i],yg[i],zg[i]]=rotx(xc,yc,zc,x[i],y[i],z[i],Rx)
140          [x[i],y[i],z[i]]=[xg[i]-xc,yg[i]-yc,zg[i]-zc]
141
142      xh,yh,xhg,yhg,hitcolor=hitpoint(x,y,z) #——returns xh,yh,xhg,yhg
143
144      plotsystem(xg,yg,zg,xh,yh,xhg,yhg,hitcolor) #——plot
145
146 def ploty(xc,yc,zc,Ry):    #——transform & plot Ry system
147      for i in range(len(x)):
148          [xg[i],yg[i],zg[i]]=roty(xc,yc,zc,x[i],y[i],z[i],Ry)
149          [x[i],y[i],z[i]]=[xg[i]-xc,yg[i]-yc,zg[i]-zc]
150
151      xh,yh,xhg,yhg,hitcolor=hitpoint(x,y,z)
152
153      plotsystem(xg,yg,zg,xh,yh,xhg,yhg,hitcolor)
154
155 def plotz(xc,yc,zc,Rz):    #——transform  &  plot  Rz  system
156      for i in range(len(x)):
157          [xg[i],yg[i],zg[i]]=rotz(xc,yc,zc,x[i],y[i],z[i],Rz)
158          [x[i],y[i],z[i]]=[xg[i]-xc,yg[i]-yc,zg[i]-zc]
159
160      xh,yh,xhg,yhg,hitcolor=hitpoint(x,y,z)
161
162      plotsystem(xg,yg,zg,xh,yh,xhg,yhg,hitcolor)
163
164 #——————————-input data and plot system
```

```
165 while True:
166         axis=input('x, y or z?: ') #——input axis of rotation (lower case)
167         if axis == 'x': #—if x axis
168                 Rx=radians(float(input('Rx Degrees?: '))) #——input degrees
169                 plotx(xc,yc,zc,Rx) #-call function plotx
170         if axis == 'y':
171                 Ry=radians(float(input('Ry Degrees?: '))) #——input degrees
172                 ploty(xc,yc,zc,Ry)
173         if axis == 'z':
174                 Rz=radians(float(input('Rz Degrees?: '))) #——input degrees
175                 plotz(xc,yc,zc,Rz)
176         if axis == ":
177                 break #—quit the program
```

Line Intersecting a Triangular Plane

Almost any flat surface can be formed by an array of triangular planes, and a curved surface can also be approximated by triangular planes (think of a geodesic dome), hence our interest in triangular planes.

Figure 5-6 shows the geometry for a line intersecting a triangular plane. The algorithms used in Listing 5-3 are mostly the same as in Listing 5-1. One difference is that the lengths of the list are, of course, shorter since the triangle has one less corner. Another is that the check on whether the hit point lies within the triangle or is out of bounds is different.

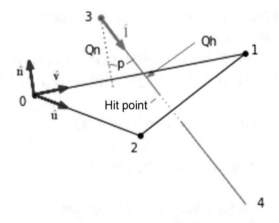

Figure 5-6. *Geometry of a line intersecting a triangular plane*

Before going on to Listing 5-3, you will develop a simple way to determine if a hit point lies within a triangle or outside of it. Figure 5-7 shows the geometry used for the out-of-bounds calculation. Listing 5-2 produces the output shown in Figure 5-8 and, with modification to the lists defining the coordinates of point 3, in Figure 5-9. In Figure 5-8, the hit is out of bounds; in Figure 5-9, it is within the triangle.

Figure 5-7 shows three triangles. The black one, defined by points 0, 1, and 2, is the base triangle, the one you are concerned with. It has area A. The triangle defined by points 0, 1, and 3 (the hit point) has area A1. The third triangle between point 0, 3, and 2 has area A2. It is easy to see that if A1+A2>A, the hit point is out of bounds; if A1+A2<A, it is in bounds. If you can calculate the areas of the three triangles, you will have an easy way to determine if the hit point is within or outside of the base triangle. To do so, you rely on a simple expression for determining the area of a triangle:

$$s = (a+b+c)/2 \qquad\qquad (5\text{-}54)$$

$$A = \sqrt{s(s-a)(s-b)(s-c)} \qquad\qquad (5\text{-}55)$$

where a, b, and c are the lengths of the three sides of the triangle and A is its area. This is known as Heron's formula, named after Heron of Alexandria, a Greek engineer and mathematician circa 10 AD - 70 AD.

This relation is put to use in Listing 5-2 and later in Listing 5-3. In Listing 5-2, most of the program is concerned with evaluating the lengths of the lines shown in Figure 5-7. Heron's formula is then used to calculate the three areas: A, A1, and A2. The decision whether the hit point is inside or outside of the base triangle is made in lines 114-117 of Listing 5-2. It produces Figure 5-8. Program THT2 (not shown) is the same as THT1 (Listing 5-2) but has the lists adjusted to put the hit point within the triangle. It produces Figure 5-9. The adjusted lists are

$$x=[40,30,80,55]$$

$$y=[60,10,60,45]$$

$$z=[0,0,0,0]$$

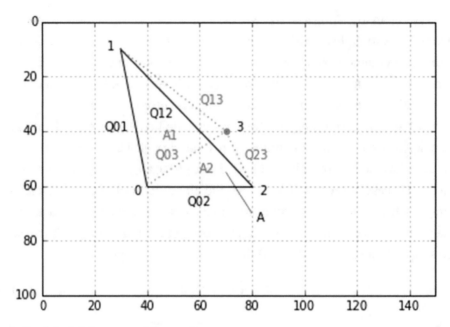

Figure 5-7. *Model for out-of-bounds test*

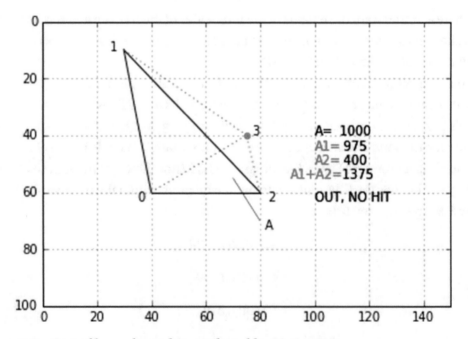

Figure 5-8. *Out of bounds, no hit produced by Listing 5-2*

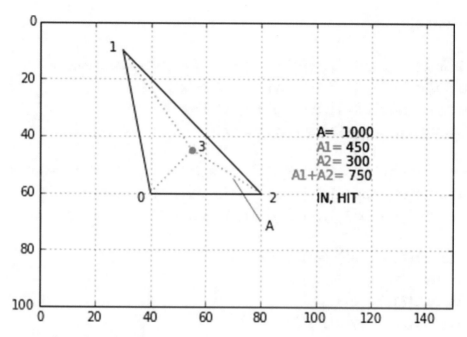

Figure 5-9. *In bounds, hit produced by modified Listing 5-2*

As you can see from these lists, the hit point has been moved to (55,45,0).

Listing 5-2. Program THT1

```
1    """
2    THT1
3    """
4
5    import matplotlib.pyplot as plt
6    import numpy as np
7    from math import sin, cos, radians, sqrt
8
9    plt.axis([0,150,100,0])
10
11   plt.axis('on')
12   plt.grid(True)
13
14   x=[40,30,80,75] #———plane
15   y=[60,10,60,40]
```

175

```
16   z=[0,0,0,0]
17
18   plt.plot([x[0],x[1]],[y[0],y[1]],color='k') #—plot plane A
19   plt.plot([x[1],x[2]],[y[1],y[2]],color='k')
20   plt.plot([x[2],x[0]],[y[2],y[0]],color='k')
21   plt.scatter(x[3],y[3],s=20,color='r')
22
23   plt.plot([x[0],x[3]],[y[0],y[3]],linestyle=':',color='r') #plot planes
24   plt.plot([x[1],x[3]],[y[1],y[3]],linestyle=':',color='r')
25   plt.plot([x[2],x[3]],[y[2],y[3]],linestyle=':',color='r')
26
27   plt.text(35,63,'0') #—label corners
28   plt.text(25,10,'1')
29   plt.text(83,63,'2')
30   plt.text(x[3]+2,y[3],'3')
31
32   a=x[1]-x[0] #—calculate dimensions
33   b=y[1]-y[0]
34   c=z[1]-z[0]
35   Q01=sqrt(a*a+b*b+c*c)
36
37   a=x[2]-x[1]
38   b=y[2]-y[1]
39   c=z[2]-z[1]
40   Q12=sqrt(a*a+b*b+c*c)
41
42   a=x[2]-x[0]
43   b=y[2]-y[0]
44   c=z[2]-z[0]
45   Q02=sqrt(a*a+b*b+c*c)
46
47   a=x[1]-x[3]
48   b=y[1]-y[3]
49   c=z[1]=z[3]
50   Q13=sqrt(a*a+b*b+c*c)
51
```

```
52   a=x[2]-x[3]
53   b=y[2]-y[3]
54   c=z[2]-z[3]
55   Q23=sqrt(a*a+b*b+c*c)
56
57   a=x[0]-x[3]
58   b=y[0]-y[3]
59   c=z[0]-z[3]
60   Q03=sqrt(a*a+b*b+c*c)
61
62   s=(Q01+Q12+Q02)/2 #—calculate areas A, A1 and A2
63   A=sqrt(s*(s-Q01)*(s-Q12)*(s-Q02))
64
65   s1=(Q01+Q03+Q13)/2
66   A1=sqrt(s1*(s1-Q01)*(s1-Q03)*(s1-Q13))
67
68   s2=(Q02+Q23+Q03)/2
69   A2=sqrt(s2*(s2-Q02 )*(s2-Q23)*(s2-Q03))
70
71   plt.arrow(70,55,10,15,linewidth=.5,color='grey') #—label area A
72   plt.text(82,73,'A',color='k')
73
74   plt.text(100,40,'A=') #—plot output
75   dle='%7.0f'%  (A)
76   dls=str(dle)
77   plt.text(105,40,dls)
78
79   plt.text(100,45,'A1=',color='r')
80   dle='%7.0f'% (A1)
81   dls=str(dle)
82   plt.text(105,45,dls)
83
84   plt.text(100,50,'A2=',color='r')
85   dle='%7.0f'% (A2)
86   dls=str(dle)
```

```
87  plt.text(105,50,dls)
88
89  plt.text(91,55,'A1+A2=',color='r')
90  dle='%7.0f'%  (A1+A2)
91  dls=str(dle)
92  plt.text(106,55,dls)
93
94  plt.text(100,40,'A=')
95  dle='%7.0f'%  (A)
96  dls=str(dle)
97  plt.text(105,40,dls)
98
99  plt.text(100,45,'A1=',color='r')
100 dle='%7.0f'% (A1)
101 dls=str(dle)
102 plt.text(105,45,dls)
103
104 plt.text(100,50,'A2=',color='r')
105 dle='%7.0f'% (A2)
106 dls=str(dle)
107 plt.text(105,50,dls)
108
109 plt.text(91,55,'A1+A2=',color='r')
110 dle="%7.0f'% (A1+A2)
111 dls=str(dle)
112 plt.text(106,55,dls)
113
114 if A1+A2 > A:
115     plt.text(100,63,'OUT, NO HIT')
116 else:
117     plt.text(100,63,'IN, HIT')
118
119 plt.show()
```

Listing 5-3 plots the hit point between a line and a triangle. It is similar to Listing 5-1 except it uses the inside or outside test developed above. Examples of output are shown in Figures 5-10, 5-11, and 5-12. One difference worth noting is in the calculation of the unit vector $\hat{n}$, which is perpendicular to the plane of the triangle. In Listing 5-1, this was found by taking the cross product of $\hat{u}$ with $\mathbf{v}$. Since the angle between $\hat{u}$ and $\hat{v}$ was 90°, this produced a unit vector that was normal to both of them, which implies normal to the plane, and of magnitude 1. This is because $|\hat{u}\times\hat{v}|=|\hat{u}||\hat{v}|\sin(\alpha)$ where α is the angle between $\hat{u}$ and $\hat{v}$. When α equals 90°, $|\hat{u}\times\hat{v}|=(1)(1)(1)=1$.

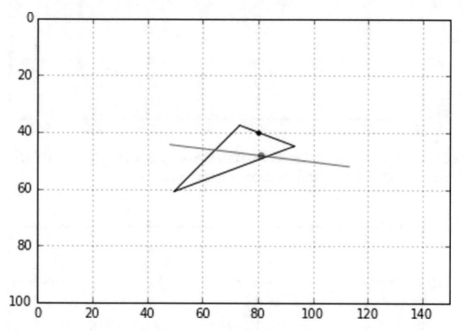

Figure 5-10. *In-bounds hit. x[3]=-60, x[4]=70, y[3]=-20, y[4]=20, z[3]=15, z[4]=0, Rx=-90, Ry=45, Rz=20 (produced by Listing 5-3)*

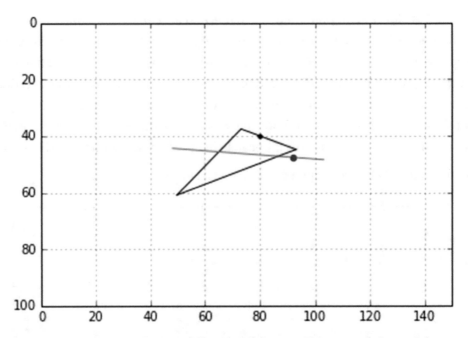

Figure 5-11. *Out-of-bounds hit. x[3]=-60, x[4]=40, y[3]=-20, y[4]=5, z[3]=15, z[4]=0, Rx=-90, Ry=45, Rz=20 (produced by Listing 5-3)*

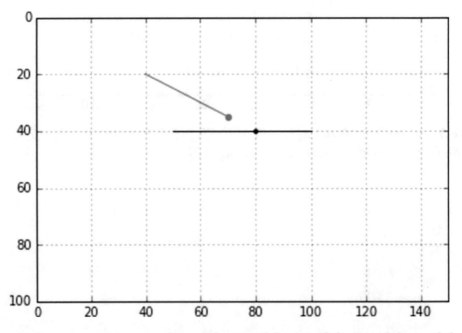

Figure 5-12. *Line too short, no hit. x[3]=-40, x[4]=-10, y[3]=-20, y[4]=-5, z[3]=15, z[4]=0, Rx=0, Ry=0, Rz=0 (produced by Listing 5-3)*

However, with a general **non-right angle triangle**, the angle is not 90° so the vector resulting from the cross product, while normal to the plane, does not have a value of 1; in other words, it is not a *unit* vector. The algorithm between lines 88 and 91 makes the correction by normalizing $\hat{n}$'s components. It does this by dividing each of them by the magnitude of $\hat{n}$. In line 88, **magn** is the magnitude of $\hat{n}$ *before* normalization of the vector's components. Depending on the angle α, its value will be somewhere between 0 and 1. Dividing each component of $\hat{n}$ by **magn** makes $\hat{n}$ a unit vector.

Listing 5-3. Program LTP

```
1    """
2    LTP
3    """
4
5    import numpy as np
6    import matplotlib.pyplot as plt
7    from math import sin, cos, radians,sqrt
8
9    #————————————fill lists with starting coordinates
10   xg=[ ]
11   yg=[ ]
12   zg=[ ]
13
14   xc=80 #————————center coordinates
15   yc=40
16   zc=40
17
18   x=[-10,-30,20,-40,-10]
19   y=[0,0,0,-20,-5]
20   z=[0,30,0,15,0]
21
22   for i in range(len(x)):
23           xg.append(x[i]+xc)
24           yg.append(y[i]+yc)
25           zg.append(z[i]+zc)
26
```

```
27  #————————————define  rotation  functions
28  def rotx(xc,yc,zc,xp,yp,zp,Rx):
29      (same as in prior programs)
30
31  def  roty(xc,yc,zc,xp,yp,zp,Ry):
32      (same as in prior programs)
33
34  def rotz(xc,yc,zc,xp,yp,zp,Rz):
35      (same as in prior programs)
36
37  #————————————define  system  plotting  functions
38  def plotsystem(xg,yg,zg,xh,yh,xhg,yhg,hitcolor):
39      plt.plot([xg[0],xg[1]],[yg[0],yg[1]],color='k')  #————plot plane
40      plt.plot([xg[1],xg[2]],[yg[1],yg[2]],color='k')
41      plt.plot([xg[2],xg[0]],[yg[2],yg[0]],color='k')
42      plt.plot([xg[3],xg[4]],[yg[3],yg[4]],color='g') #———plot line
43      plt.scatter(xc,yc,s=10,color='k') #———plot center of rotation
44
45      if hitcolor=='g':
46          plt.scatter(xg[4],yg[4],s=20,color=hitcolor)
47      else:
48          plt.scatter(xhg,yhg,s=20,color=hitcolor) #————plot
            hit point
49
50      plt.axis([0,150,100,0]) #———replot axes and grid
51      plt.axis('on')
52      plt.grid(True)
53      plt.show() #———plot latest rotation
54
55  #————————————calculate hit point coordinates and color
56  def hitpoint(x,y,z):
57      a=x[4]-x[3]
58      b=y[4]-y[3]
59      c=z[4]-z[3]
60      Q34=sqrt(a*a+b*b+c*c)  #———distance point 3 to 4
61
```

```
62        lx=a/Q34 #——unit vector components point 3 to 4
63        ly=b/Q34
64        lz=c/Q34
65
66        a=x[2]-x[0]
67        b=y[2]-y[0]
68        c=z[2]-z[0]
69        Q02=sqrt(a*a+b*b+c*c) #——distance 0 to 3
70
71        ux=a/Q02 #——unit vector 0 to 3
72        uy=b/Q02
73        uz=c/Q02
74
75        a=x[1]-x[0]
76        b=y[1]-y[0]
77        c=z[1]-z[0]
78        Q01=sqrt(a*a+b*b+c*c) #——distance 0 to 1
79
80        vx=a/Q01 #——unit vector 0 to 1
81        vy=b/Q01
82        vz=c/Q01
83
84        nx=uy*vz-uz*vy #——normal unit vector
85        ny=uz*vx-ux*vz
86        nz=ux*vy-uy*vx
87  #————————-correct magnitude of unit vector ^n
88        magn=sqrt(nx*nx+ny*ny+nz*nz)
89        nx=nx/magn
90        ny=ny/magn
91        nz=nz/magn
92  #————————————
93        a=x[3]-x[0] #——vector components 0 to 3
94        b=y[3]-y[0]
95        c=z[3]-z[0]
96
```

```
97        Qn=(a*nx+b*ny+c*nz) #——perpendicular distance 3 to plane
98
99        cosp=lx*nx+ly*ny+lz*nz #——cos of angle p
100       Qh=abs(Qn/cosp) #——distance 4 to hit point
101
102       xh=x[3]+Qh*lx #——hit point coordinates
103       yh=y[3]+Qh*ly
104       zh=z[3]+Qh*lz
105
106       xhg=xh+xc #——global hit point coordinates
107       yhg=yh+yc
108       zhg=zh+zc
109
110 #——————————————out of bounds check
111       a=x[1]-x[2]
112       b=y[1]-y[2]
113       c=z[1]-z[2]
114       Q12=sqrt(a*a+b*b+c*c)
115
116       a=x[1]-xh
117       b=y[1]-yh
118       c=z[1]-zh
119       Q1h=sqrt(a*a+b*b+c*c)
120
121       a=x[2]-xh
122       b=y[2]-yh
123       c=z[2]-zh
124       Q2h=sqrt(a*a+b*b+c*c)
125
126       a=x[0]-xh
127       b=y[0]-yh
128       c=z[0]-zh
129       Q0h=sqrt(a*a+b*b+c*c)
130
131       s=(Q01+Q12+Q02)/2 #—area A
```

```
132        A=sqrt(s*(s-Q01)*(s-Q12)*(s-Q02))

133

134        s1=(Q01+Q0h+Q1h)/2 #——area A1
135        A1=sqrt(s1*(s1-Q01)*(s1-Q0h)*(s1-Q1h))

136

137        s2=(Q02+Q2h+Q0h)/2 #—area A2
138        A2=sqrt(s2*(s2-Q02)*(s2-Q2h)*(s2-Q0h))

139

140        hitcolor='r' #——if within bounds plot red hit point

141

142        if A1+A2 > A: #——if out of bounds plot blue hit point
143            hitcolor='b'

144

145        a=x[4]-x[3]
146        b=y[4]-y[3]
147        c=z[4]-z[3]
148        Q34=sqrt(a*a+b*b+c*c)

149

150        if Q34 < Qh: #——if line too short plot green at end of line
151            hitcolor='g'

152

153        return xh,yh,xhg,yhg,hitcolor

154

155 #————————————transform coordinates and plot
156 def plotx(xc,yc,zc,Rx):    #——transform & plot Rx system
157        for i in range(len(x)):
158            [xg[i],yg[i],zg[i]]=rotx(xc,yc,zc,x[i],y[i],z[i],Rx)
159            [x[i],y[i],z[i]]=[xg[i]-xc,yg[i]-yc,zg[i]-zc]

160

161        xh,yh,xhg,yhg,hitcolor=hitpoint(x,y,z) #——returns xh,yh,xhg,yhg

162

163        plotsystem(xg,yg,zg,xh,yh,xhg,yhg,hitcolor) #——plot plane, line,
           hit point

164

165        def ploty(xc,yc,zc,Ry):    #——transform & plot Ry system
```

```
166        for i in range(len(x)):
167            [xg[i],yg[i],zg[i]]=roty(xc,yc,zc,x[i],y[i],z[i],Ry)
168            [x[i],y[i],z[i]]=[xg[i]-xc,yg[i]-yc,zg[i]-zc]
169
170        xh,yh,xhg,yhg,hitcolor=hitpoint(x,y,z)
171
172        plotsystem(xg,yg,zg,xh,yh,xhg,yhg,hitcolor)
173
174 def plotz(xc,yc,zc,Rz):   #——transform & plot Rz system
175        for i in range(len(x)):
176            [xg[i],yg[i],zg[i]]=rotz(xc,yc,zc,x[i],y[i],z[i],Rz)
177            [x[i],y[i],z[i]]=[xg[i]-xc,yg[i]-yc,zg[i]-zc]
178
179        xh,yh,xhg,yhg,hitcolor=hitpoint(x,y,z)
180
181        plotsystem(xg,yg,zg,xh,yh,xhg,yhg,hitcolor)
182
183 #————————————input data and plot system
184        while True:
185            axis=input('x, y or z?: ') #——input axis of rotation
                (lower case)
186            if axis == 'x': #-if x axis
187                    Rx=radians(float(input('Rx Degrees?: ')))
                    #——input degrees of rotation
188                    plotx(xc,yc,zc,Rx) #-call function plotx
189            if axis == 'y':
190                    Ry=radians(float(input('Ry Degrees?: ')))
                    #——input degrees of rotation
191                    ploty(xc,yc,zc,Ry)
192            if axis == 'z':
193                    Rz=radians(float(input('Rz Degrees?: ')))
                    #——input degrees of rotation
194                    plotz(xc,yc,zc,Rz)
195            if axis == '':
196                    break #——quit the program
```

Line Intersecting a Circle

The determination of whether the hit point of a line intersecting the plane of a circle is within the circle is trivial. As shown in Figure 5-13, if the distance from the circle's center to the hit point is greater than the circle's radius, it lies outside the circle:

if rh > r   NO HIT

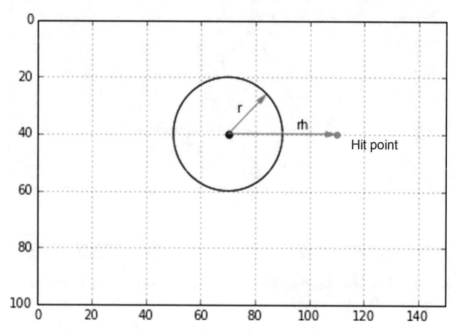

Figure 5-13. *Model for out-of-bounds test for a circle*

I won't bother writing a separate program to demonstrate this. You should be able to do that yourself by modifying Listing 5-1 or Listing 5-3. Simply fill the x[ ], y[ ], and z[ ] lists with the points defining the circle's perimeter and the line coordinates and modify the functions plotsystem and hitpoint.

Line Intersecting a Circular Sector

In this section, you develop a procedure to determine if the hit point of a line intersecting the plane of a sector of a circle is inside or outside the sector. Figure 5-14 shows the sector. It has a center at point 0 and a radius r. The hit point is at 3. rh is the distance from 0 to the hit point. Your goal is to determine if the hit point lies inside or outside the sector. (We will not be developing a full three-dimensional program here; you'll just see how the inside or outside algorithm works.) It could be easily incorporated into any of the preceding programs, such as Listing 5-3.

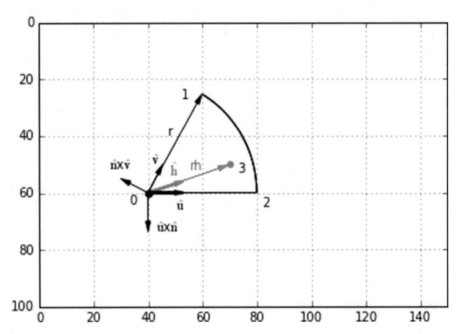

Figure 5-14. *Model for determining whether a line intersecting a circular sector is in or out of bounds. 3=hit point*

There are five unit vectors at point 0: $\hat{u}$ points from 0 to 2; $\hat{v}$ points from 0 to 1; and $\hat{h}$ from 0 to the hit point at 3. $\hat{n}$ is a unit vector normal to the plane of the sector. It is not shown since it points up and out of the plane. $\hat{u} \times \hat{n}$ is the result of the cross product of $\hat{u}$ with $\hat{n}$; $\hat{n} \times \hat{v}$ is from the cross product of $\hat{n}$ with $\hat{v}$.

Your strategy is to first determine if Rh>r, in which case the hit point is outside the sector in the radial direction. Then, recalling that the dot product of two vectors gives the projection of one on the other, you take the dot product of $\hat{h}$ with $\hat{u} \times \hat{n}$. This gives the projection of u on **u^xn^**. If positive, they point in the same direction; if negative, they point in the opposite direction. If the result is positive, the hit point is outside the sector on the 0-2 side. Then, on the other side of the sector, you take the dot product of $\hat{h}$ with $\hat{n} \times \hat{v}$. If it is positive, the hit point is out of bounds on the 0-1 side.

In Listing 5-4, the local coordinates (relative to point 0) are defined in the lists in lines 14-16. The last element in the lists defines the coordinates of the hit point, point 3. xc, yc, and zc in lines 18-20 are the global coordinates of point 0. The hit test algorithm begins in line 23. Most of it should be self-explanatory based on the previous discussion. Attention is called to lines 52-58. This is where the normal vector $\hat{n}$ is evaluated by taking the cross product of $\hat{u}$ with $\hat{v}$. As explained earlier, this produces a unit vector (magnitude 1) only if $\hat{u}$ and $\hat{v}$ are perpendicular to one another. Since the angle between them in a general sector will not necessarily be 90 degrees, the vector must be normalized. That takes place in lines 55-58. The dot product of $\hat{u} \times \hat{n}$ with $\hat{h}$ takes place in line 64, $\hat{n} \times \hat{v}$ with $\hat{h}$ in line 70. Line 72 assumes the hit color is red, which means the hit is within the sector. If A is positive, it lies outside the sector, in which case the hit color is changed to blue in line 74. Lines 76 and 77 perform the same test for the other side of the sector. Lines 79 and 80 check for the hit point lying outside the sector in the radial direction. Figures 5-15 and 5-16 show two sample runs. You can move the hit point around yourself by changing the coordinates of point 3 in the lists in lines 14-15. You change only the x and y coordinates of the hit point since it is assumed to lie in the z=0 plane, as does the sector.

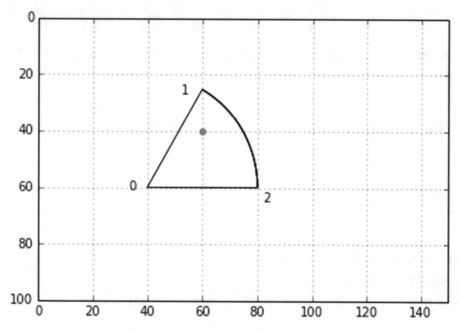

Figure 5-15. *In-bounds or out-of-bounds test produced by Listing 5-4: red=in, blue=out*

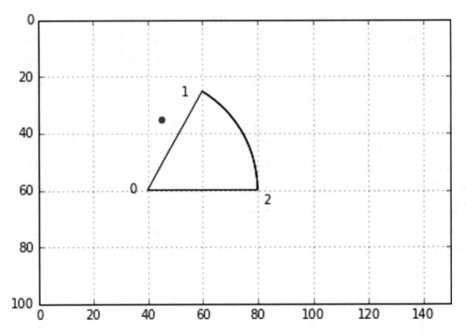

Figure 5-16. *In-bounds or out-of-bounds test produced by Listing 5-4: red=in, blue=out*

Listing 5-4. Program LCSTEST

```
1    """
2     LCSTEST
3    """
4
5    import matplotlib.pyplot as plt
6    import numpy as np
7    from math import sin, cos, radians, degrees, sqrt, acos
8
9    plt.axis([0,150,100,0])
10
11   plt.axis('on')
12   plt.grid(True)
13
14   x=[0,20,40,5]
15   y=[0,-35,0,-25]
```

```
16   z=[0,0,0,0]
17
18   xc=40
19   yc=60
20   zc=0
21
22   #———————————hit test
23   a=x[3]-x[0]
24   b=y[3]-y[0]
25   c=z[3]-z[0]
26   rh=sqrt(a*a+b*b+c*c)
27
28   a=x[3]-x[0]
29   b=y[3]-y[0]
30   c=z[3]-z[0]
31   Q0h=sqrt(a*a+b*b+c*c)
32   hx=a/Q0h #———unit vector 0 to hit point
33   hy=b/Q0h
34   hz=c/Q0h
35
36   a=x[2]-x[0]
37   b=y[2]-y[0]
38   c=z[2]-z[0]
39   Q02=sqrt(a*a+b*b+c*c)
40   ux=a/Q02 #———unit vector 0 to 3
41   uy=b/Q02
42   uz=c/Q02
43
44   a=x[1]-x[0]
45   b=y[1]-y[0]
46   c=z[1]-z[0]
47   Q01=sqrt(a*a+b*b+c*c)
48   vx=a/Q01 #———unit vector 0 to 1
49   vy=b/Q01
50   vz=c/Q01
```

```
51
52   a=uy*vz-uz*vy #——vector u xv normal to plane
53   b=uz*vx-ux*vz
54   c=ux*vy-uy*vx
55   Quxv=sqrt(a*a*b*b+c*c) #——normalize u xv
56   nx=a/Quxv
57   ny=b/Quxv
58   nz=c/Quxv
59
60   uxnx=uy*nz-uz*ny #——unit vector u xv
61   uxny=uz*nx-ux*nz
62   uxnz=ux*ny-uy*nx
63
64   A=uxnx*hx+uxny*hy+uxnz*hz #——dot product u xv with h
65
66   nxvx=ny*vz-nz*vy #——unit vector u xv
67   nxvy=nz*vx-nx*vz
68   nxvz=nx*vy-ny*vx
69
70   B=nxvx*hx+nxvy*hy+nxvz*hz #——dot product u xv with h
71
72   hitcolor='r'
73   if A>0:  #—out
74       hitcolor='b'
75
76   if B>0: #—out
77       hitcolor='b'
78
79   if rh>r: #—out
80       hitcolor='b'
81
82   plt.scatter(x[3]+xc,y[3]+yc,s=20,color=hitcolor)
83
84   #———————-plot    arc
85   r=40
```

```
86   phi1=0
87   phi2=-radians(60)
88   dphi=(phi2-phi1)/180
89   xlast=xc+r
90   ylast=yc+0
91   for phi in np.arange(phi1,phi2,dphi):
92       x=xc+r*cos(phi)
93       y=yc+r*sin(phi)
94       plt.plot([xlast,x],[ylast,y],color='k')
95       xlast=x
96       ylast=y
97
98
99   #————————-labels
100  print('rh=',rh)
101  print('r=',r)
102  plt.arrow(xc,yc,40,0)
103  plt.arrow(xc,yc,20,-35,linewidth=.5,color='k')
103  plt.text(33,61,'0')
104  plt.text(52,27,'1')
105  plt.text(82,65,'2')
106
107  plt.show()
```

Line Intersecting a Sphere

Figure 5-17, output from Listing 5-5, shows a line intersecting a sphere. The entrance and exit points are shown in red. Figure 5-18 shows the model used by Listing 5-5. The line begins at B and ends at E.

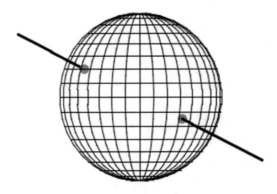

Figure 5-17. *Line intersecting a sphere, produced by Listing 5-5*

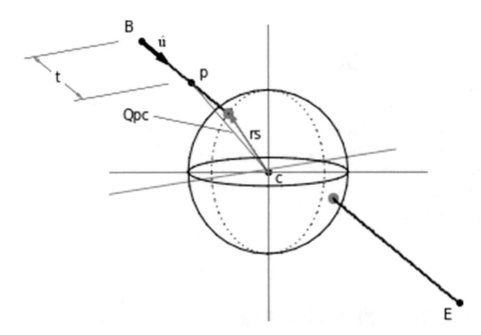

Figure 5-18. *Model for a line intersecting a sphere*

To find the entrance hit point, you start at B and move a point p incrementally along the line toward E. At each step, you calculate Qpc, the distance between p and c. If it is less than or equal to the sphere's radius rs, you have made contact with the sphere and a red dot is plotted. You continue moving p along the line inside the sphere without plotting anything (you could plot a dotted line), calculating Qpc as you go, until Qpc becomes equal to or greater than rs. At that point, p leaves the sphere and another red dot is plotted. p continues moving along the line to E, plotting black dots along the way. Instead of plotting the line with dots, you could have used short line segments as was done in prior programs.

To move p along the line, you use parameter **t**, which is the distance from B to p. To get the coordinates of p, you construct unit vector **û**, which points along the line

$$a = xe - xb \qquad (5\text{-}56)$$

$$b = ye - yb \qquad (5\text{-}57)$$

$$c = ze - zb \qquad (5\text{-}58)$$

$$Qbe = \sqrt{a^2 + b^2 + c^2} \qquad (5\text{-}59)$$

$$ux = a / Qbe \qquad (5\text{-}60)$$

$$uy = b / Qbe \qquad (5\text{-}61)$$

$$uz = c / Qbe \qquad (5\text{-}62)$$

where Qbe is the distance along the line from B to E and ux, uy, and uz are the components of **û**. The coordinates of p are thus

$$xp = xb + uxt \qquad (5\text{-}63)$$

$$yp = yb + uyt \qquad (5\text{-}64)$$

$$zp = zb + uzt \qquad (5\text{-}65)$$

Qpc is easy to determine:

$$a = xc - xp \qquad (5\text{-}66)$$

$$b = yc - yp \qquad (5\text{-}67)$$

$$c = zc - zp \qquad (5\text{-}68)$$

$$Qpc = \sqrt{a^2 + b^2 + c^2} \qquad (5\text{-}69)$$

In Listing 5-5, the sphere's center coordinates are set in lines 18-20. The sphere is composed of longitudinal (vertical) lines and latitudinal (horizontal) lines. The lists in lines 10-16 contain the local and global coordinates of the longitudes. The initial filling of these lists takes place in lines 25-38, which creates a half circle in the z=0 plane. As shown in Figure 5-19, point p lies on the circumference at coordinates xp, yp, zp where

$$xp = rscos(\phi) \qquad\qquad (5\text{-}70)$$

$$yp = rssin(\phi) \qquad\qquad (5\text{-}71)$$

$$zp = 0 \qquad\qquad (5\text{-}72)$$

They are set in lines 30-32. ϕ is the angle around the z direction. It runs from -90° to +90°. You don't need the back half of the longitudes so they are not plotted. This half circle will be rotated around the y direction to create the oval longitudes. They are 10° apart as set in line 74. Since they are rotated around the y direction only, the program contains just the rotation function roty: rotx and rotz are not needed in this model. Plotting of the longitudes takes place in lines 72-77.

The latitudes are plotted in lines 80-97. Figure 5-21 shows a front view of the sphere looking into the x,y plane. Each latitude is essentially a circle having radius rl where

$$xl = rscos(\phi) \qquad\qquad (5\text{-}73)$$

This is calculated in line 89 of the program. When viewed from the front, the latitude appears as a straight line since you are not rotating the sphere in this program.

The ϕ loop beginning at line 88 ranges ϕ from -90° to + 90° in 10° increments. At each increment a new latitude is plotted. It will have a radius given by Equation 5-73 above. The α loop beginning at line 92 sweeps across the front of the circular latitude from α=0° to 180° in 10° increments. This is illustrated in Figure 5-22, which shows the top view looking down on the x,z plane.

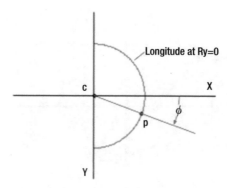

Figure 5-19. *x,y view of sphere longitude shown at starting position Ry=0. Rotation around the y direction in 10° increments will produce longitudes*

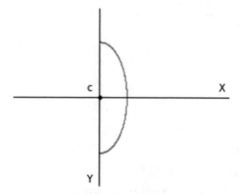

Figure 5-20. *x,y view of sphere longitude rotated by Ry=60°*

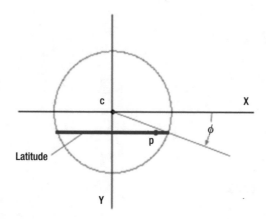

Figure 5-21. *Sphere latitude, x,y view*

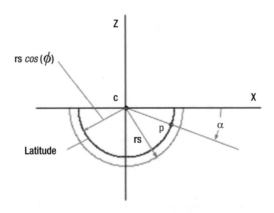

Figure 5-22. *Sphere latitude, x,z view*

Listing 5-5. Program LS

```
1    """
2    LS
3    """
4
5    import numpy as np
6    import matplotlib.pyplot as plt
7    from math import sin, cos, radians, sqrt
8
9    #———————————————lists
10   x=[ ]
11   y=[ ]
12   z=[ ]
13
14   xg=[ ]
15   yg=[ ]
16   zg=[ ]
17
18   xc=80 #—sphere center
19   yc=50
20   zc=0
21
```

```
22   rs=40 #──sphere radius
23
24   #─────────────────fill longitude lists
25   phi1=radians(-90)
26   phi2=radians(90)
27   dphi=radians(10)
28
29   for phi in np.arange(phi1,phi2,dphi):
30       xp=rs*cos(phi)
31       yp=rs*sin(phi)
32       zp=0
33       x.append(xp)
34       y.append(yp)
35       z.append(zp)
36       xg.append(xp)
37       yg.append(yp)
38       zg.append(zp)
39
40   #===============================================define rotation function
41   def roty(xc,yc,zc,xp,yp,zp,Ry):
42       a=[xp,yp,zp]
43       b=[cos(Ry),0,sin(Ry)] #────[cx11,cx12,cx13]
44       xpp=np.inner(a, b)
45       b=[0,1,0] #────[cx21,cx22,cx23]
46       ypp=np.inner(a,b) #────scalar product of a,b
47       b=[-sin(Ry),0,cos(Ry)] #────[cx31,cx32,cx33]
48       zpp=np.inner(a,b)
49       [xg,yg,zg]=[xpp+xc,ypp+yc,zpp+zc]
50       return[xg,yg,zg]
51
52   #=========================================================
53   def plotsphere(xg,yg,zg):
54       lastxg=xg[0]
55       lastyg=yg[0]
56       for i in range(len(x)):
```

```
57              if i < len(x)/2:
58                      plt.plot([lastxg,xg[i]],[lastyg,yg[i]],linewidth=1,
                        color='k')
59              else:
60                      plt.plot([lastxg,xg[i]],[lastyg,yg[i]],linewidth=1,
                        color='k')
61          lastxg=xg[i]
62          lastyg=yg[i]
63
64  #===================================================transform coordinates
65  def plotspherey(xc,yc,zc,Ry):
66      for i in range(len(x)): #————transform and plot Ry sphere
67          [xg[i],yg[i],zg[i]]=roty(xc,yc,zc,x[i],y[i],z[i],Ry)
68
69  plotsphere(xg,yg,zg)  #——plot rotated coordinates
70
71  #——————————plot longitudes
72  Ry1=radians(0)
73  Ry2=radians(180)
74  dRy=radians(10)
75
76  for Ry in np.arange(Ry1,Ry2,dRy):
77      plotspherey(xc,yc,zc,Ry)
78
79  #——————————plot latitudes
80  alpha1=radians(0)
81  alpha2=radians(180)
82  dalpha=radians(10)
83
84  phi1=radians(-90)
85  phi2=radians(90)
86  dphi=radians(10)
87
88  for phi in np.arange(phi1,phi2,dphi):
89      r=rs*cos(phi) #————————latitude radius
90      xplast=xc+r
```

```
91          yplast=yc+rs*sin(phi)
92          for   alpha   in   np.arange(alpha1,alpha2,dalpha):
93                 xp=xc+r*cos(alpha)
94                 yp=yplast
95                 plt.plot([xplast,xp],[yplast,yp],color='k')
96                 xplast=xp
97                 yplast=yp
98
99   #———————————line and hit points
100  xb=-60 #—line beginning
101  yb=-30
102  zb=-20
103
104  xe=60 #——line end
105  ye=30
106  ze=-40
107
108  a=xe-xb
109  b=ye-yb
110  c=ze-zb
111  Qbe=sqrt(a*a+b*b+c*c)  #——line length
112  ux=a/Qbe #—unit vector û
113  uy=b/Qbe
114  uz=c/Qbe
115
116  dt=1
117  for t in np.arange(0,Qbe,dt):
118         xp=xb+ux*t
119         yp=yb+uy*t
120         zp=zb+uz*t
121         Qpc=sqrt(xp*xp+yp*yp+zp*zp)
122         if Qpc > rs:
123                 plt.scatter(xp+xc,yp+yc,s=5,color='k')
124         if Qpc <= rs:
125                 plt.scatter(xp+xc,yp+yc,s=80,color='r')
```

```
126          tlast=t
127          break
128
129 for t in np.arange(tlast,Qbe,dt):
130          xp=xb+ux*t
131          yp=yb+uy*t
132          zp=zb+uz*t
133          Qpc=sqrt(xp*xp+yp*yp+zp*zp)
134          if Qpc >= rs:
135                  plt.scatter(xp+xc,yp+yc,s=80,color='r')
136          tlast=t
137          break
138
139 for t in np.arange(tlast,Qbe,dt):
140          xp=xb+ux*t
141          yp=yb+uy*t
142          zp=zb+uz*t
143          Qpc=sqrt(xp*xp+yp*yp+zp*zp)
144          if Qpc >= rs:
145                  plt.scatter(xp+xc,yp+yc,s=5,color='k')
146
147 plt.axis([0,150,100,0]) #-plot axes and grid
148 plt.axis('off')
149 plt.grid(False)
150
151  plt.show()
```

Plane Intersecting a Sphere

In this section, you will work out a technique for plotting a flat rectangular plane intersecting a sphere. Figure 5-23 shows the output of Listing 5-6; Figure 5-24 shows the model used by that listing.

The strategy here is to use the algorithms developed in the previous section for a line intersecting a sphere as your basic element. By representing the plane as a series of parallel lines, you can easily find the intersection of a plane with a sphere. Figure 5-23 shows unit vector $\hat{u}$ at corner 1. As before, this points from the beginning to end of the first line. There is also unit vector $\hat{v}$ at corner 1. This points to corner 3. By advancing along the line from 1 to 3 in small steps, you can construct lines running parallel to the first one from 1 to 2. Advancing down each of these lines in small increments of t, you can find the coordinates of points across the plane. To advance in the $\hat{v}$ direction, you introduce parameter s, which is the distance from corner 1 to the beginning of the new line. To get the coordinates of the end of that line, you perform the same operation starting at point 2 using $\mathbf{v}$ and s, as in

$$xe = x2 + vx \cdot s \tag{5-74}$$

$$ye = yr + vy \cdot s \tag{5-75}$$

$$ze = z2 + vz \cdot s \tag{5-76}$$

where xe, ye, and ze are the coordinates of the end of the line; x2, y2, and z2 are the coordinates of point 2; and vx, vy, and vz are the components of unit vector $\hat{v}$.

Incrementing down and across the plane with parameters t and s allows you to sweep across the surface of the plane. At each point p you calculate the distance from p to the center of the sphere. If it is equal to or less than the sphere's radius, you have a hit.

I won't list the entire program that produced Figure 5-23 since it is mostly similar to Listing 5-5, except for the addition of an s loop that sweeps in the $\hat{v}$ direction. Control of the program begins at line 27. Lines 27-37 define the coordinates of plane corners 1, 2, and 3. The unit vectors $\hat{u}$ and $\hat{v}$ are established in lines 39-53. Lines 55 and 56 set the scan increments in dt and ds. The loop 57-64 scans in the $\hat{v}$ direction, establishing the beginning and end coordinates of each line. Function plane, which begins at line 1, determines if there is a hit with each line and the sphere. For each s, the loop beginning at line 3 advances down the line in the $\hat{u}$ direction, calculating the coordinates xp,yp,zp of each point p along the line. Line 10 calculates the distance of p from the sphere's center. Line 11 says, if the distance is greater than the sphere's radius, plot a black dot. If it is less than or equal to the radius, line 18 plots a colorless dot. The rest of the logic up to line 24 determines if the line has emerged from the sphere, in which case plotting of black dots resumes. Results are shown in Figure 5-23.

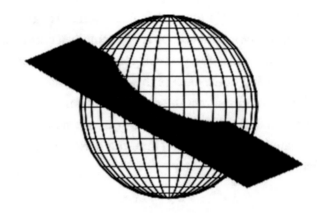

Figure 5-23. *Plane intersecting a sphere produced by Listing 5-6*

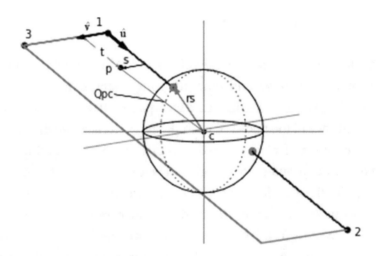

Figure 5-24. *Model for Listing 5-6*

Listing 5-6. Program PS

```
"""
PS
"""
import numpy as np
import matplotlib.pyplot as plt
from math import sin, cos, radians, sqrt

.
```

(similar to Program LS)

·

```
    #========================================================plane
1   def plane(xb,yb,zb,xe,ye,ze,Q12,dt):
2        hit='off'
3        for t in np.arange(0,Q12,dt): #——B to hit
4                xp=xb+ux*t
5                yp=yb+uy*t
6                zp=zb+uz*t
7                xpg=xc+xp
8                ypg=yc+yp
9                zpg=zc+zp
10               Qpc=sqrt(xp*xp+yp*yp+zp*zp)
11               if Qpc>=rs:
12                       plt.scatter(xpg,ypg,s=.5,color='k')
13               if Qpc<=rs:
14                   if hit=='off':
15                           hit='on'
16               if Qpc<rs:
17                   if hit=='on':
18                           plt.scatter(xpg,ypg,s=10,color=")
19               if Qpc>=rs:
20                   if hit=='on':
21                          hit='off'
22               if Qpc>rs:
23                   if hit=='off':
24                       plt.scatter(xpg,ypg,s=.5,color='k')
25
26  #————————————scan  across  plane
27  x1=-40
28  y1=-30
29  z1=-20
30
31  x2=60
32  y2=25
```

```
33   z2=-35
34
35   x3=-65
36   y3=-20
37   z3=-50
38
39   a=x2-x1
40   b=y2-y1
41   c=z2-z1
42   Q12=sqrt(a*a+b*b+c*c)
43   ux=a/Q12
44   uy=b/Q12
45   uz=c/Q12
46
47   a=x3-x1
48   b=y3-y1
49   c=z3-z1
50   Q13=sqrt(a*a+b*b+c*c)
51   vx=a/Q13
52   vy=b/Q13
53   vz=c/Q13
54
55   dt=.7 #————————scan increment
56   ds=.7
57   for s in np.arange(0,Q13,ds):
58        sbx=x1+s*vx
59        sby=y1+s*vy
60        sbz=z1+s*vz
61        sex=x2+s*vx
62        sey=y2+s*vy
63        sez=z2+s*vz
64        plane(sbx,sby,sbz,sex,sey,sez,Q12,dt)
65
66   plt.axis([0,150,100,0]) #-replot axes and grid
67   plt.axis('off')
```

```
68  plt.grid(False)
69
70  plt.show() #-plot latest rotation
```

Summary

In this chapter, you learned how to predict whether a three-dimensional line or plane will intersect a three-dimensional surface or solid object. Why bother with this? Because it is fundamental to removing hidden lines, as you will see in Chapter 6. When plotting a surface A, which may be behind another surface or object B, you may not want to display the hidden parts of A. To accomplish this task, which I call hidden line removal, you do so by plotting A with scatter dots or short line segments at each step. If a point on A is hidden by B, you do not plot it or you could substitute dot of a different color or a dashed line. To determine if it is hidden from view, you draw an imaginary line from the point on A to the observer (i.e., in the -z direction). If you can determine if that line from A intersects a surface or object B in front of it, then you will know whether or not it is hidden. While you cannot develop hidden line algorithms for every conceivable situation (you did rectangular planes, triangular planes, circular sectors, circles, and spheres here), by understanding how it is done for these objects you should, with a bit of creativity, be able to develop your own hidden line algorithms for other surfaces and objects. Perhaps the line-triangular plane is most useful since complex surfaces and objects can often be approximated by an assembly of triangles. Let's say you approximate surface B with n triangular planes. You would check each dot or line segment in A against each of the n triangles in B. You will see more about this in Chapter 6.

CHAPTER 6

Hidden Line Removal

Most of the models used in the previous chapters were essentially stick figures constructed of dots and lines. When such objects are viewed in three dimensions, it is possible to see the lines on the back side, as if the objects are transparent. This chapter is concerned with removing the lines, which are normally hidden, from objects so they appear solid.

This chapter will cover two types of situations. The first is called *intra-object* hidden line removal. This refers to removing hidden lines from a single object, such as a box. We assume that most objects are constructed of flat planes; examples are a box, a pyramid, and a spherical surface that can be approximated by planes, either rectangular or triangular. The technique you will use relies on determining whether a particular plane faces toward the viewer, in which case it is visible and is plotted, or faces away from the viewer, in which case it is not visible and is not plotted.

Inter-object hidden line removal, on the other hand, refers to a system of more than one object, such as two planes, one behind the other. Here the general approach is to use some of the ray tracing techniques that were developed in the previous chapter to find intersections between lines and surfaces. You start by drawing the back object using dots or short line segments. At each point you construct a line (ray) going toward the observer, who is in the -z direction, and see if it intersects with the front object. If it does, that point on the back object is hidden and is not plotted or it could be plotted in a different color if you want to show it while indicating it is hidden.

Box

As an example of intra-object hidden line removal, let's start off with a simple box, as shown in Figures 6-1 and 6-2. They were drawn by Listing 6-1. Figures 6-3, 6-4, and 6-5 show the model used by the program.

© Bernard Korites 2023
B. Korites, *Python Graphics*, https://doi.org/10.1007/978-1-4842-9660-8_6

In Figure 6-3, you see that the box has eight corners, numbered 0 to 7. At corner 0, there are two vectors: **V01**, which goes from corner 0 to 1, and **V03**, which goes from 0 to 3. Looking at the 0,1,2,3 face first, as the box is rotated, the strategy is to determine if it is tilted toward or away from an observer who situated is in the -z direction. If it is facing toward the observer, the edges of the face are plotted. If it is facing away from the observer, they are not plotted. How do you determine if the face is facing the observer? The cross (vector) product **V03×V01** gives a vector **N**, which is normal to the 0,1,2,3 face,

$$\mathbf{V03} = V03x\hat{\mathbf{i}} + V03y\hat{\mathbf{j}} + V03z\hat{\mathbf{k}} \tag{6-1}$$

$$\mathbf{V01} = V01x\hat{\mathbf{i}} + V01y\hat{\mathbf{j}} + V01z\hat{\mathbf{k}} \tag{6-2}$$

$$V03x = x[3] - x[0] \tag{6-3}$$

$$V03y = y[3] - y[0] \tag{6-4}$$

$$V03z = z[3] - z[0] \tag{6-5}$$

$$V01x = x[1] - x[0] \tag{6-6}$$

$$V01y = y[1] - y[0] \tag{6-7}$$

$$V01z = z[1] - z[0] \tag{6-8}$$

$$\mathbf{N} = \mathbf{V03} \times \mathbf{V01} = \begin{bmatrix} \hat{\mathbf{i}} & \hat{\mathbf{j}} & \hat{\mathbf{k}} \\ V03x & V03y & V03z \\ V01x & V01y & V01z \end{bmatrix} \tag{6-9}$$

$$\mathbf{N} = Nx\hat{\mathbf{i}} + Ny\hat{\mathbf{j}} + Nz\hat{\mathbf{k}} \tag{6-10}$$

$$\mathbf{N} = \hat{\mathbf{i}}[V03y \cdot V01z - V03z \cdot V01y] + \hat{\mathbf{j}}[V03z \cdot V01x - V03x \cdot V01z]$$
$$+ \hat{\mathbf{k}}\underbrace{[V03x \cdot V01y - V03y \cdot V01x]}_{Nz} \tag{6-11}$$

You can determine if the plane is facing toward or away from the observer by the value of Nz, **N**'s z component. Figures 6-4 and 6-5 show a plane (blue) relative to an observer. This is the side view of one of the faces of t6he box shown in Figure 6-3. The observer is on the right side of the coordinate system looking toward the +z direction. Referring to Figure 6-4, if the z component of **N**, Nz in Equation 6-11, is < 0 (i.e., pointing in the -z direction), the plane is facing the observer, it is visible to the observer, and it is plotted. If Nz is positive (i.e., pointing in the +z direction), as shown in Figure 6-5, the face is tilted away from the observer, in which case it is not seen by the observer and is not plotted. Note that you can use the full vector **V** rather than a unit vector since you are only concerned with the sign of **Nz**.

What about the other faces? The 4,5,6,7 face is parallel to 0,1,2,3 so its outward pointing normal vector is opposite to that of face 0,1,2,3. You do a similar check on whether its normal vector is pointing in the +z (don't plot) or -z (plot) direction.

The remaining faces are handled in a similar fashion. The normal to 1,2,6,5 is opposite to that of 0,3,7,4; the normal to 3,2,6,7 is opposite to that of 0,1,5,4.

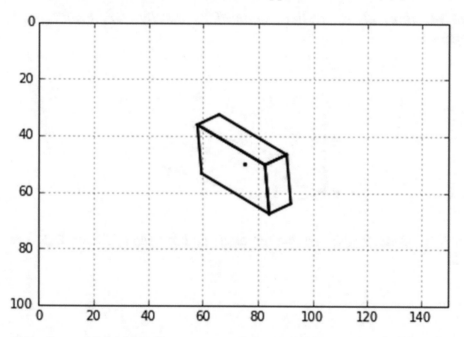

Figure 6-1. *Box with hidden lines removed: Rx=45°, Ry=45°, Rz=30° (produced by Listing 6-1)*

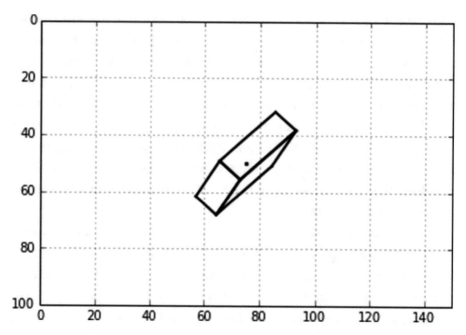

Figure 6-2. *Box with hidden lines removed: Rx=30°, Ry=-60°, Rz=30° (produced by Listing 6-1)*

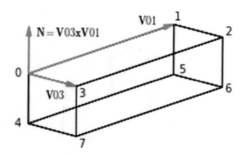

Figure 6-3. *Model for hidden line removal of a box used by Listing 6-1. N not to scale*

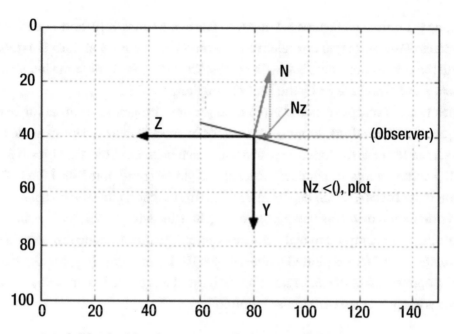

Figure 6-4. *Model for hidden line removal of a box used by Listing 6-1*

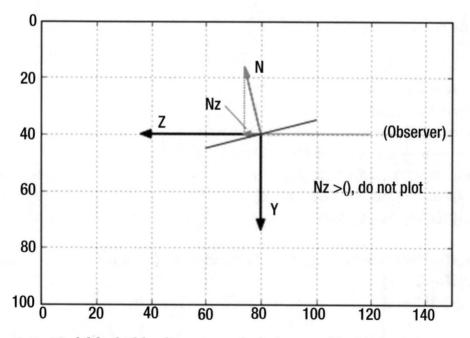

Figure 6-5. *Model for hidden line removal of a box used by Listing 6-1*

Listing 6-1 produced Figures 6-1 and 6-2. The lists in lines 9, 10, and 11 define the coordinates of the unrotated box relative to its center, which is set in lines 124-126. Lines 13-15 fill the global coordinate lists with zeroes. These lists have the same length as list x (also lists y and z) and are set by the len(x) function.

Lines 124-140 accept keyboard input as in previous programs. As an example of the sequence of operations, suppose you enter x in line 129 followed by an angle in degrees. Line 132 calls the function plotboxx, which begins at line 102. Lines 103-105 rotate the corner points and update the local and global coordinate lists. Line 107 calls function plotbox, which begins in line 40. This function plots the box in its new rotated orientation using the lists xg, yg, and zg. Starting with the 0,1,2,3 face, lines 41-47 calculate Nz, the z component of the normal vector N in line 47 using the above analysis. If Nz<=0, the 0,1,2,3 face is plotted in lines 49-52. If it is not visible (i.e., Nz>0), then you know the opposing face of 4,5,6,7 must be visible and it is plotted in lines 54-57. The other faces are processed in a similar manner.

Listing 6-1. Program HLBOX

```
1     """
2     HLBOX
3     """
4
5     import numpy as np
6     import matplotlib.pyplot as plt
7     from math import sin, cos, radians
8     #─────────────────────define  lists
9     x=[-20,20,20,-20,-20,20,20,-20]
10    y=[-10,-10,-10,-10,10,10,10,10]
11    z=[5,5,-5,-5,5,5,-5,-5]
12
13    xg=[0]*len(x) #─fill xg,yg,zg lists with len(x) zeros
14    yg=[0]*len(x)
15    zg=[0]*len(x)
16
17    #==================================================rotation functions
18    def rotx(xc,yc,zc,xp,yp,zp,Rx):
19            xpp=xp
```

```
20        ypp=yp*cos(Rx)-zp*sin(Rx)
21        zpp=yp*sin(Rx)+zp*cos(Rx)
22        [xg,yg,zg]=[xpp+xc,ypp+yc,zpp+zc]
23        return[xg,yg,zg]
24
25  def  roty(xc,yc,zc,xp,yp,zp,Ry):
26        xpp=xp*cos(Ry)+zp*sin(Ry)
27        ypp=yp
28        zpp=-xp*sin(Ry)+zp*cos(Ry)
29        [xg,yg,zg]=[xpp+xc,ypp+yc,zpp+zc]
30        return[xg,yg,zg]
31
32  def rotz(xc,yc,zc,xp,yp,zp,Rz):
33        xpp=xp*cos(Rz)-yp*sin(Rz)
34        ypp=xp*sin(Rz)+yp*cos(Rz)
35        zpp=zp
36        [xg,yg,zg]=[xpp+xc,ypp+yc,zpp+zc]
37        return[xg,yg,zg]
38
39  #================================================box plotting function
40  def plotbox(xg,yg,zg):
41        v01x=x[1]-x[0] #——0,1,2,3 face
42        v01y=y[1]-y[0]
43        v01z=z[1]-z[0]
44        v03x=x[3]-x[0]
45        v03y=y[3]-y[0]
46        v03z=z[3]-z[0]
47        nz=v03x*v01y-v03y*v01x
48        if nz<=0 :
49            plt.plot([xg[0],xg[1]],[yg[0],yg[1]],color='k',linewidth=2)
50            plt.plot([xg[1],xg[2]],[yg[1],yg[2]],color='k',linewidth=2)
51            plt.plot([xg[2],xg[3]],[yg[2],yg[3]],color='k',linewidth=2)
52            plt.plot([xg[3],xg[0]],[yg[3],yg[0]],color='k',linewidth=2)
53        else: #--plot the other side
54            plt.plot([xg[4],xg[5]],[yg[4],yg[5]],color='k',linewidth=2)
```

```
55          plt.plot([xg[5],xg[6]],[yg[5],yg[6]],color='k',linewidth=2)
56          plt.plot([xg[6],xg[7]],[yg[6],yg[7]],color='k',linewidth=2)
57          plt.plot([xg[7],xg[4]],[yg[7],yg[4]],color='k',linewidth=2)
58
59      v04x=x[4]-x[0] #——0,3,7,4 face
60      v04y=y[4]-y[0]
61      v04z=z[4]-z[0]
62      v03x=x[3]-x[0]
63      v03y=y[3]-y[0]
64      v03z=z[3]-z[0]
65      nz=v04x*v03y-v04y*v03x
66      if nz<=0 :
67          plt.plot([xg[0],xg[3]],[yg[0],yg[3]],color='k',linewidth=2)
68          plt.plot([xg[3],xg[7]],[yg[3],yg[7]],color='k',linewidth=2)
69          plt.plot([xg[7],xg[4]],[yg[7],yg[4]],color='k',linewidth=2)
70          plt.plot([xg[4],xg[0]],[yg[4],yg[0]],color='k',linewidth=2)
71      else: #——plot the other side
72          plt.plot([xg[1],xg[2]],[yg[1],yg[2]],color='k',linewidth=2)
73          plt.plot([xg[2],xg[6]],[yg[2],yg[6]],color='k',linewidth=2)
74          plt.plot([xg[6],xg[5]],[yg[6],yg[5]],color='k',linewidth=2)
75          plt.plot([xg[5],xg[1]],[yg[5],yg[1]],color='k',linewidth=2)
76
77      v01x=x[1]-x[0] #—0,1,5,4 face
78      v01y=y[1]-y[0]
79      v01z=z[1]-z[0]
80      v04x=x[4]-x[0]
81      v04y=y[4]-y[0]
82      v04z=z[4]-z[0]
83      nz=v01x*v04y-v01y*v04x
84      if nz<=0 :
85          plt.plot([xg[0],xg[1]],[yg[0],yg[1]],color='k',linewidth=2)
86          plt.plot([xg[1],xg[5]],[yg[1],yg[5]],color='k',linewidth=2)
87          plt.plot([xg[5],xg[4]],[yg[5],yg[4]],color='k',linewidth=2)
88          plt.plot([xg[4],xg[0]],[yg[4],yg[0]],color='k',linewidth=2)
89      else: #——plot the other side
90          plt.plot([xg[3],xg[2]],[yg[3],yg[2]],color='k',linewidth=2)
```

```
91        plt.plot([xg[2],xg[6]],[yg[2],yg[6]],color='k',linewidth=2)
92        plt.plot([xg[6],xg[7]],[yg[6],yg[7]],color='k',linewidth=2)
93        plt.plot([xg[7],xg[3]],[yg[7],yg[3]],color='k',linewidth=2)
94
95    plt.scatter(xc,yc,s=5,color='k') #-plot a dot at the center
96    plt.axis([0,150,100,0]) #-replot axes and grid
97    plt.axis('on')
98    plt.grid(True)
99    plt.show() #-plot latest rotation
100
101 #===============================transform coordinates and plot functions
102 def plotboxx(xc,yc,zc,Rx): #————transform & plot Rx box
103     for i in range(len(x)):
104
[xg[i],yg[i],zg[i]]=rotx(xc,yc,zc,x[i],y[i],z[i],Rx)
105         [x[i],y[i],z[i]]=[xg[i]-xc,yg[i]-yc,zg[i]-zc]
106
107     plotbox(xg,yg,zg) #————plot
108
109 def plotboxy(xc,yc,zc,Ry):
110     for i in range(len(x)): #————transform & plot Ry box
111         [xg[i],yg[i],zg[i]]=roty(xc,yc,zc,x[i],y[i],z[i],Ry)
112         [x[i],y[i],z[i]]=[xg[i]-xc,yg[i]-yc,zg[i]-zc]
113
114     plotbox(xg,yg,zg)
115
116 def plotboxz(xc,yc,zc,Rz):
117     for i in range(len(x)): #————transform  &  plot  Rz  box
118         [xg[i],yg[i],zg[i]]=rotz(xc,yc,zc,x[i],y[i],z[i],Rz)
119         [x[i],y[i],z[i]]=[xg[i]-xc,yg[i]-yc,zg[i]-zc]
120
121     plotbox(xg,yg,zg)
122
123 #————————————plot  box
124 xc=75 #-center coordinates
125 yc=50
```

```
126 zc=50
127
128 while True:
129        axis=input('x, y or z?: ') #——input axis of rotation (lower case)
130        if axis == 'x': #-if x axis
131
Rx=radians(float(input('Rx Degrees?: '))) #——input degrees of rotation
132              plotboxx(xc,yc,zc,Rx) #——call function plotboxx
133        if axis == 'y':
134
Ry=radians(float(input('Ry Degrees?: '))) #——input degrees of rotation
135              plotboxy(xc,yc,zc,Ry)
136        if axis == 'z':
137
Rz=radians(float(input('Rz Degrees?: '))) #——input degrees
138              plotboxz(xc,yc,zc,Rz)
139        if axis == ":
104            break
```

Pyramid

Listing 6-2 was used to plot Figures 6-6 and 6-7. The model used is shown in Figure 6-8. The analysis is similar to that used for the box in the previous section. The difference is there are four faces to contend with and none of them are parallel, as they were with the box, so you must process each face independently to see if it is facing toward or away from an observer. The hidden lines are plotted as dots in program lines 54-56, 67-69, and 77-79. To remove the dots, replace ":" with " " in these lines. The code in Listing 6-2 should be self-explanatory.

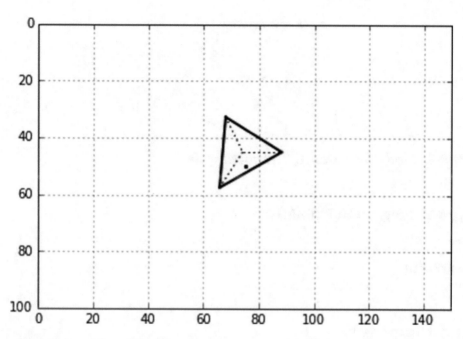

Figure 6-6. *Pyramid with hidden lines removed: Rx=30˚, Ry=45˚, Rz=0˚ (produced by Listing 6-2)*

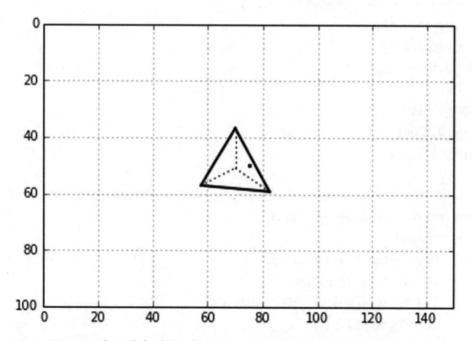

Figure 6-7. *Pyramid with hidden lines removed: Rx=30˚, Ry=45˚, Rz=-90˚ (produced by Listing 6-2)*

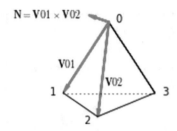

Figure 6-8. *Model for Listing 6-2. N not to scale*

Listing 6-2. Program HLPYRAMID

```
1    """
2    HLPYRAMID
3    """
4
5    import numpy as np
6    import matplotlib.pyplot as plt
7    from math import sin, cos, radians
8    #———————————————————define lists
9    x=[0,-10,0,10]
10   y=[-20,0,0,0]
11   z=[0,10,-15,10]
12
13   xg=[0]*len(x)
14   yg=[0]*len(x)
15   zg=[0]*len(x)
16
17   #==============================================define rotation function
18   def rotx(xc,yc,zc,xp,yp,zp,Rx):
19       xpp=xp
20       ypp=yp*cos(Rx)-zp*sin(Rx)
21       zpp=yp*sin(Rx)+zp*cos(Rx)
22       [xg,yg,zg]=[xpp+xc,ypp+yc,zpp+zc]
23       return[xg,yg,zg]
24
25   def roty(xc,yc,zc,xp,yp,zp,Ry):
```

```
26        xpp=xp*cos(Ry)+zp*sin(Ry)
27        ypp=yp
28        zpp=-xp*sin(Ry)+zp*cos(Ry)
29        [xg,yg,zg]=[xpp+xc,ypp+yc,zpp+zc]
30        return[xg,yg,zg]
31
32  def rotz(xc,yc,zc,xp,yp,zp,Rz):
33        xpp=xp*cos(Rz)-yp*sin(Rz)
34        ypp=xp*sin(Rz)+yp*cos(Rz)
35        zpp=zp
36        [xg,yg,zg]=[xpp+xc,ypp+yc,zpp+zc]
37        return[xg,yg,zg]
38
39  #======================================define pyramid plotting function
40
41  def plotpyramid(xg,yg,zg):
42        v01x=x[1]-x[0] #——0,1,2 face
43        v01y=y[1]-y[0]
44        v01z=z[1]-z[0]
45        v02x=x[2]-x[0]
46        v02y=y[2]-y[0]
47        v02z=z[2]-z[0]
48        nz=v01x*v02y-v01y*v02x
49        if nz<=0 :
50            plt.plot([xg[0],xg[1]],[yg[0],yg[1]],color='k',linewidth=2)
51            plt.plot([xg[1],xg[2]],[yg[1],yg[2]],color='k',linewidth=2)
52            plt.plot([xg[2],xg[0]],[yg[2],yg[0]],color='k',linewidth=2)
53        else:
54            plt.plot([xg[0],xg[1]],[yg[0],yg[1]],color='k',linestyle=':')
55            plt.plot([xg[1],xg[2]],[yg[1],yg[2]],color='k',linestyle=':')
56            plt.plot([xg[2],xg[0]],[yg[2],yg[0]],color='k',linestyle=':')
57
58        v03x=x[3]-x[0] #–0,2,3 face
59        v03y=y[3]-y[0]
60        v03z=z[3]-z[0]
```

```
61        nz=v02x*v03y-v02y*v03x
62        if nz<=0 :
63            plt.plot([xg[0],xg[2]],[yg[0],yg[2]],color='k',linewidth=2)
64            plt.plot([xg[0],xg[3]],[yg[0],yg[3]],color='k',linewidth=2)
65            plt.plot([xg[2],xg[3]],[yg[2],yg[3]],color='k',linewidth=2)
66        else:
67            plt.plot([xg[0],xg[2]],[yg[0],yg[2]],color='k',linestyle=':')
68            plt.plot([xg[0],xg[3]],[yg[0],yg[3]],color='k',linestyle=':')
69            plt.plot([xg[2],xg[3]],[yg[2],yg[3]],color='k',linestyle=':')
70
71        nz=v03x*v01y-v03y*v01x #-0,2,3 face
72        if nz<=0 :
73            plt.plot([xg[0],xg[1]],[yg[0],yg[1]],color='k',linewidth=2)
74            plt.plot([xg[0],xg[3]],[yg[0],yg[3]],color='k',linewidth=2)
75            plt.plot([xg[1],xg[3]],[yg[1],yg[3]],color='k',linewidth=2)
76        else:
77            plt.plot([xg[0],xg[1]],[yg[0],yg[1]],color='k',linestyle=':')
78            plt.plot([xg[0],xg[3]],[yg[0],yg[3]],color='k',linestyle=':')
79            plt.plot([xg[1],xg[3]],[yg[1],yg[3]],color='k',linestyle=':')
80
81        v21x=x[1]-x[2] #—1,2,3 face
82        v21y=y[1]-y[2]
83        v21z=z[1]-z[2]
84        v23x=x[3]-x[2]
85        v23y=y[3]-y[2]
86        v23z=z[3]-z[2]
87        nz=v21x*v23y-v21y*v23x
88        if nz¡0:
89            plt.plot([x[2],x[1]],[y[2],y[1]])
90            plt.plot([x[1],x[3]],[y[1],y[3]])
91            plt.plot([x[3],x[2]],[y[3],y[2]])
92
93        plt.scatter(xc,yc,s=5,color='k') #—plot a dot at the center
94        plt.axis([0,150,100,0]) #—replot axes and grid
95        plt.axis('on')
```

```
96        plt.grid(True)
97        plt.show() #-plot latest rotation
98
99  #=======================transform coordinates and plotting fucntions
100 def plotpyramidx(xc,yc,zc,Rx): #————transform & plot Rx pyramid
101       for i in range(len(x)):
102
[xg[i],yg[i],zg[i]]=rotx(xc,yc,zc,x[i],y[i],z[i],Rx)
103
[x[i],y[i],z[i]]=[xg[i]-xc,yg[i]-yc,zg[i]-zc]
104
105       plotpyramid(xg,yg,zg) #————plot
106
107 def plotpyramidy(xc,yc,zc,Ry):
108       for i in range(len(x)): #————transform & plot Ry pyramid
109             [xg[i],yg[i],zg[i]]=roty(xc,yc,zc,x[i],y[i],z[i],Ry)
110             [x[i],y[i],z[i]]=[xg[i]-xc,yg[i]-yc,zg[i]-zc]
111
112       plotpyramid(xg,yg,zg)
113
114 def plotpyramidz(xc,yc,zc,Rz):
115       for i in range(len(x)): #————transform & plot Rz pyramid
116             [xg[i],yg[i],zg[i]]=rotz(xc,yc,zc,x[i],y[i],z[i],Rz)
117             [x[i],y[i],z[i]]=[xg[i]-xc,yg[i]-yc,zg[i]-zc]
118
119       plotpyramid(xg,yg,zg)
120
121 #————————————plot pyramids
122 xc=75 #——center coordinates
123 yc=50
124 zc=50
125
126 while True:
127       axis=input('x, y or z?: ') #——input axis of rotation (lower case)
128       if axis == 'x': #——if x axis
```

```
129
Rx=radians(float(input('Rx Degrees?: '))) #——input degrees of rotation
130              plotpyramidx(xc,yc,zc,Rx) #——call function plotpyramidx
131        if axis == 'y':
132
Ry=radians(float(input('Ry Degrees?: '))) #——input degrees of rotation
133              plotpyramidy(xc,yc,zc,Ry)
134        if axis == 'z':
135
Rz=radians(float(input('Rz Degrees?: '))) #——input degrees of rotation
136              plotpyramidz(xc,yc,zc,Rz)
137        if axis == '':
138              break
```

Planes

Next is an example of inter-object hidden line removal. Figure 6-9 shows two planes, (a) and (b); Figure 6-10 shows the same two planes partially overlapping. As you will see shortly, plane (b) is actually beneath the plane (a) and should be partially obscured. Figures 6-11 shows the planes with the hidden lines of plane (b) removed. Figure 6-12 shows another example. Figure 6-13 shows an example with plane (a) rotated.

In this simple model, the two planes are parallel to the x,y plane with plane (b) taken to be located behind plane (a) (i.e., further in the +z direction). You do not need to be concerned with the z component of the planes' coordinates since you won't be rotating them out of plane, (i.e., around the x or y directions), although you will be rotating plane (a) in its plane around the z direction, but for this you do not need z coordinates.

Figure 6-14 shows the model used by Listing 6-3. Plane (a) is drawn in black, plane (b) in blue. Unit vectors $\hat{\imath}$ and $\hat{\jmath}$ are shown at corner 0 of plane (a). You use a ray tracing technique to remove the hidden lines when plane (b) or part of it is behind (a) and not visible. You do so line by line beginning with edge 0-1 of plane (b). Starting at corner 0 of plane (b), you imagine a ray emitting from that point traveling to an observer who is located in the -z direction and looking in onto the x,y plane. If plane (a) does not interfere with that ray (i.e., does not cover up that point), the dot is plotted. If plane (a) does interfere, it is not plotted. The problem thus becomes one of intersections: determining if a ray from a point on an edge of plane (b) intersects plane (a).

The edges of plane (b) are processed one at a time. Starting with corner 0, you proceed along edge 0-1 to corner 1 in small steps. Vector **H** shows the location of a point h on edge 0-1. Listing 6-3 determines the location of this point and whether or not it lies beneath plane (a) (i.e., if a ray emanating from h strikes plane (a)). If it does not, point p is plotted; if it does, p is not plotted.

In Listing 6-3, lines 14-18 establish the coordinates of the two planes in *global* coordinates, ready for plotting. Lines 21-32 define function dlinea that plots the edge lines of plane (a). It does so one edge line at a time. dlinea does not do a hidden line check on the edges of plane (a) since you are stipulating that plane (a) lies over plane (b). The calling arguments x1, x2, y1, y2 are the beginning and end coordinates of the edge line. q in line 22 is the length of that line; uxa and uya are the x and y components of a unit vector that points along the edge line from x1, y1 to x2, y2. The loop in lines 27-32 advances the point along the line from x1, y1 to x2, y2 in steps of .2 as set in line 27. hx and hy in lines 28 and 29 are the coordinates of point h along the line. hxstart and hystart permit connecting the points by short line segments, giving a finer appearance than if the points were plotted as dots.

Lines 35-38 plot the edges of plane (a) by calling function dlinea with the beginning and end coordinates of each of the four edges. Lines 40-42 establish the distance qa03 from corner 0 of plane (a) to corner 3. uxa and uya in lines 43 and 44 are the x and y components of unit vector $\hat{\mathbf{u}}$, which points from corner 0 to corner 3. Similarly, lines 46-50 give the components of $\hat{\mathbf{v}}$ a unit vector pointing from corner 0 to 1. They will be required to do the intersection check, as was done in the preceding chapter with line/plane intersections.

Function dlineb is similar to dlinea except the calling arguments now include agx[0] and agy[0], the coordinates of corner 0 of plane (a). Also, this function includes the interference check, which is between lines 64 and 71. This is labelled the inside/outside check. In line 64, a is the distance between the x coordinate of point h and the x coordinate of corner 0 of plane (a); b in line 65 is the y distance. These are essentially the x and y components of vector **H**. In line 66, the dot (scalar) product of **H** with unit vector $\hat{\mathbf{u}}$ gives up. This is the projection of **H** on the 0-3 side of plane (a). Similarly, the dot product of **H** with unit vector $\hat{\mathbf{v}}$ in line 67 gives vp, the projection of **H** on the 0-1 side of plane (a). The interference check is then straightforward and is summarized in line 68. If all questions in line 68 are true, the point is plotted in line 69 in white, which means it is invisible. If any the questions in line 68 are false, which means the point is not blocked by plane (a), line 71 plots it in black.

But why use this elaborate vector analysis? Why not just check each point's x and y coordinates as shown in Figure 6-14 against the horizontal and vertical boundaries of plane (a)? You could do that if both planes remain aligned with the x and y axes as shown. But by using the vector approach, you enable either one of the planes to be rotated about the z direction as shown in Figure 6-13.

I have simplified this model a bit by specifying that plane (b) lie under (a). In general, you may not know which plane is closer to the observer and which should be (a) and which (b). This can be accomplished by a simple check on z coordinates. In principle, the hidden line removal process would be similar to what you have done here, although the programming can get complicated trying to keep track of a large assemblage of objects.

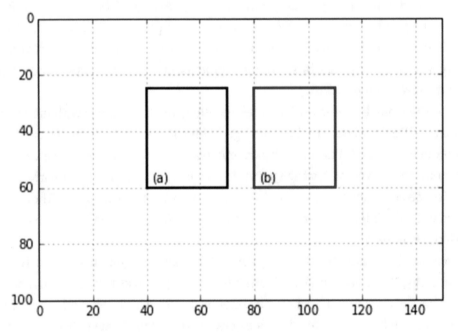

Figure 6-9. *Two planes*

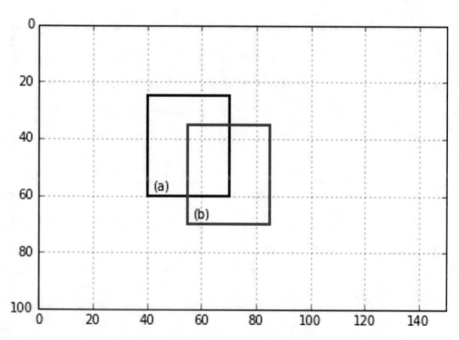

Figure 6-10. *Two planes, one partially overlapping the other, hidden lines not removed. Plane (b) is beneath (a)*

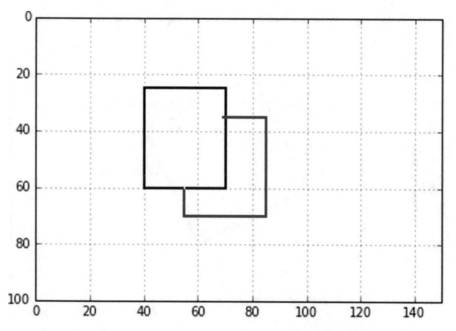

Figure 6-11. *Two planes overlapping, hidden lines removed by Listing 6-3*

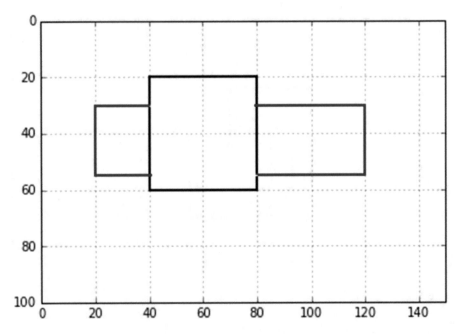

Figure 6-12. *Two planes, one overlapping the other, hidden lines removed by Listing 6-3*

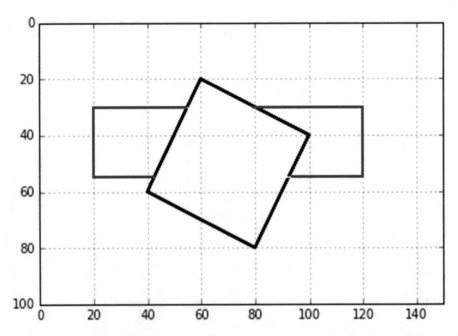

Figure 6-13. *Two planes, one at an angle and overlapping the other, hidden lines removed by Listing 6-3*

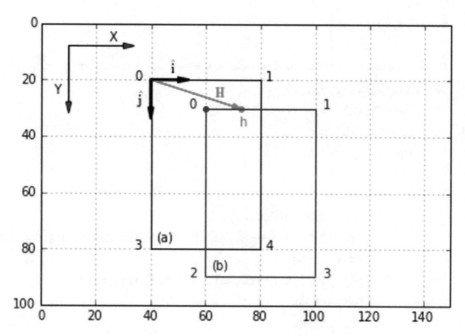

Figure 6-14. *Model for Listing 6-3*

Listing 6-3. Program HLPLANES

```
1    """
2    HLPLANES
3    """
4
5    import numpy as np
6    import matplotlib.pyplot as plt
7    from math import sqrt, sin, cos, radians
8
9    plt.axis([0,150,100,0])
10   plt.axis('off')
11   plt.grid(False)
12
13   #——————————————-define lists
14   axg=[40,80,80,40]
15   ayg=[20,20,60,60]
16
17   bxg=[20,120,120,20]
```

```
18   byg=[30,30,55,55]
19
20   #==================================================define function dlinea
21   def dlinea(x1,x2,y1,y2):
22       q=sqrt((x2-x1)**2+(y2-y1)**2)
23       uxa=(x2-x1)/q
24       uya=(y2-y1)/q
25       hxstart=x1
26       hystart=y1
27       for l in np.arange(0,q,.2):
28               hx=x1+l*uxa #——global hit coordinates along the line
29               hy=y1+l*uya
30               plt.plot([hxstart,hx],[hystart,hy],color='k')
31               hxstart=hx
32               hystart=hy
33
34   #————————————————plane (a)
35   dlinea(axg[0],axg[1],ayg[0],ayg[1]) #——plot plane (a)
36   dlinea(axg[1],axg[2],ayg[1],ayg[2])
37   dlinea(axg[2],axg[3],ayg[2],ayg[3])
38   dlinea(axg[3],axg[0],ayg[3],ayg[0])
39
40   a=axg[3]-axg[0] #——unit vector u plane (a)
41   b=ayg[3]-ayg[0]
42   qa03=sqrt(a*a+b*b)
43   uxa=a/qa03
44   uya=b/qa03
45
46   a=axg[1]-axg[0] #——unit vector v plane (a)
47   b=ayg[1]-ayg[0]
48   qa01=sqrt(a*a+b*b)
49   vxa=a/qa01
50   vya=b/qa01
51
```

```
52  #==============================================================lineb( )
53  def dlineb(x1,x2,y1,y2,ax0,ay0):
54      a=x2-x1 #——unit vector line
55      b=y2-y1
56      ql=sqrt(a*a+b*b)
57      uxl=a/ql
58      uyl=b/ql
59      hxglast=x1
60      hyglast=y1
61      for l in np.arange(0,ql,.5):
62              hxg=x1+l*uxl
63              hyg=y1+l*uyl
64              a=hxg-ax0 #——inside/outside check
65              b=hyg-ay0
66              up=a*uxa+b*uya
67              vp=a*vxa+b*vya
68              if 0<up<qa03 and 0<vp<qa01: #——is it inside (a)?
79                  plt.plot([hxglast,hxg],[hyglast,hyg],color='white')
70              else:
71                  plt.plot([hxglast,hxg],[hyglast,hyg],color='k')
72          hxglast=hxg
73          hyglast=hyg
74
75  #———————————————plot plane (b)
76  dlineb(bxg[0],bxg[1],byg[0],byg[1],axg[0],ayg[0])
77  dlineb(bxg[1],bxg[2],byg[1],byg[2],axg[0],ayg[0])
78  dlineb(bxg[2],bxg[3],byg[2],byg[3],axg[0],ayg[0])
79  dlineb(bxg[3],bxg[0],byg[3],byg[0],axg[0],ayg[0])
80
81  plt.show()
```

Sphere

In Chapter 5, you drew a sphere but did not rotate it. The planes defined by the lines on the back side were overlapped by those on the front and thus were not visible, so removing hidden lines was not an issue: it was easy to determine which lines were on the back side so just don't plot them. In this chapter, you will draw a sphere and rotate it while removing hidden lines on the back side.

Figures 6-15 and 6-18 show examples of the output from Listing 6-4, which plots a sphere with hidden lines removed. The vertical lines in Figures 6-15 and 6-16, the *longitudes*, are drawn in green; the horizontal *latitudes* are drawn in blue. The program uses a hidden line removal scheme much like the one you used before with boxes and pyramids. If the z component of a vector perpendicular to a point is positive (i.e., pointing away from an observer who is located in the -z direction), the point is not drawn; otherwise it is drawn.

In Listing 6-4, line 14 sets the length of the list g[ ] to 3. This will be used to return global coordinates xg,yg, and zg from the rotation functions rotx, roty, and rotz, which are defined in lines 24-40 (they are the same as the functions used in previous programs). The longitudes are plotted in lines 55-79. The model is the same as used in Listing 5-5 in Chapter 5. The algorithm between lines 55 and 79 calculates the location of each point on a longitude, one at a time, and rotates it. That is, each point is established and rotated separately; lists are not used other than the g[ ] list. The alpha loop starting in line 55 sweeps the longitudes from $\alpha = 0$ to $\alpha = 360$ in six-degree steps as set in lines 47-49. At each α step a longitude is drawn by the ϕ loop, which starts at -90 degrees and goes to +90 in six-degree steps. The geometry in lines 57-59 is taken from Listing 5-5. The coordinates of a point before rotation (Rx=0, Ry=0, Rz=0) are xp,yp,zp as shown in lines 57-59. This point is located on the sphere's surface at spherical coordinates α, ϕ. Line 60 rotates the point about the x direction by an angle Rx. This produces new coordinates xp, yp, zp in lines 61-63. Line 64 rotates the point at these new coordinates around the y direction. Line 68 rotates it around the z direction. This produces the final location of the point.

Next, you must determine whether or not the point is on the back side of the sphere and hidden from view. If true, it is not plotted. Lines 73-79 perform this function. First, in lines 73-75, you establish the starting coordinates of the line that will connect the first point to the second. You use lines to connect the points rather than dots since lines give a finer appearance. Line 73 asks if phi equals phi1, the starting angle in the phi loop. If it does, the starting coordinates xpglast and ypglast are set equal to the first coordinates calculated by the loop. Next, in line 76, you ask if nz, the z component of a vector from the sphere's center to the point, is less than 0. nz is calculated in line 72. If true, you know the point is visible to an observer situated in the -z direction; the point is then connected to the previous one by line 77.

The `plt.plot()` function in line 77 needs two sets of coordinates: xpglast,ypglast and xpg,ypg. During the first cycle through the loop, the starting coordinates xpglast,ypglast are set equal to xpg,ypg, meaning the first point is connected to itself so the first line plotted will have zero length. After that, the coordinates of the previous point are set in lines 78-79. Line 73 determines if it is the first point. If nz is greater than zero in line 76, the point is on the back side of the rotated sphere and is not visible so it is not plotted. The coordinates xpglast and ypglast must still be updated and this is done in lines 78-79. The latitudes are processed in much the same way, although the geometry is different, as described in Listing 5-5. The colors of the longitudes and latitudes can be changed by changing the `color='color'` values in lines 77 and 104.

When running this program, remember that the rotations are not additive as in some of the previous programs. The angles of rotation specified in lines 51-53 are the angles the sphere will end up at; they are not added to any previous rotations. To rotate the sphere to another orientation, change the values in lines 51-53.

As mentioned in the discussion on concatenation, the sequence of rotations is important. Rx followed by Ry does not give the same results as Ry followed by Rx. This program has the sequence of function calls, Rx,Ry,Rz, as specified in lines 60, 64, and 68 for longitudes and 87, 91, and 95 for latitudes. To change the order of rotation, change the order of these function calls.

The spheres shown in Figures 6-17 and 6-18 have a black background. To achieve this, insert the following lines in Listing 6-4 before any other plotting commands, for example after line 12:

```
#————————————————paint the background
for y in np.arange(1,100,1):
    plt.plot([0,150],[y,y],linewidth=4,color='k')
```

This plots black lines across the plotting window from x=0 to x=150 and down from y=1 to y=100. This fills the area with a black background. The color can be changed to anything desired. The `linewidth` has been set to 4 in order to prevent gaps from appearing between the horizontal lines. The background must be painted before constructing the sphere since you are using line segments to do that. New lines overplot old ones, so with this order the sphere line segments will overplot the background lines; otherwise the background lines would overplot the sphere.

In Figures 6-15 and 6-16, the sphere's line widths in program lines 77 and 104 is set to .5. This gives good results on a clear background but the lines are too subdued when the background is changed to black. So, along with inserting the two lines of code above, the line widths in Listing 6-4 should be changed to something greater such as 1.0. The color shown in Figures 6-17 and 6-18 is 'lightgreen'. Some colors don't plot well against a black background but color='lightgreen' seems to work; you just have to experiment.

Listing 6-4. Program HLSPHERE

```
1    """
2    HLSPHERE
3    """
4
5    import numpy as np
6    import matplotlib.pyplot as plt
7    from math import sin, cos, radians, sqrt
8
9    plt.axis([0,150,100,0])
10   plt.axis('off')
11   plt.grid(False)
12
13   #————————————————lists
14   g=[0]*3
15
16   #————————————————parameters
17   xc=80 #——sphere center
18   yc=50
19   zc=0
20
21   rs=40 #——sphere radius
22
23   #===========================================================
24   def rotx(xc,yc,zc,xp,yp,zp,Rx):
```

```
25      g[0]=xp+xc
26      g[1]=yp*cos(Rx)-zp*sin(Rx)+yc
27      g[2]=yp*sin(Rx)+zp*cos(Rx)+zc
28      return[g]
29
30  def roty(xc,yc,zc,xp,yp,zp,Ry):
31      g[0]=xp*cos(Ry)+zp*sin(Ry)+xc
32      g[1]=yp+yc
33      g[2]=-xp*sin(Ry)+zp*cos(Ry)+zc
34      return[g]
35
36  def rotz(xc,yc,zc,xp,yp,zp,Rz):
37      g[0]=xp*cos(Rz)-yp*sin(Rz)+xc
38      g[1]=xp*sin(Rz)+yp*cos(Rz)+yc
39      g[2]=zp+zc
40      return[g]
41
42  #——————————-longitudes and latitudes
43  phi1=radians(-90)
44  phi2=radians(90)
45  dphi=radians(6)
46
47  alpha1=radians(0)
48  alpha2=radians(360)
49  dalpha=radians(6)
50
51  Rx=radians(45)
52  Ry=radians(-20)
53  Rz=radians(40)
54
55  for alpha in np.arange(alpha1,alpha2,dalpha):  #——longitudes
56      for phi in np.arange(phi1,phi2,dphi):
57          xp=rs*cos(phi)*cos(alpha)
58          yp=rs*sin(phi)
59          zp=-rs*cos(phi)*sin(alpha)
```

```
60              rotx(xc,yc,zc,xp,yp,zp,Rx)
61              xp=g[0]-xc
62              yp=g[1]-yc
63              zp=g[2]-zc
64              roty(xc,yc,zc,xp,yp,zp,Ry)
65              xp=g[0]-xc
66              yp=g[1]-yc
67              zp=g[2]-zc
68              rotz(xc,yc,zc,xp,yp,zp,Rz)
69              xpg=g[0]
70              ypg=g[1]
71              zpg=g[2]
72              nz=zpg-zc
73              if phi == phi1:
74                      xpglast=xpg
75                      ypglast=ypg
76              if nz < 0:
77
plt.plot([xpglast,xpg],[ypglast,ypg],linewidth=.5,
color='g')
78              xpglast=xpg
79              ypglast=ypg
80
81   for phi in np.arange(phi1,phi2,dphi):   #———latitudes
82       r=rs*cos(phi)
83       for alpha in np.arange(alpha1,alpha2+dalpha,dalpha):
84           xp=r*cos(alpha)
85           yp=rs*sin(phi)
86           zp=-rs*cos(phi)*sin(alpha)
87           rotx(xc,yc,zc,xp,yp,zp,Rx)
88           xp=g[0]-xc
89           yp=g[1]-yc
90           zp=g[2]-zc
91           roty(xc,yc,zc,xp,yp,zp,Ry)
92           xp=g[0]-xc
```

```
93              yp=g[1]-yc
94              zp=g[2]-zc
95              rotz(xc,yc,zc,xp,yp,zp,Rz)
96              xpg=g[0]
97              ypg=g[1]
98              zpg=g[2]
99              nz=zpg-zc
100             if alpha == alpha1:
101                     xpglast=xpg
102                     ypglast=ypg
103             if nz < 0:
104
plt.plot([xpglast,xpg],[ypglast,ypg],linewidth=.5,
color='b')
105             xpglast=xpg
106             ypglast=ypg
107

108 plt.show()
```

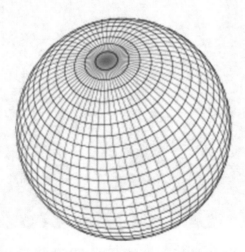

Figure 6-15. *Rotated sphere with hidden lines removed: Rx=55°, Ry=-20°, Rz=-40° (produced by Listing 6-4)*

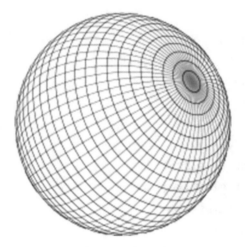

Figure 6-16. *Rotated sphere with hidden lines removed: Rx=40°, Ry=-20°, Rz=40° (produced by Listing 6-4)*

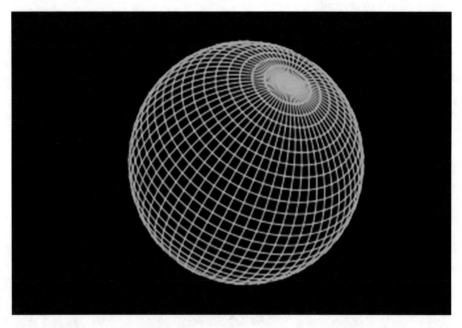

Figure 6-17. *Rotated sphere with hidden lines removed: Rx=40°, Ry=-20°, Rz=40°, black background (produced by Listing 6-4)*

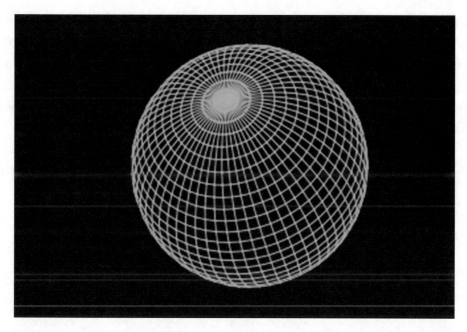

Figure 6-18. *Rotated sphere with hidden lines removed: Rx=60°, Ry=20°, Rz=10°, black background (produced by Listing 6-4)*

Summary

In this chapter, you learned how to remove hidden lines from single objects and between objects. In the case of single objects, such as the box, the pyramid, and the sphere, you were able to construct algorithms without much trouble. When removing hidden lines from separate objects, such as two planes, you relied on the technique of constructing one of the objects, the hidden or partially hidden one, using dots or short line segments that go from one dot to another. In either case, you were still dealing with dots. From a dot on one plane, you drew an imaginary line, a ray, to an observer who is positioned in the -z direction. Then you checked to see if the ray intersected the other plane. You used the line-plane intersection algorithm developed in Chapter 5. If it did intersect, the dot was hidden and it, or a line segment connected to it, was not drawn. You used two planes to explore this technique. You could have used any of the other shapes you worked with in Chapter 5. For example, you could have easily removed hidden lines from a plane beneath a circular segment by constructing the plane from dots and using the intersection algorithm from Chapter 5. However, you might not know ahead of time which object covers which. You could do a rough check to answer this question. For example, in the case of two planes, if the z coordinates of all four corners of one plane are less than the other, it is closer to the observer, in which case it may cover part of the other plane. In this case, the other plane should be checked for hidden lines.

CHAPTER 7

Shading

In this chapter, you will learn how to shade three-dimensional objects. Shading produces a much more realistic look and enhances the perception of three-dimensionality. The general idea is to first establish the direction of light rays impacting the object being illuminated and then determine the shading effect the light has on the object's surface. In the case of a box, which I will discuss next, six flat planes comprise the surface of the box. The orientation of these planes relative to the direction of the light will determine the degree of shading on each plane. To simulate shading, the planes can be filled with dots or lines. Different intensities of shading can be obtained by changing the intensity of the color of the dots or lines and by color mixing.

Normally an object being plotted will appear on a white background. If a background color is used, such as in Figure 7-13, dots or lines may be used to paint the background. Recall from Chapter 1 that new dots overplot old dots and new lines always overplot dots and old lines. This means that whether the shading is constructed of dots or lines, they will overplot the background color if it is painted with dots. The disadvantage of using dots for background color is it takes a lot of time to fill the background with dots. Lines are a better alternative in this regard and are preferred if the object can be constructed of lines. If you must use dots to shade your object, then you must use dots for your background color.

The heart of a shading program is the intensity function, which relates the amount of shading of a plane to the plane's orientation relative to the direction of the incoming light. You do not specify the position of a light source; you specify the direction of the light rays impacting the object from that source. For example, suppose the program calculates that the angle between a plane and the incoming light rays is 50 degrees. The intensity function converts this angle into a shading intensity, which is used to alter the color intensity of the lines or dots.

A considerable amount of research has been carried out on theories of shading in an effort to produce more lifelike computer-drawn images. These images often have a separate shading function for each of the primary colors (r,g,b) and take into account the color of the incident light and the reflectivity and physical characteristics of the surface

241

B. Korites, *Python Graphics*, https://doi.org/10.1007/978-1-4842-9660-8_7

material. Smooth surfaces will be highly reflective while rough, textured surfaces will scatter the incoming light, producing a higher degree of diffusivity. In your work here, you will keep it simple and use just one shading function and ignore the differences in surface features that can affect the surface's reflectivity and diffusivity, although they could easily be introduced into the program. Also, you assume the shading of a surface is dependent on only the orientation of that surface relative to the light source and not on its orientation relative to the observer who, as usual, you take to be located in the -z direction.

Shading a Box

Figures 7-1 through 7-7 show samples of output from Listing 7-1. They show a box rotated to different orientations with shading on its surfaces. They are shaded in monochrome black at different intensities ranging from black to grey to white.

Figure 7-1. Shaded box produced by Listing 7-1, Io=.8

Figure 7-2. Shaded box produced by Listing 7-1, Io=1.0

Figure 7-3. Shaded box produced by Listing 7-1, Io=1.0

Figure 7-4. *Shaded box produced by Listing 7-1, Io=1.0*

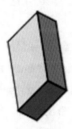

Figure 7-5. *Shaded box produced by Listing 7-1,Io=.8*

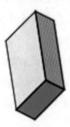

Figure 7-6. *Shaded box produced by Listing 7-1, Io=.6*

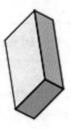

Figure 7-7. *Shaded box produced by Listing 7-1, Io=.4*

Figure 7-9 shows the model used by Listing 7-1. The light source is shown at the upper left. You do not explicitly state its location, only the direction of the light rays emanating from it. You do that by specifying lx, ly, and lz, the components of a unit vector $\hat{\mathbf{l}}$, which is aligned with the light rays. Keep in mind that $\hat{\mathbf{l}}$ is a unit vector so the following relation between its components must be observed:

$$\sqrt{lx^2 + ly^2 + lz^2} = 1 \tag{7-1}$$

Looking at the top plane of the box defined by corners 0,1,2,3, you can see a unit normal vector $\hat{\mathbf{n}}$ at corner 0. This points outward from the plane. You shade the box by drawing lines, shown in blue, which extend across the width of the plane from B to E. These lines are drawn from edge 0,1 to 3,2 and then down the plane, thus shading it. The lines on each face will have an intensity that depends on the orientation of $\hat{\mathbf{n}}$ with $\hat{\mathbf{l}}$. You get this orientation by taking the dot product of $\hat{\mathbf{n}}$ with $\hat{\mathbf{l}}$. If $\hat{\mathbf{n}}$ is facing $\hat{\mathbf{l}}$, the dot product will be negative and the intensity of the lines will be less, which means the tone will be lighter; if $\hat{\mathbf{n}}$ is facing away from $\hat{\mathbf{l}}$, the dot product will be positive, the intensity will be greater, and the tone will be darker.

This is illustrated by Figure 7-10, which shows the shading intensity, I, vs. $\hat{\mathbf{n}} \cdot \mathbf{l}$. This is a linear relation. As you will see in the next section, better results can be obtained with a non-linear relation and by mixing r,g,b colors. You can get an equation for this linear intensity function by inspection:

$$I = \frac{Io}{2} + \frac{Io}{2}\hat{\mathbf{n}} \cdot \hat{\mathbf{l}} \tag{7-2}$$

$$\boxed{I = \frac{Io}{2}\left(1 + \hat{\mathbf{n}} \cdot \hat{\mathbf{l}}\right)} \tag{7-3}$$

Note the parameter Io. It gives control over the degree of darkness in the shaded areas by increasing or decreasing the intensity of the color. The lines from B to E are plotted with the `plt.plot()` function, which includes the attribute `alpha`. By letting `alpha=I` you can control the intensity of the color. Higher values of `alpha` increase the intensity, making shaded areas appear darker; lower values of `alpha` decrease it, thus creating areas that appear lighter. Note that `alpha` may take on values from 0 to 1, hence I is limited to the same range of values. From Equation 7-3, this means that Io can have a maximum value of 1. Io=1 will give the darkest, most intense hues. To soften the image with more subtle hues, lower Io to something less than 1. To modify the function even more, the left side could be raised, which would darken the lights. If the function were horizontal, all shading would be uniform. To see the effect of Io on the shading, Figures 7-2 through 7-4 have Io=1.0. Figures 7-1, 7-5, 7-6, and 7-7 have Io=.8, .8, .6, and .4, respectively. Colors do not have to be black or primaries; they can be mixed. Figure 7-8 shows the result of using color=(r,g,b) with r=.5, g=0, b=.5,

$$color = (.5, 0, .5) \qquad (7\text{-}4)$$

which is a purple mix of equal amount of red and blue. Recall that red, green, and blue in an r,g,b mix must each have values between 0 and 1.

You have been applying your shading intensity, I, to monochrome colors. Even if you use r,g,b color mixing, it is still a monochrome shade, although not a primary color. An extension of this method would be to apply separate intensities to each of the three primary colors. For example, when an artist paints a portrait, they might render the light side of the face a light pink. To darken the shaded side, they would normally add green, the compliment of red, to the mix. If you look closely at the portraits of an accomplished artist, you will see this is usually how it is done. Rarely would one add black to the mix to darken it. In fact, many painters do not even keep a black pigment on their pallet; they achieve darker colors by mixing the hues with their compliment. The compliment of red is green; of yellow it is violet. Color mixing in painting isn't quite that simple, of course, but that is the fundamental idea. To accomplish this in your programming, suppose you are shading a red box using an r,g,b color mix. Rather than applying an intensity factor to the red to increase its intensity, thus simulating a darkening, you apply the intensity factor to the green, increasing its contribution in the r,g,b mix, thus darkening the red. For the present, in Listing 7-1 you will keep things simple and simulate shading by increasing the intensity of the color in the dark areas rather than using color mixing. This works well with a monochrome black image, although it has limitations with colored objects.

The definition of the box in Listing 7-1 is contained in the lists in lines 10, 11, and 12. Lines 14, 15, and 16 open lists for the global coordinates, which are returned by the rotation functions rotx, roty, and rotz. They have the same lengths as the x,y,z lists as specified by len(x).

A new function called shade() is defined in Listing 7-1, lines 54-84. The arguments received by shade() in line 54 are shown in Figure 7-11. When shade() is invoked for a specific plane, the box's corners must follow the order shown in Figure 7-11. As an example, the ordering for plane 1,5,6,2 is shown in Figure 7-12. Some visual gymnastics can be required to orient the six planes of the box such that they conform to the ordering in Figure 7-11. Each of the six planes are drawn and shaded separately by six calls to function shade(). They are listed in lines 88-93. The arguments of the calls are the x,y,z coordinates of points a,b,c,d, respectively. Function shade() calculates the components of unit vector $\hat{u}$ in lines 55-61 and v in lines 62-68. Components of unit vector $\hat{n}$ are calculated in lines 69-71. The dot product on $\hat{n}$ with the incoming light ray unit vector $\hat{l}$, the components of which were specified in lines 23-25, is calculated in line 72 as ndotl; the shading intensity in line 73. If nz<=0 (i.e., $\hat{n}$ is pointing toward the observer who is in the -z direction), the edges of the face are plotted in lines 75-78 and the face is shaded in loop 79-84. Line 79 ranges h, shown in Figure 7-11, from 0 to qad, the distance from corner a to d, which was calculated in line 58, in steps of 1. Lines 80-81 calculate the x and y coordinates of the beginning of the line; lines 82 and 83 get the coordinates of the end of the line. Line 84 plots the line. In line 84, alpha is equal to the intensity of the shading that was determined in line 73. The box's color is equal to clr, which was specified in line 27; for example, color='k' will give a black box. An alternative would be to mix primary colors as shown in line 28. This produces the purple box shown in Figure 7-8. To get this color, just remove the #, which indicates a comment, in line 28; otherwise, the shading will be done in black. I will discuss color mixing in more detail in the next section. The maximum intensity Io is specified in line 29. This can be anything between 0 and 1. If nz>0 (i.e., $\hat{n}$ is pointing away from the observer), the face is not plotted. The remainder of Listing 7-1 should be familiar.

Figure 7-8. *Shaded box produced by Listing 7-1, (r,g,b)=(.5,0.,5) color mixing, Io=1.0*

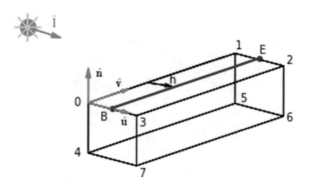

Figure 7-9. *Shading model used by Listing 7-1*

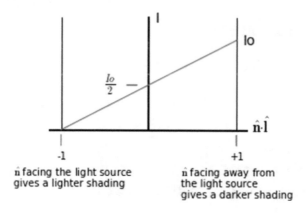

-1
n̂ facing the light source
gives a lighter shading

+1
n̂ facing away from
the light source
gives a darker shading

Figure 7-10. *Shading function*

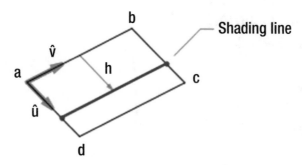

Figure 7-11. *Model of a generic plane used in Listing 7-1*

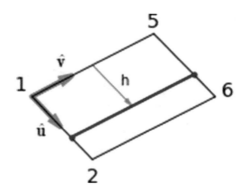

Figure 7-12. *Plane 1,5,6,2*

Listing 7-1. Program SHADEBOX

```
1    """
2    SHADEBOX
3    """
4
5    import numpy as np
6    import matplotlib.pyplot as plt
7    from math import sin, cos, radians, sqrt
8
9    #——————————————————lists
10   x=[-20,20,20,-20,-20,20,20,-20]
11   y=[-10,-10,-10,-10,10,10,10,10]
12   z=[5,5,-5,-5,5,5,-5,-5]
13
14   xg=[0]*len(x)
15   yg=[0]*len(x)
16   zg=[0]*len(x)
17
18   #————————————————parameters
19   xc=75 #——center coordinates
20   yc=50
21   zc=50
22
23   lx=.707 #——light ray unit vector components
```

```
24  ly=.707
25  lz=0
26
27  clr='k' #——use this for black monochrome images, or use another color
28  #clr=(.5,0,.5) #——use this to mix colors, this mix produces purple
29  Io=.8 #——max intensity, must be 0 < 1
30
31
#=======================================================define rotation
functions
32  def rotx(xc,yc,zc,xp,yp,zp,Rx):
33      xpp=xp
34      ypp=yp*cos(Rx)-zp*sin(Rx)
35      zpp=yp*sin(Rx)+zp*cos(Rx)
36      [xg,yg,zg]=[xpp+xc,ypp+yc,zpp+zc]
37      return[xg,yg,zg]
38
39  def roty(xc,yc,zc,xp,yp,zp,Ry):
40      xpp=xp*cos(Ry)+zp*sin(Ry)
41      ypp=yp
42      zpp=-xp*sin(Ry)+zp*cos(Ry)
43      [xg,yg,zg]=[xpp+xc,ypp+yc,zpp+zc]
44      return[xg,yg,zg]
45
46  def rotz(xc,yc,zc,xp,yp,zp,Rz):
47      xpp=xp*cos(Rz)-yp*sin(Rz)
48      ypp=xp*sin(Rz)+yp*cos(Rz)
49      zpp=zp
50      [xg,yg,zg]=[xpp+xc,ypp+yc,zpp+zc]
51      return[xg,yg,zg]
52
53  #============================================================shading
54  def shade(ax,ay,az,bx,by,bz,cx,cy,cz,dx,dy,dz):
55      a=dx-ax
56      b=dy-ay
```

249

```
57          c=dz-az
58          qad=sqrt(a*a+b*b+c*c)
59          ux=a/qad
60          uy=b/qad
61          uz=c/qad
62          a=bx-ax
63          b=by-ay
64          c=bz-az
65          qab=sqrt(a*a+b*b+c*c)
66          vx=a/qab
67          vy=b/qab
68          vz=c/qab
69          nx=uy*vz-uz*vy
70          ny=uz*vx-ux*vz
71          nz=ux*vy-uy*vx
72          ndotl=nx*lx+ny*ly+nz*lz
73          I=.5*Io*(1+ndotl)
74          if nz<=0:
75              plt.plot([ax,bx],[ay,by],color='k',linewidth=1)
76              plt.plot([bx,cx],[by,cy],color='k',linewidth=1)
77              plt.plot([cx,dx],[cy,dy],color='k',linewidth=1)
78              plt.plot([dx,ax],[dy,ay],color='k',linewidth=1)
79              for h in np.arange(0,qad,1):
80                  xls=ax+h*ux
81                  yls=ay+h*uy
82                  xle=bx+h*ux
83                  yle=by+h*uy
84
plt.plot([xls,xle],[yls,yle],linewidth=2,alpha=I,
color=clr)
85
86    #=============================================================
87    def plotbox(xg,yg,zg):
88
shade(xg[0],yg[0],zg[0],xg[1],yg[1],zg[1],xg[2],yg[2],zg[2],xg[3],yg[3],zg[3])
```

```
89
shade(xg[7],yg[7],zg[7],xg[6],yg[6],zg[6],xg[5],yg[5],zg[5],xg[4],yg[4],
zg[4])
90
shade(xg[0],yg[0],zg[0],xg[3],yg[3],zg[3],xg[7],yg[7],zg[7],xg[4],yg[4],
zg[4])
91
shade(xg[1],yg[1],zg[1],xg[5],yg[5],zg[5],xg[6],yg[6],zg[6],xg[2],yg[2],
zg[2])
92
shade(xg[3],yg[3],zg[3],xg[2],yg[2],zg[2],xg[6],yg[6],zg[6],xg[7],yg[7],
zg[7])
93
shade(xg[4],yg[4],zg[4],xg[5],yg[5],zg[5],xg[1],yg[1],zg[1],xg[0],yg[0],
zg[0])
94
95        plt.axis([0,150,100,0]) #——plot axes and grid
96        plt.axis('off')
97        plt.grid(False)
98        plt.show() #——plot latest rotation
99
100 #===========================================================
101 def plotboxx(xc,yc,zc,Rx): #———transform and plot Rx
102      for i in range(len(x)):
103
[xg[i],yg[i],zg[i]]=rotx(xc,yc,zc,x[i],y[i],z[i],Rx)
104            [x[i],y[i],z[i]]=[xg[i]-xc,yg[i]-yc,zg[i]-zc]
105
106            plotbox(xg,yg,zg) #———plot
107
108 def plotboxy(xc,yc,zc,Ry):
109      for i in range(len(x)): #———transform and plot Ry
110            [xg[i],yg[i],zg[i]]=roty(xc,yc,zc,x[i],y[i],z[i],Ry)
111            [x[i],y[i],z[i]]=[xg[i]-xc,yg[i]-yc,zg[i]-zc]
112
```

```
113              plotbox(xg,yg,zg)
114
115 def plotboxz(xc,yc,zc,Rz):
116      for i in range(len(x)): #————transform and plot Rz
117            [xg[i],yg[i],zg[i]]=rotz(xc,yc,zc,x[i],y[i],z[i],Rz)
118            [x[i],y[i],z[i]]=[xg[i]-xc,yg[i]-yc,zg[i]-zc]
119
120          plotbox(xg,yg,zg)
121
122 #———————————————————-input
123 while True:
124      axis=input('x, y or z?: ') #————input axis of rotation (lower case)
125      if axis == 'x': #-if x axis
126
Rx=radians(float(input('Rx Degrees?: '))) #————input degrees
127            plotboxx(xc,yc,zc,Rx) #————call function plotboxx
128      if axis == 'y':
129
Ry=radians(float(input('Ry Degrees?: '))) #————input degrees
130            plotboxy(xc,yc,zc,Ry)
131      if axis == 'z':
132
Rz=radians(float(input('Rz Degrees?: '))) #————input degrees
133            plotboxz(xc,yc,zc,Rz)
134      if axis == ":
135          break
```

Shading a Sphere

In the previous section, you shaded a box using a simple linear relation for the shading function where the intensity of the shading, I, was linearly related to the dot product $\hat{\mathbf{n}} \cdot \hat{\mathbf{l}}$. In this section, you will be mixing the three primary colors and controlling the intensity of each with a non-linear shading function. Results are shown in Figure 7-13, which was produced by Listing 7-2.

Figure 7-13. *Shading a sphere by color mixing with a non-linear intensity function (produced by Listing 7-2)*

Nonlinear shading functions are shown as the red, green, and blue curves in Figure 7-14; the linear one is black. The non-linear functions give more control over the shading and can produce more realistic effects. They allow you to control the shading by amplifying and extending the lighter shaded areas while more rapidly increasing the transition of intensity into the darker areas. The linear shading function is similar to the one used in Listing 7-1, except that it now starts at I=IA where IA may be greater than zero. The curves begin at I=IA and terminate at I=IB where $\hat{\mathbf{n}} \cdot \hat{\mathbf{l}}$ =+1. IA and IB are parameters that can be adjusted in Listing 7-2. IA>0 will darken the lights. This is sometimes necessary since the tones, when I=0 or close to it, may not transition well to higher regions of I; discontinuities can sometimes be observed. To correct this, start the intensity function at some small value of IA greater than 0. Increasing IA can also be a technique for reducing the brightness of light areas.

Note the difference between $\hat{\mathbf{n}} \cdot \hat{\mathbf{l}}p$ and $\hat{\mathbf{n}} \cdot \hat{\mathbf{l}}$ in Figure 7-14. To get a relation for I vs. $\hat{\mathbf{n}} \cdot \hat{\mathbf{l}}$, you let the function be of the form

$$I = C_1 + C_2 \left(\hat{\mathbf{n}} \cdot \hat{\mathbf{l}}p \right)^n \tag{7-5}$$

253

where C_1 and C_2 are constants and n is a parameter. n can be changed in the program. Noting that I=IA at $\hat{\mathbf{n}} \cdot \hat{\mathbf{l}}p = 0$,

$$IA = C_1 + C_2 (0)^n \tag{7-6}$$

$$C_1 = Ia \tag{7-7}$$

At $\hat{\mathbf{n}} \cdot \hat{\mathbf{l}}p = +2$, ($\hat{\mathbf{n}} \cdot \hat{\mathbf{l}} = +1$), I=IB,

$$IB = IA + C_2 (2)^n \tag{7-8}$$

$$C_2 = \frac{IB - IA}{2^n} \tag{7-9}$$

With $\hat{\mathbf{n}} \cdot \hat{\mathbf{l}}p = \hat{\mathbf{n}} \cdot \hat{\mathbf{l}} + 1$,

$$I = IA + (IB - IA) \left(\frac{\hat{\mathbf{n}} \cdot \hat{\mathbf{l}} + 1}{2} \right)^n \tag{7-10}$$

Equation 7-10 is your intensity function, $I(\hat{\mathbf{n}} \cdot \hat{\mathbf{l}})$. You thus have three parameters with which to adjust I: IA, which regulates the intensity of the lightest areas; IB, which adjusts the darkest areas; and n, which adjusts the transition from light to dark. Higher values of n will produce a more rapid transition. Figure 7-14 shows curves for n=1, 2, 3, and 4. When n=1, the curve becomes linear. There are no definite values for n, IA, and IB; they should be adjusted by trial and error to give visually appealing results.

Regarding colors, the background shown in Figure 7-13 is `'midnightblue'`. A good source for color samples is #`https://matplotlib.org/examples/color/named_colors.html`.

Listing 7-2 creates a sphere by plotting longitudes and latitudes as you did in Listing 6-4. In Listing 6-4, these were spaced six degrees apart. To carry out the shading in Listing 7-2, you will space the longitudes and latitudes closer together, two degrees apart. This creates 180x180=32,400 surface patches between the longitudes and latitudes. Assume each patch is flat. The intensity of color of each patch will depend on the angle between a local unit vector normal to the patch $\hat{\mathbf{n}}$ and the light source unit vector $\hat{\mathbf{l}}$ at each point on the surface. This will then be used to control the relative r,g,b contributions to the color mix. As before, you establish this relation by taking the dot product $\hat{\mathbf{n}} \cdot \hat{\mathbf{l}}$. $\hat{\mathbf{n}}$ at each point is determined quite simply by obtaining a vector from the sphere's center to the point in question on the sphere's surface and then dividing by the sphere's radius, rs. For example, suppose you are at a point p on the sphere's surface with coordinates xp,yp,zp. A vector **Vp** from the sphere's center at xc,yc,zc to p is

$$\mathbf{Vp} = (xp - xc)\hat{\mathbf{i}} + (yp - yc)\hat{\mathbf{j}} + (zp - zc)\hat{\mathbf{k}} \qquad (7\text{-}11)$$

Vp is normal to the surface at p. A unit normal vector, $\hat{\mathbf{n}}$, is then

$$\hat{\mathbf{n}} = \left(\frac{xp - xc}{rs} \right)\hat{\mathbf{i}} + \left(\frac{yp - yc}{rs} \right)\hat{\mathbf{j}} + \left(\frac{zp - zc}{rs} \right)\hat{\mathbf{k}} \qquad (7\text{-}12)$$

where rs is the sphere's radius. Taking the dot product of $\hat{\mathbf{n}}$ in Equation 7-12 with the incoming light unit vector $\hat{\mathbf{l}}$ gives $\hat{\mathbf{n}} \cdot \hat{\mathbf{l}}$, which you need to determine I from Equation 7-10.

In Listing 7-2, lines 22-24 set the components of the incoming light's unit vector. Lines 26-28 set the intensity function parameters. These values produce Figure 7-13. Lines 37-39 paint the background with dots. Lines 61-101 plot the longitudes. Note in lines 69 and 70 that dalpha and dphi have been added to alpha2 and phi2 since roundoff errors in the np.arange() function can sometimes fail to close the sphere; this assures it closes. Lines 86-92 determine the components of the $\hat{\mathbf{n}}$ at the current values of alpha and phi. Line 93 calculates the dot product $\hat{\mathbf{n}} \cdot \hat{\mathbf{l}}$; line 94 calculates the intensity.

In line 99, the attribute linewidth has been increased to 4. When combined with the angular spacing of two degrees in lines 63 and 67, this ensures there are no gaps in the surface. Also in line 99, the color statement shows red at 100 percent, green at 80 percent, and blue at 40. The (I-1) factor reflects the impact of the shading function. Recall that when the color mix is (0,0,0), black is produced; conversely, when the mix is (1,1,1), white is produced. Since you want darks where I is close to or equal to 1 (facing away from the light source), the (I-1) factor accomplishes this since it equals 0 when I=1 producing black. If you did not include the (I-1) factor, the mix (1,.8,.45) would simply produce an unshaded round rusty orange disc.

Raising B or lowering A in Figure 7-14 will increase the visual appearance of shading. Doing the reverse will decrease it.

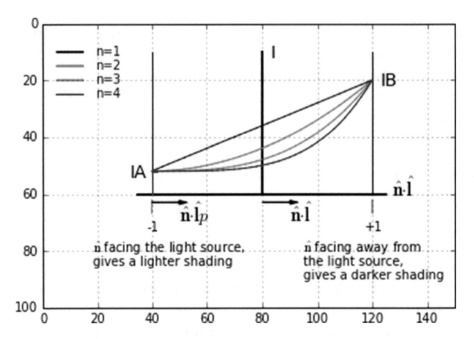

Figure 7-14. *Nonlinear shading function*

Listing 7-2. Program SHADESPHERE

```
1    """
2    SHADESPHERE
3    """
4
5    import numpy as np
6    import matplotlib.pyplot as plt
7    from math import sin, cos, radians, sqrt
8
9    plt.axis([0,150,100,0])
10   plt.axis('off')
11   plt.grid(False)
12
13   #————————————————lists
14   g=[0]*3
15
16   #————————————————parameters
```

```
17   xc=80 #——sphere center
18   yc=50
19   zc=0
20   rs=35 #——sphere radius
21
22   lx=.707 #——light ray unit vector components
23   ly=.707
24   lz=0
25
26   IA=.01 #——define curve
27   IB=1
28   n=2.0
29
30   clrbg='midnightblue' #——background color
31
32   Rx=radians(-15) #——sphere angles of rotation
33   Ry=radians(0)
34   Rz=radians(30)
35
36   #————————————paint background color
37   for x in np.arange(0,150,1):
38        for y in np.arange(0,100,1):
39             plt.scatter(x,y,s=10,color='clrbg')
40
41
#=========================================================rotation
functions
42   def rotx(xc,yc,zc,xp,yp,zp,Rx):
43        g[0]=xp+xc
44        g[1]=yp*cos(Rx)-zp*sin(Rx)+yc
45        g[2]=yp*sin(Rx)+zp*cos(Rx)+zc
46        return[g]
47
48   def roty(xc,yc,zc,xp,yp,zp,Ry):
49        g[0]=xp*cos(Ry)+zp*sin(Ry)+xc
```

```
50        g[1]=yp+yc
51        g[2]=-xp*sin(Ry)+zp*cos(Ry)+zc
52        return[g]
53
53  def rotz(xc,yc,zc,xp,yp,zp,Rz):
55        g[0]=xp*cos(Rz)-yp*sin(Rz)+xc
56        g[1]=xp*sin(Rz)+yp*cos(Rz)+yc
57        g[2]=zp+zc
58        return[g]
59
60  #——————————————longitudes
61  phi1=radians(-90)
62  phi2=radians(90)
63  dphi=radians(2)
64
65  alpha1=radians(0)
66  alpha2=radians(360)
67  dalpha=radians(2)
68
69  for alpha in np.arange(alpha1,alpha2+dalpha,dalpha):
70        for phi in np.arange(phi1,phi2+dphi,dphi):
71              xp=rs*cos(phi)*cos(alpha)
72              yp=rs*sin(phi)
73              zp=-rs*cos(phi)*sin(alpha)
74              rotx(xc,yc,zc,xp,yp,zp,Rx)
75              xp=g[0]-xc
76              yp=g[1]-yc
77              zp=g[2]-zc
78              roty(xc,yc,zc,xp,yp,zp,Ry)
79              xp=g[0]-xc
80              yp=g[1]-yc
81              zp=g[2]-zc
82              rotz(xc,yc,zc,xp,yp,zp,Rz)
83              xpg=g[0]
84              ypg=g[1]
```

```
85              zpg=g[2]
86              a=xpg-xc
87              b=ypg-yc
88              c=zpg-zc
89              qp=sqrt(a*a+b*b+c*c)
90              nx=a/qp
91              ny=b/qp
92              nz=c/qp
93              ndotl=nx*lx+ny*ly+nz*lz
94              I=IA+(IB-IA)*((1+ndotl)/2)**n
95              if phi == phi1:
96                  xpglast=xpg
97                  ypglast=ypg
98              if nz < 0:
99
plt.plot([xpglast,xpg],[ypglast,ypg],linewidth=4,
color=((1-I),.8*(1-I),.45*(1-I))
100                 xpglast=xpg
101                 ypglast=ypg
102
103 #——————————————latitudes
104 for phi in np.arange(phi1,phi2+dphi,dphi):
105     r=rs*cos(phi)
106     for alpha in np.arange(alpha1,alpha2+dalpha,dalpha):
107             xp=r*cos(alpha)
108             yp=rs*sin(phi)
109             zp=-rs*cos(phi)*sin(alpha)
110             rotx(xc,yc,zc,xp,yp,zp,Rx)
111             xp=g[0]-xc
112             yp=g[1]-yc
113             zp=g[2]-zc
114             roty(xc,yc,zc,xp,yp,zp,Ry)
115             xp=g[0]-xc
116             yp=g[1]-yc
117             zp=g[2]-zc
```

```
118                 rotz(xc,yc,zc,xp,yp,zp,Rz)
119                 xpg=g[0]
120                 ypg=g[1]
121                 zpg=g[2]
122                 a=xpg-xc
123                 b=ypg-yc
124                 c=zpg-zc
125                 qp=sqrt(a*a+b*b+c*c)
126                 nx=a/qp
127                 ny=b/qp
128                 nz=c/qp
129                 ndotl=nx*lx+ny*ly+nz*lz
130                 textbfI=IA+(IB-IA)*((1+ndotl)/2)**n
131                 if alpha == alpha1:
132                     xpglast=xpg
133                     ypglast=ypg
134                 if nz < 0:
135
plt.plot([xpglast,xpg],[ypglast,ypg],linewidth=4,
color=((1-I),.8*(1-I),.45*(1-I)))
136                     xpglast=xpg
137                     ypglast=ypg
138
139 plt.show( )
```

Summary

While adding a background color can greatly enhance the visual appearance of an object, shading can also be quite effective. In this chapter, you learned techniques for shading an object. Shading implies the presence of an illuminating light source. In your model, you used the **direction** of the light rays coming from a source but you did not specify the **position** of the source. In Listing 7-1, you explored the concept of a shading function as shown in Figure 7-10 and how it determines the intensity of shading on a plane. This depends on the orientation of the plane relative to the direction of the incoming light rays, which is determined by taking the dot product of a unit vector normal to the surface, $\hat{\mathbf{n}}$, with a unit vector pointing in the direction of the light rays, $\hat{\mathbf{l}}$. In Listing 7-2, you performed the same shading operations on a sphere. The sphere was assumed to be composed of 32,400 flat planes. However, you improved on the shading function. Whereas in Listing 7-1 you used a simple linear relation between the shading intensity and the dot product $\hat{\mathbf{n}} \cdot \hat{\mathbf{l}}$, in Listing 7-2 you used a nonlinear relation, as shown in Figure 7-14. This greatly improves the appearance of the shading. Changing the vertical positions of A and B in Figure 7-14 will increase or decrease the degree of shading. You can adjust these to obtain whatever degree of shading you prefer.

CHAPTER 8

2D Data Plotting

In this chapter, you will look at styles and techniques for plotting two-dimensional data. You will start with some simple plots and then progress to those that include multiple sets of data on the same plot. While Python contains specialized built-in functions that can be quite efficient at this, usually requiring only a few lines of code, you will find that you can embellish your plots by taking a more hands-on approach and being creative by supplementing the specialized Python functions with simple Python commands. For example, the plot in Figure 8-1 requires only three lines of specialized code after the setup and data has been entered. Figure 8-5, on the other hand, can be a challenge to create using just specialized Python commands, but that is how it has been done by Listing 8-5. The use of simple commands, plus a little creativity, can often make the job much easier and produce better results. Following simple data plots, you will move on to linear regression where you fit a straight line to a data set. You will then see how to fit non-linear mathematical functions to the data. The last thing you explore is splines. A spline is a smooth curve that passes through each data point.

Figure 8-1 shows a plot of a mathematical function. This plot was created by Listing 8-1. In it, line 13 sets the numerical range of the x axis, which in this case goes from 0 to 150 in steps of 1. This means the function will be plotted over that range. The axis definition in line 8 has the same limits, but they could be different. For example, if line 8 was plt.axis([0,200,0,100]), the width of the plotting area would be 200 but the function would still be plotted from 0 to 150. This combination would position the function plot toward the left side of the plotting area. The limit of the y axis, as specified in line 8, is 100. *As explained in Chapter 1, in the past we wanted the range of the x axis to be 150% that of the y axis. This was to ensure a square appeared as a square and not a rectangle and a circle appeared as a round circle and not an ellipse. But with data plotting, where there are usually no squares or circles, that may not be necessary.*

263

B. Korites, *Python Graphics*, https://doi.org/10.1007/978-1-4842-9660-8_8

The function being plotted is defined in line 14. This is a simple exponential function of y1 vs. x. Line 17 plots it in blue and attaches the label **y1**, which will be used by the legend() function in line 20. In line 20, loc equals the location of the legend, which can be any combination of upper, middle, lower combined with left, center, right. Here you are using 'upper left'. If you specify 'best', Python will determine the best location for it. As you can see, lines 13, 14, and 17 comprise essentially the entire plotting operation.

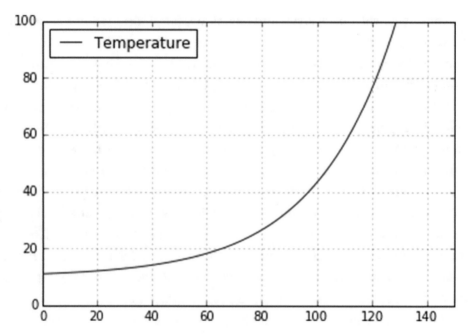

Figure 8-1. *Data plot produced by Listing 8-1*

Listing 8-1. Program DATAPLOT1

```
1   """
2   DATAPLOT1
3   """
4
5   import matplotlib.pyplot as plt
6   import numpy as np
7
8   plt.axis([0,150,0,100])
9   plt.axis('on')
```

```
10 plt.grid(True)
11
12 #————————define function y1 vs x
13 x=np.arange(0,150,1)
14 y1=10+np.exp(.035*x)
15
16 #————————plot y1 vs x
17 plt.plot(x, y1,'b',label='y1')
18
19 #————————plot the legend
20 plt.legend(loc='upper left')
21
22 plt.show()
```

In Listing 8-2, you plot two functions, y1 and y2, on the same plot. Lines 18 and 19 do the plotting. You add the labels Temperature and Pressure, which will be used by the legend() function. In line 25, you add marker='s', which plots a square at each data point of the temperature curve; marker='*' in line 26 plots a star at each point of the pressure curve. There are other marker styles available at https://matplotlib.org/api/markers_api.html.

In Figure 8-2, note that the horizontal range of the data plots (20-140) is smaller than the x axis plotting width (0-150). Having the data not bump into the edges of the plot can sometimes make it more readable. To have the data plots span the entire width of the plot, simply change line 8 to plt.axis([20,140,0,100]). Similarly, the range of the y values can be changed.

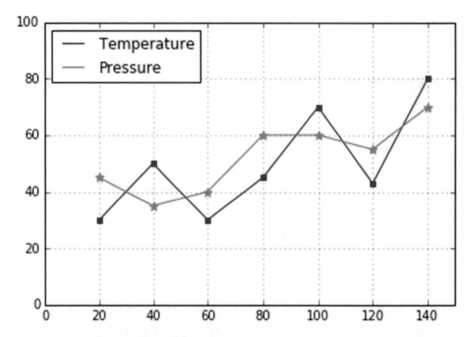

Figure 8-2. *Data plot produced by Listing 8-2*

Listing 8-2. Program DATAPLOT2

```
1    """
2    DATAPLOT2
3    """
4
5    import matplotlib.pyplot as plt
6    import numpy as np
7
8    plt.axis([0,150,0,100])
9    plt.axis('on')
10   plt.grid(True)
11
12   #————————————define data points
13   x=[20,40,60,80,100,120,140]
14   y1=[30,50,30,45,70,43,80]
15   y2=[45,35,40,60,60,55,70]
16
```

```
17 #————————————plot lines with labels
18 plt.plot(x,y1,'b',label='Temperature')
19 plt.plot(x,y2,'r',label='Pressure')
20
21 #————————————legend
22 plt.legend(loc='upper left')
23
24 #————————————add markers
25 plt.scatter(x,y1,color='b',marker='s')
26 plt.scatter(x,y2,color='r',marker='*',s=50)
27
28 plt.show()
```

In Listing 8-2, you display two functions, temperature and pressure, against one y axis. This assumes, of course, the values on the y axis are appropriate for both T and p. But what if the values of pressure were either much larger or much smaller than temperature? The plot of pressure might go off the chart or be too small to be discernible. What you need are two vertical scales, one for temperature and another for pressure.

In Listing 8-3, you lower the pressure values as shown in line 14. If plotted against the same vertical scale used for temperature, they would appear too low on the plot. You can remedy this by introducing a second vertical axis with Temperature on the left side and Pressure on the right. Lines 17-20 plot the temperature data. Line 20 allows you to change the color of the vertical tick marks to any color, red in this case. Line 21 plots a legend in the upper left corner. Lines 24-27 plot a second scale on the right side of the plot. Line 24 establishes a "twin" plotting axis. This twin includes the already established horizontal x axis plus a new vertical y axis on the right side. The rest of the commands in this group refer to this second y axis. Line 26 labels this axis as Pressure. Line 27 changes the tick marks and numbers to blue. Line 28 plots a second legend at the upper right. If you try to plot a single legend for both temperature and pressure, you find the results depend on where in the code you place the legend() function. If you use two separate legends(), as you are doing here, and locate them at the same position, say upper left, one will overwrite the other. If you try using just one legend() at the end of the code, it displays a legend with only the pressure shown. See Figure 8-3. In the next program, you will see a way around this problem.

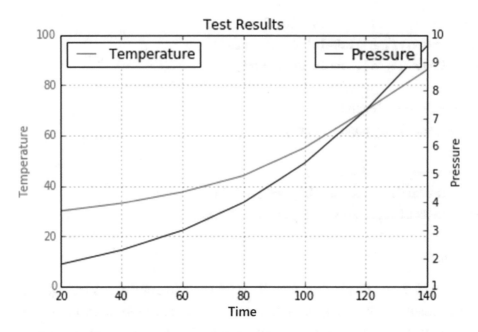

Figure 8-3. *Data plot produced by Listing 8-3*

Listing 8-3. Program DATAPLOT3

```
1   """
2   DATAPLOT3
3   """
4
5   import matplotlib.pyplot as plt
6   import numpy as np
7
8   plt.axis([0,140,0,100])
9   plt.axis('on')
10  plt.grid(True)
11
12  t=[20,40,60,80,100,120,140] #——Time
13  T=[30,33,37.5,44,55,70,86] #——Temperature
14  p=[1.8,2.3,3,4,5.4,7.3,9.6] #——Pressure
15
16  #————————Plot T vs t in red on the left vertical axis.
```

```
17 plt.plot(t,T,color='r',label='Temperature')
18 plt.xlabel('Time')
19 plt.ylabel('Temperature',color='r')
20 plt.tick}_params(axis='y',labelcolor='r')
21 plt.legend(loc='upper left')
22
23 #————Plot P vs t in blue on the right vertical axis.
24 plt.twinx()
25 plt.plot(t,p,color='b',label='Pressure')
26 plt.ylabel('Pressure', color='b')
27 plt.tick_params(axis='y', labelcolor='b')
28 plt.legend(loc='upper right')
29
30 #————title the plot
31 plt.title('Test Results')
32
33 plt.show()
```

In Listing 8-4, you try to resolve the legend() issue you encountered in the previous program. Line 12 sets up a plot called ax1 that will include a subplot. Line 14 plots a grid. Lines 8-10 set up the data lists. Line 16 labels the x axis. Line 18 plots the Temperature curve in red and names it l1. Line 20 sets the scale limits on the left vertical axis, which will range from 0 to 100. Line 21 labels it in red. Line 23 sets up a twin() second vertical axis (which includes the x axis) as ax2. Line 25 plots it in blue as the curve l2. Line 27 sets the scale limits to 0-10. Line 28 labels it. Lines 30 and 31 specify the curves that are to appear in the legend. Line 32 plots the legend. The syntax looks a bit cryptic but it works, as you can see in Figure 8-4.

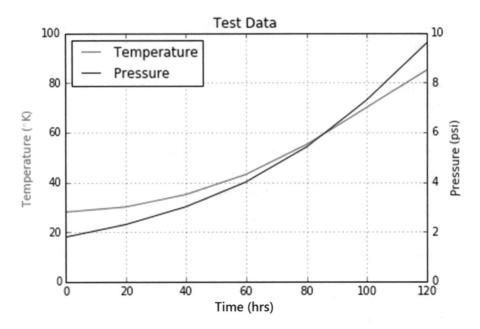

Figure 8-4. *Data plot produced by Listing 8-4*

Listing 8-4. Program DATAPLOT4

```
1   """
2   DATAPLOT4
3   """
4
5   import matplotlib.pyplot as plt
6   import numpy as np
7
8   t=[0,20,40,60,80,100,120]
9   T=[28,30,35,43,55,70,85]
10  p=[1.8,2.3,3,4,5.4,7.3,9.6]
11
12  fig, ax1 = plt.subplots() #——set up a plot ax1 with subplots
13
14  plt.grid(True) #——draw grid
15
16  ax1.set_xlabel('Time (hrs)') #——label X axis of ax1
17
```

```
18 l1=plt.plot(t,T,'r',label='Temperature') #——plot temperature in red as
   curve l1
19
20 ax1.set_ylim([0,100]) #——set Y axis limits of ax1
21 ax1.set_ylabel(r'Temperature (° K)', color='r') #——label Y axis of ax1
22
23 ax2 = ax1.twinx() #——set up ax2 as twin of ax1
24
25 l2=plt.plot(t, p, 'b',label='Pressure') #——plot pressure in blue as
   curve l2
26
27 ax2.set_ylim([0,10]) #——set Y axis limits of ax2
28 ax2.set_ylabel('Pressure (psi)', color='b') #——label Y axis of ax2
29
30 line1,=plt.plot([1],label='Temperature',color='r') #——line 1 of legend
31 line2,=plt.plot([2],label='Pressure',color='b') #
——line 2 of legend
32 plt.legend(handles=[line1,line2],loc='upper left') #——plot legend
33
34 plt.title('Test Data')
```

In Listing 8-5, you plot multiple curves while giving each its own vertical scale. Lines 12-14 define lists for time, temperature, and pressure data. In line 15, you introduce a third dependent variable, volume v. Line 17 opens a new list called pp=[ ], which will be used to vertically scale the pressure data. You could simply scale and replace the items in p=[ ] but then you would destroy the original values. That would not be a problem in this program but it's good practice to leave them unchanged in case you want to modify them later. Lines 18-19 scale the original Pressure values contained in p by a factor of 10 and append them to pp. The same is done for v in lines 21-23 where volume data is scaled by a factor of 100. Lines 25-28 plot the curves and plot a legend. Lines 30-33 plot the pressure scale on the right y-axis in blue. Lines 35-37 label the three axes. Lines 39-43 plot the volume scale values in green. Lines 45-46 plot the vertical green axis. This is accomplished by plotting the character | as text up the right side. Normally you would want to plot a single line from the vertical volume axis from top to bottom but Python does not permit plotting lines or scatter dots outside the main plotting area. It does, however, allow text. So you construct a vertical line from a series of | marks. You could add more vertical axes in this manner if you wished. See Figure 8-5.

The approach used in this program is more hands-on than before. Previous programs relied mostly on specialized Python syntax. The advantage to this approach is that it works, it's quite flexible, and it doesn't require many more lines of code. This blend of Python syntax along with a creative use of hands-on techniques is actually quite powerful. Sometimes it pays to think outside the box.

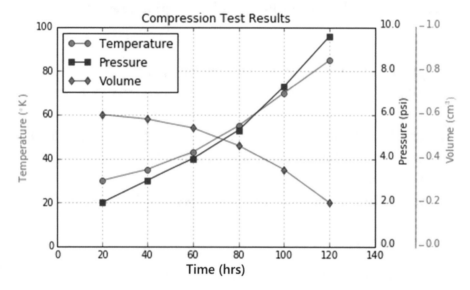

Figure 8-5. *Data plot produced by Listing 8-5*

Listing 8-5. Program DATAPLOT5

```
1    """
2    DATAPLOT5
3    """
4
5    import matplotlib.pyplot as plt
6    import numpy as np
7
8    plt.axis([0,140,0,100])
9    plt.axis('on')
10   plt.grid(True)
```

```
11
12 t=[20,40,60,80,100,120] #——time
13 T=[30,35,43,55,70,85] #——temperature
14 p=[2,3,4,5.3,7.3,9.6] #——pressure
15 v=[.6,.58,.54,.46,.35,.2] #——volume
16
17 pp=[ ] #——list for scaled pressure for plotting
18 for i in np.arange(0,len(p),1):
19        pp.append(p[i]*10) #——scale p by 10
20
21 vv=[ ] #——list for scaled volume for plotting
22 for i in np.arange(0,len(v),1):
23        vv.append(v[i]*100) #——scale volume by 100
24
25 plt.plot(t,T,color='r',label='Temperature',marker='o') #——plot
   temperature
26 plt.plot(t,pp,color='b',label='Pressure',marker='s') #——plot scaled
   pressure
27 plt.plot(t,vv,color='g',label='Volume',marker='d') #——plot
   scaled volume
28 plt.legend(loc='upper left')
29
30 for y in np.arange(0,100+1,20): #——plot pressure scale values
31      a=y/10
32      a=str(a) #——convert to string for plotting as text
33      plt.text(142,y,a,color='b')
34
35 plt.xlabel('Time (hrs)') #——label axes
36 plt.ylabel('Temperature °K',color='r')
37 plt.text(151,65,'Pressure (psi)',rotation=90,color='b')
38
39 for y in np.arange(100,-1,-20): #——plot volume scale values
40      a=y/100
41      a=str(a)
42      plt.text(162,y,a,color='g')
```

```
43        plt.text(159,y+2,'_',color='g')
44
45 for y in np.arange(1,99,3):
46        plt.text(157,y,'-',color='g')
47
48 plt.text(170,65,r'Volume (cm3)',rotation=90,color='g') #——label
   volume scale
49
50 plt.title('Compression Test Results') #—title
51
52 plt.show()
```

Linear Regression

Linear regression is the process of fitting a best straight line to a set of data points. *Best* in this context means the line has minimum error with the data points. Referring to Figures 8-6 and 8-7, the objective is to determine the parameters A and B of a straight line,

$$y = Ax + B \qquad (8\text{-}1)$$

that result in a best fit to the data points. B is the y axis intercept of the line and A is its slope. Each data point i has coordinates x_i, y_i. Each has error e_i with respect to the line. The best fit of the line to the data points will be the one where A and B result in

$$\sum_{i=1}^{n} e_i^2 = minimum \qquad (8\text{-}2)$$

where $e(i)$ is the vertical deviation of data point i from the regression line as shown in Figure 8-7, n is the number of data points. This is equivalent to bringing the RMS error to a minimum. e_i is squared in Equation 8-2 to account for negative values of e_i. It can be shown that Equation 8-2 is satisfied when

$$A = \frac{C_3 - nC_1C_2}{C_4 - nC_1C_1} \qquad (8\text{-}3)$$

$$B = C_2 - AC_1 \qquad (8\text{-}4)$$

$$C_1 = \frac{1}{n}\sum_{n=1}^{n} t_i \qquad\qquad (8\text{-}5)$$

$$C_2 = \frac{1}{n}\sum_{n=1}^{n} v_i \qquad\qquad (8\text{-}6)$$

$$C_3 = \sum_{n=1}^{n} v_i t_i \qquad\qquad (8\text{-}7)$$

$$C_4 = \sum_{n=1}^{n} t_i t_i \qquad\qquad (8\text{-}8)$$

In Listing 8-6, the regression routine has been added to Listing 8-5 beginning at line 52. It fits a regression line to the green Volume curve. Lines 55-60 calculate the coefficients C1-C4 defined above. `np.sum()` in line 55 sums the elements in list t. `np.multiply()` in line 57 multiplies the elements in lists v and t element by element, producing the list a. Line 58 then adds the elements in a. Lines 62 and 63 calculate A and B in accordance with Equations 8-3 and 8-4. Lines 65-68 plot the regression line using scatter dots; line 66 calculates values of v vs. t as vp, the plotting value of v; line 67 scales vp by 100 for plotting; line 68 does the plotting.

Equation 8-2 states that minimizing $e(i)^2$ is equivalent to minimizing the RMS value. The RMS value is

$$RMS = \left[\frac{\sum_{i=1}^{n} e(i)^2}{n}\right]^{\frac{1}{2}} \qquad\qquad (8\text{-}9)$$

This is calculated in lines 71-76. e(i) is calculated in line 73. It is squared in line 74 as ee and then summed in line 75 as sumee, producing the numerator in Equation (8-9). RMS is calculated in line 76 in accordance with Equation 8-9. It's obvious that minimizing $\Sigma e(i)^2$ is equivalent to minimizing the RMS value.

The remainder of the program places labels and values on the plot. Line 83 reduces the number of digits of vp1, the beginning value of the regression line; line 84 plots it. Lines 86-88 plot the end value. A and B (Ap and Bp) are similarly plotted in lines 90-96.

There are other ways in Python to reduce the number of digits besides the syntax used in line 83. However, if the number being shortened is negative, the minus sign may not appear on the output. This could be a problem with some versions of Python.

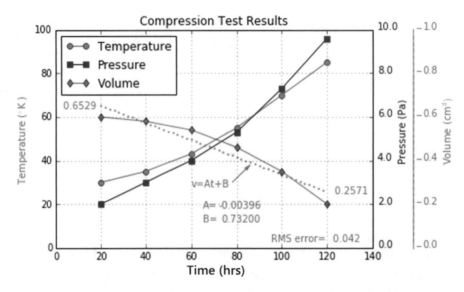

Figure 8-6. *Straight line fit to the volume curve produced by Listing 8-6*

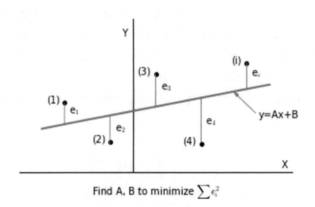

Find A, B to minimize $\sum e_i^2$

Figure 8-7. *Model used by Listing 8-6 showing data points 1,2,3,4...i with straight line fit. e_i=error from straight line for data point i*

Listing 8-6. Program REGRESSION1

```
1    """
2    REGRESSION1
3    """
     .
     .
     #——————————same as DATAPLOT5——————————
```

.

.

.

```
52 #——————————straight line fit to Volume v vs t
53 n=len(v)
54
55 c1=np.sum(t)/n #——sum values of list t and divide by n, =average of t
56 c2=np.sum(v)/n #——sum values of list v and divide by n, =average of v
57 a=np.multiply(v,t) #——multiply list v by t element by element = list a
58 c3=np.sum(a) #——sum elements of a
59 a=np.multiply(t,t) #——multiply list t by t element by element = list a
60 c4=np.sum(a) #——sum elements of a
61
62 A=(c3-n*c1*c2)/(c4-n*c1*c1) #——line parameters A and B
63 B=c2-A*c1
64
65 for tp in np.arange(t[0],t[5],2): #——plot line with scatter dots
66     vp=A*tp+B
67     vp=vp*100 #——scale vp for plotting
68     plt.scatter(tp,vp,color='g',s=1)
69
70 #——————————————calculate RMS error
71 sumee=0
72 for i in range(len(t)):
73     e=(v[i]-(A*t[i]+B))
74     ee=e*e
75     sumee=sumee+ee
76     rms=np.sqrt(sumee/n)
77
78 #——————————labels
79 plt.text(60,28,'v=At+B',color='g')
80 plt.arrow(78,30,6,6,head_length=3,head_width=1.5,color='g',linewidth=.5)
81
82 vp1=A*t[0]+B #————beginning v value of line
83 vp1='%7.4f'%(vp1) #————reduce the number of decimal places
84 plt.text(2,64,vp1,color='g') #——plot
```

```
85
86 vp2=A*t[5]+B #————end v value of line
87 vp2='%7.4f'%(vp2)
88 plt.text(122,25,vp2,color='g')
89
90 Ap='%7.5f'%(A)
91 plt.text(65,18,'A=',color='g')
92 plt.text(72,18,Ap,color='g') #——print value of A
93
94 Bp='%7.5f'%(B)
95 plt.text(65,12,'B=',color='g')
96 plt.text(73,12,Bp,color='g') #——print value of B
97
98 rms='%7.3f'%(rms)
99 plt.text(95,3,'RMS error=',color='g')
100 plt.text(123,3,rms,color='g') #——print RMS error
101
102 plt.show()
```

Function Fitting

In Listing 8-6, you plotted a straight line to fit data points that represented measurements of volume vs. time. You were fortunate that there was an analytic solution to this problem represented by Equations 8-2, 8-3, and 8-5. In this section, you will fit an arbitrary function to the same data set. The function is user-defined; that is, you can specify any function you want, whatever you think will give a good fit. In Listing 8-7, you will try the relation

$$v = Ax^2 + B \qquad\qquad (8\text{-}10)$$

As in the previous section, your task is to find the values of A and B that produce the best fit of this function to the data points. Since you want to be able to use any arbitrary function, it would obviously not be time-effective to derive a closed-form mathematical solution to the problem for every function you wish to try. Here you will use a brute force approach that involves calculating the values of the parameters A and B in Equation 8-10 for many values of A and B within the expected range of both that results in minimum RMS error. This is a hands-on approach; some insight into the problem is required. For example, inspection of the v(t) curve in Figure 8-8 and Equation 8-10 indicates that parameter B in Equation 8-10, which is the V axis (green) intercept at t=t[0], should lie somewhere between .5 and .7. Similarly, you can assume that A will be very small since Equation 8-10 involves squares of t, which have values as large as t[5]=120. You can also see by inspection that A should be negative. So you can try a range for A of -.001 to 0. Calculate the error for many combinations of values of B between .5 and .7 and A between -.001 and 0. This will give you the A and B corresponding to the almost lowest error between those ranges. I say the "almost" lowest error because, when cycling between the expected ranges of A and B, you do so in small steps. The finer those steps are, the more accurate your final solution will be. While there are automatic iteration techniques that you could use, the process described here is simpler to code but requires hands-on iteration by the user. It works as follows: after guessing initial ranges for A and B, when you get the results, you can make another run with refined values by either closing, opening, or shifting the ranges. You can also change the search increments dB (line 61) and dA (line 64). With just a few of these manual iterations you should be able to get a solution to whatever accuracy you need.

Referring to Listing 8-7, most of it is the same as Listing 8-6. Lines 59-64 define the limits of the search routine B1 and B2, which are the start and end of the B range; A1 and A2 of the A range. dB and dA are the increments. Smaller increments will give more accurate results but will require more processing time. The two nested loops beginning in lines 70 and 71 search first through the B range and then, for each value of B, through the A range. At each combination of A and B the loop starting at line 73 cycles through all the data points, len(t) (=len(v)). Line 74 calculates the error between each data point and the assumed function Equation 8-10; line 75 squares it and line 76 sums the square of the errors in accordance with Equation 8-2. The sum was initially set to zero in line 72. Line 77 says, if the sum of the squares produced by the current combination of A and B is less that the previously calculated sum, then you replace that value with the present one and set the current values of A and B to Amin and Bmin, the values that correspond to the current lowest error. When the A and B loops are first cycled, eemin in line 76 is unknown. It is set to a very high value in line 56. This ensures that the first eemin will be less. After the first cycle, it will take on the value corresponding to the latest combination of A and B that produces the lowest value of sumee. The end result of all this is the values of A and B that produce the lowest error between the data points and the assumed function. They are Amin and Bmin. Lines 86-89 plot the function using Amin and Bmin in line 87. Lines 92-97 calculate the corresponding RMS error.

Figure 8-6 shows a straight-line approximation to v(t) and the RMS error of .042, as can be seen printed on that plot. With the non-linear function Ax^2+B, the RMS error is .0132, which is considerably lower.

The remainder of the program places labels on the plot. As you can see from Figure 8-8, the limits of A and B that were set in lines 59-64 are printed in black on the plot as A1, A2, B1, and B2. The values found by the program that result in the lowest error are printed in green as Amin and Bmin. With the assumed values of A1, A2, B1, and B2 in this example, Amin and Bmin fall within the assumed range so you can be confident that you have found the near best values. But let's suppose one of the parameters, say B1, was chosen incorrectly. That is, suppose you had chosen B1=.65 with B2=.7. The result for Bmin calculated by the program would be B1=.65; that is, it would bump up against the lower B limit. That would tell you that B1 is too high and you should lower it for the next run. Similarly, if you had chosen B1=.5 with B2=.6, Bmin would bump up against the upper limit for B, indicating that you should raise B2.

There are other curve-fitting functions available similar to the one you are developing here; go to `https://docs.scipy.org/doc/scipy/reference/generated/scipy.optimize.curve_fit.html`. Others can be found with an Internet search. The one you are developing here has the advantage of being open, simple, and easy to use, plus you have control over it.

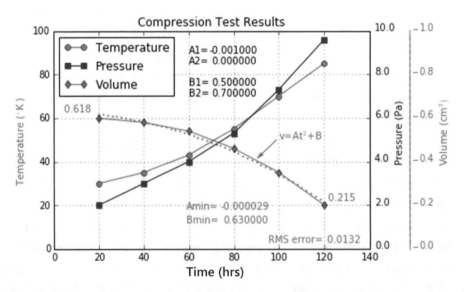

Figure 8-8. *Function fit to volume curve produced by Listing 8-7*

Listing 8-7. Program REGRESSION2

```
    """

    REGRESSION2
    """

52 #———————same as REGRESSION1———————
53
54 #————————————parabolic fit to v vs t
55 n=len(v)
56 eemin=10**10 #——starting value of eemin, deliberately set very large
57
58 #——————————loop parameters
59 B1=.5
60 B2=.7
61 dB=.001
62 A1=-.001
63 A2=0.
64 dA=.0000001
65
66 #——————————loop through all combinations of A and B
67 #——————————within ranges defined by loop parameters
68 #——————————searching for Amin, Bmin that produce
69 #——————————best fit of function to data points
70 for B in np.arange(B1,B2,dB):
71     for A in np.arange(A1,A2,dA):
72         sumee=0
73         for i in range(len(t)):
74             e=(v[i]-(A*t[i]*t[i]+B)) #——error of data point i at A, B
75             ee=e*e #——error squared
76             sumee=sumee+ee #——sum of error squared
77             if sumee < eemin: #——if sum < present minimum eemin then
78                 eemin=sumee #——set new minimum = sumee
79                 Amin=A #——set new Amin = A
80                 Bmin=B #——set new Bmin = B
81
82 #——————————Amin, Bmin above will produce best fit
```

```
 83
 84 #————————-plot best fit function with scatter dots
 85 #————————-from t[0] to t[5] in steps=2
 86 for tp in np.arange(t[0],t[5],2):
 87     vp=Amin*tp*tp+Bmin
 88     vp=vp*100 #—scale to plot
 89     plt.scatter(tp,vp,color='g',s=1)
 90
 91 #————————————calculate RMS Error
 92 sumee=0
 93 for i in range(len(v)):
 94     e=(v[i]-(Amin*t[i]*t[i]+Bmin)) #——error at each data point
 95     ee=e*e #——error squared
 96     sumee=sumee+ee #——sum of squared errors
 97     rms=np.sqrt(sumee/n) #——RMS error
 98
 99 #————————————————labels
100 plt.text(100,50,'v=At+B',color='g')
101 plt.arrow(99,50,-6.5,-6.5,head_length=3,head_width=1.5,color='g',
    linewidth=.5)
102
103 A=Amin
104 B=Bmin
105
106 vp1=A*t[0]*t[0]+B
107 vp1='%7.3f'%(vp1)
108 plt.text(2,63,vp1,color='g')
109
110 vp2=A*t[5]*t[5]+B
111 vp2='%7.3f'%(vp2)
112 plt.text(119,22,vp2,color='g')
113
114 Ap='%8.6f'%(A)
115 plt.text(59,18,'Amin=',color='g')
116 plt.text(74,18,Ap,color='g')
```

```
117
118 Bp='%8.6f'%(B)
119 plt.text(59,12,'Bmin=',color='g')
120 plt.text(75.2,12,Bp,color='g')
121
122 rms='%7.4f'%(rms)
123 plt.text(95,3,'RMS error=',color='g')
124 plt.text(120,3,rms,color='g')
125
126 A1='%8.6f'%(A1)
127 plt.text(60,90,'A1=')
128 plt.text(69,90,A1)
129
130 A2='%8.6f'%(A2)
131 plt.text(60,85,'A2=')
132 plt.text(70.2,85,A2)
133
134 B1='%8.6f'%(B1)
135 plt.text(60,75,'B1=')
136 plt.text(70.2,75,B1)
137
138 B2='%8.6f'%(B2)
139 plt.text(60,70,'B2=')
140 plt.text(70.2,70,B2)
141
142 plt.show()
```

Splines

The curves shown in Figure 8-9 are called splines. They are characterized by the fact that they pass through their respective data points, which are shown as dots. Each curve is also a "natural" spline since there is no twisting at the ends. In the parlance of calculus, the second derivative is zero at the end points.

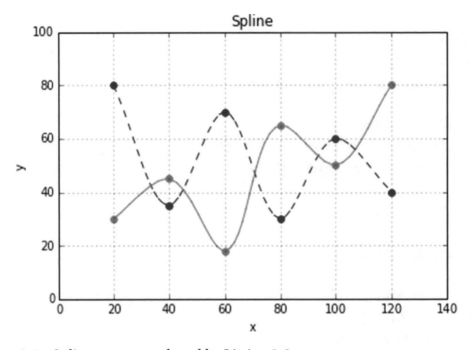

Figure 8-9. *Spline curves produced by Listing 8-8*

Splines constructed of thin slats of wood were at one time commonly used in shipbuilding where it was necessary to produce hull shapes that were smooth. In the lofting room, workers would drive nails into the floor and then bend thin strips of wood around them. The shape of the bent strip was then traced onto paper or plywood beneath. This shape was used to cut full-scale molds that were used in the construction process. The word "spline" is thought to derive from the Danish *splind* or North Frisian *splinj*, both ancient boat-building regions. After World War II, the usage of mechanical splines was replaced by mathematically derived curves in both shipbuilding and aircraft design and construction.

The mathematical relation for a spline that you will use here is called a cubic spline. It has the form of

$$x = Axq^3 + Bxq^2 + Cxq + Dx \qquad (8\text{-}11)$$

Since each point on a spline curve is defined by two coordinates x and y, you need two versions of Equation 8-11:

$$x = Axq^3 + Bxq^2 + Cxq + Dx \qquad (8\text{-}12)$$

$$y = Ayq^3 + Byq^2 + Cyq + Dy \qquad (8\text{-}13)$$

Your task is to determine the coefficients Ax → Cx and Ay → Cy. Once you have them, you will be able to plot the spline curve. To do this, you fit a separate equation for x and y within segments, that is, between adjacent data points. For example, the region between points 2 and 3 is a segment; between 3 and 4 is another segment. You also use information about the data points to the right and left of each segment.

Figure 8-10 shows a set of data points and the numbering scheme. **nop** in line 21 is the **n**umber **of** data **p**oints. There are six data points so nop=6. There are five inter-point segments. You will use lists to keep track of everything. Remember, Python wants to begin lists with the [0]th element. At point [3], which is the fourth data point, i=3, you see the length q[2] to the left and q[3] to the right. Each of these is a chord length, the straight line distance from one point to the next.

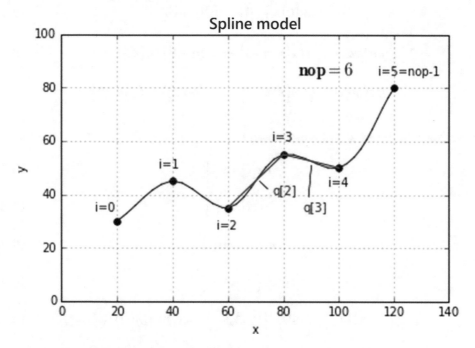

Figure 8-10. *Model used by Listing 8-8*

Referring now to just the x equation in Equation 8-12, you can define a "slope" at point [3], mx[3] as

$$mx[3] = \left(\frac{x[3] - x[2]}{q[2]} + \frac{x[4] - x[3]}{q[3]} \right) * .5 \tag{8-14}$$

This is an average at point [3] of the left "slope" and the right. I put "slope" in quotes to emphasize it is not a slope in the traditional sense such as $\Delta y / \Delta x$ but is instead each Δx (delta x) divided by a chord length q[ ]. For any point [i],

$$mx[i] = \left(\frac{x[i] - x[i-1]}{q[i-1]} + \frac{x[i+1] - x[i]}{q[i]} \right) * .5 \tag{8-15}$$

The equation for my[i] is similar. Because mx[i] and my[i] rely on coordinate values preceding and following i, separate equations are required for the first and last points, mx[0] and mx[nop-1]:

$$mx[0] = \left(x[1] - x[0] \right) / q[0] \tag{8-16}$$

$$my[0] = \left(y[1] - y[0] \right) / q[0] \tag{8-17}$$

$$mx[nop - 1] = \left(x[nop - 1] - x[nop - 2] \right) / q[nop - 2] \tag{8-18}$$

$$my[nop - 1] = \left(y[nop - 1] - y[nop - 2] \right) / q[nop - 2] \tag{8-19}$$

With these definitions, it can be shown that

$$dx[i] = x[i] \tag{8-20}$$

$$dy[i] = y[i] \tag{8-21}$$

$$cx[i] = mx[i] \tag{8-22}$$

$$cy[i] = my[i] \tag{8-23}$$

$$bx[i] = \left(3x[i+1] - 2cx[i]q[i] - 3dx[i] - mx[i+1]q[i] \right) / q[i]q[i] \tag{8-24}$$

$$by[i] = (3y[i+1] - 2cy[i]q[i] - 3dy[i] - my[i+1]q[i]) / q[i]q[i] \qquad (8\text{-}25)$$

$$ax[i] = (mx[i+1] - 2bx[i]q[i] - cx[i] / 3q[i]q[i] \qquad (8\text{-}26)$$

$$ay[i] = (my[i+1] - 2by[i]q[i] - cy[i] / 3q[i]q[i] \qquad (8\text{-}27)$$

These coefficients are based on the requirement that, at the intersection of spline segments at a data point, the locations of the splines and their slopes must match from one section to the next. Also, the rate of change of the slopes (second derivative) must match; otherwise there would be angular discontinuities in the shape of the spline. At the beginning point of the spline where i=0, there is no adjacent segment so you require that the rate of change of slope (second derivative of deflection) at that point be zero. This means that if the spline were to continue off to the left side of the first point, it would be a straight line having the same slope as the spline segment at that point. In the mechanics of beams, a bending moment called M produces a rate of change of slope y; that is, $d^2y/dx^2 \approx M$. The moment M would bend the spline at that point producing a change in slope. Since there is nothing at either end of the spline to produce a bending moment, $d^2y/dx^2 = 0$ and the slope will not be changed. This is intuitive; if a boat builder is fitting a wooden spline to a set of nails hammered into the floor, and they use a strip of wooden spline that is too long, the extra length would trail off the end straight at the same angle as the end of the spline at the last nail. This same argument holds for the end of the spline at i=nop-1; there is no constraint on its slope so the second derivative is 0. This provides a "natural" spline. You could specify other end conditions, such as clamped or twisted, in which case the coefficients above would be different.

The following equations locate a point xp,yp along the spline between points [i] and [i+1]:

$$xp = ax[i]qq^3 + bx[i]qq^2 + cx[i]qq + dx[i] \qquad (8\text{-}28)$$

$$yp = ay[i]qq^3 + by[i]qq^2 + cy[i]qq + dy[i] \qquad (8\text{-}29)$$

where qq is the length of chord i.

When Listing 8-8 plots the spline, it does so segment by segment starting with point [0] and proceeding to point [nop-1]. Referring again to Figure 8-10, if i=3, the above equations would plot the spline segment from point [3] to point [4]. To plot the entire spline from point [0] to [5], the program plots individual segments starting at [0] and going to [nop-1]. That is, the program automatically plots segments from [0] → [1], [1] → [2],.....[5] → [6].

Referring to Listing 8-8, the calculations and plotting are carried out by function spline beginning in line 17. In the function's arguments, x and y are in a list that is defined in line 73 and 74. Each x,y pair are the coordinates of a data point. clr is the color of the spline and ls is the line style. The data points are plotted in line 19. nop in line 21 is the number of data points. Lines 23-33 are zero lists of length nop. You fill these lists by calculating values item by item. You could have defined empty lists to begin with and appended elements later. By defining the list lengths now, you avoid appending. Either way will work; it's just a matter of preference.

Lines 35-38 calculate the chord lengths q[i]. Line 40 and 41 calculate the slopes at the beginning of the spline. Lines 43-45 calculate the average slopes at 0<i<nop-1. Line 47-48 calculate the slope at the end of the spline. Lines 51-59 evaluate the coefficients in Equations 8-28. Lines 62-70 plot the spline as line segments.

Control of the program takes place in lines 73-83. Here you are plotting two splines. The set of data points for the first spline are contained in the lists in lines 73 and 74. The color and line style desired are set in lines 75 and 76. Line 77 invokes function spline. The second spline is created in a similar manner in lines 79-83. More splines could be added by adding more of these routines.

It's an easy matter to print out the x,y values within the range of a spline segment. For example, suppose you want the coordinates of points within the segment between points [2] and [3]. Insert the following lines at line 71:

```
if i==2:
    print(xp,yp)
```

This will print the coordinate's values up to point [3] where i will then become equal to 3.

Listing 8-8. Program SPLINE2D

```
1    """
2    SPLINE2D
3    """
4
5    import matplotlib.pyplot as plt
```

```
6   import numpy as np
7   from math import sqrt
8
9   plt.axis([0,140,0,100])
10  plt.axis('on')
11  plt.grid(True)
12
13  plt.xlabel('x')
14  plt.ylabel('y')
15  plt.title('2D Splines')
16
17  def spline(x,y,clr,ls):
18
19      plt.scatter(x,y,s=30,color=clr)
20
21      nop=len(x)
22
23      q=[0]*nop
24      mx=[0]*nop
25      my=[0]*nop
26      cx=[0]*nop
27      cy=[0]*nop
28      dx=[0]*nop
29      dy=[0]*nop
30      bx=[0]*nop
31      by=[0]*nop
32      ax=[0]*nop
33      ay=[0]*nop
34
35      for i in range(1,nop): #——chords q(i)
36          a=x[i]-x[i-1]
37          b=y[i]-y[i-1]
38          q[i-1]=sqrt(a*a+b*b)
39
40      mx[0]=(x[1]-x[0])/q[0]
```

```
41        my[0]=(y[1]-y[0])/q[0]

42

43        for i in range(1,nop-1): #————average m[i]
44            mx[i]=((x[i]-x[i-1])/q[i-1]+(x[i+1]-x[i])/q[i])*.5
45            my[i]=((y[i]-y[i-1])/q[i-1]+(y[i+1]-y[i])/q[i])*.5

46

47        mx[nop-1]=(x[nop-1]-x[nop-2])/q[nop-2]
48        my[nop-1]=(y[nop-1]-y[nop-2])/q[nop-2]

49

50 #————————-calculate coefficients
51        for i in range(0,nop-1):
52            dx[i]=x[i]
53            dy[i]=y[i]
54            cx[i]=mx[i]
55            cy[i]=my[i]
56            bx[i]=(3*x[i+1]-2*cx[i]*q[i]-3*dx[i]-mx[i+1]*q[i])/(q[i]*q[i])
57            by[i]=(3*y[i+1]-2*cy[i]*q[i]-3*dy[i]-my[i+1]*q[i])/(q[i]*q[i])
58            ax[i]=(mx[i+1]-2*bx[i]*q[i]-cx[i])/(3*q[i]*q[i])
59            ay[i]=(my[i+1]-2*by[i]*q[i]-cy[i])/(3*q[i]*q[i])

60

61 #————————plot the spline
62        xplast=x[0]
63        yplast=y[0]
64        for i in range(0,nop-1):
65            for qq in np.arange(0,q[i],4):
66                xp=ax[i]*qq*qq*qq+bx[i]*qq*qq+cx[i]*qq+dx[i]
67                yp=ay[i]*qq*qq*qq+by[i]*qq*qq+cy[i]*qq+dy[i]
68                plt.plot([xplast,xp],[yplast,yp],linewidth=1,color=clr,
                    linestyle=ls)
69                xplast=xp
70                yplast=yp

71

72 #————————————control
73 x=[20,40,60,80,100,120]
74 y=[80,35,70,30,60,40]
```

```
75 clr='b'
76 ls='-'
77 spline(x,y,clr,ls)
78
79 x=[20,40,60,80,100,120]
80 y=[30,45,18,65,50,80]
81 clr='g'
82 ls='-'
83 spline(x,y,clr,ls)
84
85 plt.show()
```

Summary

This chapter covered a range of data plotting techniques: plotting simple points and functions, multiple functions on the same plot, labeling axes with multiple functions, linear regression where you fit a straight line to a data set, function fitting where you fit a user-defined function to a data set, and splines where you fit a smooth curve that passes through each data point. While there are many data plotting routines available within the Python community, which you can find with an Internet search, the approach here has been more hands-on. By understanding how to do it yourself, with a little creativity you can produce plots customized to your own needs. In Chapter 9, you will extend what you have done here to three dimensions.

CHAPTER 9

3D Data Plotting

Extrapolating the techniques developed in Chapter 8, which were used to produce two dimensional splines, to three dimensions is easy: all you need to do is add a few lines to the program. These lines are the bold highlighted lines in Listing 9-1, Program SPLINE3D, particularly those in function plotspline() from lines 89 to 161. They introduce the z coordinate in a syntax that is essentially the same as used for the x and y coordinates.

Control of Listing 9-1 begins at line 175. The first set of data points are defined by lists x, y, and z in lines 175-177. These have been nullified with the # symbol but are left in place should you want to use them. They produce Figure 9-1. The active lists in lines 179-181 produce Figures 9-2 through 9-4. nop in line 183 is the number of data points. This equals len(x) which, of course, equals len(y) and len(z). The list g in line 85 holds the values returned by the rotation functions rotx(), roty(), and rotz(). The coordinates of the center of rotation xc, yc, and zc are defined in lines 187-189.

The angles of rotation Rxd, Ryd, and Rzd in lines 191-193 could use some explanation. Referring to Figure 9-5, the coordinate system on the right defines the data points and the spline in their rotated (Rxd,Ryd,Rzd) and translated (xc,yc,zc) orientations. The system on the left shows the global coordinate system, which is the one that should be used when specifying rotations. The x and y directions are defined by the plt.axis() function in line 9. Since this is a right-handed coordinate system, the +z direction points *out* of the screen. As an example, a positive rotation around the z direction, Rzd, would rotate the figure on the right in the *counter-clockwise* direction.

Grid lines are shown on the plot primarily as an aid in location for xc,yc,zc. When axes such as the x and z axes in Figure 9-4 lie in the plotting plane, they can be used as a measure of data point and spline coordinate values. However, when the plot is rotated, as in Figure 9-3, they do not give true measures but may be used as an aid when locating the center, xc,yc,zc.

© Bernard Korites 2023
B. Korites, *Python Graphics*, https://doi.org/10.1007/978-1-4842-9660-8_9

Lines 200-210 plot the axes that define the data points and the spline by invoking function plotaxis() that goes from line 33 to 43. Each is 30 units long. The list g in line 43 holds the coordinates of the end of each axis. Line 202 plots the x axis; similarly for the y and z axes.

Without rotation (i.e., Rxd=Ryd=Rzd=0) the axes will appear as on the left side of Figure 9-5. When plotting data, we normally think of z as being a function of x and y (i.e., z=z(x,y)) and we prefer the z axis to point up. To accomplish this, we must rotate the coordinate system such that z points up. As an example, in Figure 9-4, Rx=-90,Ry=0,Rz=0. These values are shown in the upper right corner of the plot. This takes the +z axis, which pointed out of the screen in the unrotated position, and turns it counter-clockwise around the x axis so that it now points upward. +y now points into the screen. This is a good starting orientation. Subsequent rotations around this orientation can give a three-dimensional view. Keep in mind, however, that this program has been hard-wired to give rotations in the sequence Rx,Ry,Rz. For example, in function plotdata(), which begins at line 46, line 51 does the Rx rotation. The Ry rotation is next in line 55, and then Rz in line 59.

The data points are plotted in line 213, which invokes function plotdata(). This function is straightforward. Each data point is rotated amount Rx, then Ry, and then Rz in lines 51, 55, and 59. Each point is plotted as a green scatter dot in line 66. Line 64 plots the first point in red. Lines 68-86 plot grey lines from each point down to the x,y plane. The top of each line has the same global plotting coordinates as the data point g[0],g[1]. The z coordinate g[3] is not needed for plotting. The local coordinate of each line's bottom has the same local x,y coordinates as the data point, but now the local z coordinate is zero as specified in line 72. You need these local coordinates to rotate the bottom point of each line. Lines 73, 77, and 81 do the rotations. Line 83 plots the first point in red; line 86 plots the remainder of the points in black with the lines plotted in grey.

Next, the spline is plotted in line 217, which invokes function plotspline(). The color is set in line 216. This function is identical to the spline plotting algorithm used in the previous chapter with the exception of the addition of the z axis lines set in bold in the program listing.

The bottoms of the vertical lines are next connected by a spline by invoking function plotbottomspline() in line 221. The color is set in line 220. plotbottomspline() opens lists for the x, y, and z coordinates of each point: xbottom[ ], ybottom[ ], and zbottom[ ]. The items in each are initially set to zero. They are equated to the x and y data point coordinates in lines 168-171. Since the z coordinate lies in the x,y plane, it is set equal to zero in line 171. These are all local coordinates. Line 172 invokes function plotspline(), which was used to plot the main spline, with the arguments being the local coordinates of the bottom points. As before, plotspline() will perform the rotations and will plot the spline. The remainder of the program prints data and labels on the plot.

Listing 9-1. Program SPLINE3D

```
1    """
2    SPLINE3D
3    """
4
5    import matplotlib.pyplot as plt
6    import numpy as np
7    from math import sqrt, radians, sin, cos
8
9    plt.axis([0,150,0,100])
10   plt.axis('on')
11   plt.grid(True)
12
13
#================================================rotation transformations
14   def rotx(xp,yp,zp,Rx):
15        g[0]=xp+xc
16        g[1]=yp*cos(Rx)-zp*sin(Rx)+yc
17        g[2]=yp*sin(Rx)+zp*cos(Rx)+zc
18        return[g]
19
20   def roty(xp,yp,zp,Ry):
21        g[0]=xp*cos(Ry)+zp*sin(Ry)+xc
22        g[1]=yp+yc
23        g[2]=-xp*sin(Ry)+zp*cos(Ry)+zc
24        return[g]
25
26   def rotz(xp,yp,zp,Rz):
27        g[0]=xp*cos(Rz)-yp*sin(Rz)+xc
```

```
28        g[1]=xp*sin(Rz)+yp*cos(Rz)+yc
29        g[2]=zp+zc
30        return[g]
31
32    #===========================================================plot axis
33    def plotaxis(xp,yp,zp,Rx,Ry,Rz):
34        rotx(xp,yp,zp,Rx) #–Rx rotation
35        xp=g[0]-xc
36        yp=g[1]-yc
37        zp=g[2]-zc
38        roty(xp,yp,zp,Ry) #–Ry rotation
39        xp=g[0]-xc
40        yp=g[1]-yc
41        zp=g[2]-zc
42        rotz(xp,yp,zp,Rz) #–Rz rotation
43        return[g]
44
45    #=========================================plot data points
46    def plotdata(x,y,z,Rx,Ry,Rz):
47        for i in range(0,nop):
48            xp=x[i]
49            yp=y[i]
50            zp=z[i]
51            rotx(xp,yp,zp,Rx)
52            xp=g[0]-xc
53            yp=g[1]-yc
54            zp=g[2]-zc
55            roty(xp,yp,zp,Ry)
56            xp=g[0]-xc
57            yp=g[1]-yc
58            zp=g[2]-zc
59            rotz(xp,yp,zp,Rz)
60            xp=g[0]-xc
61            yp=g[1]-yc
62            zp=g[2]-zc
```

```
63          if i==0: #——plot first point red
64              plt.scatter(g[0],g[1],s=25,color='r')
65          else:
66              plt.scatter(g[0],g[1],s=25,color='g')
67          #————plot vertical lines from data points to the x,y plane
68          xt=g[0] #-global line top coords=rotated data point coords
69          yt=g[1]
70          xp=x[i] #—coords of line bottom (zp=0) before rotation)
71          yp=y[i]
72          zp=0
73          rotx(xp,yp,zp,Rx) #——rotate bottom coords
74          xp=g[0]-xc
75          yp=g[1]-yc
76          zp=g[2]-zc
77          roty(xp,yp,zp,Ry)
78          xp=g[0]-xc
79          yp=g[1]-yc
80          zp=g[2]-zc
81          rotz(xp,yp,zp,Rz)
82          if i==0: #————plot first bottom point red
83              plt.scatter(g[0],g[1],s=25,color='r')
84          else:
85              plt.scatter(g[0],g[1],s=25,color='k')
86          plt.plot([xt,g[0]],[yt,g[1]],color='grey') #——plot line
87
88  #=======================================================plot spline
89  def plotspline(x,y,z,Rx,Ry,Rz,clr):
90      q=[0]*nop
91      mx=[0]*nop
92      my=[0]*nop
93      mz=[0]*nop
94      cx=[0]*nop
95      cy=[0]*nop
96      cz=[0]*nop
97      dx=[0]*nop
```

```
98       dy=[0]*nop
99       dz=[0]*nop
100      bx=[0]*nop
101      by=[0]*nop
102      bz=[0]*nop
103      ax=[0]*nop
104      ay=[0]*nop
105      az=[0]*nop
106
107      for i in range(1,nop): #——chords q(i)
108          a=x[i]-x[i-1]
109          b=y[i]-y[i-1]
110          c=z[i]-z[i-1]
111          q[i-1]=sqrt(a*a+b*b+c*c) #——nop=6 gives q[5]
112
113      mx[0]=(x[1]-x[0])/q[0] #——mx[0]
114      my[0]=(y[1]-y[0])/q[0] #——my[0]
115      mz[0]=(z[1]-z[0])/q[0] #——mx[0]
116
117      for i in range(1,nop-1): #——average m[i]
118          mx[i]=((x[i]-x[i-1])/q[i-1]+(x[i+1]-x[i])/q[i])*.5
119          my[i]=((y[i]-y[i-1])/q[i-1]+(y[i+1]-y[i])/q[i])*.5
120          mz[i]=((z[i]-z[i-1])/q[i-1]+(z[i+1]-z[i])/q[i])*.5
121
122      mx[nop-1]=(x[nop-1]-x[nop-2])/q[nop-2] #—mx[nop-1]
123      my[nop-1]=(y[nop-1]-y[nop-2])/q[nop-2] #—my[nop-1]
124      mz[nop-1]=(z[nop-1]-z[nop-2])/q[nop-2] #—mz[nop-1]
125
126      #———————calculate coefficients
127      for i in range(0,nop-1):
128          dx[i]=x[i]
129          dy[i]=y[i]
130          dz[i]=z[i]
131          cx[i]=mx[i]
132          cy[i]=my[i]
133          cz[i]=mz[i]
```

```
134          bx[i]=(3*x[i+1]-2*cx[i]*q[i]-3*dx[i]-mx[i+1]*q[i])/(q[i]*q[i])
135          by[i]=(3*y[i+1]-2*cy[i]*q[i]-3*dy[i]-my[i+1]*q[i])/(q[i]*q[i])
136          bz[i]=(3*z[i+1]-2*cz[i]*q[i]-3*dz[i]-mz[i+1]*q[i])/(q[i]*q[i])
137          ax[i]=(mx[i+1]-2*bx[i]*q[i]-cx[i])/(3*q[i]*q[i])
138          ay[i]=(my[i+1]-2*by[i]*q[i]-cy[i])/(3*q[i]*q[i])
139          az[i]=(mz[i+1]-2*bz[i]*q[i]-cz[i])/(3*q[i]*q[i])
140
141      #──────────plot spline between data points
142      for i in range(0,nop-1):
143          for qq in np.arange(0,q[i],2):
144              xp=ax[i]*qq*qq*qq+bx[i]*qq*qq+cx[i]*qq+dx[i]
145              yp=ay[i]*qq*qq*qq+by[i]*qq*qq+cy[i]*qq+dy[i]
146              zp=az[i]*qq*qq*qq+bz[i]*qq*qq+cz[i]*qq+dz[i]
147              rotx(xp,yp,zp,Rx) #──Rx rotation
148              xp=g[0]-xc
149              yp=g[1]-yc
150              zp=g[2]-zc
151              roty(xp,yp,zp,Ry) #──Ry rotation
152              xp=g[0]-xc
153              yp=g[1]-yc
154              zp=g[2]-zc
155              rotz(xp,yp,zp,Rz) #──Rz rotation
156              if qq==0: #─plot first point red
157                  xplast=g[0]
158                  yplast=g[1]
159              plt.plot([xplast,g[0]],[yplast,g[1]],linewidth=.7,
                 color=clr)
160              xplast=g[0]
161              yplast=g[1]
162
163  #==============================================plot bottom spline
164  def plotbottomspline(x,y,z,Rx,Ry,Rz,clr):
165      xbottom=[0]*nop
166      ybottom=[0]*nop
167      zbottom=[0]*nop
```

```
168     for i in range(0,nop):
169         xbottom[i]=x[i]
170         ybottom[i]=y[i]
171         zbottom[i]=0
172     plotspline(xbottom,ybottom,zbottom,Rx,Ry,Rz, clr)
173
174 #=====================================================control
175 #x=[20,40,60,80] #–LOCAL coords-Fig(3D Spline 1)
176 #y=[30,30,30,30]
177 #z=[15,33,28,17]
178
179 x=[10,30,65,60,80,95,130,140 #–LOCAL coordinates-Figs
    (3D Splines 2,3 and 4)
180 y=[20,35,50,32,60,50,65,60]
181 z=[42,30,22,28,45,55,55,55]
182
183 nop=len(x) #–number of data points
184
185 g=[0]*3 #–global plotting coords returned by rotx, roty and rotz
186
187 xc=80 #–origin of X,Y,Z coordinate system
188 yc=20
189 zc=10
190
191 Rxd=-100 #–rotations of X,Y,Z system degrees
192 Ryd=-135
193 Rzd=8
194
195 Rx=radians(Rxd) #——rotations of X,Y,Z system radians
196 Ry=radians(Ryd)
197 Rz=radians(Rzd)
198
199 #———————————plot X,Y,Z axes
200 plotaxis(30,0,0,Rx,Ry,Rz) #–plot X axis
201 plt.plot([xc,g[0]],[yc,g[1]],linewidth=2,color='k')
```

```
202 plt.text(g[0]-5,g[1]-1,'X')
203
204 plotaxis(0,30,0,Rx,Ry,Rz) #—plot Y axis
205 plt.plot([xc,g[0]],[yc,g[1]],linewidth=2,color='k')
206 plt.text(g[0],g[1]-5,'Y')
207
208 plotaxis(0,0,30,Rx,Ry,Rz) #—plot Z axis
209 plt.plot([xc,g[0]],[yc,g[1]],linewidth=2,color='k')
210 plt.text(g[0]-2,g[1]+3,'Z')
211
212 #————————————plot data
213 plotdata(x,y,z,Rx,Ry,Rz)
214
215 #————————————plot spline
216 clr='g' #————————-spline color
217 plotspline(x,y,z,Rx,Ry,Rz,clr)
218
219 #————————————plot bottom spline
220 clr='b' #————————bottom spline color
221 plotbottomspline(x,y,z,Rx,Ry,Rz,clr)
222
223 #————————————labels
224 plt.text(120,90,'Rx=')
225 Rxd='%7.1f'%(Rxd)
226 plt.text(132,90,Rxd)
227
228 plt.text(120,85,'Ry=')
229 Ryd='%7.1f'%(Ryd)
230 plt.text(132,85,Ryd)
231
232 plt.text(120,80,'Rz=')
233 Rzd='%7.1f'%(Rzd)
234 plt.text(132,80,Rzd)
235
```

```
236 plt.text(90,90,'xc=')
237 xc='%7.1f'%(xc)
238 plt.text(100,90,xc)
239
240 plt.text(90,85,'yc=')
241 yc='%7.1f'%(yc)
242 plt.text(100,85,yc)
243
244 plt.text(90,80,'zc=')
245 zc='%7.1f'%(zc)
246 plt.text(100,80,zc)
247
248 plt.text(4,90,'x')
249 plt.text(7,90,x)
250 plt.text(4,85,'y')
251 plt.text(7,85,y)
252 plt.text(4,80,'z')
253 plt.text(7,80,z)
254
255 plt.title('3D Spline 4')
256
257 plt.show()
```

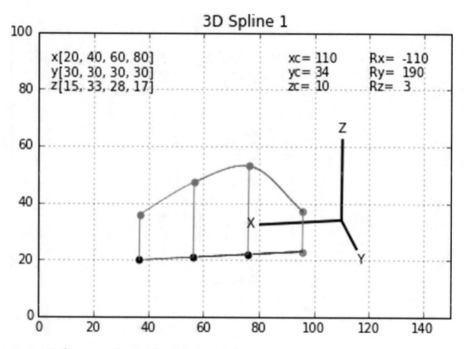

Figure 9-1. *Spline produced by Listing 9-1*

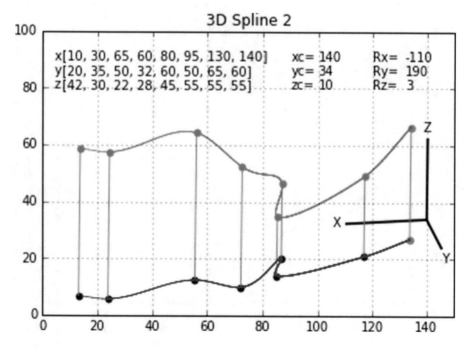

Figure 9-2. *Spline produced by Listing 9-1*

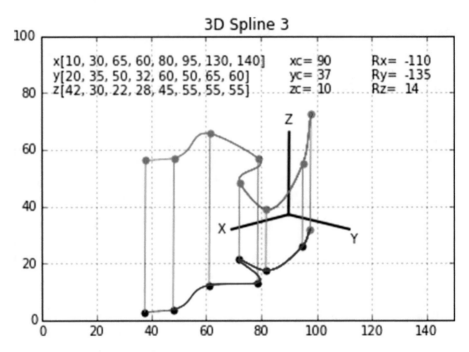

Figure 9-3. *Spline produced by Listing 9-1*

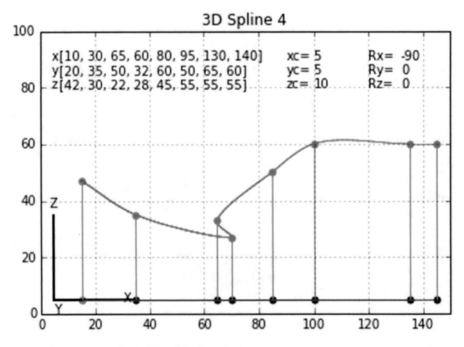

Figure 9-4. *Spline produced by Listing 9-1*

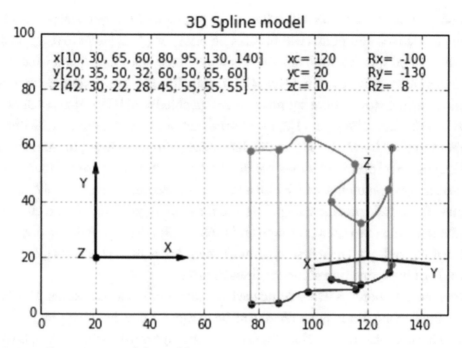

Figure 9-5. *Rotation model used by Listing 9-1*

3D Surfaces

In the previous section, you saw how to connect data points with splines in three dimensions. In this section, you will use those techniques to create a three-dimensional surface. Figure 9-6 shows a surface $z=z(x,y)$. It is defined by 16 data points in the x,y,z space. To give the appearance of a surface, these points are connected to one another by splines. The green splines connect the points in the y direction and the blue ones connect in the x direction. Since you already know how to create splines in three dimensions, the problem becomes one of arranging the data points in the proper order.

Listing 9-2 is similar to Listing 9-1 although some of the features of that program have been deleted for simplicity; you do not draw vertical lines from the data points to the x,y plane and you do not plot the projection of the splines on the x,y plane.

The essence of Listing 9-2 is contained in the "control" section beginning in line 140. The 16 data points shown in Figure 9-6 are defined by the lists in lines 168-182. The first group of points in the lists in lines 168-170 defines the data points shown in the first y-direction spline (green). This spline lies in the y,z plane where x=0. The points x1[ ], y1[ ],z1[ ] refer to the four points within this spline; x2[ ],y2[ ],z2[ ] refer to the points within the second spline, and so on. The first point in the first spline lies at 0,0,0. These coordinates are specified as x1[0],y1[0],z1[0] in lines 168-170. The second point in this first spline lies at 0,10,43. These coordinates are specified as x1[1],y1[1],z1[1]. Similarly, x1[2],y1[2],z1[2] and x1[3],y1[3],z1[3] refer to the third and fourth points in the first y-direction spline. Lines 187-190 plot the data points with these lists as arguments by invoking function plotdata(). Lines 194-197 invoke the function plotspline(), again with these lists as arguments, which plots the first y-direction spline. Lines 172-174 along with lines 188 and 195 plot the data points and the second green spline at x=20 and so on for the remaining two splines at x=40 and x=60. To plot the x-direction splines, you do the same thing, only you must first redefine the coordinate lists. This takes place in lines 200-214. The blue splines are plotted in lines 218-221.

Of course, the coordinate lists could each contain more than four items. The data points defined in the lists in lines 170-184 all lie in a grid. They don't have to.

While it works, the methodology used here to arrange the data for plotting is very cumbersome. It also requires a lot of coding. It is being done this way here to illustrate the procedure used. It could be shortened quite a bit by the use of arrays, which you will use in the next section.

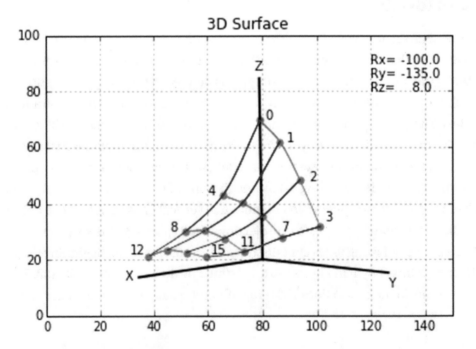

Figure 9-6. *Surface produced by Listing 9-2*

Listing 9-2. Program SURFACE3D

```
1    """
2    SURFACE3D
3    """
4
5    import matplotlib.pyplot as plt
6    import numpy as np
7    from math import sqrt, radians, sin, cos
8
9    plt.axis([0,150,0,100])
10   plt.axis('on')
11   plt.grid(True)
12
13
#=====================================================rotation
transformations
14   def rotx(xp,yp,zp,Rx):
15       g[0]=xp+xc
16       g[1]=yp*cos(Rx)-zp*sin(Rx)+yc
17       g[2]=yp*sin(Rx)+zp*cos(Rx)+zc
18       return[g]
19
20   def roty(xp,yp,zp,Ry):
21       g[0]=xp*cos(Ry)+zp*sin(Ry)+xc
22       g[1]=yp+yc
23       g[2]=-xp*sin(Ry)+zp*cos(Ry)+zc
24       return[g]
25
26   def rotz(xp,yp,zp,Rz):
27       g[0]=xp*cos(Rz)-yp*sin(Rz)+xc
28       g[1]=xp*sin(Rz)+yp*cos(Rz)+yc
29       g[2]=zp+zc
30       return[g]
31
32   #============================================================plot axis
```

```
33   def plotaxis(xp,yp,zp,Rx,Ry,Rz):
34       rotx(xp,yp,zp,Rx) #——Rx rotation
35       xp=g[0]-xc
36       yp=g[1]-yc
37       zp=g[2]-zc
38       roty(xp,yp,zp,Ry) #——Ry rotation
39       xp=g[0]-xc
40       yp=g[1]-yc
41       zp=g[2]-zc
42       rotz(xp,yp,zp,Rz) #——Rz rotation
43       return[g]
44
45   #=======================================================plot data
46   def plotdata(x,y,z,Rx,Ry,Rz):
47       for i in range(0,nop):
48           xp=x[i]
49           yp=y[i]
50           zp=z[i]
51           rotx(xp,yp,zp,Rx)
52           xp=g[0]-xc
53           yp=g[1]-yc
54           zp=g[2]-zc
55           roty(xp,yp,zp,Ry)
56           xp=g[0]-xc
57           yp=g[1]-yc
58           zp=g[2]-zc
59           rotz(xp,yp,zp,Rz)
60           xp=g[0]-xc
61           yp=g[1]-yc
62           zp=g[2]-zc
63           plt.scatter(g[0],g[1],s=25,color='g')
64
65   #=======================================================plotspline( )
66   def plotspline(x,y,z,Rx,Ry,Rz,clr):
67       q=[0]*nop
```

```
68      mx=[0]*nop
69      my=[0]*nop
70      mz=[0]*nop
71      cx=[0]*nop
72      cy=[0]*nop
73      cz=[0]*nop
74      dx=[0]*nop
75      dy=[0]*nop
76      dz=[0]*nop
77      bx=[0]*nop
78      by=[0]*nop
79      bz=[0]*nop
80      ax=[0]*nop
81      ay=[0]*nop
82      az=[0]*nop
83
84      for i in range(1,nop): #-chords q(i)
85          a=x[i]-x[i-1]
86          b=y[i]-y[i-1]
87          c=z[i]-z[i-1]
88          q[i-1]=sqrt(a*a+b*b+c*c) #-nop=6 gives q[5]
89
90      mx[0]=(x[1]-x[0])/q[0] #-mx[0]
91      my[0]=(y[1]-y[0])/q[0] #-my[0]
92      mz[0]=(z[1]-z[0])/q[0] #-mx[0]
93
94      for i in range(1,nop-1): #-average m[i]
95          mx[i]=((x[i]-x[i-1])/q[i-1]+(x[i+1]-x[i])/q[i])*.5
96          my[i]=((y[i]-y[i-1])/q[i-1]+(y[i+1]-y[i])/q[i])*.5
97          mz[i]=((z[i]-z[i-1])/q[i-1]+(z[i+1]-z[i])/q[i])*.5
98
99      mx[nop-1]=(x[nop-1]-x[nop-2])/q[nop-2] #-mx[nop-1]
100     my[nop-1]=(y[nop-1]-y[nop-2])/q[nop-2] #-my[nop-1]
101     mz[nop-1]=(z[nop-1]-z[nop-2])/q[nop-2] #-mz[nop-1]
102
```

```
103         #—————————calculate coefficients
104         for i in range(0,nop-1):
105             dx[i]=x[i]
106             dy[i]=y[i]
107             dz[i]=z[i]
108             cx[i]=mx[i]
109             cy[i]=my[i]
110             cz[i]=mz[i]
111             bx[i]=(3*x[i+1]-2*cx[i]*q[i]-3*dx[i]-mx[i+1]*q[i])/(q[i]*q[i])
112             by[i]=(3*y[i+1]-2*cy[i]*q[i]-3*dy[i]-my[i+1]*q[i])/(q[i]*q[i])
113             bz[i]=(3*z[i+1]-2*cz[i]*q[i]-3*dz[i]-mz[i+1]*q[i])/(q[i]*q[i])
114             ax[i]=(mx[i+1]-2*bx[i]*q[i]-cx[i])/(3*q[i]*q[i])
115             ay[i]=(my[i+1]-2*by[i]*q[i]-cy[i])/(3*q[i]*q[i])
116             az[i]=(mz[i+1]-2*bz[i]*q[i]-cz[i])/(3*q[i]*q[i])
117
118         #—————————plot splines between data points
119         for i in range(0,nop-1):
120             for qq in np.arange(0,q[i],2):
121                 xp=ax[i]*qq*qq*qq+bx[i]*qq*qq+cx[i]*qq+dx[i]
122                 yp=ay[i]*qq*qq*qq+by[i]*qq*qq+cy[i]*qq+dy[i]
123                 zp=az[i]*qq*qq*qq+bz[i]*qq*qq+cz[i]*qq+dz[i]
124                 xp=g[0]-xc
125                 yp=g[1]-yc
126                 zp=g[2]-zc
127                 roty(xp,yp,zp,Ry) #-Ry rotation
128                 xp=g[0]-xc
129                 yp=g[1]-yc
130                 zp=g[2]-zc
131                 rotz(xp,yp,zp,Rz) #-Rz rotation
132                 if qq==0:
133                     xplast=g[0]
134                     yplast=g[1]
135                 plt.plot([xplast,g[0]],[yplast,g[1]],linewidth=.7,color=clr)
136                 xplast=g[0]
137                 yplast=g[1]
138
```

```
139 #=======================================================control
140 g=[0]*3 #—global plotting coords returned by rotx, roty and rotz
141
142 xc=80 #—origin of X,Y,Z coordinate system
143 yc=20
144 zc=10
145
146 Rxd=-100 #-rotations of X,Y,Z system degrees
147 Ryd=-135
148 Rzd=8
149
150 Rx=radians(Rxd) #—rotations of X,Y,Z system radians
151 Ry=radians(Ryd)
152 Rz=radians(Rzd)
153
154 #———————————————plot X,Y,Z axes
155 plotaxis(60,0,0,Rx,Ry,Rz) #—plot X axis
156 plt.plot([xc,g[0]],[yc,g[1]],linewidth=2,color='k')
157 plt.text(g[0]-5,g[1]-1,'X')
158
159 plotaxis(0,60,0,Rx,Ry,Rz) #—plot Y axis
160 plt.plot([xc,g[0]],[yc,g[1]],linewidth=2,color='k')
161 plt.text(g[0],g[1]-5,'Y')
162
163 plotaxis(0,0,60,Rx,Ry,Rz) #—plot Z axis
164 plt.plot([xc,g[0]],[yc,g[1]],linewidth=2,color='k')
165 plt.text(g[0]-2,g[1]+3,'Z')
166
167 #————————define 4 sets of data points at different values of X
168 x1=[0,0,0,0] #——LOCAL coords
169 y1=[0,10,20,30]
170 z1=[50,43,30,14]
171
172 x2=[20,20,20,20]
173 y2=y1
```

311

```
174 z2=[25,23,19,12]
175
176 x3=[40,40,40,40]
177 y3=y1
178 z3=[14,15,13,9]
179
180 x4=[60,60,60,60]
181 y4=y1
182 z4=[7,10,10,9]
183
184 nop=len(x1) #——number of data points
185
186 #————————————plot data points
187 plotdata(x1,y1,z1,Rx,Ry,Rz)
188 plotdata(x2,y2,z2,Rx,Ry,Rz)
189 plotdata(x3,y3,z3,Rx,Ry,Rz)
190 plotdata(x4,y4,z4,Rx,Ry,Rz)
191
192 #————————————plot Y direction splines
193 clr='g' #————spline color
194 plotspline(x1,y1,z1,Rx,Ry,Rz,clr)
195 plotspline(x2,y2,z2,Rx,Ry,Rz,clr)
196 plotspline(x3,y3,z3,Rx,Ry,Rz,clr)
197 plotspline(x4,y4,z4,Rx,Ry,Rz,clr)
198
199 #————redefine the data points at different values of y
200 xx1=[0,20,40,60]
201 yy1=[y1[3],y2[3],y3[3],y4[3]]
202 zz1=[z1[3],z2[3],z3[3],z4[3]]
203
204 xx2=xx1
205 yy2=[y1[2],y2[2],y3[2],y4[2]]
206 zz2=[z1[2],z2[2],z3[2],z4[2]]
207
208 xx3=xx1
209 yy3=[y1[1],y2[1],y3[1],y4[1]]
```

```
210 zz3=[z1[1],z2[1],z3[1],z4[1]]
211
212 xx4=xx1
213 yy4=[y1[0],y2[0],y3[0],y4[0]]
214 zz4=[z1[0],z2[0],z3[0],z4[0]]
215
216 #————————————plot X direction splines
217 clr='b' #————————spline color
218 plotspline(xx1,yy1,zz1,Rx,Ry,Rz,clr)
219 plotspline(xx2,yy2,zz2,Rx,Ry,Rz,clr)
220 plotspline(xx3,yy3,zz3,Rx,Ry,Rz,clr)
221 plotspline(xx4,yy4,zz4,Rx,Ry,Rz,clr)
222
223 #————————————labels
224 plt.text(120,90,'Rx=')
225 Rxd='%7.1f'%(Rxd)
226 plt.text(130,90,Rxd)
227
228 plt.text(120,85,'Ry=')
229 Ryd='%7.1f'%(Ryd)
230 plt.text(130,85,Ryd)
231
232 plt.text(120,80,'Rz=')
233 Rzd='%7.1f'%(Rzd)
234 plt.text(130,80,Rzd)
235
236 plt.title('3D Surface')
237
238 plt.show()
```

3D Surface Shading

In the previous section, you constructed a surface by connecting data points with splines. You did not use arrays but relied on a cumbersome system of numbering. While this kept the procedure open and easy to understand, it led to too many lines of code. In this section, you will use the same data set but with two differences: first, you will connect the data points by straight lines; second, you will use arrays to organize your plotting. When you see how simple and elegant the use of arrays can be, you may question which method is the easiest to code and to follow.

Using the same three-dimensional data set as you used in the previous section, the array that defines the data is,

$$
\begin{aligned}
A = np.array([\ &\overbrace{[0,0,50]}^{A[0]=point\,0},\ \ \overbrace{[0,10,43]}^{A[1]=point\,1},\ [0,20,30],\ \overbrace{[0,30,14]}^{A[i]=point\,i}, \\
&[20,0,25],[20,10,23],[20,20,19],[20,30,12], \\
&[40,0,14],[40,10,15],[40,20,13],[40,30,9], \\
&[60,0,7],\ \ [60,10,10],[60,20,10],[60,30,9]\ ])
\end{aligned}
$$

(9-1)

This array is used by Listing 9-3 to produce Figure 9-7. The numbering scheme used to relate A to the surface points is shown in Figure 9-8.

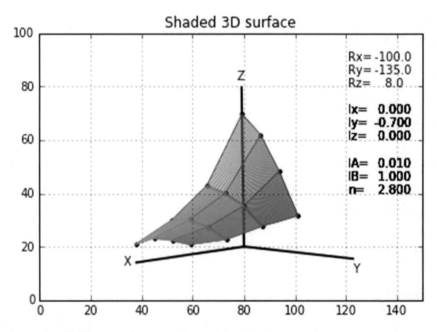

Figure 9-7. *Shaded 3D surface produced by Listing 9-3*

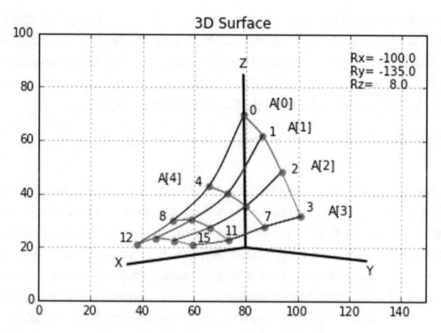

Figure 9-8. *Data point numbering scheme used in Listing 9-3*

Each element in A is a list. There are 16 lists: A[0] through A[15]. List i is referenced as A[i] where i=0→15. For example, A[3]=[0,30,14]. Each list i defines the x,y,z coordinates of data point i. That is

$$A[i,1] = x(i) \tag{9-2}$$

$$A[i,2] = y(i) \tag{9-3}$$

$$A[i,3] = z(i) \tag{9-4}$$

For example, the first point, point 0, has coordinates

$$A[0,1] = x(0) = 0 \tag{9-5}$$

$$A[0,2] = y(0) = 0 \tag{9-6}$$

$$A[0,3] = z(0) = 50 \tag{9-7}$$

This method replaces the list numbering system used in the previous section.

Referring to Figure 9-8, to get the z coordinate of the fourth data point, which is numbered 3, you access the third element of the *fourth* list of array A by letting i=3, j=2. As with lists, the numbering of elements within arrays begins at 0 so the coordinates of the fourth data point are contained in list i=3. The z component is the third element in that list, j=2. Thus the z coordinate of the fourth data point is A[3,2], so

```
print(A[3,2])
14
```

The numbering scheme in Figure 9-8 starts at point 0, which is at the upper corner of the surface at x=0, y=0, z=50, and proceeds in the y direction for a total of 4 data points. It then advances to a new value of x for another grouping of 4 y-direction points. This gives a total of 16 data points. Other numbering schemes could be used. You could, for example, have started at the same point but proceeded in the x direction first rather than the y direction. Or you could have started at a different corner of the surface. As you will see, whatever numbering scheme is chosen, it will have an impact on subsequent operations on that data.

The surface is composed of quadrangles, which are called *patches*. You will be shading these patches. Each patch is defined by four data points. Since they are located in three-dimensional space, the patches will, in general, not be flat. Also, since the sides can have arbitrary lengths, the patches will not necessarily be rectangular. The basic shading techniques used in previous chapters (i.e., coloring the patches by drawing lines across them) will be used but the technique must be modified.

Figure 9-9 shows the model. This is a generic oblique patch defined by four corners numbered 0 → 3. q03 and q12 are the lengths of the sides from 0 → 3 and 1 → 2. As mentioned, these sides are three-dimensional and are not necessarily parallel. As was done in previous chapters on shading, you fill in the patch with color by drawing lines across the quadrangle. The blue lines shown are examples. As shown in Figures 9-10 and 9-11, the algorithm you will be developing here will work with any quadrilateral.

To plot the lines, all you have to do is determine the starting position S of each line along side 0,3 and the end position E alongside 1,2. Since these sides may have different lengths, the distance q of S from point 0 alongside 0,3 is not the same as the distance of E from point 1 down along side 1,2. The starting point of the lines S begin at the top of the patch (corner 0) at q=0 and proceed to the bottom at q=q03. To get the corresponding position of E down side 1,2, you ratio the distance q by q12/q03. A line is then drawn between S and E. The blue lines shown in Figure 9-9 are 70%, 80%, and 90% of the way down both sides of the patch.

The unit vector $\hat{n}$ shown in Figure 9-9 is not required for the line drawing but will be needed when you determine the intensity of coloring. This is done as before by taking the dot product of $\hat{n}$ with a light source unit vector $\hat{l}$.

In Listing 9-3, the numbers of the generic patch corners, 0→3 in Figure 9-9, are replaced by the appropriate numbers for each patch on the surface from array A. The array is defined in the control section in lines 164-167. Line 169 gives the number of data points in A, which is equal to the number of lists, each list defining the location of a point. In this case, nop=16. The data points are plotted in lines 172-194. This simple routine, which illustrates a benefit of using arrays, replaces the data plotting function used in prior programs. Lines 178-185 connect the four y direction points by lines of color clr specified in line 177. Function plotline() does the line plotting. Lines 188-194 do the same in the x direction.

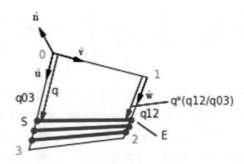

Figure 9-9. Patch model used in Listing 9-3

The patches are shaded in lines 197-205 by invoking function shade(), which begins in line 65. The arguments are arranged to conform to the generic patch corners shown in Figure 9-9. Lines 197-199 shade the first row of patches in the y direction. The first patch has its upper left corner at A[0,0], the second patch at A[1,0], and so on. In the first cycle through the loop, with i=0, lines 198 and 199 give the following patch corner coordinates, which are used as parameters in the call to function shade:

$A[0, 0] = x[0] = x0 = 0 \; corner \; 0$

$A[0, 1] = y[0] = y0 = 0$

$A[0, 2] = z[0] = z0 = 50$

$A[1, 0] = x[1] = x1 = 0 \; corner \; 1$

$A[1, 2] = y[1] = y1 = 10$

$$A[1, 3] = z[1] = z1 = 43$$

$$A[5, 0] = x[5] = x2 = 0 \ corner \ 2$$

$$A[5, 1] = y[5] = y2 = 20$$

$$A[5, 2] = z[5] = z2 = 30$$

$$A[4, 0] = x[4] = x3 = 0 \ corner \ 3$$

$$A[4, 1] = y[4] = y3 = 30$$

$$A[4, 2] = z[4] = z3 = 14$$

In function shade(), the arguments in line 65 coincide with the above patch corners 0,1,2 and 3,

$$\left(\underbrace{x0, \ y0, \ z0}_{corner \ 0}, \underbrace{x1, \ y1, \ z1}_{corner \ 1}, \underbrace{x2, \ y2, \ z2}_{corner \ 2}, \underbrace{x3, \ y3, \ z3,}_{corner \ 3} \right)$$

where $A[0]$, $A[1]$, $A[2]$, $A[3]$ label the four corner groups.

When i=1, these same program lines give the corner coordinates for the next patch in the y direction, which has corners 1, 2, 6, and 5. These correspond to the generic patch corners 0, 1, 2, and 3. The remaining cycles of the loop shade the remaining two patches in the y direction. Lines 200-202 and 203-205 advance in the x direction and perform the same operation, thus shading all nine patches.

You may be wondering why the for loop in line 197, for i in range(0,3):, uses the index *3* instead of *2*. After all, there are only three y direction patches to shade; 0 → 3 would seem to give four. It has to do with the workings of the range() function. In general, the syntax is range(start, stop, step). If no step is specified, it is assumed to be 1. Range will start at start, go to stop in steps of step, but it will *not* return the value at stop. In line 197, 0 is the start value and 3 is the stop value. This will return i=0, 1, and 2, but *not* 3. This was explained in Chapter 1. You can try this for yourself:

```
for i in range(0,3):
    print(i)
0
1
2
```

It is tempting to think of stop as the number of values to be returned, but it isn't. For example,

```
for i in range(1,3):
    print(i)
1
2
```

If the start value is not specified, it is automatically set to 0:

```
for i in range(3):
    print(i)
0
1
2
```

In this text, I usually included the start value for clarity but I do not usually specify the step value unless it is different from 1.

In function shade(), lines 66-92 evaluate the unit vectors $\hat{\mathbf{u}}$, $\hat{\mathbf{v}}$, $\hat{\mathbf{w}}$, and $\hat{\mathbf{n}}$

Lines 94-96 specify the components of $\hat{\mathbf{l}}$, the incoming light direction unit vector, as was done in prior shading programs. Line 98 takes the dot product of $\hat{\mathbf{n}}$ with $\hat{\mathbf{l}}$. Line 100-103 defines the shading function and establishes the light intensity, I, impacting the patch. Line 105 mixes the r,g,b colors. Lines 107-115 plot the lines across the patch. Line 117 plots the lines. Note that the lines have the color established in line 105.

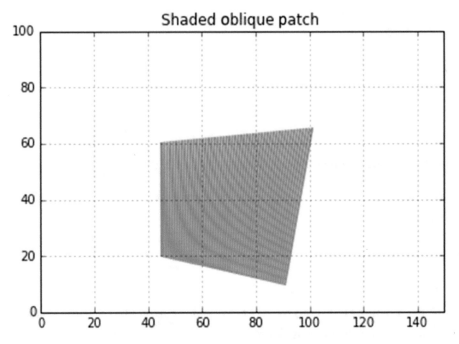

Figure 9-10. *Shaded oblique patch*

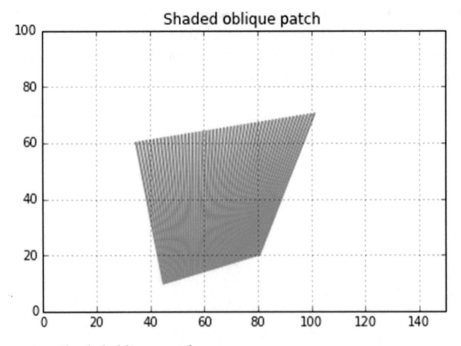

Figure 9-11. *Shaded oblique patch*

Listing 9-3. Program SHADEDSURFACE3D

```
1    """
2    SHADEDSURFACE3D
3    """
4
5    import matplotlib.pyplot as plt
6    import numpy as np
7    from math import sqrt, radians, sin, cos
8
9    plt.axis([0,150,0,100])
10   plt.axis('on')
11   plt.grid(True)
12
13   #========================================rotation transformations
14
15   #————same as Listing 9-2, Program SURFACE3D————
16
17   #=========================================================plot axes
18
19   #————same as Listing 9-2, Program SURFACE3D————
20
21   #=========================================================plot point
22   def plotpoint(xp,yp,zp,Rx,Ry,Rz,clr):
23       rotx(xp,yp,zp,Rx)
24       xp=g[0]-xc
25       yp=g[1]-yc
26       zp=g[2]-zc
27       roty(xp,yp,zp,Ry)
28       xp=g[0]-xc
29       yp=g[1]-yc
30       zp=g[2]-zc
31       rotz(xp,yp,zp,Rz)
32       plt.scatter(g[0],g[1],s=10,color=clr)
33
34   #=========================================================plotline
```

321

```
35   def plotline(xb,yb,zb,xe,ye,ze,Rx,Ry,Rz,clr):
36       rotx(xb,yb,zb,Rx) #——rotate line beginning coordinates
37       xb=g[0]-xc
38       yb=g[1]-yc
39       zb=g[2]-zc
40       roty(xb,yb,zb,Ry)
41       xb=g[0]-xc
42       yb=g[1]-yc
43       zb=g[2]-zc
44       rotz(xb,yb,zb,Rz)
45       xb=g[0]
46       yb=g[1]
47       zb=g[2]
48
49       rotx(xe,ye,ze,Rx) #——rotate line end coordinates
50       xe=g[0]-xc
51       ye=g[1]-yc
52       ze=g[2]-zc
53       roty(xe,ye,ze,Ry)
54       xe=g[0]-xc
55       ye=g[1]-yc
56       ze=g[2]-zc
57       rotz(xe,ye,ze,Rz)
58       xe=g[0]
59       ye=g[1]
60       ze=g[2]
61
62   plt.plot([xb,xe],[yb,ye],linewidth=.7,color=clr)
63
64   #==================================================shade
65   def shade(x0,y0,z0,x1,y1,z1,x2,y2,z2,x3,y3,z3,Rx,Ry,Rz,clr):
66       a=x3-x0
67       b=y3-y0
68       c=z3-z0
69       q03=np.sqrt(a*a+b*b+c*c)
70       ux=a/q03
```

```
71      uy=b/q03
72      uz=c/q03
73
74      a=x1-x0
75      b=y1-y0
76      c=z1-z0
77      q02=sqrt(a*a+b*b+c*c)
78      vx=a/q02
79      vy=b/q02
80      vz=c/q02
81
82      a=x2-x1
83      b=y2-y1
84      c=z2-z1
85      q12=np.sqrt(a*a+b*b+c*c)
86      wx=a/q12
87      wy=b/q12
88      wz=c/q12
89
90      nx=uy*vz-uz*vy
91      ny=uz*vx-ux*vz
92      nz=ux*vy-uy*vx
93
94      lx=0
95      ly=-.7
96      lz=0
97
98      ndotl=nx*lx+ny*ly+nz*lz
99
100     IA=.01
101     IB=1
102     n=2.8
103     I=IA+(IB-IA)*((1-ndotl)/2)**n
104
105     clr=(1-I,.4*(1-I),.6*(1-I))
106
```

```
107      r=q12/q03
108      dq=q03/50
109      for q in np.arange(0,q03+1,dq):
110          xb=x0+ux*q
111          yb=y0+uy*q
112          zb=z0+uz*q
113          xe=x1+wx*q*r
114          ye=y1+wy*q*r
115          ze=z1+wz*q*r
116
117          plotline(xb,yb,zb,xe,ye,ze,Rx,Ry,Rz,clr)
118
119      plt.text(121,70,'lx=')
120      lx='%7.3f'%(lx)
121      plt.text(130,70,lx)
122
123      plt.text(121,65,'ly=')
124      ly='%7.3f'%(ly)
125      plt.text(130,65,ly)
126
127      plt.text(121,60,'lz=')
128      lz='%7.3f'%(lz)
129      plt.text(130,60,lz)
130
131      plt.text(121,50,'IA=')
132      IA='%7.3f'%(IA)
133      plt.text(130,50,IA)
134
135      plt.text(121,45,'IB=')
136      IB='%7.3f'%(IB)
137      plt.text(130,45,IB)
138
139      plt.text(121,40,'n=')
140      n='%7.3f'%(n)
141      plt.text(130,40,n)
142
```

```
143 #=========================================================control
144 g=[0]*3 #----global plotting coords returned by rotx, roty and rotz
145
146 xc=80 #----origin of X,Y,Z coordinate system
147 yc=20
148 zc=10
149
150 Rxd=-100 #----rotations of X,Y,Z system degrees
151 Ryd=-135
152 Rzd=8
153
154 Rx=radians(Rxd) #----rotations of X,Y,Z system radians
155 Ry=radians(Ryd)
156 Rz=radians(Rzd)
157
158 #----------------------plot X,Y,Z axes
159
160 #--------same as Listing 9-2, Program SURFACE3D--------
161
162 #--------------------define data point array A
163
164 A=np.array([ [0,0,50],   [0,10,43],  [0,20,30],  [0,30,14],
165              [20,0,25], [20,10,23], [20,20,19], [20,30,12],
166              [40,0,14], [40,10,15], [40,20,13], [40,30,9],
167              [60,0,7],  [60,10,10], [60,20,10], [60,30,9] ])
168
169 nop=len(A) #----number of data points
170
171 #----------------------plot data points
172 clr='k'
173 for i in range(0,16):
174     plotpoint(A[i,0],A[i,1],A[i,2],Rx,Ry,Rz,clr)
175
176 #--------------------connect data points in Y direction
177 clr='k' #----------line color
```

```
178 for i in range(0,3):
179     plotline(A[i,0],A[i,1],A[i,2],A[i+1,0],A[i+1,1],A[i+1,2],
        Rx,Ry,Rz,clr)
180 for i in range(4,7):
181     plotline(A[i,0],A[i,1],A[i,2],A[i+1,0],A[i+1,1],A[i+1,2],Rx,Ry,
        Rz,clr)
182 for i in range(8,11):
183     plotline(A[i,0],A[i,1],A[i,2],A[i+1,0],A[i+1,1],A[i+1,2],
        Rx,Ry,Rz,clr)
184 for i in range(12,15):
185     plotline(A[i,0],A[i,1],A[i,2],A[i+1,0],A[i+1,1],A[i+1,2],
        Rx,Ry,Rz,clr)
186
187 #———————————connect data points in X direction
188 clr='k' #————————line color
189 for i in range(0,4):
190     plotline(A[i,0],A[i,1],A[i,2],A[i+4,0],A[i+4,1],A[i+4,2],
        Rx,Ry,Rz,clr)
191 for i in range(4,8):
192     plotline(A[i,0],A[i,1],A[i,2],A[i+4,0],A[i+4,1],A[i+4,2],
        Rx,Ry,Rz,clr)
193 for i in range(8,12):
194     plotline(A[i,0],A[i,1],A[i,2],A[i+4,0],A[i+4,1],A[i+4,2],
        Rx,Ry,Rz,clr)
195
196 #————————————shade patches
197 for i in range(0,3):
198     shade(A[i,0],A[i,1],A[i,2],A[i+1,0],A[i+1,1],A[i+1,2],A[i+5,0],
199         A[i+5,1],A[i+5,2],A[i+4,0],A[i+4,1],A[i+4,2],Rx,Ry,Rz,clr)
200 for i in range(4,7):
201     shade(A[i,0],A[i,1],A[i,2],A[i+1,0],A[i+1,1],A[i+1,2],A[i+5,0],
202         A[i+5,1],A[i+5,2],A[i+4,0],A[i+4,1],A[i+4,2],Rx,Ry,Rz,clr)
203 for i in range(8,11):
204     shade(A[i,0],A[i,1],A[i,2],A[i+1,0],A[i+1,1],A[i+1,2],A[i+5,0],
205         A[i+5,1],A[i+5,2],A[i+4,0],A[i+4,1],A[i+4,2],Rx,Ry,Rz,clr)
206
```

```
207 #――――――――――――――labels
208 plt.text(121,90,'Rx=')
209 Rxd='%7.1f'%(Rxd)
210 plt.text(130,90,Rxd)
211
212 plt.text(121,85,'Ry=')
213 Ryd='%7.1f'%(Ryd)
214 plt.text(130,85,Ryd)
215
216 plt.text(121,80,'Rz=')
217 Rzd='%7.1f'%(Rzd)
218 plt.text(130,80,Rzd)
219
220 plt.title('Shaded 3D Surface')
221
222 plt.show()
```

Summary

In this chapter, you saw how to plot data in three dimensions. To do so, you changed the usual orientation of your axes with z pointing into the screen to z pointing up; x and y are in the horizontal plane. This is the common way of displaying data where Pz=f(Px,Py) and Px, Py, and Pz are the coordinates of a data point. In Listing 9-1, you connected the data points by splines. As an aid to visualization, you projected the spline down onto the x,y plane. It could be projected onto the other coordinate planes without much difficulty. The 3D spline algorithm you used is an extrapolation of the 2D spline presented in Chapter 8. In Listing 9-2, you constructed a surface by connecting points by splines in the x and y directions. Then you shaded the three-dimensional surface. This required connecting the data points by straight lines rather than splines. The result was an assemblage of oblique patches, which are not necessarily planar; each of them may be twisted out of plane. You learned how to shade the surface by shading each patch. This required the development of an algorithm capable of shading a non-planar oblique quadrilateral. The shading was carried out by plotting lines across the surface of each patch; the intensity of the color was determined by the orientation of the patch with respect to the direction of the illuminating light rays.

CHAPTER 10

Demonstration Saturn

In this chapter, you will apply some of the techniques developed in previous chapters to produce some interesting images of the planet Saturn. They should give you some idea of the things that can be accomplished with Python graphics plus a bit of creative geometry.

Saturn

Saturn is famous for its rings. While Jupiter, Uranus, and Neptune also have rings, Saturn's are the largest, brightest, and most well-known in our solar system. They consist of particles as small as dust up to boulder-sized objects. The rings are thought to have originated when a comet or a large asteroid collided with one of Saturn's moons, shattering both into small pieces. Saturn has been known from ancient times but in 1610 Galileo was the first to observe it with a telescope. The planet is named after Saturn, the Roman god of agriculture, as is our sixth day, Saturday, Saturn's Day.

Listing 10-1 builds on an earlier program, SHADESPHERE from Listing 7-2 from Chapter 7. That program is left mostly intact here except for the introduction of algorithms that construct Saturn's rings and the shadow of the planet that is cast on the rings. The model that creates the rings is shown in Figure 10-6.

Figures 10-1 through 10-5 show images produced by Listing 10-1. They are at different angles of orientation, which are listed in the captions. Also listed are the unit vector components of the incoming light rays. For example, lx=+.707, ly=+.707, lz=0 indicates the light is coming from a light source in the upper left quadrant; if lx were negative, such as lx=-1, ly=0, lz=0, this would indicate a light source coming from the right. When specifying lx, ly, and lz, be sure they conform to a <u>unit</u> vector as mentioned earlier.

329

© Bernard Korites 2023
B. Korites, *Python Graphics*, https://doi.org/10.1007/978-1-4842-9660-8_10

In the images, please notice the shadow cast by the planet on the rings, especially in Figure 10-5, which shows the curvature of the planet's body. The geometry that does that is shown in Figure 10-7.

Figure 10-8 shows how easily an image can be magnified. With the change of just a few lines of code, you can create a telescopic image.

For comparison, a photographic image of Saturn, courtesy of Jet Propulsion Lab and NASA, can be found at `www.jpl.nasa.gov/spaceimages/?search=saturn&category=#submit`.

Figure 10-1. *Saturn with rings and shadow 1: Rx=-20, Ry=0, Rz=-10, lx=1, ly=0, lz=0 (produced by Listing 10-1)*

Figure 10-2. *Saturn with rings and shadow 2: Rx=-8, Ry=0, Rz=30, lx=.707, ly=.707, lz=0 (produced by Listing 10-1)*

Figure 10-3. *Saturn with rings and shadow 3, Rx=-20, Ry=0, Rz=25, lx=.707, ly=.707, lz=0 (produced by Listing 10-1)*

Figure 10-4. *Saturn with rings and shadow 4: Rx=-10, ry=0, Rz=25, lx=-.707, ly=-.707, lz=0 (produced by Listing 10-1)*

Figure 10-5. *Saturn with rings and shadow 5: Rx=20, Ry=0, Rz=30, lx=-1, ly=0, lz=0 (produced by Listing 10-1)*

Figure 10-6 shows the model used to construct the rings. In Chapter 7, you developed the shaded sphere algorithm by first creating an upright sphere. That is, the longitudes were vertical and the latitudes were horizontal (i.e., parallel to the x,z plane). From this starting orientation, you rotated the sphere around the x, y, and z axes. You do a similar thing here for the rings. You create horizontal rings, which are parallel to the x,z plane, and then rotate them through the same angles along with the spherical planet body. The rings lie in a plane that passes through the sphere's center so both the sphere and the rings have the same center of rotation. The rings are, in a sense, attached to the body of the planet and both rotate as one object.

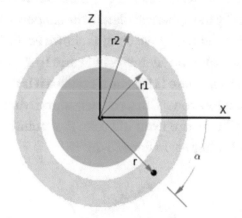

Figure 10-6. *Rings model: top view of planet and rings looking down on the x,z plane with Rx=0, Ry=0, Rz=0*

The ring band is drawn as a series of adjacent concentric circles, each of which is composed of short line segments. Referring to Figure 10-6 and Listing 10-1, program lines 42 and 43 set the inner and outer radii of the rings. Line 44 sets the distance between circles. The rings are divided into seven annular bands (not shown in Figure 10-6) to accommodate different colors; their width is deltar in line 45.

The bands are composed of short line segments. Each line segment is rotated and plotted separately. Line 48 starts a radial direction loop from r1 to r2 plotting the circle segments. Line 49 starts a loop plotting in the circumferential direction. Lines 50-61 do the rotating producing global plotting coordinates xpg and ypg in lines 62 and 63. The rotation functions rotx, roty, and rotz are the same as in previous programs.

Next, you set the colors of the segments. The rings are arranged in bands of different colors, which are a result of their physical composition as seen in the NASA image. This is done in lines 66-75. The first band, which goes from r=r1 to r1+deltar, has color `clr=(.63,.54,.18)` and so on for the remaining bands. You omit the fifth band, which is empty; the background color shows through. The sixth band is twice as wide as the others. This provides the colors for the seven bands.

For a given light direction, in most orientations, the planet's body will cast a shadow on the rings. Referring to Figure 10-7, your objective is to determine if a point on the band, p, lies inside or outside the planet's shadow zone. The spherical planet casts a circular shadow. The shadow's diameter will equal the size of the planet, or more precisely, the sphere's "great circle." This is the largest circle that can be obtained by cutting a sphere with a plane through its center. It's like cutting an orange in half; what you see is the orange's great circle. In Figure 10-7, the shadow could also be caused by a circular disk of this size as by the spherical planet; the shadow will have the same size in either case. The side view of Saturn's great circle is shown as the heavy line that passes through the plane's center. From the geometry in Figure 10-7, you can see that if p lies in a position such that $|\mathbf{B}| > rs$, where rs is Saturn's radius, it is outside the shadow zone; if $|\mathbf{B}| < rs$, p is inside the shadow zone. Once you determine where p is, if it is inside the shadow zone, when you plot the rings you will color that point grey. If it is outside, you will give it one of the band colors set in lines 66-75.

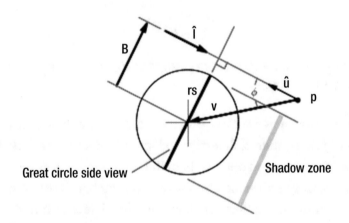

Figure 10-7. *Shadow model*

Your job now is to get $|\mathbf{B}|$ for a given position of p. You see from Figure 10-7 that

$$|B| = |V| sin(\phi) \tag{10-1}$$

You know that

$$V \times \hat{u} = |V||\hat{u}| sin(\phi) \tag{10-2}$$

where

$\hat{u} =$ -Î Î. Combining the above equations with $|\hat{u}|$=1

$$B = V \times \hat{u} \tag{10-3}$$

$$|B| = |V \times \hat{u}| \tag{10-4}$$

In Listing 10-1, line 78 establishes the length of the incident light vector, Î. This should equal 1, but it may not if the components entered in lines 23-25 do not compute to 1 (i.e., $\sqrt{lx^2 + ly^2 + ly^2} \neq 1$). Lines 79-81 then reestablish the components if necessary by scaling them up or down. Lines 82-84 establish the components of vector **V**. Lines 85-87 compute components of **B**. Line 88 gives its magnitude magB=|**B**|. Line 89 determines if p lies within the shadow zone. If it does, line 90 is executed. This is the dot product of **V** with Î Î . It determines whether p lies on the side of the planet that is toward the light source, in which case it is opposite the dark side of the planet and not in the shadow zone. This is necessary since the shadow algorithm in lines 78-89 does not make this distinction. If p does lie on the dark side and is within the shadow zone, the color is set to a medium grey in line 91.

You will notice in the images above that there is a dark band within the rings. This is because Saturn's rings have a void in that band: there are no particles there to reflect light; what you see is the background color, 'midnightblue', showing through. This creates a problem since the shadow color will overplot the background color in that void. Lines 93 and 94 reestablish it as 'midnightblue'.

Now that the band colors have been established, you can plot the rings. This is done by plotting short line segments. Lines 97-99 compute the starting location of the first segment. Referring to Figure 10-6, lines 100-101 determine if the segment is in front of the planet, in which case it is plotted. Lines 103-108 determine if it is behind the planet, in which case it is not plotted. This is done by calculating the distance c of the point's global coordinates from the planet's center. Line 107 says if c is greater than the sphere's radius times 1.075, then plot the segment. The factor of 1.075 is included to prevent the line segments from nibbling into the sphere's edges. But sometimes it can create too large a gap so you can reduce this if necessary. It is necessary to go through the above logic; otherwise the front visible segments, which are within the radius of the sphere, won't be plotted.

Two things can be noted regarding the above images produced by Listing 10-1. First is the color. The NASA photographic image shows a greyish hue, almost devoid of color. But many observers of Saturn have described it as having a golden hue, hence my choice of colors. As any photographer knows, capturing an object's true colors in a photographic image is difficult; so much depends on the color of the incident light and the image-capturing medium. Perhaps it is best to rely on the observations of stargazers. If you do not agree with the colors in the images produced by Listing 10-1, you can tinker with them by altering the clr definitions in the program. The second thing to notice is the curvature of the shadow that follows the planet's curvature in Figure 10-5. It shows that the shading algorithm works as expected.

Regarding use of the program, you can change the direction of the incident light in lines 23-25 and the angles of rotation in lines 31-33. Listing 10-1 takes a while to run so be patient.

Listing 10-1. Program SATURN

```
1    """
2    SATURN
3    """
4
5    import numpy as np
6    import matplotlib.pyplot as plt
7    from math import sin, cos, radians, sqrt
8
9    plt.axis([0,150,100,0])
10   plt.axis('off')
11   plt.grid(False)
12
13   print('running')
14   #————————————parameters
15   g=[0]*3
16
17   xc=80 #——sphere center
18   yc=50
```

```
19  zc=0
20
21  rs=25 #——sphere radius
22
23  lx=-1 #——light ray unit vector components
24  ly=0
25  lz=0
26
27  IA=0
28  IB=.8
29  n=2
30
31  Rx=radians(-20)
32  Ry=radians(0)
33  Rz=radians(30)
34
35  #————same as SHADESPHERE————
36
37  #————————rings
38  alpha1=radians(-10)
39  alpha2=radians(370)
40  dalpha=radians(.5)
41
42  r1=rs*1.5
43  r2=rs*2.2
44  dr=rs*.02
45  deltar=(r2-r1)/7 #——ring band width
46
47  #————————rotate ring point p which is at r, alpha
48  for r in np.arange(r1,r2,dr):
49      for alpha in np.arange(alpha1,alpha2,dalpha):
50          xp=r*cos(alpha)
51          yp=0
52          zp=-r*sin(alpha)
53          rotx(xc,yc,zc,xp,yp,zp,Rx)
```

```
54          xp=g[0]-xc
55          yp=g[1]-yc
56          zp=g[2]-zc
57          roty(xc,yc,zc,xp,yp,zp,Ry)
58          xp=g[0]-xc
59          yp=g[1]-yc
60          zp=g[2]-zc
61          rotz(xc,yc,zc,xp,yp,zp,Rz)
62          xpg=g[0]
63          ypg=g[1]
64
65  #----------------select ring band color
66      if r1 <= r < r1+1*deltar:
67          clr=(.63,.54,.18)
68      if r1+1*deltar <= r <= r1+2*deltar:
69          clr=(.78,.7,.1)
70      if r1+2*deltar <= r <= r1+3*deltar:
71          clr=(.95,.85,.1)
72      if r1+3*deltar <= r <= r1+4*deltar:
73          clr=(.87,.8,.1)
74      if r1+5*deltar <= r <= r1+7*deltar:
75          clr=(.7,.6,.2)
76
77  #----------------shadow
78      magu=sqrt(lx*lx+ly*ly+lz*lz)
79      ux=-lx/magu
80      uy=-ly/magu
81      uz=-lz/magu
82      vx=xc-xpg
83      vy=yc-ypg
84      vz=zc-zpg
85      Bx=uy*vz-uz*vy
86      By=uz*vx-ux*vz
```

```
87      Bz=ux*vy-uy*vx
88      magB=sqrt(Bx*Bx+By*By+Bz*Bz)
89      if magB < rs: #————————if in the shadow region
90          if vx*lx+vy*ly+vz*lz <= 0: #——if v points toward light source
91              clr=(.5,.5,.2) #——shadow color
92
93      if r1+4*deltar <= r <= r1+5*deltar: #——overplot empty band
94          clr='midnightblue' #——with background color
95
96  #——————————————————-plot line segment
97      if alpha == alpha1:
98          xstart=xpg
99          ystart=ypg
100     if zpg <= zc: #-front (z axis points into the screen)
101         plt.plot([xstart,xpg],[ystart,ypg],linewidth=2,color=clr)
102
103     if zpg >= zc: #-back
104         a=xpg-xc
105         b=ypg-yc
106         c=sqrt(a*a+b*b)
107         if c > rs*1.075: #——plot only the visible portion of rings
108             plt.plot([xstart,xpg],[ystart,ypg],linewidth=2,color=clr)
109         xstart=xpg
110         ystart=ypg
111
112 plt.show()
```

Figure 10-8 shows an image of Saturn magnified and shifted off-center. This is easily done by changing a few lines of input specifications in Listing 10-1. Figures 10-1 through 10-5 were done with various values of angles of rotation Rx, Ry, and Rz in Listing 10-1. Also, the center of Saturn was placed at approximately the center of the plotting area. The light direction specified by lx, ly, and lz in lines 23-25 comes from the right. So how did we get the magnified telescopic image shown in Figure 10-8 with the center of the planet off-center?

Figure 10-8. *Saturn magnified: Rx=20, Ry=0, Rz=30, lx=-1, ly=0, lz=0 (produced by Listing 10-1 with modifications as shown in the script below)*

It only required changing a few lines in Listing 10-1. These are shown in bold below. In line 9, the values in the plt.axis function have been changed to ([0,75,50,0]). In the previous images of Saturn they were equal to ([0,150,100,0]); here they are half what they were before. The plt.axis() function determines the *numerical* size of the plotting area (i.e., the lengths of the x and y axes). It does not change the *physical* size of the plotting area that appears on your monitor. By cutting these axes *numerically* in half, you are essentially doubling the size of the image inside. This assumes, of course, that the numbers that define the image *within* the plotting area remain unchanged. Note that in line 9 the length of the x-axis, which is 75, is 50% greater than that of the y-axis, which is 50. This retains the ratio of 150%, which eliminates distortions, giving you a round sphere instead of an ellipse. This was discussed in Section 1.17.2. You can see in lines 23-25 that the light direction goes from right to left, in the negative x direction. The radius of Saturn's body is **rs=25** in line 21. You can see that if you reduce the numerical values of the x and y axes, as you have done, a sphere that keeps its numerical value of the radius at 25 will appear larger. Rs is unchanged from the previous images of Saturn. The center of the planet has been moved off-center in lines 17 and 18. Obviously, there are parts of the image that lie outside the plotting area but are clipped off by the boundaries of the plotting area. Fortunately, Python does not plot or worry about things that lie outside the plotting area so, while a program may call for something to be plotted out-of-bounds, Python will ignore it. The program takes a few minutes to run so, if you're as impatient as I am, then line 13 lets you know it is running. There are a few other notes that are printed as the different operations are initiated. When the program is finished, the image of Saturn will pop up on the screen (see Figure 10-9). If you want to create a different degree of magnification, just change line 9; reduce the numbers to increase the magnification and increase the numbers to decrease the magnification, which will give a more distant view. Remember to keep x at 150% of y in line 9.

```
9    plt.axis([0,75,50,0])
10   plt.axis('off')
11   plt.grid(False)
12
13   print('running')
14   #————————————parameters
15   g=[0]*3
16
17   xc=80 #——sphere center
18   yc=50
19   zc=0
20
21   rs=25 #——sphere radius
22
23   lx=-1 #——light ray unit vector components
24   ly=0
25   lz=0
26 # ————————same as SHADESPHERE————
```

Figure 10-9. *Python enjoys the view from Enceladus, Saturn's sixth largest moon.*
Enceladus is covered by a layer of pure ice, making it one of the most reflective
bodies in our solar system. Beneath the ice there is thought to be water, making this
moon of great interest to the scientific community. This image was produced by
Listing 10-2

Listing 10-2 uses code that was developed in previous chapters. Saturn is the same
as before except it is positioned off-center and the axes definitions have been changed
(increased) to produce a more distant view. Earth in the distance is just a large, light blue
scatter dot. Enceladus uses the same sphere-producing algorithm as Saturn but without
the rings. The distant stars are just white scatter dots placed and sized at random. Every
time the program is run, the pattern will change. The section of code that produced them is

```
for ns in np.arange(1,20):              #--------20 stars
    x = random.randint(0,300)           #--------random x position of
                                        each star
    y = random.randint(0,175)           #--------random y position of
                                        each star
    t=[.5,1,1.5,2,2.5,3,3.5,4,4.5,5,5.5]     #-------size picked at
                                        random from this list
    ss = random.choice(t)
    plt.scatter(x,y,s=ss,color='white')
```

The green Python was produced using splines as shown in Chapter 8. The spline is
set up and then a line passes through points that have been specified. The line thickness
equals 7. This produces a reasonably smooth curve.

Listing 10-2. Saturn From Enceladus

```
#------------Saturn From Enceladus
import numpy as np
import matplotlib.pyplot as plt
from math import sin, cos, radians, sqrt
import random

plt.axis([0,300,200,0])
plt.axis('off')
plt.grid(False)

print('running')
#-------------lists
g=[0]*3

xc=250                  #---sphere center
yc=100
zc=0

rs=25                   #---sphere radius

lx=1                    #---light ray unit vector components
ly=0
lz=0

IA=0
IB=.8
n=2

Rx=radians(-20)
Ry=radians(0)
Rz=radians(-20)

#--background color
print('  background color')

for x in range(0,300,4):
    for y in range(0,200,4):
        plt.scatter(x,y,s=50,color='k')
```

```python
#-------------distant Earth, stars
plt.scatter(60,40,s=100,color='lightblue')

#====================rotation functions
def rotx(xc,yc,zc,xp,yp,zp,Rx):
    g[0]=xp+xc
    g[1]=yp*cos(Rx)-zp*sin(Rx)+yc
    g[2]=yp*sin(Rx)+zp*cos(Rx)+zc
    return[g]

def roty(xc,yc,zc,xp,yp,zp,Ry):
    g[0]=xp*cos(Ry)+zp*sin(Ry)+xc
    g[1]=yp+yc
    g[2]=-xp*sin(Ry)+zp*cos(Ry)+zc
    return[g]

def rotz(xc,yc,zc,xp,yp,zp,Rz):
    g[0]=xp*cos(Rz)-yp*sin(Rz)+xc
    g[1]=xp*sin(Rz)+yp*cos(Rz)+yc
    g[2]=zp+zc
    return[g]

#-------------longitudes
print('  Saturn longitudes')

phi1=radians(-92)
phi2=radians(92)
dphi=radians(2)

alpha1=radians(0)
alpha2=radians(360)
dalpha=radians(.5)

for alpha in np.arange(alpha1,alpha2+dalpha,dalpha):  #----longitudes
    for phi in np.arange(phi1,phi2+dphi,dphi):
        xp=rs*cos(phi)*cos(alpha)
        yp=rs*sin(phi)
        zp=-rs*cos(phi)*sin(alpha)
        rotx(xc,yc,zc,xp,yp,zp,Rx)
```

```python
        xp=g[0]-xc
        yp=g[1]-yc
        zp=g[2]-zc
        roty(xc,yc,zc,xp,yp,zp,Ry)
        xp=g[0]-xc
        yp=g[1]-yc
        zp=g[2]-zc
        rotz(xc,yc,zc,xp,yp,zp,Rz)
        xpg=g[0]
        ypg=g[1]
        zpg=g[2]
        a=xpg-xc
        b=ypg-yc
        c=zpg-zc
        qp=sqrt(a*a+b*b+c*c)
        nx=a/qp
        ny=b/qp
        nz=c/qp
        ndotl=nx*lx+ny*ly+nz*lz
        I=IA+(IB-IA)*((1+ndotl)/2)**n
        if phi == phi1:
            xpglast=xpg
            ypglast=ypg
        if nz < 0:
            plt.plot([xpglast,xpg],[ypglast,ypg],linewidth=4,color=(.80*(1-
            I),.75*(1-I),.1*(1-I)))
        xpglast=xpg
        ypglast=ypg

print('  Saturn latitudes')

for phi in np.arange(phi1,phi2+dphi,dphi):    #----latitudes
    r=rs*cos(phi)
    for alpha in np.arange(alpha1,alpha2+dalpha,dalpha):
        xp=r*cos(alpha)
        yp=rs*sin(phi)
```

345

```python
        zp=-rs*cos(phi)*sin(alpha)
        rotx(xc,yc,zc,xp,yp,zp,Rx)
        xp=g[0]-xc
        yp=g[1]-yc
        zp=g[2]-zc
        roty(xc,yc,zc,xp,yp,zp,Ry)
        xp=g[0]-xc
        yp=g[1]-yc
        zp=g[2]-zc
        rotz(xc,yc,zc,xp,yp,zp,Rz)
        xpg=g[0]
        ypg=g[1]
        zpg=g[2]
        a=xpg-xc
        b=ypg-yc
        c=zpg-zc
        qp=sqrt(a*a+b*b+c*c)
        nx=a/qp
        ny=b/qp
        nz=c/qp
        ndotl=nx*lx+ny*ly+nz*lz
        I=IA+(IB-IA)*((1+ndotl)/2)**n
        if alpha == alpha1:
            xpglast=xpg
            ypglast=ypg
        if nz < 0:
            plt.plot([xpglast,xpg],[ypglast,ypg],linewidth=4,color=(.80*(1-
            I),.75*(1-I),.1*(1-I)))
        xpglast=xpg
        ypglast=ypg

#---------rings and shadows
print('  Saturn rings and shadow')

alpha1=radians(-10)
alpha2=radians(370)
```

```
dalpha=radians(.5)

r1=rs*1.5
r2=rs*2.2
dr=rs*.02
deltar=(r2-r1)/7

for r in np.arange(r1,r2,dr):
    for alpha in np.arange(alpha1,alpha2,dalpha):
        xp=r*cos(alpha)
        yp=0
        zp=-r*sin(alpha)
        rotx(xc,yc,zc,xp,yp,zp,Rx)
        xp=g[0]-xc
        yp=g[1]-yc
        zp=g[2]-zc
        roty(xc,yc,zc,xp,yp,zp,Ry)
        xp=g[0]-xc
        yp=g[1]-yc
        zp=g[2]-zc
        rotz(xc,yc,zc,xp,yp,zp,Rz)
        xpg=g[0]
        ypg=g[1]
        zpg=g[2]
#-------ring colors
        if r1 <= r < r1+1*deltar:
            clr=(.63,.54,.18)
        if r1+1*deltar <= r <= r1+2*deltar:
            clr=(.78,.7,.1)
        if r1+2*deltar <= r <= r1+3*deltar:
            clr=(.95,.85,.1)
        if r1+3*deltar <= r <= r1+4*deltar:
            clr=(.87,.8,.1)
        if r1+5*deltar <= r <= r1+7*deltar:
            clr=(.7,.6,.2)
```

```
#-------shadow
        magu=sqrt(lx*lx+ly*ly+lz*lz)
        ux=-lx/magu
        uy=-ly/magu
        uz=-lz/magu
        vx=xc-xpg
        vy=yc-ypg
        vz=zc-zpg
        Bx=uy*vz-uz*vy
        By=uz*vx-ux*vz
        Bz=ux*vy-uy*vx
        magB=sqrt(Bx*Bx+By*By+Bz*Bz)
        if magB < rs:    #----------if in the shadow region
            if vx*lx+vy*ly+vz*lz <= 0:    #---if v pointing toward
            light source
                clr=(.4,.4,.1)            #---shadow color

        if r1+4*deltar <= r <= r1+5*deltar:  #---overplot with
        background color
            clr='k'

#-----------plot line segment
        if alpha == alpha1:
            xstart=xpg
            ystart=ypg
        if zpg <= zc:         #---front
            plt.plot([xstart,xpg],[ystart,ypg],linewidth=2,color=clr)
        if zpg >= zc:         #--back
            a=xpg-xc
            b=ypg-yc
            c=sqrt(a*a+b*b)
            if c > rs*1.090: #-----plot only visible part of ring
                plt.plot([xstart,xpg],[ystart,ypg],linewidth=2,color=clr)
        xstart=xpg
        ystart=ypg
```

```
#--------------Moon
xc=50                   #---sphere center
yc=400
zc=50

rs=240                  #---sphere radius

Rx=radians(-20)
Ry=radians(0)
Rz=radians(-20)

#---------      --------------Enceladus longitudes
print(' Moon longitudes')

phi1=radians(-92)
phi2=radians(92)
dphi=radians(2)

alpha1=radians(0)
alpha2=radians(360)
dalpha=radians(.5)

for alpha in np.arange(alpha1,alpha2+dalpha,dalpha):  #----Enceladus
longitudes
    for phi in np.arange(phi1,phi2+dphi,dphi):
        xp=rs*cos(phi)*cos(alpha)
        yp=rs*sin(phi)
        zp=-rs*cos(phi)*sin(alpha)
        rotx(xc,yc,zc,xp,yp,zp,Rx)
        xp=g[0]-xc
        yp=g[1]-yc
        zp=g[2]-zc
        roty(xc,yc,zc,xp,yp,zp,Ry)
        xp=g[0]-xc
        yp=g[1]-yc
        zp=g[2]-zc
        rotz(xc,yc,zc,xp,yp,zp,Rz)
```

```
            xpg=g[0]
            ypg=g[1]
            zpg=g[2]
            a=xpg-xc
            b=ypg-yc
            c=zpg-zc
            qp=sqrt(a*a+b*b+c*c)
            nx=a/qp
            ny=b/qp
            nz=c/qp
            ndotl=nx*lx+ny*ly+nz*lz
            I=IA+(IB-IA)*((1+ndotl)/2)**n
            if phi == phi1:
                xpglast=xpg
                ypglast=ypg
            if nz < 0:
                plt.plot([xpglast,xpg],[ypglast,ypg],linewidth=4,
                color=(.90*(1-I),.9*(1-I),.9*(1-I)))
            xpglast=xpg
            ypglast=ypg

#----Moon latitudes
print('  Moon latitudes')

for phi in np.arange(phi1,phi2+dphi,dphi):    #----latitudes
    r=rs*cos(phi)
    for alpha in np.arange(alpha1,alpha2+dalpha,dalpha):
        xp=r*cos(alpha)
        yp=rs*sin(phi)
        zp=-rs*cos(phi)*sin(alpha)
        rotx(xc,yc,zc,xp,yp,zp,Rx)
        xp=g[0]-xc
        yp=g[1]-yc
        zp=g[2]-zc
        roty(xc,yc,zc,xp,yp,zp,Ry)
        xp=g[0]-xc
```

```python
        yp=g[1]-yc
        zp=g[2]-zc
        rotz(xc,yc,zc,xp,yp,zp,Rz)
        xpg=g[0]
        ypg=g[1]
        zpg=g[2]
        a=xpg-xc
        b=ypg-yc
        c=zpg-zc
        qp=sqrt(a*a+b*b+c*c)
        nx=a/qp
        ny=b/qp
        nz=c/qp
        ndotl=nx*lx+ny*ly+nz*lz
        I=IA+(IB-IA)*((1+ndotl)/2)**n
        if alpha == alpha1:
            xpglast=xpg
            ypglast=ypg
        if nz < 0:
            plt.plot([xpglast,xpg],[ypglast,ypg],linewidth=4,
            color=(.90*(1-I),.9*(1-I),.9*(1-I)))
        xpglast=xpg
        ypglast=ypg
#-----------python
print('  python')

#Listing 8-8. SPLINE2D

def spline(x,y,clr,ls):
    nop=len(x)
    plt.scatter(x,y,s=5,color=clr)
    q=[0]*nop
    mx=[0]*nop
    my=[0]*nop
    cx=[0]*nop
    cy=[0]*nop
```

```
dx=[0]*nop
dy=[0]*nop
bx=[0]*nop
by=[0]*nop
ax=[0]*nop
ay=[0]*nop

for i in range(1,nop):                #---chords q(i); nop=6 gives q[5]
    a=x[i]-x[i-1]
    b=y[i]-y[i-1]
    q[i-1]=sqrt(a*a+b*b)

mx[0]=(x[1]-x[0])/q[0]            #---mx[0]
my[0]=(y[1]-y[0])/q[0]            #---my[0]

for i in range(1,nop-1):                 #---average m[i]
    mx[i]=((x[i]-x[i-1])/q[i-1]+(x[i+1]-x[i])/q[i])*.5
    my[i]=((y[i]-y[i-1])/q[i-1]+(y[i+1]-y[i])/q[i])*.5

mx[nop-1]=(x[nop-1]-x[nop-2])/q[nop-2]    #---mx[nop-1]
my[nop-1]=(y[nop-1]-y[nop-2])/q[nop-2]    #---my[nop-1]

#----calculate coefficients
for i in range(0,nop-1):
    dx[i]=x[i]
    dy[i]=y[i]
    cx[i]=mx[i]
    cy[i]=my[i]
    bx[i]=(3*x[i+1]-2*cx[i]*q[i]-3*dx[i]-mx[i+1]*q[i])/(q[i]*q[i])
    by[i]=(3*y[i+1]-2*cy[i]*q[i]-3*dy[i]-my[i+1]*q[i])/(q[i]*q[i])
    ax[i]=(mx[i+1]-2*bx[i]*q[i]-cx[i])/(3*q[i]*q[i])
    ay[i]=(my[i+1]-2*by[i]*q[i]-cy[i])/(3*q[i]*q[i])

#--------------plot the spline
xplast=x[0]
yplast=y[0]
```

```
    for i in range(0,nop-1):
        for qq in np.arange(0,q[i],2):
            xp=ax[i]*qq*qq*qq+bx[i]*qq*qq+cx[i]*qq+dx[i]
            yp=ay[i]*qq*qq*qq+by[i]*qq*qq+cy[i]*qq+dy[i]
            plt.plot([xplast,xp],[yplast,yp],linewidth=7,color='#698B69',lin
            estyle=ls)
            xplast=xp
            yplast=yp
            if i==2:
                print(i,xp,yp)

    plt.scatter(52,160,s=10,color='#698B69')
    plt.scatter(94,143,s=5,color='#698B69')

    plt.plot([43,40],[156,168],linewidth=2,color='#698B69')
    plt.plot([46,40],[156,168],linewidth=2,color='#698B69')
    plt.plot([44,40],[156,168],linewidth=2,color='#698B69')

    #plt.plot([70,80],[165,165],linewidth=1,color='g')

    plt.scatter(59,154,s=37,color='#698B69')
    plt.scatter(44,156,s=24,color='#698B69')
#-----------control
x=[60,65,75,80,85,85,94]
y=[155,161,164,163,164,145,143]
clr='g'
spline(x,y,clr,ls='--')

#-------------stars
print('  stars')

for ns in np.arange(1,20):
    x = random.randint(0,300)
    y = random.randint(0,175)
    t=[.5,1,1.5,2,2.5,3,3.5,4,4.5,5,5.5]
    ss = random.choice(t)
    plt.scatter(x,y,s=ss,color='white')
```

```
#-----------showing
print('  showing (wait)')
plt.show()
print('  almost done')
```

Summary

In this chapter, you learned a bit about the planet Saturn and how its rings were formed. You saw how to construct Saturn's body and shade it as you did earlier in Program SHADESPHERE in Chapter 7 (Listing 7-2). Adding the rings was easy; you created them from annular rings whose plane passes through the planet's body's center. With all angles of rotation equal to zero, you started off by creating the rings such that they lie parallel to the x,z plane. When you rotated or translated the planet's body, you rotated and translated the rings along with it. In a sense, the body and the rings acted as one unit. Then, using simple geometry, you constructed an algorithm that showed the shadow cast on the rings by Saturn's body. You also learned how to easily magnify or shrink an image by simply changing a few numbers in the plt.axis() function. This changes the definition of the numerical scale of the axes while the numerical values that describe Saturn and its rings remain unchanged. This has the effect of magnifying the image as shown in Figure 10-8, making it look closer. The image can be made smaller by doing the opposite, in which case it would look further away as in Figure 10-9. In Listing 10-2, you used random functions to position the distant stars and you used splines, discussed in Chapter 8, to create Python enjoying the view from Enceladus. Enceladus was created from the same algorithm that was used to create Saturn although the position of the center of the moon (out of the plotting area) and the moon's radius and color were chosen to give the icy grey image seen.

CHAPTER 11

Electrons, Photons and Hydrogen

Why are we concerned with electrons, photons, and hydrogen? As you will see here and in Chapter 12, the Sun is composed mostly of hydrogen whose electrons produce the photons that strike our planet, heating it (sometimes more than we would like). We need to understand how electrons generate photons and how they give photons the different frequencies that comprise the spectrum of electromagnetic energy. You saw some of this in Chapter 10 where you looked at Max Planck's spectrum. For this discussion of atomic activity, we will use as our model the hydrogen atom, which is the simplest of all atoms, is the most abundant element in the universe; is the lightest element; and has been well studied over the years. In addition, hydrogen comprises most of the Sun's mass. Its photon-producing electrons are responsible for virtually all of the Sun's energy output.

We all know basically what atoms look like; or do we? An atom consists of a nucleus, which is surrounded by electrons. Hydrogen (H) has only one electron. The nucleus of hydrogen contains one proton and no neutrons. All other atomic nuclei contain both protons and neutrons. The **atomic number** is the number of protons in the nucleus. Since H has only one proton, its atomic number is 1. The **mass number** of an atom is the number of protons plus neutrons in the nucleus. Since H has no neutrons in its nucleus, only one proton, its mass number is equal to 1. Its atomic number is also 1.

Protons and neutrons are composed of **gluons** and **quarks**; both are assumed to be indivisible. If you are wondering where the name "quark" came from, it can be attributed to a line from James Joyce's novel *Finnegan's Wake*:

"*Three quarks for Muster Mark.*"

The nucleus is held together in a tightly bound packet by strong intramolecular nuclear forces of attraction. It is now believed that all atomic particles (protons, neutrons, electrons, and all the rest) are not simple point masses but exhibit both

© Bernard Korites 2023
B. Korites, *Python Graphics*, https://doi.org/10.1007/978-1-4842-9660-8_11

particle and wave properties, known as wave-matter. The region between the nucleus and the surrounding electrons is empty space.

The pictures of atoms many of us remember seeing in textbooks are usually wrong in the way they depict the size of the nucleus relative to the overall size of the atom. The nucleus is usually shown to be too big. If we could enlarge an atom to the size of a football stadium, the nucleus would be about as large as a marble in the center of the playing field. Almost all the mass of an atom is concentrated in its nucleus, which has an immense density on the order of 10^{17} kg/m3. This is not its total mass, of course; it is its density in mass per unit volume. To put this in human terms, the nucleus would have the same density if we compressed 6 billion 4,000 pound automobiles into a box one foot on a side. The old concept of electrons being like little moons orbiting the nucleus is also wrong, as you will see.

Human investigation into the structure of matter has gone through numerous iterations beginning with Greek philosophers in 450-550 BC up to our present understanding of the atom which is called the **Standard Model**. Many dedicated and highly skilled researchers have participated in this evolution over several centuries. It is difficult to pin down exactly when some breakthrough occurred and who was responsible for it since oftentimes their work overlapped. Throughout this journey, much interest has been focused on the electron since this is the particle that is responsible for chemical reactions and the production of photons that give us light and heat.

The following is a brief timeline of atomic research:

- In about the year 450 BC, a Greek philosopher named Democritus thought all matter was made up of small, indivisible particles, which he called *atomos* and we now call atoms.

- A hundred years later, Aristotle thought Democritus' idea of an atomos was incorrect. He believed that the universe was divided into two parts: the terrestrial region on our planet and the celestial region of space. He thought all matter in the universe was composed of a continuum of substances. In the terrestrial region, all matter was made of a combination of four substances: *earth, fire, air,* and *water;* in the outer regions of the universe he thought everything was made of a fifth substance he called *quintessence.* Aristotle's ideas persisted for another 1,000 years.

- In the early years of the 17th century, a British scientist named John Dalton based on his research into chemical compounds and the behavior of gases, brought back the notion of the atom. There was no other concept that could explain what he was observing in the laboratory. However, his idea that atoms are small, solid particles was flawed. We now know, of course, they are not.

- In the late 17th century, another British physicist named J. J. Thompson discovered the electron, which he named. He realized that, since atoms are electrically neutral, there must be something there to cancel out the negative charge of the electrons. His idea was that an atom was a spherical mass of positively charged matter in which were located small negatively charged electrons, like plums in a pudding. Not surprisingly, this is known as the Plum Pudding Model. Thompson also discovered that electricity is the flow of negatively charged particles. This was important at the time since the prevailing thought was that electric current was similar to light.

- By the late 1800s, scientists realized atoms were so small they could not be observed optically. Using the laws of thermodynamics, about which much was known at that time, they concluded that the approximate diameter of an atom is about 1×10^{-8} cm.

- In 1861, Scottish physicist and mathematician James Clerk Maxwell published an early form of his famous equations which describe electric and magnetic fields. These equations form the foundation of classical field theory, also known as electrodynamics. While an important set of equations, they were later shown to be an approximation of theories developed through quantum mechanics.

- In 1888, a Swedish physicist named Johannes Rydberg developed a formula that matched the observed wavelengths of the spectral lines of alkali metals. His formulation involved a constant called the Rydberg Constant that calibrated his formula to the observed lines very accurately.

- In 1899, New Zealand physicist Ernest Rutherford eliminated Thompson's plum pudding model with his discovery of the nucleus. He did this by irradiating a thin film of gold with positively charged particles, which he called alpha particles. He discovered that most of the alpha particles passed right through the foil while some of them bounced back. This led to his idea that most of the atom is empty space, a positively charged nucleus surrounded by small negatively charged electrons. He predicted the existence of the neutron but never discovered it. He thought electrons revolved around the nucleus in random circular orbits, like planets orbiting a sun. Rutherford's model is known as the Planetary Model. We now know that this model was simplistic; there is a lot more to it.

- On December 14, 1900, Max Planck, a German physicist, presented his theory of black-body radiation, something that had confounded scientists up until that time. Planck's equation, which you will see more of in Chapter 12, describes the power spectrum of light and other forms of electromagnetic radiation. It is based on the idea that light is not a continuum, as Maxwell had asserted, but is composed of photons, individual packets of energy having the characteristics of both a particle and a wave. As you will see shortly, photons are produced by electrons changing their energy state.

- In 2013, the Higgs Boson, also known as the Higgs particle, or simply the Higgs, was discovered at CERN (near Geneva in Switzerland). The Higgs is thought to give the other particles their mass.

Where are we now in our understanding of the atom? At this time we are left with the Standard Model. While it works well and gives good agreement with experiments, it still does not answer all questions. At times it gives strange results. It seems a bit too convoluted, too fragile, too patched together. You don't have to be a professional particle physicist to get the feeling something is not quite right with it.

The Standard Model is not fully accepted by many physicists as being the final answer. Paul Dirac, Nobel Prize-winning physicist known for his contributions to quantum mechanics and quantum electrodynamics said, *"we have not yet solved the problem."* On the other hand, Carlo Rovelli, one of the founders of the loop gravity theory, says of the Standard Model, *"it may not be very elegant, but it works. Perhaps it is we who have not yet learned to look at it from just the right point of view."*

While the subject is fascinating, it is not necessary for us to worry about the details of the Standard Model. We need only be concerned with the atom as far as it is involved with the production of light and heat and other forms of electromagnetic radiation and that comes down to understanding the electron, its energy states, and its role in the production of photons.

In 1925, Erwin Schrodinger, addressing the wave side of the matter-wave duality, derived a partial differential equation that describes a wave function that is central to the wave nature of all atomic particles. This equation is a fundamental postulate of quantum mechanics and has played a central role in the development of our understanding of the electron and of all atomic particles.

His equation is based on the idea that electrons are actually standing matter-waves that encircle the nucleus. Imagine a piano string: the lowest harmonic, the string's fundamental natural frequency, has the longest wavelength. Now imagine an atomic scale piano string wrapped around the nucleus. Its fundamental wave would simulate the lowest frequency, the ground state of its energy. The fundamental wave has the lowest energy. Higher harmonics of vibration correspond to higher notes on the piano wire which, if wrapped around the nucleus, would simulate higher energy levels. Only waves having the correct wavelength can fit evenly around the nucleus. This means the harmonics, and thus the energy levels, can have only discrete values.

Schrodinger's waves are not strings like piano wires but are three-dimensional waves that surround the nucleus. The solutions to his wave equation, which are called eigenfunctions, define these standing waves. There is more than one solution to the equation, hence more than one eigenfunction is possible. Each defines a **quantum state**. These waves are in constant motion so we cannot say where an electron is at any specific time. All we can determine is the *probability* that it is at a certain place at a certain time.

Schrodinger's proposal that an electron exists in the form of a wave was later interpreted by Max Born as a probability amplitude whose square is equal to a probability density. This gave rise to the term **probability cloud**. This is not to say that the electron is a cloud; we are saying the probability of finding an electron at a specific point in space resembles a cloud pictorially. We cannot say exactly where an electron is within that cloud at any particular instant. All we can say is it is in there somewhere.

Figure 11-1 shows a hydrogen atom with its nucleus (red). In this image, the nucleus is depicted as much larger than it should be. Surrounding it is its one electron traveling around within its probability cloud (grey) in its lowest energy state which is called the *ground state*. This is called the **1s** orbital, the "s" indicating it is spherical and 1 indicates it is in the first and lowest energy state. The electron lives within this probability cloud. It will spend about 90 percent of its time here, most of it closer to the nucleus. The darker areas are where the electron spends most of its time; that is, the probability of finding it within the darker region is higher than in the lighter-shaded areas further away from the nucleus. This makes sense since the nucleus carries a positive charge while the electron is negative so they attract one another. The code in Listing 11-1 drew Figure 11-1.

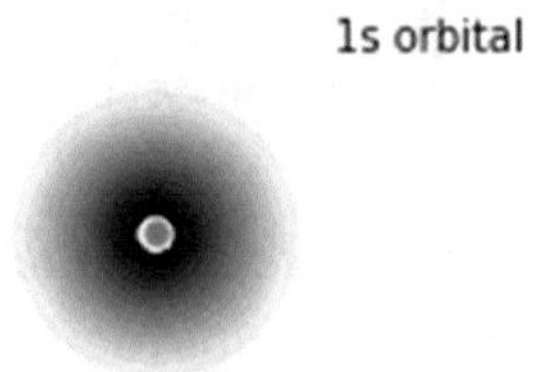

1s orbital

Figure 11-1. *A hydrogen atom with its one electron in its 1s energy state, called the ground state, the lowest*

Listing 11-1. *Program 1s orbital*

```
#---------------------------------program 1s orbital
import numpy as np
import matplotlib.pyplot as plt

plt.axis([-75,75,-50,50])

plt.axis('off')
plt.grid(False)

plt.scatter(0,0,s=25,color='r') #-------nucleus

r1=3
r2=16
dr=1
phi1=0
phi2=360.*np.pi/180.
dphi=2.*np.pi/180.
```

```
for r in np.arange(r1,r2,dr):
    for phi in np.arange(phi1,phi2,dphi):
        x=r*np.cos(phi)
        y=r*np.sin(phi)
        clr=(r-r1)/(r2-r1) #intensity decreases linearly
                           #from the nucleus
        plt.scatter(x,y,s=5,color=(clr,clr,clr))
plt.text(20,20,'1s orbital')

plt.show()
```

In Listing 11-1, in the scatter() function, the r,g,b colors are equally mixed as the variable CLR. They are all zero when r=r1, which gives black; when they all equal 1, they produce white. (See the section on color mixing in Chapter 1). The distribution of probability shown is linear from the nucleus. It is depicted that way here for pictorial purposes.

Figure 11-2 shows the orbital of the next higher energy state. This is the 2s level, which means it is spherical and in the second energy level. It extends further from the nucleus than the 1s state. Notice it is still spherical, as indicated by the s in the label, but is further from the nucleus due to its higher energy. This was drawn by Listing 11-2.

2s orbital

Figure 11-2. A hydrogen atom with one 2s energy electron. It is similar to the 1s but the probability cloud is larger due to its higher energy. The listing that produced this is similar to Listing 11-1 except the definition of CLR is different; the radius of the outer limit of the probability cloud has been increased

There are 3s, 4s, and higher spherical electron states possible with increasingly higher energy levels associated with each. The further the electron is from the nucleus, the higher its energy. An analogy is that a brick that is 10 feet off the ground has more potential energy than one 2 feet high. It takes energy to lift a brick 10 feet high. As you will see, in our atom, if we think of an electron as being a brick, the energy to raise its energy will be supplied by impacting photons.

It is important to recognize that an energy state's probability cloud, as depicted in Figures 11-1, 11-2, and 11-3 is *not* an electron; it is an <u>available energy state</u>, an orbital probability cloud. It simply shows where it is most probable to find an electron if it were to occupy that energy state. The various probability clouds show the states that are available to the electron as its energy is raised.

If we think in terms of energy shells, the first shell has one available energy state, the 1s orbital, as shown in Figure 11-1. The second has four; the 2s orbital is shown in Figure 11-2 plus three (x,y,z) p orbitals shown in Figure 11-3 (if we include the z-axis orbital which is not shown). This doesn't mean that hydrogen's one electron will occupy all four possible orbitals at one time; it merely means these four orbitals are *available* to the electron if it has the proper energy. If an electron in the 1s ground state acquires enough additional energy, it might flip into the 2s orbital *or* into one of the three p orbitals. It's as if you were checking into a hotel that has four rooms available on the second floor. You only need one of them.

You might ask, how many energy levels are there available to an electron? The answer: there is theoretically no limit. That doesn't mean, of course, that there could be as many as an infinite number of electrons in a hydrogen atom. We are talking about *possible* energy states that are *available* to the hydrogen atom's one electron if it is pushed up into higher energy levels. In reality, if an electron acquires enough energy, it may break away from its host nucleus. As shown in Figure 11-5, this is called the break-free energy and gives rise to the photoelectric effect.

We might expect the differences between the energy levels of states to be equal, but they are not. At low energy levels, the only orbital available to an electron is the 1s state, the ground state. As its energy increases, the 2s, 3s, 4s, and higher spherical orbitals become available to it. But at the 2 energy level, the p orbitals also become available. Shown in Figure 11-3 are two energy level 2 p orbitals, abbreviated as 2p (2 indicating the energy level and p the configuration).

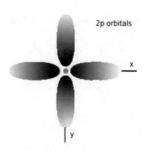

Figure 11-3. *px and py orbitals produced by Listing 11-2. These are both 2p orbitals indicating they are at the second energy level and are in the p configuration. A third pz orbital is available at this energy level but is not shown. This was produced by Listing 11-2*

Listing 11-2. Program 2p Orbital

```
#--------------------------------------------2p orbitals
import numpy as np
import matplotlib.pyplot as plt

plt.axis([-75,75,50,-50])

plt.axis('off')
plt.grid(False)
plt.scatter(0,0,s=40,color='r') #---------------nucleus

#-------------------------------------bottom orbital
a=4.
b=15.
xp1=-a
xp2=a
dx=.2

for xp in np.arange(xp2,xp1,-dx):
    yp1=b*(1-xp**2./a**2.)**.5
    yp2=-yp1
    for yp in np.arange(yp2,yp1,dx):
        clr=1-(-yp+b+4)/(2*b+4)
        plt.scatter(xp,yp+b+5,s=60,color=(clr,clr,clr))
```

```python
#----------------------------------------------top orbital
a=4.
b=15.
xp1=-a
xp2=a
dx=.2

for xp in np.arange(xp2,xp1,-dx):
    yp1=b*(1-xp**2./a**2.)**.5
    yp2=-yp1
    for yp in np.arange(yp2,yp1,dx):
        cl=1-(yp+b+4)/(2*b+4)
        plt.scatter(xp,yp-b-5,s=60,color=(cl,cl,cl))

#----------------------------------------------left orbital
a=15.
b=4.
xp1=-a
xp2=a
dx=.2

for xp in np.arange(xp1,xp2,dx):
    yp1=b*(1-xp**2./a**2.)**.5
    yp2=-yp1
    for yp in np.arange(yp1,yp2,-dx):
        clr=1-(xp+a+4.)/(2.*a+4.)
        plt.scatter(xp-a-5.,yp,s=60,color=(clr,clr,clr,clr))

#----------------------------------------------right orbital
a=15.
b=4.
xp1=-a
xp2=a
dx=.2

for xp in np.arange(xp2,xp1,-dx):
    yp1=b*(1-xp**2./a**2.)**.5
    yp2=-yp1
```

```
    for yp in np.arange(yp2,yp1,dx):
        clr=(xp+a+4.)/(2.*a+4.)
        plt.scatter(xp+a+5.,yp,s=60,color=(clr,clr,clr))

#------------------------------------------------axes
plt.arrow(37,0,10,0)
plt.arrow(0,37,0,10)
plt.text(42,-3,'x')
plt.text(3,43,'y')

plt.text(20,-30,'2p orbitals')

plt.show()
```

pz orbitals can also exist along with the py and px orbitals. They will align themselves with the z axis but are not shown in the illustration. Electrons flow into the lowest energy orbitals, which are closest to the nucleus, first. Then they fill the higher orbitals as their energy increases.

The orbitals shown here are called *principal quantum* and are designated by the letter n. There are other orbitals: *orbital angular momentum,* I, and *magnetic quantum,* m. They all have energy states and will release a photon when an electron drops from one energy state to a lower one.

As energy levels increase, orbital configurations get very complicated very quickly. The situation gets even more complicated when dealing with multi-atom molecules. The main points to be made here are the following: electrons are depicted in probability clouds or states; the clouds themselves are not electrons, just probability clouds, and these clouds have different shapes as energies increase; the differences between energy states are not constant but decrease with energy, as shown in Figure 11-5.

The number of electrons orbiting a nucleus always has an integer value (i.e., 1,2,3,...). Electrons can jump between energy states. If an existing electron is struck by a single photon, it may jump up to the next state and the incoming photon is annihilated, its energy going into pushing the existing electron up to a higher energy level, as shown in Figure 11-4 (b), in keeping with the principle of conservation of energy.

Electron energy states can decrease as well as increase. When an electron drops to a lower energy state, it emits a photon that will have the same energy, which is equal to the difference between the energy level the electron had and the one it drops to. See Listing 11-3. This is shown in Figure 11-4 (a).

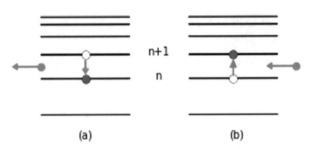

Figure 11-4. *In (a), an electron drops to a lower energy level and emits a photon. The energy lost by the electron goes into the emitted photon. In (b), an incoming photon strikes an electron bumping it up to the next higher energy level. The photon's energy goes into the electron. The photon is annihilated*

Listing 11-3. Emission and Absorption of a Photon

```
#-------------------------------program emission (a) and absorption (b)
of a photon

import numpy as np
import matplotlib.pyplot as plt

plt.axis([-150,150,-100,100])
plt.axis('off')
plt.grid(False)

#------------------------------------------(a) energy levels
plt.arrow(-100,66,75,0)
plt.arrow(-100,60,75,0)
plt.arrow(-100,50,75,0)
plt.arrow(-100,35,75,0)
plt.arrow(-100,15,75,0)
plt.arrow(-100,-15,75,0)

#------------------------------------------(b) energy levels
plt.arrow(25,66,75,0)
plt.arrow(25,60,75,0)
plt.arrow(25,50,75,0)
plt.arrow(25,35,75,0)
plt.arrow(25,15,75,0)
plt.arrow(25,-15,75,0)
```

```
#--------------------(a) electron dropping one energy state
plt.scatter(-62.5,35,s=50,color='k')
plt.scatter(-62.5,35,s=40,color='white')
plt.scatter(-62.5,15,s=50,color='k')
plt.scatter(-62.5,15,s=40,color='b')

#--------------------(b) electron rising one energy state
plt.scatter(62.5,35,s=50,color='k')
plt.scatter(62.5,35,s=40,color='b')
plt.scatter(62.5,15,s=50,color='k')
plt.scatter(62.5,15,s=40,color='white')

#---------------------------------------arrows and labels
plt.scatter(-100,25,s=39,color='r')
plt.arrow(-100,25,-20,0,head_length=4,head_width=5,color='r')

plt.scatter(100+15,25,s=39,color='r')
plt.arrow(100+15,25,-20,0,head_length=4,head_width=5,color='r')

plt.text(-10,35,'n+1')
plt.text(-4,15,'n')

plt.arrow(-62.5,30,0,-7,head_length=4,head_width=5,color='r')
plt.arrow(62.5,17,0,7,head_length=6,head_width=5,color='r')

plt.text(-69,-50,'(a)')
plt.text(59,-50,'(b)')

plt.show()
```

Figure 11-4 is drawn by Listing 11-3. The listing should be easy to understand. One feature is worth noting, however. The empty white circles representing electrons at their initial state were drawn by first placing a black scatter() dot and then over that a white one of slightly smaller diameter. This leaves a black ring surrounding the white dot. In Chapter 1, you learned that new dots overplot old ones so this is an easy way to have a white dot visible against a white background.

Electrons can occupy only certain stable orbits called *stationary states*. Each orbit has an energy associated with it called its *energy state*. The lowest energy state is the *ground state*. When an electron has an energy higher than the ground state it is said to be excited. When an electron drops from one energy state, n having energy En, to a lower one, n-1 having energy En-1, it emits a quantum of energy $\Delta E=En-En-1$, which is equal to the difference in energies. This packet of energy becomes a photon and is emitted by the atom as a unit of electromagnetic energy. This is shown in Figure 11-4 (a). This was anticipated by Max Planck in 1900 and by Einstein in 1905. Conversely, when an electron is hit by a photon having exactly the correct energy, it jumps to a higher energy state, as shown in Figure 11-4 (b).

Conservation of energy requires that the energy of the ejected photon must be the same as the change in energy of the electron as it drops from one state to another. Conversely, when struck by a photon, the increase in energy of the electron equals that of the incoming photon, which is annihilated in the process. In accordance with Einstein's equivalence of mass and energy through the famous equation $E=Mc^2$, the striking photon's mass M is converted into the energy required to bump the electron up to the next energy level.

Occasionally an electron may get hit hard enough by a photon that pushes it beyond the *break-free energy*. This may cause the electron to break free from its host nucleus. In that case, the electron's excess energy is converted into kinetic energy, forcing it to fly away from its host nucleus. This gives rise to the photoelectric effect.

The electron energy levels are not uniformly spaced. As shown in Figure 11-5, the spacings become smaller at higher energies. This is because the relation between energies is given by

$$E_n = \frac{E_{n=1}}{n^2} \qquad (11\text{-}1)$$

Where $E_{n=1}$ = -13.6, the ground state. Thus we have the following:

Quantum number		Energy
1	$E_1 = -13.6/1$	-13.6
2	$E_2 = -13.6/4$	-3.4
3	$E_3 = = -13.6/9$	-1.5
4	$E_4 = -13.6/16$	-.85
6	$E_5 = -13.6/25$	-.54

You can see, for example, the energy of a photon produced by an electron that drops from state 3 to state 2 is (-1.5)-(-3.4) = 1.9 ev where 1 ev (electron volt) equals

$$6 \times 10^{-19} \, J \tag{11-2}$$

This equation is based on the work of Johannes Rydberg 1n 1888 and Niels Bohr.

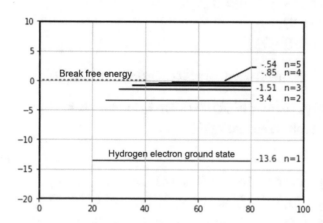

Figure 11-5. *Energy level of a hydrogen atom's electron showing the ground state and the break-free energy. This figure was produced by Listing 11-4*

Listing 11-4. Energy of a Hydrogen Atom's Electron

```
#------------------------------------------------------Figure 11-6
import numpy as np
import matplotlib.pyplot as plt

plt.axis([0,100,-20,10])
plt.axis('on')
plt.grid(True)

#------------------------------------------hydrogen ground state
plt.arrow(20,-13.6,60,0)
#------------------------------------------higher energy states
plt.arrow(25,-3.4,55,0)
plt.arrow(30,-1.511,50,0)
plt.arrow(35,-.85,45,0)
plt.arrow(40,-.544,40,0)
plt.arrow(45,-.378,35,0)
plt.arrow(50,-.278,30,0)
```

```
plt.text(82,-13.6,'-13.6    n=1')
plt.text(82,-3.4,'-3.4      n=2')
plt.text(82,-1.51,'-1.51    n=3')

plt.text(82,1.,'   -.85    n=4')
plt.text(82,2.5,'   -.54    n=5')
plt.arrow(80,2.3,2,0)
plt.arrow(80,2.3,-10,-2.3)

plt.text(23,-13,'    hydrogen electron ground state')

plt.arrow(0,0,40,0,color='b',linewidth=2,linestyle=':')
plt.text(8,.6,'break free energy')

#--------------------------------------------------------frame
plt.plot([0,0],[-20,10],linewidth=3,color='k')
plt.plot([0,100],[10,10],linewidth=3,color='k')
plt.plot([100,100],[10,-20],linewidth=3,color='k')
plt.plot([100,0],[-20,-20],linewidth=3,color='k')
plt.show()
```

What about the frequency of an emitted photon? This is responsible for the color of the light we see as well as for the "colors" we can't see such as UV and infrared. We can calculate the wavelength (equivalent to the frequency) of the photon that is emitted by an electron that drops from one energy level to another as in

$$v = \frac{\Delta E}{h} \tag{11-3}$$

where h is Planck's Constant.

The units of wavelength are typically nanometers (1 nm = 10^{-9} m). So you see that the energy of a photon is dependent on the energy that an electron gives up when it drops from one state to another. This is, of course, a consequence of the principle of conservation of energy. You also see that the emitted photon's wavelength (or frequency) is also dependent on the electron's energy drop.

Summary

You learned about the hydrogen atom, atomic structure and how photons are generated, and where photons get their energy and their frequency. You also saw how to use Python graphics to produce images of electron probability clouds. You can probably guess where all this is leading. In Chapter 12, you will see how photons emitted by the Sun due to changes in the energy state of its immense number of hydrogen atoms and electrons are what produces the Sun's solar power that irradiates the Earth.

CHAPTER 12

Demonstration: The Sun

This chapter demonstrates how you can use Python to plot and label curves that represent mathematical functions. Our focus of interest will be the Sun. We will plot Max Planck's spectrum of radiation, which will be used to represent the energy spectrum emitted by the Sun. Then we will calculate the Sun's total power output and the amount that reaches Earth, which is called the *solar constant*. The scientific aspects of this section are quite interesting, as is the history of their development. The major benefit from a Python programming aspect is seeing how Python can be used to set up plots, perform numerical integration, display numerical data, and put labels and notes on the plots. Plus you will learn some interesting facts about solar physics. Much of this chapter relates to photons, which were discussed in Chapter 11. All illustrations in this chapter were produced using Python.

The Earth-Sun Model

Listing 12-1 was used to produce Figure 12-1.

© Bernard Korites 2023
B. Korites, *Python Graphics*, https://doi.org/10.1007/978-1-4842-9660-8_12

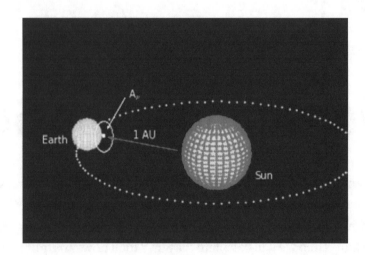

Figure 12-1. *The Earth-Sun model produced by Listing 12-1. AU, the distance from the Earth to the Sun, is known as an Astronomical Unit. Ap is an imaginary circular disk having the same diameter as the Earth. It is used to determine the amount of the Sun's energy that is received by the Earth*

Listing 12-1. Program EARTHSUN

```
"""

EARTHSUN
"""

import matplotlib.pyplot as plt
import numpy as np
from math import radians, sin, cos, sqrt
plt.axis([-100,150,-100,150])
plt.grid(False)
plt.axis('off')
sfx=2.5/3.8
#————————————————background
for x in range(-100,150,2):
    for y in range(-100,150,2):
        plt.scatter(x,y,s=40,color='midnightblue')
phimin=0.
phimax=2.*np.pi
dphi=phimax/100.
rs=40.
```

```
re=20.
ys=15.
ye=2.
xos=50.
yos=0.
zos=0.
#————————————Sun's core
plt.scatter(xos,yos,s=4300,color='yellow')
#————————————Sun horizontals
rx=radians(20)
for ys in np.arange(-rs,rs,5):
    for phi in np.arange(phimin,phimax,dphi):
        rp=np.sqrt(rs*rs-ys*ys)
        xp=rp*np.sin(phi)
        yp=ys
        zp=rp*np.cos(phi)
        px=xos +sfx*xp*1. +yp*0. +zp*0.
        py=yos +xp*0. +yp*np.cos(rx) -zp*np.sin(rx)
        pz=zos +xp*0. +yp*np.sin(rx) +zp*np.cos(rx)
        if pz > 0 :
            plt.scatter(px,py,s=1,color='red')
#————————————Sun verticals
alphamin=0.
alphamax=2.*np.pi
dalpha=alphamax/30.
for alpha in np.arange(alphamin,alphamax,dalpha):
    for phi in np.arange(phimin,phimax,dphi):
        xp=rs*np.sin(phi)*np.sin(alpha)
        yp=rs*np.cos(phi)
        zp=rs*np.sin(phi)*np.cos(alpha)
        px=xos +sfx*(xp*1. +yp*0. +zp*0.)
        py=yos +xp*0. +yp*np.cos(rx) -zp*np.sin(rx)
        pz=zos +xp*0. +yp*(np.sin(rx)) +zp*np.cos(rx)
        if pz > 0 :
            plt.scatter(px,py,s=1,color='red')
```

```
#————————————Earth's clouds
xoe=-50.
yoe=20.
zoe=-10.
plt.scatter(xoe,yoe,s=800,color='white')
#———————————— Earth horizontals
rx=20.*np.pi/180.
dphi=phimax/100.
for ys in np.arange(-re,re,2):
    for phi in np.arange(phimin,phimax,dphi):
        rp=np.sqrt(re*re-ys*ys)
        xp=rp*np.sin(phi)
        yp=ys
        zp=rp*np.cos(phi)
        px=xoe +sfx*(+xp*1. +yp*0. +zp*0.)
        py=yoe +xp*0. +yp*np.cos(rx) -zp*np.sin(rx)
        pz=zoe +xp*0. +yp*(np.sin(rx)) +zp*np.cos(rx)
        if pz > 0 :
            plt.scatter(px,py,s=.1,color='#add8e6')
#————————————Earth verticals
alphamin=0.
alphamax=2.*np.pi
dalpha=alphamax/30.
for alpha in np.arange(alphamin,alphamax,dalpha):
    for phi in np.arange(phimin,phimax,dphi):
        xp=re*np.sin(phi)*np.sin(alpha)
        yp=re*np.cos(phi)
        zp=re*np.sin(phi)*np.cos(alpha)
        px=xoe +sfx*(xp*1. +yp*0. +zp*0.)
        py=yoe +xp*0. +yp*np.cos(rx) -zp*np.sin(rx)
        pz=zoe +xp*0. +yp*(np.sin(rx)) +zp*np.cos(rx)
        if pz > 0 :
            plt.scatter(px,py,s=.1,color='#add8e6')
plt.arrow(xos-rs*sfx-3,yos+2,xoe-(xos-rs*sfx)+re+3,yoe-yos-6.2,color='r',
                        head_length=4.,head_width=3.)
```

```
plt.text(-14,16,'1 AU',color='white')
plt.text(80,-29,'Sun',color='white')
plt.text(-84,10,'Earth',color='white')
#————————————————front orbit
deltamin=0.*np.pi/180.
deltamax=195.*np.pi/180.
ddelta=deltamax/60.
for delta in np.arange(deltamin,deltamax,ddelta):
    r=108./sfx
    xp=r*np.cos(delta)
    yp=0.
    zp=r*np.sin(delta)
    px=xos +sfx*(xp*1. +yp*0. +zp*0.)
    py=yos +xp*0. +yp*np.cos(rx) -zp*np.sin(rx)
    pz=zos +xp*0. +yp*(np.sin(rx)) +zp*np.cos(rx)
    plt.scatter(px,py,s=1,color='white')
#————————————————back orbit
deltamin=220.*np.pi/180.
deltamax=360.*np.pi/180.
for delta in np.arange(deltamin,deltamax,ddelta):
    r=108./sfx
    xp=r*np.cos(delta)
    yp=0.
    zp=r*np.sin(delta)
    px=xos +sfx*xp*1. +yp*0. +zp*0.
    py=yos +xp*0. +yp*np.cos(rx) -zp*np.sin(rx)
    pz=zos +xp*0. +yp*(np.sin(rx)) +zp*np.cos(rx)
    plt.scatter(px,py,s=1,color='white')
#————————————————Ap disc
xoc=xoe+re*sfx
yoc=yoe-2.5
zoc=zoe
rc=.83*re
phi1=0
phi2=2*np.pi
```

```
dphi=(phi2-phi1)/200
ry=-25*np.pi/180
for phi in np.arange(phi1,phi2,dphi):
    xc=xoc
    yc=rc*np.sin(phi)
    zc=rc*np.cos(phi)
    px=xoc+zc*np.sin(ry)
    py=yoc+yc
    pz=zoc+zc*np.cos(ry)
    plt.scatter(px,py,s=.03 ,color='white')
plt.scatter(xoe+re*sfx,yoe-2,s=6,color='white')
plt.arrow(-20,60,(xoe+re*sfx)+24,(yoe+re/2)-60-2,color='white',
                            linewidth=.5,head_width=2.,head_length=3)
plt.text(-18,60,'Ap',color='white')
plt.show()
```

Facts About the Sun

The Sun's diameter is roughly 1392x10³ kilometers or about 865,000 miles. By comparison, Earth's average diameter is 12,742 km or 7,918 miles, about 109 times smaller. We use the term *average diameter* since the Earth is not a perfect sphere. It is flattened out a bit from the North Pole to the South Pole due to centrifugal force caused by the Earth's rotation about its axis. This makes the equatorial diameter 12,756 km or 7,926 miles while its polar diameter is 12,714 km or 7,898 miles. On a volume basis, the Sun is 1,303,782 times larger than Earth.

The Sun is about 93,000,000 miles from Earth, which is shown in Figure 12-1. At the speed of light, which is about 186,000 miles per second, radiation emitted by the Sun takes about 500 seconds or 8 minutes to reach Earth.

The Sun is a star, but it is not the largest star out there. Red giants have diameters 10 to 40 times that of our Sun. There are stars that are one-tenth its size. If the Sun was hollow, we could to fit 64,000,000 of our Moons inside it.

Our Sun, as well as other stars, is composed mostly of hydrogen. There is a lot of hydrogen in our Sun: 4.4 followed by 30 zeros pounds of it. Hydrogen is the lightest element in the periodic table and is the most abundant chemical substance in the

Universe. Most active stars, such as our Sun, are composed primarily of hydrogen in the plasma state. Plasma, one of the most common forms of matter in the universe, is a strange electrically neutral medium of unbound positively and negatively charged particles swirling around in a soupy stew.

At the Sun's center is a plasma core. This is a result of the tremendous pressure exerted by the gravitational attraction of the surrounding hydrogen, which pulls the mass inward toward the center. Every second, deep inside the core where temperatures are about 15 million degrees Kelvin and higher, and pressures are a million times greater than on the surface of the Earth, 600 million tons of this plasma are being converted into helium through a multi-step proton-proton fusion chain reaction, which produces helium plus a tremendous amount of heat and energy. The core extends out from the center to about 25% of the Sun's radius. At the surface, temperatures are about 5800°K.

The tremendous heat within the core causes the particles to emit photons. Each photon travels a short distance, about one micrometer, before it is absorbed by another molecule. This creates an increase in the energy of that molecule, which stimulates the release of another photon, and so on. When a photon migrates about 20% of the way to the Sun's surface, it is transported the rest of the way mostly by convection. It takes about 100,000 years of emissions and absorptions for the original photon to migrate to the surface where it escapes and is finally radiated off into space.

The Sun's radiation is not constant. Solar flares can occur, which eject clouds of electrons, ions, and atoms into space. The energy released in a burst is of the order of 160,000,000,000 megatons of TNT. These clouds can reach Earth one or two days later, disrupting radio and tv transmissions and, some believe, contributing to global warming and climate change.

Photons and the Sun

The Sun, like all radiating bodies, emits electromagnetic energy in the form of photons. We know that photons are emitted at different frequencies or, equivalently, wavelengths—a wavelength being inversely proportional to frequency, as in

$$\lambda = \frac{S_m}{v} \tag{12-1}$$

where λ is the wavelength, s_m is the speed of light within the medium, and v is the frequency of a wave traveling in that medium. Since we are concerned primarily with light traveling through empty space (i.e., from the Sun to Earth), $s_m=c$ where c is the speed of light in empty space, Equation 12-1 thus becomes

$$\lambda = \frac{c}{v} \qquad\qquad (12\text{-}2)$$

A function such as solar power, when represented over a range of frequencies or wavelengths, is called a *spectrum*. In the case of electromagnetic radiation, we are mostly concerned with the power of light at different frequencies, or equivalently, wavelengths. This is called a *power spectrum*. An example is the curve shown in Figure 12-2 where the *power spectral density*, often called simply the *power spectrum*, $S(\lambda)$, is plotted vs. wavelength λ. This curve originated from Equation 12-3.

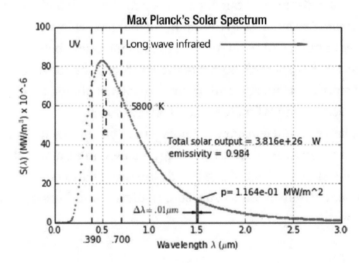

Figure 12-2. *Max Planck's Solar Spectrum produced by Listing 12-3's Program PLANCK'SSOLARSPECTRUM*

Most of the frequencies emitted by the Sun, which range from high frequency, short wavelength ultraviolet (UV) to low frequency, long wavelength infrared, are invisible to our human eyes. We are able to see only a small range of the spectrum which, fortunately for us, lies near the peak of the Sun's emitted power spectrum. This must have pleased our hunter-gatherer ancestors since it enabled them to hunt and gather earlier and later in the day. While we can thank the shape of the Sun's power spectrum for this, it is also a characteristic of our eyes' biology which, if we believe Charles Darwin, likely evolved through natural selection to be optimized at the frequencies near the Sun's maximum power output. Our eyes have also evolved to see the different frequencies as colors. The only animal that cannot see colors is a fish called a skate, a flat fish that lives on the bottom of oceans. This is because it has no cones in its eyes.

Max Planck's Black Body Radiation

As you have seen, light is photons. But what is a photon? We know that photons are quantized forms of electromagnetic energy. But in the late 19th century, that was still a mystery. There were many attempts to explain the light spectrum that was emitted from heated materials. For example, when we heat up an iron poker, at first we don't see any change in color but then, after a certain temperature is reached, we visually observe it glowing through a progression of colors: dull red, brighter red, orange, yellow, white, blue, and then violet. These colors correspond to different frequencies of the electromagnetic radiation emitted by the object. Early attempts to explain this phenomenon were based on the classical theory at that time called Maxwell's Equations. They describe an electromagnetic field where the electromagnetic energy is assumed to be a smooth continuum. Despite many attempts, this approach failed to explain what was being observed.

Many scientists at the time struggled with this problem. Then in 1900, Max Planck, a German physicist, sent a postcard to a colleague. On the back he had written an equation that accurately described the spectrum. Plank's breakthrough was to assume, contrary to the prevailing theories at the time, that the electromagnetic field was not a continuum of energy. Rather, he guessed that electromagnetic energy exists in discrete packets and not as a continuous field, as was assumed by Maxwell's equations. This led to his breakthrough formulation, shown in Equation 12-3. He presented his idea to the German Physical Society on December 14, 1900, a date that has become known as the birth of quantum mechanics. His equation is known as the *blackbody radiation formula*. You will see more of it later.

In 1901, Planck published his results in an article in *Annalen der Physik* in which he hypothesized that electromagnetic energy could only be released by a source, such as the Sun, or by a hot iron poker, in the form of discrete packets of energy rather than as continuous waves. Since it was known that light exhibits wave characteristics, in 1905 Albert Einstein extended this idea by suggesting Planck's discrete "packets" could only exist as discrete "*wave*-packets." He called such a packet a *Lichtquant* or "light quantum."

Later, in 1928, Arthur Compton used the term "photon" which derives from *Phos*, the Greek word for light. Phos was also the Greek god of Venus, which is the brightest planet in the early morning sky before the Sun rises to dim it. General Custer's Native American scouts called him *"The Son of the Morning Star,"* probably because of his predilection for attacking at sunrise while Venus was still visible in the early morning sky.

Planck also assumed that the source of the wave packets are thermally excited charges, each emitting a packet of electromagnetic energy, a photon, at a particular frequency. The more charges emitting photons at the same frequency, the greater the power of the emitted light at that frequency. He further theorized that the energy of a wave packet could only occur at specific fixed energy levels or states.

Where do photons come from? An atom has a nucleus, which is surrounded by electrons. The electrons exist in discrete energy states. When an electron drops to a state having lower energy, for whatever reason, the atom emits a photon. Because of the law of conservation of energy, the energy lost to the atom by the change of state of the electron is manifested by the emission of the energy of the photon.

Returning to 1900, the equation Planck wrote on the back of a postcard, which predicts the power spectrum of light $S(\lambda)$ emitted by a black body, is

$$S(\lambda) = \frac{2\pi c^2 h}{\lambda^5} \frac{\varepsilon}{e^{\frac{hc}{\lambda kT}} - 1} \quad J/s/m^3 = W/m^3 \tag{12-3}$$

where c is the speed of light (m/s), h is Planck's Constant (J·s), λ is the wavelength (m), k is Boltzman's Constant (J/K), T is the temperature (K), and ε is the emissivity of the radiating body's surface. ε is essentially a measure of the effectiveness of a surface's radiating ability. It can range from 0 to 1. As you might imagine, there was a lot of thought behind the development of this equation.

Over the past 100+ years, this relation has withstood the test of time and gives very accurate results. Displayed in Figure 12-2, it is often referred to as *Planck's black body radiation formula*. It applies equally well to all radiating bodies as well as the Sun. Even though the Sun certainly does not *look* like a black body, as far as its radiation characteristics are concerned it behaves like one—a very hot one. As an analogy, you might think of the Sun as being a very hot (about 5800 °K) black stove glowing very brightly.

Figure 12-2 shows the solar output spectrum (red curve) of the Sun as predicted by Equation 12-3. This is called a power spectral density, or simply a power spectrum. Each point on the curve gives the power density $S(\lambda)$ at a corresponding wavelength λ. The green band shown in Figure 12-2 will be explained later.

The Sun's Total Power Output

The quantity $S(\lambda)$ displayed in Figure 12-2 is a *power density*. What is a *power density* and how does it differ from a simple power? Notice in Equation 12-3 that the units of $S(\lambda)$ are power per cubic volume. These are the units of a density. You might think of this "density" as analogous to mass density, which has units of mass per cubic volume. In the case of $S(\lambda)$ you are dealing with a power density $J/s/m^3 = W/m^3$.

The feature of Equation 12-3 that makes the power spectrum resemble the Sun's output, and not that of any other black body, is the temperature T. For the Sun, T is approximately 5800 °K. To get the power emitted by the Sun, $P(\lambda)$, over a bandwidth λ_1 to λ_2, it is necessary to sum $S(\lambda)$ across that band. In calculus, this amounts to taking the integral of S vs. λ, which is equivalent to finding the area under the $S(\lambda)$ curve between these limits.

$$P_{\lambda_1 \to \lambda_2} = \int_{\lambda_1}^{\lambda_2} S(\lambda)\,d\lambda \quad J/s/m^2 = W/m^2 \tag{12-4}$$

With Equation 12-3 this becomes

$$P_{\lambda_1 \to \lambda_2} = 2\pi c^2 h \int_{\lambda_1}^{\lambda_2} \frac{\lambda^{-5}\varepsilon}{e^{\frac{hc}{\lambda kT}} - 1}\,d\lambda \quad J/s/m^2 = W/m^2 \tag{12-5}$$

Equation 12-5 gives the power emitted by the Sun over the bandwidth λ_1 to λ_2. It equals the integral of $S(\lambda)$ times the infinitesimally small bandwidth $d\lambda$ across that range. In other words, if you pick a point along the $S(\lambda)$ curve, as shown in Figure 12-3, and multiply it by $d\lambda$ and then sum (integrate) all those values from λ_1 to λ_2, you get the total electromagnetic power emitted by the wavelengths in the waveband λ_1 to λ_2. This is the area under the $S(\lambda)$ curve from λ_1 to λ_2.

To get the power generated by the entire solar spectrum, you integrate
Equation 12-5 from wavelengths beginning at $\lambda=0$ and extending to $\lambda=\infty$. For those who
prefer to integrate Equation 12-5 mathematically, I show how to do so in Appendix B:
Planck's Radiation Law and the Stefan-Boltzmann Equation. The Stefan-Boltzmann
Equation is a closed-form solution to the integration of Planck's Equation (12-3) from
zero to infinity. Integration is simply finding the area under the $S(\lambda)$ curve.

To carry out the integration numerically, replace the infinitesimally small wave band
$d\lambda$ with a small band of finite width $\Delta\lambda$ and replace the integral with a summation, as in

$$P(\lambda)=2\pi c^2 h \sum_{i=1}^{i=N} \frac{1}{\lambda_i^5} \frac{\varepsilon}{e^{\frac{hc}{\lambda_i kT}}-1} \Delta\lambda \quad J/s/m^2 = W/m^2 \qquad (12\text{-}6)$$

where i refers to the ith band centered at λ_i and N is the number of bands of width $\Delta\lambda$
between λ_i and λ_N. A typical band of width $\Delta\lambda$ is illustrated in Figure 12-3. The width of
the band shown is exaggerated for illustrative purposes. In reality, it should appear much
narrower.

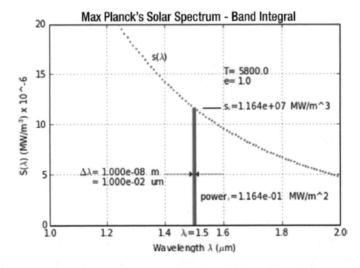

Figure 12-3. *Numerical integration of power $S(\lambda)d\lambda$ emitted by spectrum band$_i$
across a .01 μm bandwidth at $\lambda_i=1.5$ (produced by Listing 12-2)*

Equation 12-6 is an approximation to Equation 12-5 because it assumes the value
of $S(\lambda)$ is constant across the width of each band $\Delta\lambda$. However, if $\Delta\lambda$ is chosen small
enough, the curve $S(\lambda_i - \Delta\lambda/2) \rightarrow S(\lambda_i + \Delta\lambda/2)$ can be approximated by the constant
value $S(\lambda_i)$ across the bandwidth $\Delta\lambda$, in which case the results can be quite accurate. With

this simple integration scheme, the power in the band equals the band's rectangular area. While there are more sophisticated integration schemes you could use, this one is simple, easy to program, and adequate for our purposes.

Let's calculate the power P(λ) emitted by the wavelengths across the small band $\Delta\lambda$. Figure 12-3 shows an enlargement of the band shown in Figure 12-2 centered at λ=1.5 um. This might be considered a typical band in Equation 12-4. Listing 12-2 evaluates the power generated by the wavelengths across this bandwidth. The curve S(λ) has been generated according to Equation 12-3. According to this simplified integration scheme, the power generated by this band, which is just its rectangular area, is given by

$$P(\lambda) = S(\lambda)\Delta\lambda \quad J/s/m^2 = W/m^2 \tag{12-7}$$

In Listing 12-2, which plots Figure 12-3, the area of the band is calculated according to Equation 12-7. The magnitude of $\Delta\lambda$ is arbitrary. In the program, it is the parameter dla, which is set to .01x10^{-6} meters or .01 μm. Whether $\Delta\lambda$ is large or small, the power it emits will be the power radiated by the wavelengths across that bandwidth. Wider bandwidths will generate proportionally more power, narrower ones less. Later, when you do a numerical integration of the area under the entire S(λ) curve to get the total power radiated by the Sun across its entire spectrum, choosing a small value of $\Delta\lambda$ will lead to more accurate results.

In Figure 12-3, the band is shown centered at λ=1.5 um. The corresponding value of S, as calculated by the program, is 1.164x10^7 MW/m^3. With a bandwidth of .01 μm, which equals 1.0x10^{-8} meters, the power generated by this band is (1.164x10^7)x(1x10^{-8})=.1164 MW/m^2, about what a small power plant produces.

Note that the units of S(λ) will be consistent with those of the input parameters: speed of light, Planck's Constant, Boltzman's Constant, and wavelength λ. The units of these parameters should be consistent with one another. To avoid confusion, in this work you will keep all of these quantities in the spatial dimension of meters when evaluating Equation 12-3. S(λ) will then have the units (J/s)/m^3, which is the same as W/m^3. If the output is needed in another power dimension, such as kW or MW, the conversion can be done after S(λ) has been evaluated by multiplying S(λ) in watts by 10^{-3} to get kilowatts or 10^{-6} to get megawatts. When calculating power emitted across a waveband, the width of that band $\Delta\lambda$ should also be in meters. For example, 1.5μm should be specified as 1.5x10^{-6}m. Conversion from meters back to micrometers μm for display or other purposes later can be done by multiplying λ meters by 10^{+6}. This is shown in Listing 12-2 in the section plot s curve in line lag=la*10**6.

In Figure 12-3, S_i is shown with a value of 1.164×10^7 MW/m³. The S(λ) axis indicates a value of 11.64 MW/m³x10⁻⁶, which indicates that the value of 11.64 has been multiplied by 10⁻⁶ for display purposes. This would make its actual value $11.64 \times 10^{+6}$, which equals the value calculated by the program. This is displayed on the plot as $1.164 \times 10^{+7}$ MW/m³.

In Listing 12-2, which created Figure 12-3, the section plot S curve solves Equation 12-3 for values of wavelength la, which go from la=lamin to lamax in increments dla. The comments within the code trace the evolution of the units of S. As given by Equation 12-3, when the parameters are as indicated in section **establish parameters**, the units of S start off as Joules/second per cubic meter (remember S(λ) is a density). Since one Joule per second defines the watt, the units are watts per cubic meter. These are converted to megawatts per cubic meter and then scaled to be plotted against the vertical axis in the units (MW/m³)x10⁻⁶ as the variable sg. The 10⁻⁶ factor indicates the actual values have been multiplied by that amount. Next, the green band is plotted and the values of temperature and emissivity are displayed.

The value of S(λ) at λ=1.5 is calculated using Equation 12-3, converted to MW/m³, and then multiplied by the bandwidth dl=.01x10⁻⁶ to get pl MW/m², the power within that bandwidth. The remainder of the program displays the data and cleans up the plot.

Listing 12-2. Program BANDINTEGRAL

```
"""

BANDINTEGRAL
"""

import numpy as np
import matplotlib.pyplot as plt
#----------------------------------------------------- set up axes
ymax=20
plt.axis([1.,2.,0,ymax])
plt.xlabel('Wavelength $\lambda$ ($\mu$m)')
plt.ylabel('S($\lambda$) (MW/m$^{3}$) x 10$^{-6}$')
plt.grid(True)
plt.title('Max Planck's Solar Spectrum - Band Integral')
#----------------------------------------------- establish parameters
c=2.9979*(10.**8)              # speed of light in a vacuum m/s
h=6.63*(10.**-34)              # Planck's Constant J.s
kb=1.38*(10**-23)              # Boltzmann's Constant J/K
```

```python
t=5800.                          # temperature K
e=1.0                            # emissivity
lamin=.01*10**-6                 # starting wavelength m
lamax=2.*10**-6                  # ending wavelength m
dla=.01*10**-6                   # incremental wavelength m
#——————————————————————————————— plot s curve
for la in np.arange(lamin,lamax,dla):
    a1=2.*np.pi*c*c*h/(la**5.)
    a2=h*c/(la*kb*t)
    sl=e*a1/(np.exp(a2)-1.)                  # J/s/m^3 = W/m^3
    sl=sl*10**-6                             # MW/m^3
    slg=sl*10**-6                            # scale plot at 10^-6 scale
    lag=la*10**6                             # scale to plot at 10^6 scale
    plt.scatter(lag,slg,s=1,color='r')
#———————————————————————————-——— plot band
plt.plot([1.495,1.495],[0.,11.64],color='g')
plt.plot([1.4975,1.4975],[0.,11.64],color='g')
plt.plot([1.5,1.5],[0,11.64],color='g')
plt.plot([1.5025,1.5025],[0.,11.64],color='g')
plt.plot([1.5005,1.505],[0.,11.64],color='g')
#——————————————————————————————— plot temperature and emissivity
d=str(t)
plt.text(1.6,15,'T=')
plt.text(1.65,15,d)
plt.text(1.6,14,'e=')
d=str(e)
plt.text(1.65,14,d)
#——————————————————— calculate s and band power pl at lambda=1.5
la=1.5*10**-6
a1=2.*np.pi*c*c*h/(la**5.)
a2=h*c/(la*kb*t)
sl=e*a1/(np.exp(a2)-1.)   # J/s/m^3 = W/m^3
sl=sl*10**-6             # MW/m^3
dl=.01*10**-6            # bandwidth m
pl=sl*dl
```

```
#————————————————————————— plot results and labels
plt.plot([1.53,1.59],[11.6,11.6],'k')
plt.text(1.6,11.5,'si=')
d='%7.3e'%(sl)
plt.text(1.65,11.5,d)
plt.text(1.83,11.5,'MW/m^3')
plt.arrow(1.4,5,.085,0,head_width=.5,head_length=.01,linewidth=.2)
plt.arrow(1.6,5,-.085,0,head_width=.5,head_length=.01,linewidth=.2)
plt.text(1.15,5,'$\Delta \lambda$=')
dle='%7.3e'% (dl)
dls=str(dle)
plt.text(1.18,5,dls)
plt.text(1.35,5,'m')')
plt.text(1.145,4,'=')
dl=dl*10**6
dle='%7.3e'%(dl)
dls=str(dle)
plt.text(1.18,4,dls)
plt.text(1.35,4,'um')
plt.text(1.35,16.5,'s($\lambda$)')
plt.text(1.52,2.5,'power$_{i}$=')
pl='%7.3e'%(pl)
pl=str(pl)
plt.text(1.65,2.5,pl)
plt.text(1.823,2.5,'MW/m^2')
plt.text(1.45,-1.1,'$\lambda_{i}$=1.5')
plt.show()
```

Next, let's look at Max Planck's entire black body spectrum as shown in Figure 12-2. It's titled "Max Planck's *Solar* **Spectrum**" since the temperature used is that of the Sun, approximately 5800° K.

The program that produced this plot, Listing 12-3, follows the logic in the preceding program, Listing 12-2, but here you sum the individual band powers from $\lambda=.01 \times 10^{-6}$ to $10. \times 10^{-6}$ meters (.01μm to 10.μm) (1000 bands) to get the area under the entire (almost) $S(\lambda)$ curve. The band you looked at in Listing 12-2 is shown at $\lambda=1.5$ um.

The process used here is to simply advance along wavelengths, calculate the value of S(λ) at each wavelength, multiply it by $\Delta\lambda$ to get the power within that band, and then sum the power generated by each band in accordance with Equation 12-6. This will give you the total power emitted by all wavelengths.

You extend the range of integration to 10×10^{-6} meters in order to get a more accurate measure of the total power under the S(λ) curve. This will be the approximate total spectral power emitted by each square meter of the Sun's surface. Then you multiply that by the Sun's spherical surface area to get the total power emitted by the Sun, which is known as the *solar luminosity*. In Figure 12-3, it is called the *total solar output*. As shown on the plot, its value as calculated by the program is 3.816×10^{26} watts. This is in close agreement with published values. An Internet search finds values ranging from 3.83×10^{26} to 3.85×10^{26} watts. Your value of 3.81 is 1% less than the 3.83 value. Presumably, this is because you truncated your numerical integration without going closer to infinity with the wavelength. The further out you go, the larger your number will be.

Many researchers use e=1.0 for emissivity, which is an idealization that assumes the Sun is a perfect radiator (you can assume it isn't). Here you use an emissivity of e=.984. When you use Planck's spectrum to calculate the solar constant, which has been measured by satellite, you must either reduce the temperature of the Sun in your calculations or lower its emissivity to less than 1.0 in order to get the results to agree with the measured values. If you choose to stay with a Sun temperature of 5800°K, then you must lower the emissivity to .984 in order to obtain agreement. Another option, as you will see, is to keep e=1.0 and lower the Sun's temperature to 5777° K.

Listing 12-3. Program PLANCKSSOLARSPECTRUM

```
"""

PLANCKSSOLARSPECTRUM
"""

import numpy as np
import matplotlib.pyplot as plt
#————————————————————————————— set up axes
ymax=100
plt.axis([0,3,0,ymax])
plt.xlabel('Wavelength _ (_m)')
plt.ylabel('S(λ) (MW/m^{3}) x 10^-6')
plt.grid(True)
```

```
plt.title('Max Planck's Solar Spectrum')
#------------------------------------------- establish parameters
c=2.9979*(10.**8)              # speed of light in a vacuum m/s
h=6.63*(10.**-34)              # Planck's Constant J.s
kb=1.38*(10**-23)              # Boltzmann's Constant J/K
e=.984                         # emissivity
t=5800.                        # K
lamin=.01*10**-6               # m
lamax=10.*10**-6               # m
dla=.01*10**-6                 # m
st=0.                          # set area under s curve to zero
#------------------------------------------- plot s curve and calculate area
for la in np.arange(lamin,lamax,dla):
    a1=2.*np.pi*c*c*h/(la**5.)
    a2=h*c/(la*kb*t)
    sl=e*a1/(np.exp(a2)-1.)                  # W/m^3
    sl=sl*10**-6                             # MW/m^3
    bandarea=sl*dls                          # band area MW/m^2
    st=st+bandarea                           # sum band areas MW/m^2
    slg=sl*10**-6                            # scale to plot
    lag=la*10**6                             # scale to plot
    plt.scatter(lag,slg,s=1,color='r')
#------------------------------------------- multiply the Sun's surface area
ds=1.39*10**9              # Sun's diameter m
spas=np.pi*ds**2.         # Sun's spherical area m^2
to=spas*st                # Sun's total output MW
to=to*10**6               # Sun's total output W
#------------------------------------------------- plot results
plt.text(.8,58.,'5800')
plt.text(1.05,58, '°K')
plt.plot([.39,.39],[-0.,100.],'b-')
plt.plot([.7,.7],[-0.,100.],'b-')
plt.text(.3,-10,'.390')
plt.text(.6,-10,'.700')
plt.text(.15,90.,'UV')
plt.text(.8,90.,'long wave infrared')
```

```python
plt.arrow(1.75,91.,.8,0.,head_width=1.,head_length=.1,color='r')
plt.text(1.2,40.,'total solar output =')
so='dd=str(so)
plt.text(2.1,40,dd)
plt.text(2.7,40,'W')
plt.text(1.2,34,'emissivity =')
e=str(e)
plt.text(1.8,34,e)
plt.text(.5,75.,'v')
plt.text(.53,70.,'i')
plt.text(.5,65.,'s')
plt.text(.53,60.,'i')
plt.text(.5,55.,'b')
plt.text(.53,50.,'l')
plt.text(.5,45.,'e')
plt.plot([1.49,1.49],[0.,11.61],color='g')
plt.plot([1.5,1.5],[0.,11.61],color='g')
plt.plot([1.51,1.51],[0.,11.61],color='g')
#——————————— calculate s at la=1.5x10^-6 m and band power pband
laband=1.5*10**-6
a1=2.*np.pi*c*c*h/(laband**5.)
a2=h*c/(laband*kb*t)
sband=a1/(np.exp(a2)-1.)
sband=sband*10**-12
pband=sband*dla # MW/sq meter
pband=pband*10**6 # W/sq meter
#—————————————————————— plot band
plt.plot([1.55,1.7],[12.5,15.],color='k')
plt.text(1.72,14.,' p=')
pband='pband=str(pband)
plt.text(1.9,14,pband)
plt.text(2.4,14,'MW/m^2')
plt.arrow(1.35,5,.1,0,head_width=1, head_length=.05, ec='k', fc='k')
plt.arrow(1.65,5,-.1,0,head_width=1, head_length=.05, ec='k', fc='k')
plt.text(.82,4.9,' $\Delta\lambda$ = :01$\mu m$' )
plt.show()
```

Earth's Irradiance

Figure 12-4 shows the spectrum of solar radiation that reaches Earth. Figure 12-1 shows the Earth orbiting the Sun. This is the model used to calculate the amount of the Sun's total power output that is intercepted by Earth, the *solar constant*. The distance between the two orbs is an average of 1 AU, about 93,000,000 miles. It varies during an orbit. The circular disk labeled A_p has an area equal to the Earth's cross-section. The solar power intercepted by A_p is what irradiates the Earth and is responsible for heating the Earth.

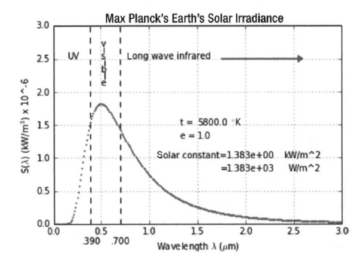

Figure 12-4. *Spectrum of solar power reaching Earth, the Earth's solar irradiance, produced by Listing 12-3, which has been modified by inclusion of the inverse square law shown in Equation 12-10*

Notice how much lower the values are than in Figure 12-2. This is because the power *intensity* of the Sun's output that reaches Earth and is intercepted by A_p diminishes over the distance from Sun to Earth according to the inverse square law of

$$P_p = P_s \left(\frac{r_s}{r_{es}} \right)^2 \tag{12-8}$$

where p_s is the intensity of power at the Sun's surface, p_p is the *intensity* intercepted by A_p, r_s is the radius of the Sun, and r_{es} is the distance from the Sun to the Earth. The total power intercepted by A_p is thus

$$P_p = A_p P_p \tag{12-9}$$

$$P_p = A_p P_s \left(\frac{r_s}{r_{es}} \right)^2 \tag{12-10}$$

When Equations (12-8) through (12-10) are included in Listing 12-3's Program PLANCKSSOLARSPECTRUM, the spectrum reduces to Figure 12-4. Again, notice how much lower the values are than in Figure 12-2 as a result of the inverse square law.

P_p, which is the solar power reaching the top of the Earth's atmosphere, is called the *solar constant*. It is not really a constant, though, because the orbit of the Earth around the Sun is elliptical, not circular, so the Earth-to-Sun distance is not constant. Everything is averaged to arrive at a number for the solar constant. Its value as measured by satellite is about **1361 W/m²**. This is equivalent to about 13 100W light bulbs per square meter. Note that this is at satellite altitude, well above Earth's atmospheric effects. About 30% of this is reflected off the Earth's surface and atmosphere by albedo effects such as snow, ice, clouds, and water. A lot simply reflects off, especially near Earth's poles. The remainder is absorbed by the Earth. But much of that is reradiated back into space, allowing the planet to reach a thermal equilibrium (like the Sun, the Earth is also a hot (warm) body and exhibits its own thermal radiation out into space). But some of what should be reradiated back into space is blocked by greenhouse gasses including CO_2, methane, and water vapor. That has always been the case. If it was not, the Earth would be a very cold place. It is the greenhouse gasses that keep the Earth at a livable temperature. The problem is, these gasses have been increasing in recent years, producing an increase in Earth's global temperature. All this is, as we know, being actively investigated by climate researchers.

Summary

In this chapter, you learned about the Sun, the physics of energy production within the Sun, photons, solar radiation, Max Planck's black body radiation equation, numerical integration, and Python's ability to construct technical illustrations. Of special note are the techniques used to scale variables for plotting. You also learned about the Sun's irradiation of Earth and its impact on the warming of our planet. You learned how to build images such as Figures 12-1 and 12-2.

CHAPTER 13

Climate Change

This topic brings to mind a line from William Shakespeare's *Julius Caesar,*

"The fault, dear Brutus, is not in the stars, but in ourselves"

As you saw in Chapter 12, the Earth is continually being irradiated and warmed by the Sun. This is, of course, a good thing. Without a sustained influx of solar radiation, which provides the heat energy necessary to maintain our planet at a livable temperature, our Earth would quickly cool down to an unlivable temperature. Life on this planet would cease. We would become just another cold rock drifting through space. So when we talk about excessive "global warming" we should remember it isn't totally the Sun's fault; it's the changes in our atmosphere, which are presumably man-made, that are causing too much of the Sun's energy to become trapped by greenhouse gasses. This, in turn, is leading to increases in global temperatures, changes in our climate, rising sea levels, and other undesirable effects. Our goal is to understand this phenomenon and what is causing it.

First, we must recognize that there are many people who dispute the idea that global warming is being caused by human activity, whether it is the result of solar activity, or whether it is in fact warming all. Even if it is warming, some say, not to worry, the climate has changed drastically many times in the past. So let's examine some historic evidence and some contemporary facts and see where they take us.

First, let's discuss global cooling. The Earth has cooled in the past, which is indisputable. Nobody disputes the "Little Ice Age" that occurred during the Middle Ages when temperatures dropped by as much as two degrees Celsius, or 3.6 degrees Fahrenheit. This occurred during the Middle Ages, extending to as late as the 1800s. It was responsible for trapping the Vikings in Greenland and Iceland where many perished from the effects of the cold. There is plenty of other scientific and anecdotal evidence that shows the Earth has experienced periods of cooling before. But most of these periods have been relatively short-term, on the order of years rather than decades. They were caused largely by aerosols that were injected into the atmosphere by volcanic activity and forest fires. Aerosols are small particles of contaminants and ash that reflect incoming solar radiation back out into space, like many tiny mirrors. The result is a lowering of temperatures.

On the other hand, there is certainly plenty of evidence that the Earth has warmed in the past and is likely still warming. Much of this is anthropogenic, the result of human activity, mostly the burning of massive amounts of carbon-based fuels.

Where does the energy in carbonaceous fuels come from, the energy sources that we have been so eagerly mining and drilling? Imagine this planet 500 million years ago, when the first plant life began to grow, probably in the form of pond scum. Animal life is thought to have begun about the same time. Imagine the Sun is shining in the sky and its photons are irradiating the leaves of the plants and the pond scum in the water and other organic life forms. Focusing on a leaf as a typical form of vegetation, during the day, the Sun's photons strike the leaf, pumping up the energy of the organic molecules that comprise it. At night, after the Sun has set, the leaf is still warm, maybe even hot; but gradually the energy in its molecules dissipates and so it cools. In the morning it returns almost to the state it had the previous morning. But it retains some of the solar energy it acquired the day before, mostly in chemical form. This cycle is repeated, day after day, year after year. The energy of the organic molecules continues to increase. After the leaf dies, its remains contain the solar energy accumulated over its lifetime. Now multiply this cycle for decades, centuries, tens of thousands of years until the residue of that leaf, and an uncountable number of leaves like it, is covered by silt, mud, lava, or whatever material forms our Earth's outer layers, compressing our leaves and other energetic plant life under hundreds and thousands of feet of mud, dirt, rocks, and sedimentary materials at high temperature and pressure, until they turn into oil, combustible gasses, and coal, which we drill and mine and burn. Basically, we are drilling, mining, and burning off, in just a few centuries, hundreds of thousands of years of solar energy. Much of the byproducts of that burning-CO_2, methane, and other greenhouse gasses-have been accumulating in our planet's atmosphere since the Industrial Revolution began around 1740.

It's difficult to believe that pumping huge amounts of carbonaceous materials into the atmosphere over all the years since 1740 isn't having some effect on our planet's temperature. You might think that's ok, we have cooling from volcanic eruptions and forest fire aerosols and warming from greenhouse gases, so what's the problem? Don't they tend to balance out? No, they do not. The problem is aerosols return to Earth after only a few years of floating in the atmosphere while greenhouse gases stay aloft and persist for decades. Also, a volcanic eruption, or a major forest fire, is usually a one-time short-term event whereas emissions of greenhouse gases (GHGs) are continual and they build up in the atmosphere causing ever-increasing levels of GHGs with increasing levels of global warming. They can stay in the atmosphere for many decades.

An important factor in this discussion is the Earth's *albedo*. The etymology of the word is that it comes from the Late Latin C. 19th century word "*albus,*" which means "whiteness." In the context of climate studies, it refers to the Earth's ability to reflect solar irradiation back into space. It is a cooling factor.

Climate Cooling

Let's review some factors that cause climate cooling. The Sun's energy, in the form of photons, travels across the 93 million miles that separate Earth from the Sun. It reaches the outer extremities of our atmosphere. Some of that energy bounces off various features of the atmosphere, especially clouds. The remainder reaches the Earth's surface. Some of that is absorbed, largely by the oceans, while some is reflected back into space by albedo effects. The total percentage reflected is about 30 percent of the energy that reaches the outer atmosphere. If the albedo was greater, more would be reflected away into space; this would lead to a cooling effect.

Albedo

Albedo refers to the "whiteness" or reflecting ability of various features on Earth. Table 13-1 lists some typical sources and values of albedo. It should be noted that features affecting the albedo at the north and south polar extremities (snow, ice, sea surface) have less effect on the planetary albedo since the incoming solar radiation impacts these regions at a shallower angle; the energy mostly glances off. Changes in surface albedos in these regions, such as the melting of ice, have less effect on the planetary albedo for the same reason. While some of the values in Table 13-1 appear to be large, their effect on the planetary albedo may be relatively small because they cover less surface area or they are near the poles. To calculate the planetary albedo from these figures, we need to know the surface area covered by each of these features and the angle of incidence of the Sun's rays. Any significant increase in the albedo of any of these features could lead to climate cooling, especially if it occurred in regions near the equator. On the other hand, a decrease could lead to warming.

Table 13-1. *Albedo of various surface features*

Feature	Albedo %
Fresh snow	42-83
Ice	32-38
Sand	21-43
Water	6-8
Soil	7-34
Forest	5-14
Desert	27-29
Clouds	36-78
Vegetation	11-24

Sunspots

Sunspots are another possible source of climate change. They are dark regions on the Sun's surface that appear and disappear in cycles averaging about 11 years in duration. The number of sunspots that appear correlates with periods of heightened solar activity and solar flares. At low points in the 11-year cycle about six sunspots will typically appear, sometimes none. At high points, a large number may appear. The question is, do sunspots themselves affect the Earth's climate or are they harbingers of some other solar activity that does?

For hundreds of years, even up to this time, people have tried to establish a correlation between sunspot activity and such things as the movement of stock and commodity prices. It would seem logical to conclude that large, dark sunspots should decrease the amount of radiation leaving the Sun, akin to painting a dark spot on the side of a light bulb. It would seem this would partially block some radiation and would correlate with cold periods of the Earth's climate. For the investment-minded, this should correlate with low crop yields and higher commodity prices. Conversely, if this hypothesis is correct, one would think a lack of sunspots would allow more radiation to escape from the Sun, which should correlate with warm periods on Earth. Surprisingly, however, during the 61-year period between 1639 and 1700, no sunspots were reported by observers yet this was during one of the coldest periods in recent history, the Little Ice Age, which lasted roughly from 1300 to 1850. This spell of no sunspot activity was reported by astronomers E.W Maunder and F.G Sporer and is known as The Maunder Minimum.

On the other hand, radiocarbon dating of tree rings, which measures the amount of Carbon 14 (14C), does correlate well with past solar activity. 14C is produced in the Earth's atmosphere by cosmic rays. It is a radioactive isotope of carbon. Its presence in organic materials is the basis of a radiocarbon dating method. This is affected by solar activity. When sunspots are at a maximum, some cosmic rays are blocked, leading to lower levels of 14C. Conversely, during times of low sunspot activity, we would expect to find an increase in the production of atmospheric 14C and its appearance in tree rings. And that is, in fact, the case. During the Medieval Warm Period, from about 1110-1250AD, which preceded the onset of the Little Ice Age by only 50 years, levels of 14C in tree rings fell, implying there was an increase in sunspot and solar activity during that time. Oddly, while the light-blocking black-spot-on-a-light-bulb theory would predict a drop in temperatures, just the opposite happened. During the period from AD 1100 to 1710, the level of 14C found in tree rings varies considerably, reaching a peak in 1690, well within the time span of the 1639-1700 Maunder Minimum, a period of low sunspot activity. According to the light-blocking theory, we would have expected a warming period but again, just the opposite happened: the Little Ice Age.

It may be that sunspots, as harbingers of increased solar activity, do, in fact, indicate a coming change in Earth's climate. But these effects may be delayed by a period of time. For example, cold periods may lead to more sea ice, which then drifts south, cooling local climates, but this takes time. Or warm periods can melt polar ice, the cold water then flowing south, upsetting climates and diverting ocean currents. This also takes time. The impact of these time delays complicates attempts to understand past and present climate changes. These are all topics of active research.

Figure 13-1 shows a new monster sunspot named AR2529, several times larger than Earth. It appeared in the spring of 2016. This photo was taken by the Heliospheric Observatory (SOHO). Could this sunspot predict a new period of increasing solar activity and be the start of a new period of climate change? When you see the size of a sunspot, even a monster like this, it is hard to believe that by itself it could have much impact on our climate.

Figure 13-1. *Sunspot AR2529. It is barely visible but the sunspot is there at about 2:30, halfway from the center. It is difficult to imagine something that small could affect our climate*

So do sunspots affect our climate? While we have seen through historic records of 14C a correlation between the two, we must remember that correlation does not necessarily imply causation. There may be some relationship but it may be dwarfed by other influences, especially in our modern age with measurable global warming being caused by CO_2, water vapor, and methane.

Aerosols

Table 13-1 showed that the Earth's planetary albedo is affected by planetary surface features such as ice, sand, water, and vegetation. It is also affected by aerosols, which are small particles of soot, smoke, dust, and ash in the atmosphere that increase the Earth's reflectivity and hence its albedo. Aerosols act like micro-mirrors that reflect incoming sunlight back into space. Typical sources are the burning of biomass, such as forest fires; windblown dust from dry, arid regions, such as deserts; and industrial pollution primarily from the burning of fossil fuels. The oceans are also a source of atmospheric aerosols in the form of bubbles that rise from the water's surface. As the water evaporates in the atmosphere, small particles of salt are left suspended in the atmosphere. Another very large contribution comes from volcanic eruptions.

The amount of aerosols in the atmosphere varies with location. City air may contain 160,000 particles per cubic meter, mostly soot. Clean air over a landmass may hold 3,000 pcm. Levels in the atmosphere can go as low as 300 pcm. Volcanoes are a major source of aerosols. The massive amounts that are spewed into the air from an erupting volcano can have a very strong effect on climate. They spread more or less uniformly around the globe in a matter of months.

Vivid displays of color caused by atmospheric aerosols can also occur from anthropogenic sources such as pollutants over cities. In the late 1800s, coal was a principal source of heat and energy fueling the Industrial Revolution. Claud Monet was an astute observer of atmospheric effects as can be seen in his 1899 painting *Charing Cross Bridge, The Thames*. His painting of colorful, pea soup fog over London shows the effect of smog particles that were produced by the incomplete combustion of coal.

While producing dramatic local effects, aerosols of this type tend to remain close to their source before being rained out of the atmosphere and returning to the ground and thus do not contribute much to cooling on a global scale. Looking at Monet's sunlight struggling to penetrate the gloom, it's easy to see how aerosols can shield us from solar radiation. Who would have thought coal smog could be beautiful?

When particulate aerosols rise into the troposphere they can act as condensation sites for water vapor. These droplets, when viewed from above, have a whitish hue. These lighter-toned aerosols also increase the albedo but primarily over that local area, which can lead to local cooling. Darker-toned particulates, however, can do the opposite, absorbing solar irradiation and leading to local warming. The interplay between aerosols (their color, altitude in the atmosphere, cloud formation, local albedo changes, local production of water vapor, etc.) is very complex. There is little consensus as to their net effect on climate change on a global basis. The exception to this is the aerosols released from volcanic eruptions since these produce enormous volumes of particles that tend to rise high into the atmosphere where they are carried great distances across the globe by high-altitude winds.

Most aerosols do not remain in the atmosphere for more than a few years. With the exception of volcanic gases and ash, their effect on the climate is mostly local and transient. Volcanic eruptions, on the other hand, may have been responsible for some of the more dramatic cooling periods witnessed in the past. A major eruption can have climate consequences lasting for five years or longer. If several volcanoes erupt one after another, the combined effects can last for decades.

Volcanoes

Volcanic eruptions have injected enormous amounts of aerosols high into the atmosphere in the past and have been major causes of global atmospheric disruption over the history of the planet. For example, a volcanic eruption by Iceland's Laki volcano in 1783 caused the temperatures in the eastern United States to drop 4.8°C, which was below the 225-year average. These extreme temperature drops are believed to have been the result of the large amount of haze-producing SO_2 that was released. The sulfur in the SO_2 combines with water vapor in the stratosphere to form dense clouds of sulfuric acid droplets. These act as micro-mirrors, reflecting solar irradiation back into space. These aerosols can take several years to settle out. In the meanwhile, they decrease the global mean temperature by increasing the Earth's albedo.

In 1815, Mount Tambora on the island of Sumbawa in the Dutch East Indies (present-day Indonesia) erupted in a massive explosion, producing what is believed to be the largest volcanic eruption in the last 10,000 years. There were 92,000 casualties. The eruption earned a rating of 7.0 on the Volcanic Explosivity Index (VEI), which is an open-ended measure of the explosive strength of an eruption. The scale is logarithmic so every incremental jump in value means a 10-fold increase. After the Mount Tambora event, global temperatures decreased by an average of 0.53°C, resulting in widespread crop failures and what is known as "*the year without a summer*" in the eastern U.S. and Europe. The following year, 1816, was the second coldest year on record in New Hampshire since the 1400s.

On June 15, 1991, Mount Pinatubo in the Philippines erupted with a VEI of 6.0. A month later Mount Hudson in southern Chile erupted with a VEI of 5+. Alaska's Mount Spurr next decided to erupt with a VEI of 4.0 followed by Mount Lascar in Chile also with a VEI of 4.0. The aerosol plumes from these eruptions spread around the globe. Over the first half of 1991, the level of stratospheric aerosols rose sharply, producing a global mean temperature drop of almost 1°C.

In 1452-1453, Kuwae in Vanuatu erupted, then Billy Mitchel around 1580, followed by Huaynaputima in 1600. Normally the cooling effect of a volcanic eruption perturbs the global climate for only a few years. But during the 150-year period from 1452 to the early 1600s, the long-term cold spell caused by these eruptions occurring one after another allowed sea ice in the North Atlantic to develop and drift south. This is thought to have maintained cold oceanic and climate conditions long after the volcanic aerosols had become depleted, thus contributing to the cooling at that time.

These events may have been what produced the Little Ice Age, which was a dramatic cooling during the Middle Ages. It was severe enough to have driven the Vikings from Greenland and Iceland. Crop failures caused by the extreme cold combined with sea ice drifting and packing against the coast of Greenland are thought to have been factors in the decline of the Viking population. Ships from Europe couldn't break through the newly formed sea ice to bring supplies and rescue.

A number of theories have been proposed to account for the Little Ice Age including variations in Earth's orbit around the Sun, changes in the Sun's solar activity, changes in ocean current flow, persistence and movement of sea ice, and volcanic activity. It would appear that all these events may have combined and been responsible, to one extent or another, for the dramatic cooling during that time. Nature can be complicated.

Along with cooling, aerosols can produce dramatic visual changes in the appearance of the atmosphere, especially brilliant sunsets. Landscape painters have captured many of these in regions far from the volcanic eruption. The explosive eruption of Krakatoa in 1883, one of the largest volcanic eruptions ever, spewed a massive amount of aerosols into the atmosphere. The event was followed by deep red sunsets throughout Europe and the Western Hemisphere. It is believed to have been the inspiration for Edvard Munch's painting *Der Schrei der Natur* (*The Scream of Nature)*, which was later shortened to *The Scream*.

Munch writes in his diary in 1892,

> *"One evening I was walking along a path, the city was on one side and the fjord below. I was tired and ill. I stopped and looked out over the fjord, the Sun was setting, and the clouds turning blood red. I sensed a scream passing through nature; it seemed to me that I heard a scream. I painted this picture, painted the clouds as actual blood. The color shrieked. This became 'The Scream.'"*

The Krakatoa eruption was so violent that it ruptured the eardrums of sailors aboard ships 40 miles away in the Sunda Strait. It could be heard 3,000 miles away. It released approximately 20 million tons of sulfur into the atmosphere, producing a global winter. Temperatures were lowered by an average of 1.2°C for five years. The energy released is estimated to have been the equivalent of 200 megatons of TNT (Nagasaki was 15 kilotons). The ensuing pressure wave was recorded by gauges around the world. The volcanic ash released was thrust into the atmosphere to an estimated height of 80km (50 miles).

Climate Warming

You have seen evidence of climate cooling, primarily from volcanic aerosols. Now you will see some facts about climate warming.

While atmospheric aerosols, primarily from volcanic eruptions, have been shown to produce atmospheric cooling, unless several eruptions occur back to back, they have generally had a short-term effect, on the order of months or years. On the other hand, the accumulation of greenhouse gases in the atmosphere that cause global warming can persist for decades and possibly centuries. Although there are other greenhouse gases besides CO2, we focus on CO2 because it is the one we have the most control over.

Why do CO_2, methane, and other GHGs store so much energy while other simpler atoms such as hydrogen do not? It's because they are larger, more complex molecules; a passing photon rising from the Earth's surface has a larger target. Also, when a photon hits a molecule such as methane, the more complex structure of the methane molecule has more mechanisms to store the energy, primarily from the various atoms comprising the molecule straining and vibrating against their intramolecular bonds.

An important feature of the rise in global temperatures vs. CO2 correlation is that, unlike the short-term effects of cooling from aerosols, CO2 and global temperature increases are a long-term problem because atmospheric CO2 doesn't go away for decades, possibly centuries. Here are more facts:

- The eight warmest global temperatures recorded have occurred since 2014. The warmest year ever recorded was 2016.

- It is estimated that the temperature of the layer of atmosphere closest to the Earth's surface, the bottom of the troposphere, rose almost .3°C from 1960 to the late 1980s. This is startling when one compares it to a total global warming of 5°C since the last ice age.

- A climatologist at NOAA said, "Either my data set is full of holes or something drastic is going on, It's so dramatic, it's unbelievably warm."

- The level of CO2 in the atmosphere is only about 421 pp or .0004%. But it is generally recognized that GHG has caught the most attention. We continue to produce it in immense quantities. Other GHGs such as oxides of nitrogen, methane, ozone, and CFC also contribute but for now, CO2 is getting most of the attention.

- In May of 2016, India recorded it highest temperature ever, 124°F.

- During the summer of 2016, a phenomenon occurred in the Midwest part of the United States called a *heat dome*. Many believe this can be attributed to *corn sweat*. What is corn sweat? Plants, like corn, absorb groundwater through their roots. This is pulled up through the plant by capillary action where it contributes to the plant's growth. Much of that water escapes from the plant's leaves and goes into the atmosphere through a process called *transpiration*. This adds to the local atmospheric water vapor, which is a strong GHG, along with evaporation from lakes and rivers, and other water surfaces. These processes, taken together, are called *evapotranspiration*. As an illustration of the magnitude of this effect, one acre of corn plants, which are ubiquitous in the Midwest, can sweat off 3,000 to 4,000 gallons of water each day. This adds to humidity levels, increasing the dew point by as much as 5 to 10 degrees F. This increases the misery level for people living in the area during hot summer months. The corn sweat causes a form of local heat-trapping called a heat dome.

Measuring Climate Data

There is an army of people around the world gathering data to study climate change. Just to mention a few in the United States, we have observatories like Mona Lao on the Big Island in Hawaii; ice cores being taken in the Northern and Southern oceans; sediment cores being taken in oceans, seas, and lakes everywhere; and institutions and organizations such as NOAA, Scripps in California, Woods Hole Oceanographic in Massachusetts, Lamont-Doherty Earth Observatory in New York, and NASA.

One of the more interesting and surprising observatories is a small Icelandic container ship that normally you wouldn't give a second thought about. This is the M.V. Skogafoss, shown in Figure 13-2.

Figure 13-2. *The Icelandic container ship M.V. Skogafoss southbound in the Cape Cod Canal. From a painting by the author.*

The Skogafoss is a small Icelandic container ship that has been designed to service small ports along the Canadian Maritimes and the East Coast of the United States. She was named after a waterfall, the Skogafoss, on the Skoga River in Iceland. Notice on the port side the cranes that are used to load and unload containers in small ports that do not have container handling facilities. Starting at her home port in Reykjavik, she travels south as far as Florida, probably distributing Icelandic fish along the way down and returning to Reykjavik full of fruits and vegetables. Then she repeats the cycle, over and over. The reason for our interest in her is that she is outfitted with an extensive array of scientific equipment that measures environmental parameters of interest to climate scientists. As Skogafoss travels, this data is sent in real time to NOAA. Since she normally travels the same route, her measurements are of special importance since they allow the detection of changes in the environment over time. Very smart. We can assume there are other ships, probably aircraft as well, gathering data for NOAA.

The Piston Corer

Core samples of marine sediment are important to climate scientists since they can reveal events far back in the past. The standard *piston corer* is an important tool for capturing and retrieving cores in the benthic environment. It is reliable, inexpensive, and easy to use if you have the shipboard machinery capable of lowering it over the side and to the bottom, even in rough weather, and then pulling it out of the sediment and back to the ship where the core sample is removed for later examination. In the ocean environment, a substantial ship is usually required.

As icebergs float along the coasts of Canada, occasionally they run aground and sever an underwater communications or utility cable. The John Cabot, a Canadian ice-breaker-cable-repair ship, has a large wheel on her bow and powerful winches. She dredges up the severed ends of the broken cable and splices them back together. Because of her capabilities, she was chartered by Woods Hole Oceanographic Institution to help scientists attempt to take the world's longest core sample in sediment in the North Atlantic. The author served as Chief Engineer on the expedition. Sediment cores give us the opportunity to essentially look back in time; the longer the core, the further back you can look.

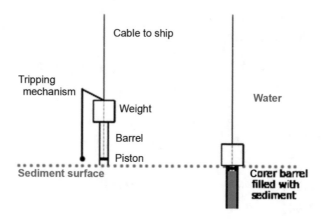

Figure 13-3. *Operation of a piston corer produced by Listing 13-1*

Shown in Figure 13-3 is a typical piston corer. It is a simple but effective device, lowered to the bottom by a cable that is tied to a ship above. As shown on the left, before penetrating the sediment a clamp holds the corer to the cable in this position. The piston inside the barrel is near the tip. When the corer hits the bottom, a tripping mechanism releases the clamp holding it to the cable and it falls. The weight inside the box above pushes the barrel into the sediment, filling it with sediment. Because the piston is held in place by the cable at the top of the sediment, it stays at the surface, creating a vacuum inside the falling barrel. This draws the sediment into the barrel rather than pushing it aside. After retrieving the corer, the sediment sample inside, which is held inside a plastic liner in the barrel, is removed and cut in half, exposing the core for various types of tests and examinations.

Listing 13-1 draws Figure 13-4.

Listing 13-1. Operation of a Piston Corer

```
#----------------------------Listing 13-1, piston corer
import numpy as np
import matplotlib.pyplot as plt

plt.axis([-75,75,50,-50])

plt.axis('off')
plt.grid(False)

#-------------------------------sediment surface
for x in np.arange(-65,65,3):
    plt.scatter(x,20,s=5,color="g")

#---------------------------------------left corer
plt.arrow(-30,0,0,-10) #--------------weight
plt.arrow(-20,0,0,-10)
plt.arrow(-30,-10,10,0)
plt.arrow(-30,0,10,0)

plt.arrow(-27,0,0,20) #----------------barrel
plt.arrow(-23,0,0,20)

plt.plot([-26.5,-24],[17,17],linewidth=3,color='k')  #--piston

plt.arrow(-25,-10,0,-40,linewidth=.5)  #------------cable
plt.arrow(-25,-10,0,27,linewidth=.5,linestyle=':')

plt.arrow(-25,-10,-10,-5) #-----tripping mechanism
plt.plot([-35,-35],[-15,17],color='k')
plt.scatter(-35.04,17,s=20,color='k')

plt.text(-20,-40,'cable to ship')#-----labels
plt.text(-18, -5,'weight')
plt.text(-20,9,'barrel')
plt.text(-20,18,'piston')
plt.text(-64,-18,'tripping')
plt.text(-64,-13,'mechanism')
```

```
#-----------------------------------------right corer
plt.arrow(30,20,0,-10) #--------------weight
plt.arrow(40,20,0,-10)
plt.arrow(30,10,10,0)
plt.arrow(30,20,10,0)

plt.arrow(33,20,0,20,linewidth=4,head_length=0) #-----------------barrel
plt.arrow(37,20,0,20,linewidth=4,head_length=0)

plt.plot([33.5,36],[21,21],linewidth=3,color='k')   #--piston

plt.arrow(35,10,0,-60,linewidth=.5)   #-------------cable
plt.arrow(35,10,0,30,linewidth=.5,linestyle=':')

for y in np.arange(23,40,1): #-------------fill barrel with sediment
    plt.plot([33.5,36],[y,y],linewidth=3,color='g')

    plt.text(44,25,'corer barrel')
    plt.text(44,30,'filled with')
    plt.text(44,35,'sediment')

    plt.text(45,-10,'water', color='b')
    plt.text(-65,25,'sediment surface',color='g')

#-------------------------------------------labels
plt.arrow(-25,-10,-10,-5) #-----tripping mechanism
plt.plot([-35,-35],[-15,17],color='k')
plt.scatter(-34.9,s=20,color='k')

plt.text(-20,-40,'cable to ship')#-----labels
plt.text(-18, -5,'weight')
plt.text(-20,9,'barrel')
plt.text(-20,18,'piston')
plt.text(-64,-18,'tripping')
plt.text(-64,-13,'mechanism')

plt.show()
```

The Global Energy Balance

Figure 13-4 shows the basics of the Earth's global energy balance. Proceeding from left to right, irradiation q from the Sun strikes the Earth. When it hits the top of the atmosphere, it is equal to the solar constant, q, about 1.37×10^3 W/m². As it passes through the atmosphere and strikes the Earth, aerosols and clouds plus various albedo features of the Earth's surface reflect about 30% of q back into space. The remaining 70% heats the Earth. The Earth, being a warm/hot body, reradiates some of its thermal energy in the form of infrared radiation, IR. The influx of energy to the Earth is thus,

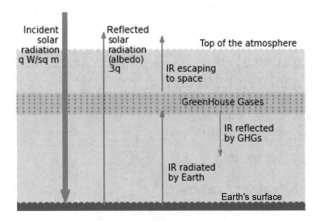

Figure 13-4. *The global energy balance*

$$\text{INFLUX} = \pi a^2 q(1-A) \qquad (13\text{-}1)$$

where a=.637x10⁷ meters is the mean radius of Earth, A=.3 is the average albedo, and q=1.37x10³ W/m². A is a function of the light-reflecting properties of the Earth's atmosphere and surface reflecting properties. For example, clouds, dust, and other aerosols in the atmosphere may reflect or absorb light depending on their specific characteristics. Surface ice and snow reflect it, dark jungles absorb it, and so on. Table 13-1 shows values for various surface features. Taken together, the net effect is that about 30% of the incoming light is reflected back into space. This number has been confirmed by satellite.

For the Earth's average temperature to remain more or less constant, the influx in Equation 13-1 must be balanced by an equal amount of outgoing thermal radiation. According to the Stefan-Boltzmann Law, the thermal radiation emitted by the planet is

$$\text{OUTFLUX} = 4\pi a^2 \sigma T_e^4 \tag{13-2}$$

where σ is the Stefan-Boltzmann Constant = 5.67×10^{-8} (Watts/m^{2}K^4) and T_e is the Earth's surface temperature.

In Equation 13-1, πa^2 is the cross-sectional area of Earth. This is the area facing the Sun and is what captures the Sun's radiation. In Equation 13-2, $4\pi a^2$ is the total global surface area of Earth; this is what radiates thermal energy out into space.

Since INFLUX = OUTFLUX at thermal equilibrium, combining Equations 13-1 and 13-2,

$$\pi a^2 q (1-A) = 4\pi a^2 \sigma T_e^4 \tag{13-3}$$

After rearranging,

$$T_e = \left(\frac{q(1-A)}{4\sigma} \right)^{1/4} \tag{13-4}$$

With the values of q, σ and A stated above, Equation 13-4 gives a value for Earth's equilibrium temperature T_e=255°K. This is -18°C, well below freezing. However, the observed global temperature averaged over time and surface area is about +14°C or 287°K. This is 32°C greater than predicted above. The difference is due to the greenhouse effect. Without it we would all have frozen long ago. Also, note that the greenhouse gases in the atmosphere are more transparent to the frequencies of light which comprise the incoming solar radiation than to the outgoing thermal infrared (IR) radiation.

As you can see with the simple model displayed in Figure 13-1, if there were no greenhouse gases or clouds or aerosols in the atmosphere, the IR would pass out into space and the Earth would reach a thermal equilibrium temperature lower than what is today. But the GHGs capture some of the IR energy that is trying to leave. A smaller amount thus passes through the GHGs and escapes to outer space. The part captured by the GHGs excites their molecules, allowing them to store the energy, like little glowing light bulbs which shine some of that energy back at Earth. This is the mechanism by which some of the energy is reradiated back to Earth. There have always been GHGs in the atmosphere. It's the excess amount, produced mostly during the past century, that has been creating an excess amount of IR returning to Earth. This is what causes global warming. It results in an amount of heating reaching the Earth's surface that is above what has been necessary to sustain global equilibrium temperatures in the past.

Listing 13-2 draws Figure 13-5.

In Figure 13-5, the words identifying the arrows are right justified when they appear to the left of an arrow while those appearing to the right are left justified. The left-justified lines are easy. But how do we do the right justified ones? In the "text" section in the script below, the bold lines show how. The "s" says what is to be justified; the "rjust" says to the right, the number in the parentheses says how much space to leave.

Listing 13-2.   Draws Figure 13-5

```
s='incident'
plt.text(-74,-40,s.rjust(10))

#-------------------------------global energy balance
import numpy as np
import matplotlib.pyplot as plt

plt.axis([-75,75,50,-50])

plt.axis('off')
plt.grid(False)

#--------------------------------------------------sky
for x in np.arange(-75,75,3):
    for y in np.arange(-30,47,2):
        plt.scatter(x,y,s=50,color='lightblue')

#-----------------------------------------------ground
for x in np.arange(-75,75,3):
    for y in np.arange(50,47,-2):
        plt.scatter(x,y,s=50,color='#A52A2A')

#----------------------------------greenhouse gases
for x in np.arange(-75,75,3):
    for y in np.arange(0,-10,-2):
        plt.scatter(x,y,s=50,color='lightgreen')
for x in np.arange(-75,75,3):
```

```
    for y in np.arange(0,-10,-2):
        plt.scatter(x,y,s=1,color='green')

#-----------------------------------------------arrows
plt.arrow(-50,-50,0,91,linewidth=5,head_length=3,head_width=2,color='r')
plt.arrow(-30,48,0,-85,linewidth=1,head_length=3,head_width=2,color='r')
plt.arrow(-0,48,0,-45,linewidth=1,head_length=3,head_width=2,color='r')
plt.arrow(-0,-10,0,-25,linewidth=1,head_length=3,head_width=2,color='r')
plt.arrow(30,0,0,20,linewidth=1,head_length=3,head_width=2,linestyle=':',color='r')

#-----------------------------------------------text
plt.text(20,-33,'top of the atmosphere')
plt.text(10,-3,'GreenHouse Gases')
plt.text(30,45,'Earths surface')
s='incident'
plt.text(-74,-40,s.rjust(10))
s='solar'
plt.text(-74,-35,s.rjust(12))
s='radiation'
plt.text(-74,-30,s.rjust(10))
plt.text(-74,-25,'q W/sq m')

plt.text(-28,-40,'reflected')
plt.text(-28,-35,'solar')
plt.text(-28,-30,'radiation')
plt.text(-28,-25,'(albedo)')
plt.text(-28,-20,'.3q')

plt.text(3,30,'IR radiated')

plt.text(3,35,'by Earth')

plt.text(32,10,'IR reflected')
plt.text(32,15,'by GHGs')

plt.text(2,-20,'IR escaping')
plt.text(2,-15,'to space')

plt.show()
```

The Rising Oceans

Will the melting of floating icebergs cause ocean water levels to rise? No, it will not. Floating icebergs have already displaced the water; when they melt, they just go from ice back to liquid. The berg's ice projecting above the water surface just compensates for the lighter density of ice vs. water. When the berg melts, it will shrink by the amount of ice projecting above the surface. It will not add any volume to the water. The real problem is the melting of ice that is not floating in the oceans but is supported by land as ice sheets and glaciers. Another significant contributor to rising sea levels is the thermal expansion of water as its temperature increases. In this section, you will assess how much we can expect the sea level to rise due to the thermal expansion of the seawater.

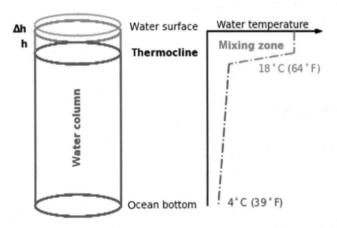

Figure 13-5. *Water column with thermocline showing the rise in water level Δh caused by an increase in water temperature. Drawn by Listing 13-3*

Shown in Figure 13-5 is what oceanographers refer to as a water column. This is an imagined column of water from the sea surface to the bottom. The red portion is the part above the thermocline, which is the depth of rapid transition from warmer to colder water. What creates the thermocline? Because of its lower density, warmer water rises to the top of the water column. This is called the mixing zone since wave action and surface currents mix the water in this zone. It is mostly separated from the water below by its lower density. Also, the mixing effect of wave action and surface currents only influences the water close to the surface. As water temperature increases in the mixing zone, the water in this zone will expand. This will cause the water level at the surface to rise. The question is, how much will it rise?

We will assume that only the water above the thermocline will be affected. This is a major question in climate science; to what depth is the water affected by global warming and how much will it warm? We will assume for now that only the water above the thermocline is affected although thermocline depths can change and vary widely depending on location.

The coefficient of *volumetric* thermal expansion of water, β, gives the amount a volume of water will increase with temperature. It is not a constant but increases with temperature. This means that as the water gets warmer, its *rate* of swelling will also increase. The coefficient of thermal expansion for seawater is about $2.3 \times 10^{-4}/°C$ at an average water temperature of 18°C. It will be greater for temperatures above 18°C. This value of β, which is for seawater, is somewhat higher than for freshwater due to the presence of salt ions that are dissolved in the water. They tend to repel one another and increase β.

Before heating, the volume of water above the thermocline is

$$Vo = Ah \qquad (13\text{-}5)$$

where Vo is the unheated volume of the water above the thermocline, A is the cross-sectional area of the water column, and h is the depth from the surface to the thermocline. After heating, the volume is $Vo+\Delta V$ where ΔV is the change in volume. The change in volume is

$$\Delta V = \beta Vo\Delta T = \beta Ah\Delta T \qquad (13\text{-}6)$$

where ΔV is the change in volume and ΔT is the change in temperature. Since the water in the water column is constrained by the surrounding water (it's all expanding), ΔV has nowhere to go but up, so the change in height, Δh, is

$$\Delta h = \frac{\Delta V}{A} \qquad (13\text{-}7)$$

$$\Delta h = \beta h\Delta T \qquad (13\text{-}8)$$

Inserting $\beta=2.3\times10^{-4}/°C$ and $\Delta T=1.0°C$ into Equation 13-8 we get the following values for the rise in sea level for different values of thermocline depth h:

Assumed Thermocline Depth h (m)	Ocean Surface Rise Δh (cm) for ΔT=1.0°C
75	1.7
200	4.6
1000	230

There isn't much uncertainty in this model or this calculation; it's quite straightforward. The only question is the depth we assume for the thermocline. It seems unlikely that we will see the oceans warming a full degree C to a depth of 1000 meters (6000 feet) any time soon. So if we expect a warming of 1°C to a depth of 200 meters, we are looking at a sea level rise of about 4.6 cm. If we expect a temperature increase to the thermocline of about 2°C, we may be looking at a sea level rise of 9-10 cm sometime in the future caused by swelling of the ocean's waters.

Before we forget, we still have to cope with one of the most critical effects of climate change: the melting of land-supported ice and snow and its runoff into the oceans. Greenland looks to be an especially problematic area in this regard. According to the National Snow and Ice Data Center (NSIDC.org), at its thickest point, the Greenland Ice Sheet measures over 3 kilometers (1.9 miles) thick and contains about 2.9 million cubic kilometers (696,000 cubic miles) of ice. If the entire Greenland Ice Sheet melted and the water found its way to the oceans, sea levels would rise about 7.4 meters (24 feet).

Listing 13-3. The Rising Oceans

```
plt.text(43,-22,r'18$^\circ$C (64$^\circ$F)',color='r')
        ^\circ is the temperature symbol. This line says 18°C (64°F)
plt.text(-42,20,'water column',rotation=90,weight='bold',color='b')
        The rotation=90 attribute rotates the text 90 degrees.
        The weight=bold attribute makes the text bold.
plt.text(-70,-40,'\u0394h', weight='bold')
        The \u0394 is Unicode for Δ

#--------------------------------------------------Listing 13-11 The
Rising Oceans
import numpy as np
```

```python
import matplotlib.pyplot as plt

plt.axis([-75,75,50,-50])

plt.axis('off')
plt.grid(False)

a=20
b=5
p1=0
p2=180*np.pi/180
dp=.2*np.pi/180

#---------------------------------------------------------------Ellipse
xplast=a
yplast=0
for p in np.arange(p1,p2,dp):
    xp=np.abs(a*b*(b*b+a*a*(np.tan(p))**2.)**-.5)
    yp=np.abs(a*b*(a*a+b*b/(np.tan(p))**2.)**-.5)
    if p>np.pi/2.:
        xp=-xp
    plt.plot([xplast-40,xp-40],[yplast-40,yp-40],color='r')
    plt.plot([xplast-40,xp-40],[-yplast-40,-yp-40],color='r')
    xplast=xp
    yplast=yp

#---------------------------------------------------------------Ellipse
xplast=a
yplast=0
for p in np.arange(p1,p2,dp):
    xp=np.abs(a*b*(b*b+a*a*(np.tan(p))**2.)**-.5)
    yp=np.abs(a*b*(a*a+b*b/(np.tan(p))**2.)**-.5)
    if p>np.pi/2.:
        xp=-xp
    plt.plot([xplast-40,xp-40],[yplast-40+10,yp-40+10],color='b')
    plt.plot([xplast-40,xp-40],[-yplast-40+10,-yp-40+10],color='b')
    xplast=xp
    yplast=yp
```

```
    plt.plot([-60,-60],[-40,-30],color='r')
    plt.plot([-20,-20],[-40,-30],color='r')

#--------------------------------------------------------------Ellipse
xplast=a
yplast=0
for p in np.arange(p1,p2,dp):
    xp=np.abs(a*b*(b*b+a*a*(np.tan(p))**2.)**-.5)
    yp=np.abs(a*b*(a*a+b*b/(np.tan(p))**2.)**-.5)
    if p>np.pi/2.:
        xp=-xp
    plt.plot([xplast-40,xp-40],[yplast+40,yp+40],color='b')
    plt.plot([xplast-40,xp-40],[-yplast+40,-yp+40],color='b')
    xplast=xp
    yplast=yp

    plt.plot([-60,-60],[-30,40],color='b')
    plt.plot([-20,-20],[-30,40],color='b')

    plt.plot([-60,-60],[-30,40],color='b')
    plt.plot([-20,-20],[-30,40],color='b')

#--------------------------------------------------------------Ellipse
xplast=a
yplast=0
for p in np.arange(p1,p2,dp):
    xp=np.abs(a*b*(b*b+a*a*(np.tan(p))**2.)**-.5)
    yp=np.abs(a*b*(a*a+b*b/(np.tan(p))**2.)**-.5)
    if p>np.pi/2.:
        xp=-xp
    plt.plot([xplast-40,xp-40],[yplast-43,yp-43],linestyle='-.',color='r')
    plt.plot([xplast-40,xp-40],[-yplast-43,-yp-43],linestyle='-.',color='r')
    xplast=xp
    yplast=yp

    plt.plot([-60,-60],[-30,40],color='b')
    plt.plot([-20,-20],[-30,40],color='b')
```

```
#------------------------------------------------------------Temperature  axis
plt.plot([20,20],[-40,40],color='k')
plt.arrow(20,-40,50,0,head_length=3,head_width=2,color='k')

#------------------------------------------------------------Thermocline
plt.plot([60,60],[-40,-30],linestyle='-.',color='r')
plt.plot([60,30],[-30,-25],linestyle='-.',color='r')
plt.plot([30,25],[-25,40],linestyle='-.',color='b')

#------------------------------------------------------------labels
plt.text(25,-42,'water temperature',color='k')
plt.text(-15,-41,'water surface')
plt.text(25,-32,'mixing zone',weight='bold',color='r')
plt.text(-16,41,'ocean bottom')

plt.text(43,-22,r'18$^\circ$C (64$^\circ$F)',color='r')
plt.text(29,40,r'4$^\circ$C (39$^\circ$F)',color='b')

plt.text(-42,20,'water column',rotation=90,weight='bold',color='b')
plt.text(-14,-29,'thermocline',weight='bold', color='k')

plt.text(-67,-33,'h', weight='bold')
plt.text(-70,-40,'\u0394h', weight='bold')

plt.show()
```

The Global Climate Model

The simple global climate model shown in Figure 13-6 represents the Earth as a lumped mass having a uniform temperature and uniformly distributed thermal properties. Even though we know these are not uniformly distributed, it is a fair representation if we take them to be effective global averages. We assume the Earth has reached a state of thermal equilibrium and its temperature is not changing under the influence of whatever GHGs are present in the atmosphere. But how much will Earth's temperature change if the GHGs change? We can write the following equation:

$$C\frac{\Delta T}{dt} + \lambda \Delta T = \Delta Q \tag{13-9}$$

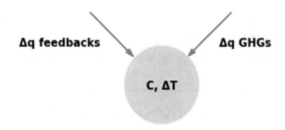

Figure 13-6. *A simple global climate model*

C is the Earth's heat capacity; ΔQ is the additional heating caused by a change in GHGs; ΔT is the temperature change caused by ΔQ; and $\lambda \Delta T$ is the influence of albedos. Equation 13-10 is saying the increase in heating, ΔQ, caused by a change in GHGs is going into heating the Earth plus albedo effects. I highlight the word *change* to emphasize that, in the above equation, we are concerned with *changes* in atmospheric levels of GHG and T. Rewriting (13-10)

$$C\frac{\Delta T}{dt} = \Delta Q - \lambda \Delta T \tag{13-10}$$

The quantity $\lambda \Delta T$ is a feedback term. It represents the albedo processes that occur in response to ΔQ. When λ is positive, we see from Equation 13-11 that the term $\lambda \Delta T$ <u>subtracts</u> from ΔQ, providing less heating and a cooling effect.

If we restrict this discussion to CO_2 being the only GHG that will change, then regarding vegetation, an increase in CO_2 in the atmosphere would result in additional growth of vegetation, which absorbs CO_2. This would decrease CO_2 levels and subtract from the greenhouse effect (positive λ, negative feedback). If λ is negative, it will add to the heating. For example, the melting of reflective snow and ice exposes darker material beneath such as tundra. This has a warming effect (negative λ, positive feedback). The total λ is a summation of IR radiation and albedos,

$$\lambda = \lambda_{IR} + \lambda_{vegetation\ growth} + \lambda_{cloud\ cover} + \lambda_{melting\ of\ snow\ and\ ice} + \ldots \tag{13-11}$$

Table 13-2 shows some albedos. These numbers should be considered rough estimates, useful for illustrative purposes. They will presumably be refined and more will be known with further research.

Table 13-2. *Albedos*

Feature	IR Radiation (W/m²)/°K	Albedo λ (W/m²)/°K
IR emission into space	+3.7	
Water vapor	-1.3	-.24
Cloud cover	unknown	Unknown
Cloud top height	unknown	Unknown
Melting Ice and snow	unknown	-.26
Vegetation growth	unknown	Unknown
Total	**+2.4**	**-.5**

Why isn't the IR emission into space that arises from the additional heating caused by an increase in GHGs larger? After all, 30% of the Sun's irradiation is reradiated back into space by Earth's albedos. Why is the IR reradiation from the temperature increase caused by GHG so small? It is because as the IR rises from Earth's surface, some of it is reflected back down by the GHGs; they reflect some of their additional stored heat back to the Earth's surface where it is reradiated back into the GHGs and so on. This reduces the amount of heat that leaves Earth.

Data about albedo effects is scattered. As an example, the albedo of vegetation growth depends on the type of vegetation, where it is growing, the season of the year, and other factors. Perhaps it is too soon to give it an average number for such an albedo on a global scale. The same is true for ice and snow.

Earth's heat capacity C is also uncertain. Earth stores energy in the atmosphere, the ground, and in water, mainly the oceans. Here are some numbers:

Component	C (Watt-years)/(m²°K)
Ground to 3 meters	.04
Atmosphere	.3
Oceans: surface to 45 meters	4.0
Oceans: 45-450 meters	40
Oceans: 450-bottom meters	300

The role played by the oceans in storing energy is very important and overwhelms the other components. And this is strongly a function of the depth of water we assume is storing the energy. As explained earlier, most heating of seawater takes place above the thermocline. If we assume this is at a depth of 45 meters, we will take 4.0 as the figure to use for that component. The value of C we will use is therefore

$$C = .04 + .3 + 4.0 = 4.34 \qquad (13\text{-}12)$$

Next we will turn our attention to ΔQ, the additional atmospheric heating caused by an increase in the level of CO_2 in the atmosphere. The units of ΔQ are Watts/m². In 1990, the level of CO_2 was 350 ppm. It is estimated to increase to 600 ppm sometime between 2030 and 2080. If we take 2055 as the year that level is reached, we can write the following relation for CO_2 vs t in years:

$$CO_2(t) = 350 + \frac{600 - 350}{65} t = 350 + 3.84\, t \qquad (13\text{-}13)$$

where t is the time in years from 1990. Thus we see that, with the above estimates, the rate of increase of CO_2 in the atmosphere will be about 3.84 ppm per year. It is known that the additional heat trapped In the atmosphere increases logarithmically with CO_2,

$$\Delta Q = 4 = A \ln\left(\frac{CO_2(t)}{CO_2(t=0)}\right) = A \ln(2) \qquad (13\text{-}14)$$

where A is a constant. It is also calculated that increases in CO_2 add about 4 Watts/m² to ΔQ for every doubling of CO_2. Thus,

$$4 = A \ln(2) \qquad (13\text{-}15)$$

$$A = 5.77 \qquad (13\text{-}16)$$

Combing the above, Equation 13-15 becomes

$$\Delta Q = 5.77 \ln\left(\frac{350 + 3.84t}{350}\right) \qquad (13\text{-}17)$$

$$\Delta Q = 5.77 \ln(1 + .011t) \qquad (13\text{-}18)$$

Rewriting Equation (13-10),

$$\frac{\Delta T}{dt} + \frac{\lambda}{C}\Delta T = \frac{\Delta Q}{C}$$
(13-19)

With Equation (13-19),

$$\frac{d\Delta T}{dt} + \frac{\lambda}{C}\Delta T = \frac{5.77}{C}\ln\left(1+.011t\right)$$
(13-20)

Over a time span of 100 years the function ln(1+.011t) on the right side of Equation (13-21) is almost linear. It can be approximated by

$$\ln\left(1+.011t\right) \cong .00742\,t$$
(13-21)

Inserting (13-22) into (13-21),

$$\frac{d\Delta T}{dt} + \frac{\lambda}{C}\Delta T = .0428\,\frac{t}{C}$$
(13-22)

This equation is easily solved by Laplace transforms. Transforming both sides,

$$S\Delta T(s) - \Delta T(0) + \frac{\lambda}{C}\Delta T(s) = \frac{.0428}{C}\frac{1}{s^2}$$
(13-23)

ΔT(0) is the temperature change at time=0 (1990), which we are taking as our reference point, so

$$\Delta T(0) = 0$$
(13-24)

Rearranging (3-24) gives us

$$\Delta T(s) = \frac{.0428}{C}s^2\left(s + \lambda/C\right)$$
(13-25)

Taking the inverse of (13-26) by partial fractions

$$T(t) = \frac{.0428\tau^2}{C}\left[\frac{t}{\tau} - \left(1 - e^{-t/\tau}\right)\right]$$
(13-26)

where $\tau = C/\lambda$ is the time constant (years). τ is a measure of how fast or slowly the system responds to an input. A larger value of τ implies a larger thermal inertia. For example, if there is a surge in GHG heating at time t=0, the resulting temperature change ΔT will reach 63.2% of its full value when t=τ. If τ is larger, the system will take longer to reach that amount. In our model, which is represented by Equation 13-26, $\tau = C/\lambda$. The larger the Earth's heat capacity, the longer it will take ΔT to reach its final value since more of the heat input caused by the surge in GHG is being absorbed by Earth, mostly by the oceans. Choosing a greater depth for the thermocline gives a larger C and a larger time constant.

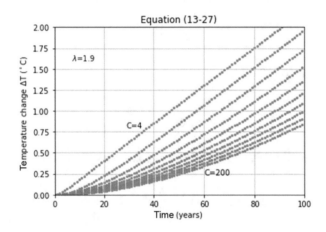

Figure 13-7. *Solution of Equation 13-26, produced by Listing 13-4*

Figure 13-7 shows the solution of Equation 13-26, produced by Listing 13-4. C is the Earth's heat capacity (watt-years/m²-°K). λ=1.9 is the sum of the Earth's albedos (watts/m²-°K). It is assumed there occurs a doubling of CO_2 in the atmosphere at time t=0. This increase in CO_2 adds about 4 Watts/m² of additional global warming which produces a global temperature increase ΔT as shown above for various values of C. For example, the value C=4 corresponds to a change in the heating of the oceans to a thermocline depth of 45 meters. After 20 years' time, the Earth's global average temperature would be expected to rise by about .40°C above the temperature at t=0. As expected, for greater values of C, the Earth's temperature change responds more slowly. Heat capacity C thus acts as a thermal inertia; it slows things down. It is emphasized that this analysis and the results shown are very uncertain due to the lack of reliable data for almost all the parameters involved. This analysis is presented to show a simple methodology for making climate predictions. See Listing 13-4.

Listing 13-4. Display of Equation 13-26

```
#----------------------Listing 13-12 display of equation 13-26
import numpy as np
import matplotlib.pyplot as plt

plt.axis('on')
plt.grid(True)

plt.axis([0,100,0,2])

#--------------------------------------------------------------------solution
lam=1.9 #----lambda

for c in np.arange(4,200,20): #---c=Earth's heat capacity
    tau=c/lam #------------------tau-time constant
    for t in np.arange(0,100,1):        #----t=time
        dt=(.0428*tau*tau/c)*((t/tau)-(1.0-np.exp(-t/tau)))
        #-temperature change
        plt.scatter(t,dt,s=5,color='r')

#------------------------------------------------------------labels
plt.xlabel('time (years)')
plt.ylabel('temperature change \u0394T ($^\circ$C)')
plt.text(7,1.60,r'$\lambda$=1.9')

plt.title('Equation (13-27)')
plt.text(60,.24,'C=200')
plt.text(29,.8,'C=4')

plt.show()
```

Summary

You reviewed the history of Earth's temperature fluctuations—the heatings and the coolings. You saw evidence of this in paintings of artists of the past. You also saw how environmental data is collected today. You learned that the most troubling threat posed by global warming is Greenland with its 1.9 mile thick icesheet. What happens when it melts and we have to cope with a sea level rise of 24 feet? We can learn as much as we can, but what are we going to do about it? The cause of this problem is undisputable; it is anthropogenic. It looks like the solution will also have to be anthropogenic. Reducing greenhouse gases rising into the atmosphere may be one solution, but what about all the CO_2, methane, and all the other GHGs that are already up there? Electric vehicles will help, but the electricity has to come from somewhere. Windmills and solar panels will help but what happens when the wind doesn't blow and the Sun doesn't shine? There has to be a backup system for such an event, or a lot of batteries, which means we will have to have parallel energy systems of renewables and fuel-powered. This will cause electricity to be much more expensive, radically changing our lifestyle. Or, and this may be inevitable, we may have to go back to nuclear power. As the problem is anthropogenic, the solution will likely have to be anthropogenic as well.

CHAPTER 14

Population Dynamics

This chapter contains several programs that simulate population dynamics in population biology and ecology. It could be a population of people, whales, or aphids, any population that experiences growth that occurs in discrete steps or in a continuous process.

Sequential Growth

Program GGROWTH plots the change in size of a population that follows a sequential growth process. The change in size of the population from one generation to the next occurs in discrete steps, in a sequence, and there is no overlap between generations. The human population of the United State, for example, is not an example of sequential growth since the overall size of the population is changing continuously. Populations of perennial plants are an example of sequential growth since each generation grows during a well-defined growing season, the time between generations being one year.

Equation 14-1 (a geometric equation) is an elementary model that can be used to describe this type of growth process:

$$N(i) = (ggr) N(i-1) \qquad (14\text{-}1)$$

This says the size of the population in the ith generation is simply a multiple of the size of the preceding (i-1) generation. The quantity ggr is called the geometric growth rate. It equals the difference between births and deaths from one generation to the next:

$$ggr = births - deaths \qquad (14\text{-}2)$$

© Bernard Korites 2023
B. Korites, *Python Graphics*, https://doi.org/10.1007/978-1-4842-9660-8_14

Equations 14-1 and 14-2 form an elementary model since they assume

- The growth *rate* does not depend on the size of the population.

- The growth rate does not depend on the population's age structure.

- The size of generation (i) depends only on ggr and the size of generation (i-1). The delayed effects of generations more than one year previous are ignored. See Figure 14-1.

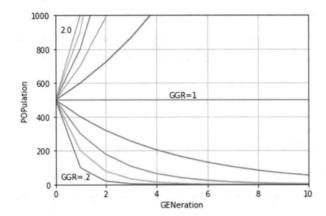

Figure 14-1. *Population vs. generations for 10 geometric growth rates ranging from .2 – 2.0 in steps of .2. The starting population is 500. When GGR=1, there is no change in the population with generations since we have defined GGR according to Equation 14-1. If GGR < 1, each successive generation will be smaller than the preceding one so the population will eventually go extinct. For GGR > 1, the population will increase indefinitely. As can be seen from the GGR=2 curve, with GGR=2 the population doubles in one generation going from 500 to 1000. This graphic was produced by Listing 14-1*

In the section "Lists" below, the generation gen[ ] and population pop[ ] lists are defined. gen has 11 elements including the initial 0th one. They are defined sequentially as 0, 1, 2......10. The pop list has the same number of elements but the values shown are dummies; they just serve to define the number of elements in the pop list and will be replaced. The first loop cycles the geometric growth rate, ggr, from .2 to 2 in steps of .2. The value shown in the for ggr loop in section "Lists" is 2.01, not 2.0, because Python rounds off errors and that final value will be missed without the .01 added to 2.0. pop[0] is the starting population. Lists, including plotting with lists, are discussed in Chapter 1. The heart of this program is the equation pop[i]=pop[i-1]*ggr, which takes the population from one generation to the next.

Listing 14-1.   Geometric Growth Rate

```
#----------------------------------------------------------Listing GGR
import numpy as np
import matplotlib.pyplot as plt

plt.axis([0,10,0,1000])
plt.axis('on')
plt.grid(True)

#---------------------------------------------Lists
gen=[0,1,2,3,4,5,6,7,8,9,10]
pop=[0,1,2,3,4,5,6,7,8,9,10]

for ggr in np.arange(.2,2.01,.2): #pop vs gen for 10 GGRs
    pop[0]=500                    #--initial population
    for i in np.arange(1,11):     #-calculate POP for 11 gen's
        pop[i]=pop[i-1]*ggr       #-----Eqn (14-1)

    plt.plot(gen,pop)    #--plot pop vs gen for 11 values of GGR

#--------------------------labels
plt.xlabel('GENeration')
plt.ylabel('POPulation')
plt.text(4.5,515,'GGR=1')
plt.text(.2,30,'GGR=.2')
plt.text(.2,900,'2.0')

plt.show()
```

Plants

Plant growth is an example of sequential growth with age dependence. Program PLANTS plots the change in the population of perennial plants which come up every year. The growth model here includes the influences of the past two generations including differences in seed production, survival, and germination rates. This concept could easily be extended to include more than two generations or other types of populations that follow a sequential growth model with more elaborate age-dependent properties.

Each summer the growing season produces a new generation of plants. Starting with a population N(0), the following summer you will have N(1) plants. During the next summer, you will have N(2) plants and so on such that during the ith growing season you will have N(i) plants. These will all be elements of the N[] list.

At the end of each summer, the population leaves behind **spr,** seeds per plant. Spr is called the seed production rate. During the following winter, a quantity of these seeds will die from the weather and other environmental factors such as disease and predation. The fraction of seeds that survive the winter is **wsr**, the winter survival rate. During the following spring only a fraction of these surviving seeds will germinate and produce new plants. These are "one-year seeds." They germinate at the rate of **grl** plants per seed. Some of these seeds will survive two years. These are called "two-year seeds" and they germinate and produce new plants at the rate **gr2** plants per seed. (Assume seeds more than two years old do not germinate.)

Program PLANTS plots the growth or decline in the plant population for specified values of the above parameters. It also plots the number of seeds available for germination at the beginning of each summer growing season.

Equation 14-3 is the growth model for this process. It expresses the relation between the number of plants during the ith growing season, N(i), and the number during the preceding two seasons, N(i-1) and N(i-2):

$$N(i) = (gr1)(wsr)(spr)N(i-1) + (gr2)(wsr)(1-gr1)(wsr)(spr\}n(i-2)$$

$$= (\text{contribution of 1 year seeds}) + (\text{contribution of 2 year seeds}) \qquad (14\text{-}3)$$

While Equation 14-3 looks complicated, it can be easily understood by examining the two terms on the right side. The first is the contribution of one-year seeds (those dropped in the soil in year (i-1)) to the plant population in growing season i. The second is the contribution of two-year seeds (those dropped in year (i-2). Table 14-1 explains this.

Table 14-1. *Explaining the Equation*

(spr)N(i-1)	Number of seeds produced by plants at the end of the previous growing season
(wsr)(spr)N(i-1)	Number of seeds that survived the previous winter (one-year seeds)
(gr1)(wsr)(spr)N(i-1)	Number of one-year seeds that germinate to produce new plants during the ith growing season
(spr)N(i-2)	Number of seeds produced two seasons ago
(wsr)(spr)N(i-2)	Number that survived the winter two winters ago
(1-gr1)(wsr)(spr)N(i-2)	Number that survived the winter two winters ago and did not germinate the following growing season
(wsr)(1-gr1)(wsr)(spr)N(i-2)	Number of these that survived the following winter (two-year seeds)
(gr2)(wsr)(1-gr1)(wsr)(spr)N(i-2)	Number of two-year seeds that germinated to produce new plants during the ith growing season

Spr (seed production rate) and wsr (winter survival rate) are assumed to be the same for both generations (i-1) and (i-2). Germination rates gr1 and gr2 are different since you would expect older gr2 seeds to have a lower rate of germination. See Figure 14-2.

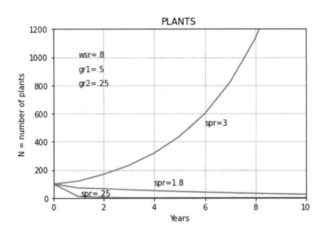

Figure 14-2. *The growth in a population of plants for three different seed production rates (spr). Winter survival rate wsr=.8, germination rate for the previous generation gr1=.5, for the second previous generation gr2=.25. Curves show that for a spr = .25, the population will quickly die out; for spr = 1.8, it will eventually die out; and for spr = 3, the population will grow. These curves are dependent on the winter survival rate (wsr) and growth rates for the two previous generations (gr1 and gr2). Produced by Listing 14-2, PLANTS*

Listing 14-2. Program PLANTS

```
#--------------------------------------------------------------PLANTS
import numpy as np
import matplotlib.pyplot as plt

plt.axis([0,10,0,1200])
plt.axis('on')
plt.grid(True)

wsr=.8
gr1=.5
gr2=.25

#------------------------------------------Lists
gen=[0,1,2,3,4,5,6,7,8,9,10]
N=[0,1,2,3,4,5,6,7,8,9,10]
```

```
#------------------------------------------------------------spr=.25
spr=.25
N[0]=100
N[1]=spr*wsr*gr1*N[0]
N[2]=spr*wsr*gr1*N[1]+spr*wsr*wsr*gr2*(1-gr1)*N[0]
for i in np.arange(3,11,1):
    N[i]=spr*wsr*gr1*N[i-1]+spr*wsr*wsr* gr2*(1-gr1)*N[i-2]

plt.plot(gen,N, color='g')

#------------------------------------------------------------spr=1.8
spr=1.8
N[0]=100
N[1]=spr*wsr*gr1*N[0]
N[2]=spr*wsr*gr1*N[1]+spr*wsr*wsr*gr2*(1-gr1)*N[0]
for i in np.arange(3,11,1):
    N[i]=spr*wsr*gr1*N[i-1]+spr*wsr*wsr* gr2*(1-gr1)*N[i-2]

plt.plot(gen,N, color='g')

#------------------------------------------------------------spr=3
spr=3
N[0]=100
N[1]=spr*wsr*gr1*N[0]
N[2]=spr*wsr*gr1*N[1]+spr*wsr*wsr*gr2*(1-gr1)*N[0]
for i in np.arange(3,11,1):
    N[i]=spr*wsr*gr1*N[i-1]+spr*wsr*wsr* gr2*(1-gr1)*N[i-2]

plt.plot(gen,N, color='g')

#--------------------------labels
plt.xlabel('Years')
plt.ylabel('N = number of plants')
plt.text(6,515,'spr=3')
plt.text(4,90,'spr=1.8')
plt.text(1.1,13,'spr=.25')
```

```
plt.text(1,1000,'wsr=.8')
plt.text(1,900,'gr1=.5')
plt.text(1,800,'gr2=.25')

plt.title('PLANTS')

plt.show()
```

Insects

In this section, you consider the case of a population that follows a sequential growth model where the net growth rate (births-deaths) is not constant but is dependent on the size of the population. As the size increases, there will be increased competition for food between the members of the population, improved efficiency of predators, and so on, causing the death rate to increase and the birth rate to decrease. As a result, the net birth rate will decrease. As an example, consider a population of aphids that follows a growth model of the following form:

$$N(i+1) = g\big[N(i)\big]N(i) \tag{14-4}$$

$$gr\big[N(i)\big] = a\text{-}bN(i) \tag{14-5}$$

where gr[N(i)] is the net growth rate (births-deaths) and a and b are constants.

If there is no effect of population size on the growth *rate* gr, b will be zero and a will be equivalent to ggr, the geometric growth rate as defined in Listing 14-1. That is the *intrinsic* growth rate that occurs when there is no influence on the growth rate from population size. The parameter b in Equation 14-5, which accounts for the influence of population size on growth rate, will normally be greater than zero, implying that the net growth rate decreases as the population size increases. If b is negative, the rate of growth will increase with population size, a condition you could define as explosive growth. b will normally be much smaller than a since it is multiplied by N(i) in Equation 14-5 and N(i) is normally a large number. Inserting Equation 14-5 into Equation 14-4 gives the growth model

$$N(i+1) = \big[a - bN(i)\big]N(i) \tag{14-6}$$

Example 1 is shown in Figure 14-3.

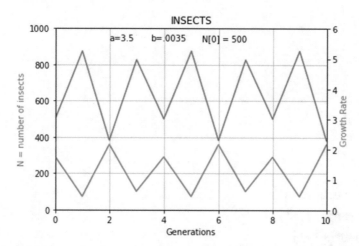

Figure 14-3. *This plot shows the population of insects that follow the growth model Equations 14-5 and 14-6. It was produced by Listing 14-3. The population starts off at 500. As it increases to the first generation, the growth rate gr in Equation 14-5 decreases such that after the first generation the population decreases. The population size N is shown in green and the growth rate gr is shown in red. As N decreases, the growth rate increases. Then the population recovers and the cycle starts again*

Of interest in this listing is the method of setting up and labeling dual vertical axes. The relevant lines are shown in bold.

Listing 14-3. Program INSECTS

```
#------------------------------------------------------------INSECTS
import numpy as np
import matplotlib.pyplot as plt

plt.axis([0,10,0,1000])
plt.axis('on')
plt.grid(True)

#-------------------------------------------Lists
gen=[0,1,2,3,4,5,6,7,8,9,10]
N=[0,1,2,3,4,5,6,7,8,9,10]
```

```
gr=[0,1,2,3,4,5,6,7,8,9,10]

a=3.5
b=.0035
N[0]=500

gr[0]=a-b*N[0]
N[1]=gr[0]*N[0]
gr[1]=a-b*N[1]
N[2]=gr[1]*N[1]

plt.xlabel('Generations')
for i in np.arange(2,11,1):
    gr[i-1]=a-b*N[i-1]
    N[i]=gr[i-1]*N[i-1]
    print(i,'gr[i-1]=',gr[i-1],N[i])

gr[10]=a-b*N[10]

plt.ylabel('N = number of insects', color='g')
plt.plot(gen,N,color='g')

plt.twinx()
plt.ylabel('Growth Rate',color='r')
plt.axis(ymax=6)
plt.plot(gen,gr,color='r')

#---------------------------------------------------------title
plt.title('INSECTS')
plt.show()
```

Example 2:

Try another run but this time with the following numbers:

$$N[0] = 100$$
$$a=3.25$$
$$b=.0034$$

Except for the size of the initial population N[0], these numbers are the same as before but they produce a much different response. See Figure 14-4.

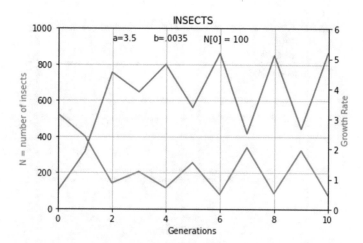

Figure 14-4. *The nature of the response has changed from oscillatory to one that exhibits a rapid rise to almost a steady state in only two generations. It then continues on as oscillatory. Since parameters a and b in this example are almost the same as in Example 1, you can infer that you are near some sort of a transition point*

Example 3:

Here you extend the number of generations to 50 and look at the response for a = 2.7, 3.0, 3.3, and 3.5. See Figures 14-4 through 14-8.

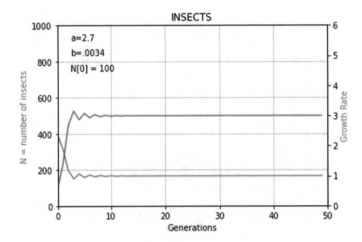

Figure 14-5. *Here a=2.7. The response starts off oscillatory but dies out to a steady state; the growth rate decreases to a steady state of 1. As you would expect in the steady state, the population neither increases nor decreases*

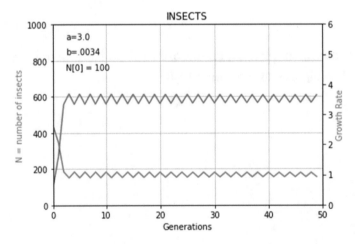

Figure 14-6. *Here a=3.0. The population rises to slight oscillations around a steady state of about 590*

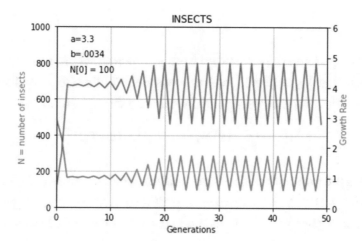

Figure 14-7. *Here a=3.3. The population rises to a steady state of about 680 and then changes into violent oscillations*

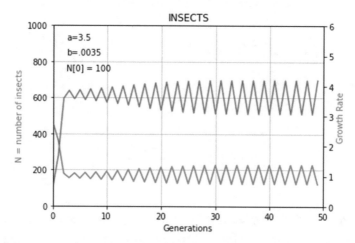

Figure 14-8. *Here both the population and the growth rate gradually build up to increasing oscillations*

It appears that slight changes in population size interact with the size-dependent growth rate to induce oscillations in the population. In fact, it can be shown that a value of a=3.0 is the transition point. When a is above 3.0, oscillations or chaotic behavior will result. When a is less than 3.0, oscillations may not occur or, if they do, they will eventually die out.

Whales

The following analysis and data are taken from *Mathematical Biology* by J.D. Murray (Springer-Verlag, New York; 1989). The International Whaling Commission models the population dynamics of the baleen whale by the following equation:

$$N(t) = (1 - mr)N(t-1) + R[N(t-TD)]1 \qquad (14\text{-}7)$$

where N(t) is the population of sexually mature whales at time t, mr is the mortality rate, and (1-mr)N(t-1) is the fraction of whales that survive from year to year. Note that N(t) is not the entire population of baleen whales; it is the population of only the sexually mature ones. It takes several (TD) years for newborn whales to reach maturity. The second term on the right is the number of whales who were born TD years earlier and who are just reaching maturity and contributing to the population of adults at time t. This term, which introduces a time delay TD into the dynamics, is

$$R[N(t-TD)] = \frac{1}{2}(1-mr)^{TD} N(t-TD)\left\{ P + Q\left[1 - \left(\frac{N(t-TD)}{K} \right)^{z} \right] \right\} \qquad (14\text{-}8)$$

The quantity

$$\left\{ P + Q\left[1 - \left(\frac{N(t-TD)}{K} \right)^{z} \right] \right\} \qquad (14\text{-}9)$$

is the *fecundity* (number of offsprings produced per adult female) of female whales at time t-TD. K is the equilibrium population that would result with no harvesting and P is the equilibrium fecundity that occurs when N(t-TD) = K. Q and z are parameters that account for the changes in fecundity with change in population. The fecundity decreases when the population rises above the equilibrium value of K and increases when populations fall below equilibrium. It reaches a maximum when the population falls to very low values.

The fecundity is multiplied by the number of adult females in the population of adult whales at time t-TD. Assuming there are as many females as males, this is N(t-TD)/2. Thus the quantity

$$\frac{N(t-TD)}{2}\left\{P+Q\left[1-\left(\frac{N(t-TD)}{K}\right)^{z}\right]\right\} \tag{14-10}$$

is the number of offspring produced in the year t-TD. Since these baby whales must survive TD years in order to reach maturity at time t, you multiply the above by $(1-mr)^{TD}$ to get the number of baby whales that survive to maturity and contribute to the population in year t.

Typical numbers for the parameters are

mr = .04

TD = 6

K = 600,000

Q = .9

P is not independent but is related to mr and TD since, at equilibrium

$$N(t) = N(t-1) = K \tag{14-11}$$

Inserting Equation 14-11 into Equation 14-7 with Equation 14-8 gives

$$P = 2mr(1-mr)^{-TD} \tag{14-12}$$

Using the values above you get

$$P = .102 \tag{14-13}$$

Listing 14-4 calculates P automatically using Equation 14-12. See Figure 14-9.

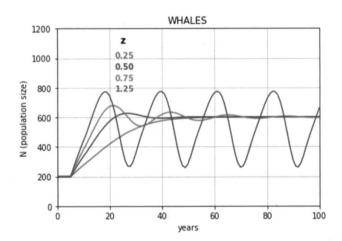

Figure 14-9. *This figure was drawn by Listing 14-4. It shows the growth in the population of baleen whales that have reached sexual maturity after TD=6 years. N is the population of sexually mature whales. In this figure, you assume their numbers are unchanged while they grow to maturity. This is the horizontal line from 0 to TD, which is six years in Listing 14-4. After that time, they join the rest of the whale population and contribute to its growth. The parameters Q and z determine the fecundity, the number of offspring produced per adult female whale, of the adult whale population. The response is quite sensitive to z as shown above where the growth curves transition from smooth (green and blue) to oscillatory (red and purple) as z increases. This is to be expected since z is a strong parameter in Equation 14-10, which gives the number of offspring produced in the year t-TD*

Listing 14-4. Program WHALES

```
#-----------------------------------------------------------WHALES
import numpy as np
import matplotlib.pyplot as plt

plt.axis([0,100,0,1200])
plt.axis('on')
plt.grid(True)

#-----------------------------------------Lists
gen=[]
n=[]
```

```
for i in range(101):
    gen.append(i)
    n.append(i)

#-----------------------------------------------------parameters
mr=.04
TD=6
K=600
Q=.9
nstart=200

#---------------------------------------------------axes
plt.axis([0,100,0,1200])
plt.axis('on')
plt.grid(True)

#----------------------------------------------- starting values
for i in range(0,6,1):
    gen[i]=i
    n[i]=nstart

#------------------------------------------------analysis
p=2*mr*(1-mr)**-TD

z=.25
for i in np.arange(TD,101,1):
    a=(1-mr)*n[i-1]
    b=.5*n[i-TD]*(1-mr)**TD
    c=p+Q*(1-(n[i-TD]/K)**z)
    n[i]=a+b*c
    gen[i]=i
plt.plot(gen,n,color='g')

z=.50
for i in np.arange(TD,101,1):
    a=(1-mr)*n[i-1]
    b=.5*n[i-TD]*(1-mr)**TD
    c=p+Q*(1-(n[i-TD]/K)**z)
```

```
    n[i]=a+b*c
    gen[i]=i
plt.plot(gen,n,color='b')

z=.75
for i in np.arange(TD,101,1):
    a=(1-mr)*n[i-1]
    b=.5*n[i-TD]*(1-mr)**TD
    c=p+Q*(1-(n[i-TD]/K)**z)
    n[i]=a+b*c
    gen[i]=i
plt.plot(gen,n,color='r')

z=1.25
for i in np.arange(TD,101,1):
    a=(1-mr)*n[i-1]
    b=.5*n[i-TD]*(1-mr)**TD
    c=p+Q*(1-(n[i-TD]/K)**z)
    n[i]=a+b*c
    gen[i]=i
plt.plot(gen,n,color='purple')

#-------------------------------------------------------labels
plt.title('WHALES')
plt.xlabel('years')
plt.ylabel('N (population size)')

plt.text(24,1100,'z',size='large',fontweight='bold',color='k')
plt.text(22,1000,'0.25', fontweight='bold',color='g')
plt.text(22,925,'0.50', fontweight='bold',color='b')
plt.text(22,850,'0.75', fontweight='bold',color='r')
plt.text(22,775,'1.25', fontweight='bold',color='brown')

plt.show()
```

Summary

In this chapter, you learned how to model and plot the growth of a population. Four Python programs were developed: GGROWTH plots the change in size of a population that follows a sequential growth process; PLANTS charts growth according to a sequential growth process with age dependence; INSECTS concerns where the growth rate is dependent on the size of the population; and WHALES covers where the growth rate of a population of baleen whales follows dynamics specified by the International Whaling Commission. You also saw how to plot population dynamics on charts having two vertical axes.

CHAPTER 15

Resource Management

This chapter is about the development of programs that simulate various principles and techniques for the management of resources that are subject to harvesting. Examples are fisheries, wildlife, and so on. All programs assume logistic growth of the population.

Program LG: Logistic Growth with No Harvesting

This program plots the change in size of a population that follows a logistic growth process. There is no harvesting in this model. Growth is assumed to proceed in a continuous fashion rather than in discrete steps. Such a process is representative of populations where generations overlap as opposed to those where reproduction takes place only at distinct time intervals. The equation for this process is

$$\frac{dN}{dt} = RN\left(1 - \frac{N}{K}\right) = f(N) \tag{15-1}$$

where t is time, N is the population size in units of the species (such as number of trees, acres of biomass, number of fish, etc.), R is the net intrinsic growth rate (births minus deaths), and K is the carrying capacity of the environment.

Program LG plots the solution N vs t from Equation (15-1). It also plots f(N)=dN/dt, the growth rate function, vs. N. See Figure 15-1.

© Bernard Korites 2023
B. Korites, *Python Graphics*, https://doi.org/10.1007/978-1-4842-9660-8_15

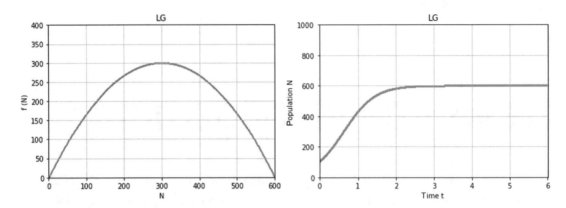

Figure 15-1. *Plots of the logistic growth rate function f(N) vs N (green) and population N vs. time t (red)*

Figure 15-1 was drawn by Listing 15-1, Program LG. There is no harvesting (i.e., H=0 in Listing 15-2, Program CHR). As you will see in the next section, Program CHR does incorporate harvesting. Parameters here are R=2, K=600, and Nstart=100. N grows to a steady state value of 600, which is where f(N) equals 0. f(N)=0 implies there is no further growth either up or down. The N vs. t curve (red) has an inflection point at about N=300. This is consistent with the transition of the f(N) vs. the N curve (green) from a positive slope to a negative one at N=300.

Listing 15-1. Program LG - Logistic Growth, No Harvesting

```
#-----------------------------------------------------------Listing LG
import numpy as np
import matplotlib.pyplot as plt

#----------------------------------------f(N) vs N
plt.axis([0,600,0,400])

plt.axis('on')
plt.grid(True)

R=2.          #----population growth rate
K=600.        #----carrying capacity of the environment

for N in np.arange(0,600,1):
    f=R*N*(1-N/K)                        #--------growth rate function f(N)
    plt.scatter(N,f,s=1,color='g')
```

```
plt.title('LG')
plt.ylabel('f (N)')
plt.xlabel('N')

plt.show()


#---------------------------------------N vs t (time)
plt.axis([0,6,0,1000])

plt.axis('on')
plt.grid(True)

Nstart=100.     #----------------starting size of the population
dt=.01              #---------------time increment
tmax=10.      #--------------maximum time

f=R*Nstart*(1-Nstart/K)          #------starting value of growth rate
function
N=Nstart+f*dt                    #----------population size at time dt
for t in np.arange(dt,tmax,.01):
        f=R*N*(1-(N)/K)
        N=N+f*dt
        plt.scatter(t,N,s=3,color='r')

plt.title('LG')
plt.ylabel('population N')
plt.xlabel('time t')

plt.show()
```

Program CHR: Logistic Growth with Constant Rate Harvesting

Figure 15-2 shows plots of growth rate function f(N) vs. N (green) and population N vs. time t (red) with a *constant rate of harvesting* equal to 100 as shown by the horizontal red line in the f vs. N plot. Parameters are R=2, K=600, and Nstart=100. This was drawn by the code in Listing 15-2 called Program CHR.

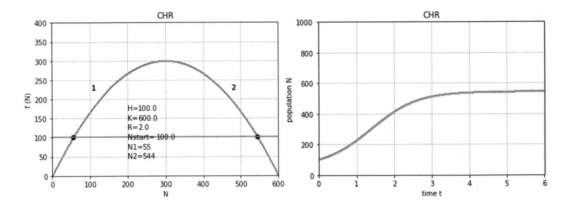

Figure 15-2. Drawn by Listing 15-2

What is a constant rate of harvesting? Think of a fishing boat, or a fleet of boats, catching codfish on Georges Bank, a relatively shallow area of the Continental Shelf between Cape Cod and Sable Island. If the fleet caught fish cumulatively at a more or less constant rate, that would be *constant rate harvesting*. Notice the population N does not reach K=600, the carrying capacity of the environment, as it did in the previous section where there was no harvesting. Figure 15-3 shows this program with Nstart=120, which is less than H, which equals 200. You can see the population goes quickly to 0. This is because the population never has the size necessary to overcome the harvesting rate H=200.

In the figure of f(N) vs. N, the black dots show the intersection of the growth function, which is a parabola, and the harvesting line H. This is a graphical solution to the equation

$$RN\left(1-\frac{N}{K}\right)=H \tag{15-2}$$

where the left side is a parabola and the right side is a horizontal line. Equation 15-2 can be rewritten as a quadratic equation:

$$N^2-KN+\frac{KH}{R}R=0 \tag{15-3}$$

This equation has two roots, N1 and N2. They are calculated in the program and used to plot the two black dots, which indicate the two solutions. They represent harvesting *equilibrium points*. Notice in the N vs. time curve that the population stabilizes at about N=545. This is consistent with the second equilibrium point, N2.

450

The net growth rate is the intrinsic growth rate minus the harvesting rate:

$$\text{Net Growth Rate} = RN\left(1 - \frac{N}{K}\right) - H \tag{15-4}$$

The net growth rate is the difference between the green parabola and the harvesting line shown in red. For a starting population level Nstart, which equilibrium point will be reached depends on the initial population level's value and the value of H. If it starts off below the left equilibrium point, the net growth rate will be negative and the population will decrease to zero. If it is above that level, the net growth rate will be positive and the population will grow to the equilibrium point on the right. The left equilibrium point is unstable since it doesn't matter how much the population is below or above that point, it will drop to extinction or grow to the right equilibrium point. The right point is stable since even small perturbations about it will cause the population to return to it. This can be seen from Equation 15-4 where the net growth rate can be positive depending on the relative values of the intrinsic growth rate and the harvesting rate. If positive, N will increase; if negative, it will decrease. If positive or negative, N will always go to the second equilibrium point. In Listing 15-2, parameters H and Nstart have been changed to produce the plots shown in Figure 15-3. N1 and N2 indicate the position of the equilibrium points along the N axis.

Figures 15-3 and 15-4 illustrate the *instability* of the first equilibrium point; Figures 15-5 and 15-6 indicate the *stability* of the second. Perturbation in N or H about the first equilibrium point will result in either extinction or growth of the population to the second equilibrium point. Perturbations about the second point result in a return of the population to that equilibrium.

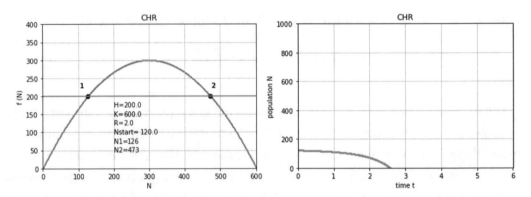

Figure 15-3. *N1=126 is the N location of point 1, the left equilibrium point and N2=473 of the right equilibrium point. These values were calculated within the program. Let Nstart = 120, just below N1 (i.e., to the left of point 1). According to the above discussion, you see on the right that the population goes to extinction as expected*

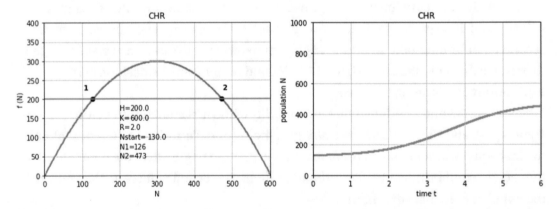

Figure 15-4. *Here Nstart is just to the right of N1 (i.e., greater than N1), the first equilibrium point. As expected, in the right plot the population is growing toward the second equilibrium point at N2=473*

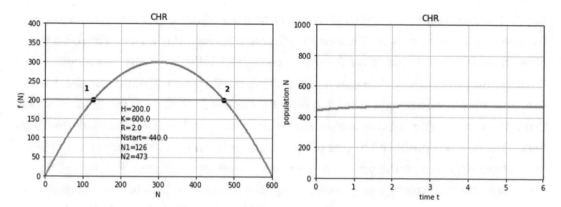

Figure 15-5. *Here you shift your attention to the second equilibrium point, which has a population value of N2=473. You start at Nstart=440, less than N2, the N value of the second equilibrium point. As expected, N vs. t shows the population initially trying to make up the difference and move from Nstart=440 toward the equilibrium value of 473*

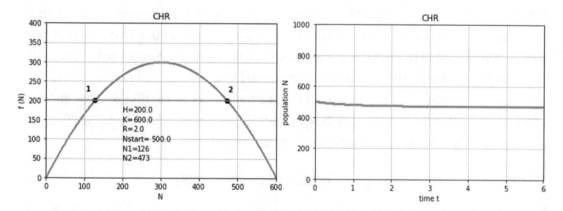

Figure 15-6. *Here you start at Nstart=500, just greater than the N value of the second equilibrium point. As expected, N vs. t shows the population decreasing and again moving toward the second point*

As a personal anecdote, if you have ever seen Penobscot Bay in Maine, which is 40 miles long and 20 miles wide, you would expect it must be full of fish. In the summer, there are plenty of migratory fish (mackerel, bluefish, and stripers) but there are no bottom fish (no cod, no haddock, and no flounder). I once spent a day bottom fishing there, among the rocks and islands. Caught nothing, not a bite, not even a nibble. The place seemed to be dead, beautiful but dead. A few years later I was aboard a schooner sailing down the

Bay in a pleasant summer southwest breeze. I asked the captain, why are there no fish in Penobscot Bay? He answered, "because the place was fished out years ago. The fish are gone, the habitat went next, and neither ever came back." Plenty of lobstahs though.

Regarding the side-by-side layout of the above plots, it was <u>not</u> done with the use of subplots. Subplots do not always give satisfactory results and they can be difficult to use. Doing it the old-fashioned way is often easier and gives good results. In the side-by-sides here, each pair was produced by one program, either LG or CHR. Python prints the two plots vertically, one over the other. Each one was saved separately as a file. To do this, right-click one of the plots, select Save, and specify a file name. This is done for each of the two plots and they are saved with separate file names. Then load MS Word or a similar word processing program. This entire book has been composed with MS Word. In Word, put your cursor where you want the plots to appear and click. Select Insert and then Table. Select the two boxes on the upper left of the dialog matrix. This gives a one-row, two-column table. Two empty boxes will appear on your Word page. Click one of them. Then click Insert again and select one of the two plots you saved. After it pops up in the frame box, adjust its size with the frame that appears around it, usually by dragging one of the corners. Then do the same to put the second plot in the second box. Finally, if you want to remove the frame lines, click the icon at the upper left of the table and select whatever you want to do with the frame lines.

Parameters Nstart and H have been changed to produce the various images above. Lines N1 and N2 in the listing solve the quadratic Equation 15-3 for N1 and N2. To try a different set of parameters, change their value in the program.

Listing 15-2. Logistic Growth - Constant Rate Harvesting

```
#------------------------------------------------------------Listing CHR
import numpy as np
import matplotlib.pyplot as plt
import math

#----------------------------------------f(N) vs N
plt.axis([0,600,0,400])

plt.axis('on')
plt.grid(True)
```

```
R=2.
K=600.
H=200.
Nstart=500.

for N in np.arange(0,600,1):
    f=R*N*(1-N/K)
    plt.scatter(N,f,s=1,color='g')

plt.text(103,223,'1',fontweight='bold')
plt.text(475,223,'2',fontweight='bold')


#---------------------------------------harvesting line
plt.plot([0,600],[H,H],color='r')

a=1
b=-K
c=K*H/R
N1=(-b-(b*b-4*a*c)**.5)/(2*a)    #-----------see Equation (15-3)
N2=(-b+(b*b-4*a*c)**.5)/(2*a)
N1=math.trunc(N1)  #-----trunc() is part of the math library that was
imported above.
N2=math.trunc(N2)  #-----trunc() removes the decimal places.

plt.scatter(N1,H,s=40,color='k')
plt.scatter(N2,H,s=40,color='k')

#-------------------------------------------labels
plt.title('CHR')
plt.ylabel('f (N)')
plt.xlabel('N')

#-------------------Print parameters on the plot
plt.text(200,170,'H=')
plt.text(227,170,str(H))    #----the str() function converts
                            #----the numeric H to a string enabling it to
                            be plotted on the plot.
```

```
plt.text(200,145,'K=')
plt.text(227,145,str(K))

plt.text(200,120,'R=')
plt.text(227,120,str(R))

plt.text(200,95,'Nstart=')
plt.text(275,95,str(Nstart))

plt.text(200,70,'N1=')
plt.text(238,70,str(N1))

plt.text(200,45,'N2=')
plt.text(238,45,str(N2))

plt.show()


#----------------------------------------N vs t (time)
plt.axis([0,6,0,1000])

plt.axis('on')
plt.grid(True)

dt=.01
tmax=6.

f=R*Nstart*(1-Nstart/K)
N=Nstart+f*dt
for t in np.arange(0,tmax,dt):
        f=R*N*(1-N/K)-H
        N=N+f*dt
        plt.scatter(t,N,s=3,color='r')

#-------------------------------------------labels
plt.title('CHR')
plt.ylabel('population N')
plt.xlabel('time t')

plt.show()
```

Summary

This chapter is about the development of programs that simulate various principles and techniques for the management of resources that are subject to harvesting. Examples are fisheries and wildlife. All programs assume logistic growth of the population. Two Python programs were developed. Program LG plots the change in size of a population that follows a logistic growth process. There is no harvesting in this model. Growth is assumed to proceed in a continuous fashion rather than in discrete steps. Such a process is representative of populations where generations overlap as opposed to those where reproduction takes place only at distinct time intervals. Program CHR plots the change in size of a population that follows a logistic growth process but is subject to a constant rate of harvesting. It shows how in this model there are two equilibrium points: one is unstable and the other is stable. Small perturbations about the unstable one can drive the population to extinction or to the stable point while perturbation about the stable point drive the population back to that point. These are important conditions that must be understood when setting harvesting policies.

CHAPTER 16

Ecological Diversity and Butterflies

What is ecological diversity? There are two components to ecological diversity. The first is species *richness*, which is simply the number of different species that are present in a community or population. In a population of butterflies, for example, these species might be Monarchs, Black Swallowtails, or Painted Ladies. Each is considered to be a separate species. The more species that are present in a particular environment, the richer the diversity of species within that environment. The second component of ecological diversity is relative *abundance*, which refers to the number of individuals that comprise each of the species present. Ten Monarch butterflies mean the species Monarch butterfly has an abundance of ten. Richness and abundance are terms frequently encountered in the study of ecological diversity.

Many studies of ecological diversity indices are concerned with only the species richness (i.e., the number of different species present in the population). A healthy environment could be expected to support a rich community, one where a wide variety of species are present. An environment that is harsh, on the other hand, whether due to extreme conditions such as extremely low or high temperatures, lack of moisture, or pollution, may be able to support only a few hardy species.

Butterflies are an important component of our ecology. They can be an important indicator of our ecosystem's health, changes within an ecosystem that may be due perhaps to local development, changes in atmospheric conditions, or climate change. Butterflies are also pollinating insects responsible, along with honeybees, for producing a third of the world's crops. They are also relatively abundant in the right places, easy to observe and identify, and are usually well-described in readily available field guides. Butterfly stalking makes a great hobby (at least Vladimir Nabakov, a noted lepidopterist, thought so). And if you have never seen a chrysalis, a fat, ugly, green, snail-like creature, morph into a beautiful Monarch butterfly right before your eyes, you are in for a treat. It's almost unbelievable. First, out of the slime pops a fully-formed wing, then....

In this chapter, you develop a program called RANK-ABUNDANCE that displays the results of a sampling in terms of the richness and abundance found. These quantities are representative of the environment's diversity. The term *diversity*, as it relates to ecology, refers to (1) the number of different species in a community, called the richness, and (2) the relative abundance of each species, or the way in which the population of individuals is distributed among the species. In some communities, a few dominant species may contain most of the individuals while in others a more even or equitable distribution may be the case.

As an example, consider a freshwater pond. Assume a period of sampling the fish in the pond produces 50 smallmouth bass and 5 trout. Even though they are all fish, the bass and trout represent different species. We would say the population of fish in that pond is not very rich since only two species, bass and trout, were found. We would also say the relative abundance of the species is not very diverse since the number of bass far outweighs the number of trout. A richer and more diverse population would be 50 bass, 40 trout, 40 sunfish, 45 perch, and 20 pickerel. In this example, we would have five species with a more equitable distribution of the number of fish between the species groups.

The rank of a species does not necessarily mean its number. It could be its biomass, the area of ground covered, the number of shellfish per acre, oak trees per acre, and such.

The RANK-ABUNDANCE program plots the number of species and their abundance in descending rank order based on their sample size. The sample size is a loosely defined variable that refers to *sampling effort* such as the number of trees sampled, acres of land, the length of time a trap is left open, the number of Black Swallowtail butterflies found, and so on. In the pond example above, we might have spent one day dragging the pond with a net to come up with the number of fish cited. If we had spent two days, we would presumably have netted more fish and the distribution of the species among the total pond population would likely have changed.

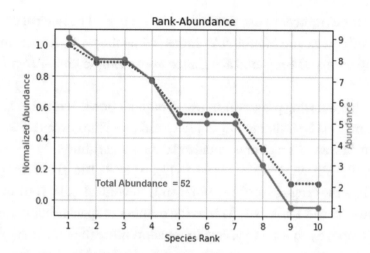

Figure 16-1. *Typical rank abundance chart*

Figure 16-1 might result from a morning field trip to a local meadow to find butterflies of different species and to count the number of each species found. On the horizontal axis, the numbers refer to the species in descending rank order. That is, number 1, the most abundant species, might represent Monarchs. It has rank 1 since more Monarchs were found than any other species. Looking at the first green dot on the left and the vertical axis on the right, 9 Monarchs were found. Each green dot represents, in descending order, the other species found. As can be seen from the horizontal axis, a total of 10 different species of butterflies were found. The total number of butterflies found on this trip was 52. The blue data points represent the normalized abundance; all abundance values are divided by the maximum, in this case by 9, the number of Monarchs. The program finds the most abundant species, automatically normalizes the other data, and plots the chart.

What can we infer from this chart? Without doing any statistical analysis, we can see there is moderately good richness; 10 species were found during a morning walk. If only 3 were found, the richness would be questionable. The abundance is not bad either; the total abundance of 52 is reasonably well-proportioned among the 10 species. In general, we could say that if the normalized abundance curve (blue) dropped off steeply, the abundance would not be equitably distributed among the species since most of the total abundance of 52 would be taken up by only a few species. If the curve was nearly horizontal, that would approach near-perfect distribution of abundance since there would be nearly an equal number of each species, similarly for the un-normalized green data.

There are various indices in use that serve as measures of ecological diversity, such as Margalef's Index and Menhinick's Index. While they will give a number, more information can perhaps be gleaned at a glance from a simple Rank-Abundance chart as above.

There are other charting programs in use. A popular one is Whittaker's Rank-Abundance chart. This is similar to our Rank-Abundance chart except it does not plot the raw abundance data and its plot of normalized data is logarithmic.

Program RANK-ABUNDANCE is shown as Listing 16-1. The plt.axis([.5,10.5,-.1,1.1]) defines the range of the horizontal and left vertical axes. The horizontal x axis, which is the Species Rank axis, defines the number of species being considered; it is set 10 here. Suppose you want to visit your meadow more than once, say for 10 days in a row. You will likely discover more species than the 10 found the first day so you might want to double the number of ranks to 20. The abundance of each species will also likely increase but that won't affect the normalized abundance since the maximum will always be one. But it will likely affect the vertical green scale on the right, which shows the abundance of each species.

The lists hold the raw input data and the sorted and normalized data. If you add more data, you will have to increase the size of these lists. R=[ ] holds the species ranks (horizontal axis); A=[ ] holds the abundance data (right green vertical); SA=[ ] is the sorted species abundance; and NSA=[ ] is the normalized sorted abundance data (left blue vertical). These will be the A[ ] data sorted into reverse (high to low) rank order with the statement SA=sorted(A,reverse=True) then normalized by finding the maximum in the list with the operator maxa=max(A) and dividing all elements in SA by maxa to get NSA[ ].

These lists are set to each hold 10 values. For larger samples, they will have to be increased. Rather than typing lots of zeros to define the list sizes, it is easier to use the structure A[0]*20, for example, which establishes the size of A to 20 and fills it with zeros.

Listing 16-1. Rank Abundance

```
#-------------------------------------------------------------Rank-Abundance
import numpy as np
import matplotlib.pyplot as plt
import math
```

```
plt.axis([.5,10.5,-.1,1.1])
plt.axis('on')
plt.grid(True)
plt.xticks(np.arange(1,11,1))
plt.xlabel('Species Rank')
plt.ylabel('Normalized Abundance',color='b')

#---------------------------------------------------------------lists
R=[1,2,3,4,5,6,7,8,9,10] #-----------------Species Rank
A=[5,8,1,5,5,7,3,9,8,1] #---------------------------Species Abundance
SA=[0,0,0,0,0,0,0,0,0,0]   #------------------sorted species abundance
NSA=[0,0,0,0,0,0,0,0,0,0]  #-------normalized sorted species abundance

#-----------------------------------sort Abundance descending order
SA=sorted(A,reverse=True) #-----------------------------reverse order

maxa=max(A) #-----------------------------------find maximum Abundance
for i in range(0,10,1):
    NSA[i]=SA[i]/maxa  #-------------------normalize sorted abundance

for i in range(0,10,1):   #-----------------------------------------plot
    plt.scatter(R[i],NSA[i],color='b')
    plt.plot(R,NSA,color='b',linestyle=':')

#--------------------------plot abundance on the right vertical axis
plt.twinx()
plt.ylabel('Abundance',color='g')

for i in range(0,10,1):
    plt.scatter(R[i],SA[i],color='g')
    plt.plot(R,SA,color='g')

#----------------------------------------------------total abundance
TA=sum(A)
TA=str(TA)
plt.text(2,2,'total abundance = ',color='g', fontweight='bold')
plt.text(5.1,2,TA,color='g',fontweight='bold')
```

```
#-----------------------------------------------------------labels
plt.title('Rank-Abundance')
plt.xlabel('Species Rank')

plt.show()
```

Summary

With this brief excursion into the field of ecological diversity, you have learned about the importance of *rank* and *abundance*. You have seen how to construct a plot with two vertical axes; how to get the sum of the elements in a list using sum(A); how to convert a numeric variable such as **TA** to a string using TA=str(TA) so that it can be plotted; and how to sort a string such as A into ascending rank order using SA=sorted(A) or into descending rank order using SA=sorted(A,reverse=True). You have also learned something about butterflies and their importance to our environment both as indicators of our environment's health and for their role, along with bees, in pollination. Like Vladimir Nabakov, you might decide to try butterfly collecting. We don't pin them to boards anymore, we capture their image with our phones.

APPENDIX A

Where to Get Python

There are several places on the Internet where you can download various versions of Python. I use Anaconda with Spyder[2] and Python 3.5. This is available for download from Continuum Analytics at `https://docs.continuum.io/anaconda/install`.

It's free and easy; just follow the instructions. While I use Python 3.5, I recommend using the latest version.

An icon should appear on your desktop. If it doesn't, look in your list of installed programs and drag it to the desktop. Double-click it to get the environment to run. You will be entering Python script in the left pane. After entering code for a program, click the Run button at the top or press the F5 key on your keyboard. You may be told to open a new console. Click the Consoles button at the top then select the "Open an IPython console" option to do so. Try to run it again. Results should appear in the pane at the lower right.

There is a pane at the upper right that shows the state of variables. I never use it; in fact, I close it to allow more room for output. If I want to see what a particular variable is doing, I usually put a `print` statement in the program. The variable's history will appear in the output pane.

If you find your program is doing unexpected things, it can sometimes help to open a new console and rerun the program.

© Bernard Korites 2023
B. Korites, *Python Graphics*, https://doi.org/10.1007/978-1-4842-9660-8

APPENDIX B

Planck's Radiation Law and the Stefan-Boltzmann Equation

In Chapter 10, you were introduced to Max Planck's famous equation of black body radiation:

$$S(\lambda) = \frac{2\pi c^2 h}{\lambda^5} \frac{\varepsilon}{e^{\frac{hc}{\lambda kT}} - 1} \quad J/s/m^3 = W/m^3 \tag{B-1}$$

The power emitted by a surface over a bandwidth $\lambda_1 \to \lambda_2$ is

$$P_{\lambda_1 \to \lambda_2} = \int_{\lambda_1}^{\lambda_2} S(\lambda) d\lambda \quad J/s/m^2 = W/m^2 \tag{B-2}$$

With Equation B-1, this becomes

$$P_{\lambda_1 \to \lambda_2} = 2\pi c^2 h \int_{\lambda_1}^{\lambda_2} \frac{\lambda^{-5}\varepsilon}{e^{\frac{hc}{\lambda kT}} - 1} d\lambda \quad J/s/m^2 = W/m^2 \tag{B-3}$$

In Chapter 10, you numerically integrated Equation B-3. Here you will mathematically integrate it and show that it can be used to derive the Stefan-Boltzmann Law of black-body radiation:

$$p = \frac{\varepsilon 2\pi^5 k_B^4}{15 h^3 c^2} T^4 \tag{B-4}$$

B. Korites, *Python Graphics*, https://doi.org/10.1007/978-1-4842-9660-8

where T is the surface's absolute temperature, p is power radiated per unit area, k_B is Boltzmann's Constant, h is Planck's Constant, c is the speed of light, and ϵ is the surface's emissivity. The power radiated from a surface of area A is then

$$P = pA = \varepsilon A \sigma T^4 \tag{B-5}$$

where

$$\sigma = \frac{2\pi^5 k_B^4}{15 h^3 c^2} = 5.6696x10^{-8} \quad W / m^2 / K^4 \tag{B-6}$$

σ is known as the Stefan-Boltzmann Constant. Equation B-4 relates power intensity radiated by a surface to the fourth power of its temperature, T. This equation is commonly used in science and engineering.

To carry out the integration that results in Equation B-4, you start with Planck's radiation equation:

$$S(\lambda) = \frac{2\pi hc^2}{\lambda^5} \frac{\varepsilon}{e^{\frac{hc}{\lambda \kappa_B T}} - 1} \tag{B-7}$$

You want to integrate this from λ=0 to λ=∞ to get the total power per unit area p radiated by all wavelengths. Letting $C_1 = \epsilon 2\pi hc^2$ and $C_2 = \frac{k_B T}{h}$, you get

$$p = C_1 \int_0^\infty \frac{\lambda^{-5} d\lambda}{e^{\frac{1}{C_2 \lambda}} - 1} \tag{B-8}$$

If you make the following substitutions,

$$x = C_2 \lambda, \quad dx = C_2 d\lambda \tag{B-9}$$

After a little fussing around, you have

$$p = C_1 C_2^4 \int_0^\infty \frac{dx}{x^5 \left(e^{\frac{1}{x}} - 1 \right)} \tag{B-10}$$

Using the well-known :) relation

$$\int_0^{\infty} \frac{dx}{x^5 \left(e^{\frac{1}{x}} - 1 \right)} = \frac{\pi^4}{15} \tag{B-11}$$

and substituting C_1 and C_2 into Equation B-10, you get

$$p = \frac{\varepsilon 2\pi^5 k_B^4}{15 h^3 c^2} T^4 \tag{B-12}$$

which is the same as Equation B-4 above.

Graphics and Math Functions Commonly Used in Graphics Programming with Examples

```
import math
import numpy as np
import matplotlib.pyplot as plt
from numpy import sin, cos,
radians....

from math import log, log10, e,
exp, pow, sqrt

  log(n)= log of n to the base e

  log10(n)=log of n to the base 10

  e=Euler's number=2.718

  exp(n)=e to the nth power=e^n
```

```
plt.scatter(x,y,attributes)
  s=size
  color='color')
  alpha=0-1 (intensity)
  plt.scatter(2,7,s=10,color='k', alpha=.7)

plt.plot([x1,x2],[y1,y2],attributes)
  linewidth = width  1,2,3,4,5,6,7,8....
  'color' = 'k', 'r', 'g', ' b'.......
  linestyle = :,  -.,  -
  plt.plot([2,3],[9,6],linewidth=5,
  "LINE STYLE" = ':',color='k')
```

B. Korites, *Python Graphics*, https://doi.org/10.1007/978-1-4842-9660-8

APPENDIX C   GRAPHICS AND MATH FUNCTIONS COMMONLY USED IN GRAPHICS PROGRAMMING
            WITH EXAMPLES

---

pow(a,b)=a to the power b:

pow(a,b)=a^b

sqrt(n)=square root of n = n$^{.5}$

abs(y) *absolute value of y.*
It is a built-in Python

  function and does not
  need to be imported

plt.axis([x1,x2,y1,y2])
  plt.axis([2,3,0,9])
    horizontal axis goes from
    2 to 3
    vertical axis goes from 0
    to 9
plt.axis ('on')
plt.axis('off')

plt.arrow(x,y,dx,dy,*attributes*)
  linewidth=*width*
  head_length=*length*
  head_width=*width*
  color='*color*'
  plt.arrow(4,5,7,7,linewidth=4,head_
  length=4, head_width=2,color='r')

color='k' *black*
color='b' *blue*
color='r' *red*
color='c' *cyan*
color='g' *green*
color='m' *magenta*
color='y' *yellow*
color='grey' or 'gray' *gray*
color='lightblue' *lightblue*
color='midnightblue' *midnight blue*

plt.grid(True,attributes) T *must*
be upper case
  plt.grid(True,color='b')
plt.grid(False)   F *must be upper case*

SA=sorted(A) *sorts list A low to high. Gives new list SA.*
SA=sorted(A,reverse=True) *sorts list A high to low gives*
a new list SA.

---

plt.title('title')	ta=sum(A) *sums elements in list A*
plt.title('title',color='color')	sa=str(a) *converts numeric a to a string for plotting*
plt.title('this is my chart	a=57
title',color='y')	sa=str(a)
	plt.text(3,7,sa,color='k',fontweight='bold')
plt.xlabel('x axis label')	
plt.xlabel('this is my x axis	X=[x1,x2,x3]
label',color='g')	Y=[y1,y2,y3]
plt.ylabel('y axis label')	plt.plot(x,y,attributes)
	Connects x1,y1 to x2,y2 to x3,y3 with lines.
	Both lists must have the same number of elements
plt.xticks(xmin,xmax,dx)	If numpy has been imported as
plt.xticks(0,70,10,color='r')	" import numpy as np" then
plt.yticks(ymin,ymax,dy)	x=np.radians(y)
	Converts y in degrees to x in
plt.xticks(np.	radians
arange(xmin,xmax,dx)	
plt.yticks(np.	If radians has been imported as
arange(ymin,ymax,dy)	"from numpy import radians" then
	x=radians(Y)
	x=np.inner(A,B)
	A and B are lists (vectors) of length n
	X=the scalar or dot product or the two
	lists
	=A[0]*B[0]+A[1]*B[1]+A[2]*B[2]+......
	A[n]*B[n]
	It is a Numpy function
Plt.show()	g=[0]*10 *opens list g having 10 elements*
	each equal to 0
	g=[0,0,0,0,0,0,0,0,0,0] *does the same*
	x=len(g) x=*the length of list g*

APPENDIX D

Setting up the Plotting Axes with plt.axis()

Problems can arise if the definitions of directions of the plotting axes specified by the `plt.axis()` function are not compatible with the definitions of directions in your analyses and Python program. Recall that the x,y,z directions of the axes must follow the right-hand rule. Rotate x into y through the smaller angle between the two and the z direction will be in the direction that would be taken by a right-handed screw turned clockwise. That is normally what you would be careful to do in your mathematical analyses and in your plotting commands. However, you must take care to see that the directions of the axes on Python's plotting screen follow the same directions as in your analysis and program. If they do not, problems can arise such as figures appearing upside-down, or right to left when they should be left to right, and rotations turning the wrong way. Regarding rotations, this is a particularly common problem with rotations about the z-axis direction.

Screen axes directions are normally specified through the `plt.axis([x1,x2,y1,y2])` function. For example, with `plt.axis([-75,+75,-50,+50])`, this will put the 0,0 coordinate in the center of the plotting area; the x-axis will go from left to right; the y-axis will go _up_. If you had set up the graphics commands in your Python program assuming the y-axis points _down_ (following the right-hand rule this makes the z-axes go _into_ the screen), your image will appear upside down. This is because you had set up the screen y-axis to point up in the `plt.axis()` function, which is opposite to what you had assumed in your program.

With rotations, let's assume you had, as above, set up the `plt.axis()` function to have the screen x-axis point from left to right while the y-axis points _up_ (the z-axis points out of the screen) but in your analysis and in your Python program your y-axis points _down_ (z-axis points into the screen). If you now specify in your program a rotation in the +Rz direction (i.e., a rotation about the z-axis which follows the right-hand rule) with

© Bernard Korites 2024
B. Korites, *Python Graphics*, https://doi.org/10.1007/978-1-4842-9660-8

the z-axis pointing out of the screen, the rotation would appear to go counter-clockwise while with the z-axis pointing into the screen, it will go clockwise. There's nothing wrong with rotations going clockwise or counterclockwise, as long as that is what you intend.

Normally, x would go from left to right, y would go down, and z would go into the screen. To get a clockwise Rz rotation with a positive number for Rz specified, use the following transformation in two dimensions:

$$Xp = xp*cos(Rz)\ yp*[-sin(Rz)]$$
$$Yp = xp*sin(Rz)\ yp*cos(Rz)$$

where xp and yp are the coordinates of the unrotated point p, which is located at the outer end of the line; Xp and Yp are the rotated coordinates. Figures D-1 and D-2 show rotating the coordinates of point p at the end of the line.

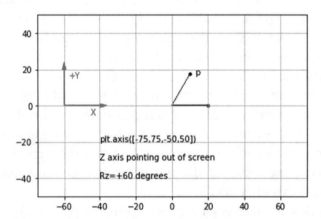

Figure D-1. *The black line starts out horizontal. After applying a positive rotation Rz, the line (dotted) rotates in the counter-clockwise direction. This is because, as defined in the plt.axis() function, the Y axis points up; this causes Z to point out of the screen making a positive Rz appear to turn counter-clockwise.*

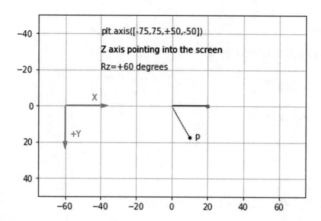

Figure D-2. *Here the +Y axis points down. Z, therefore, points into the screen; a +Rz rotation turns the line clockwise in accordance with the right-hand-rule.*

So you see that the direction of rotation seen on the screen is dependent not only on the mathematical analysis and on the programming but also on the directions of the coordinate axes as specified in the plt.axis() function. They must agree with one another.

Both Figures D-1 and D-2 were produced by Listing D-1.

Listing D-1. Code for Figures D1 and D2

```
#-------------------------------Listing D-1
import numpy as np
import matplotlib.pyplot as plt
from math import sin, cos, cos, radians

#------------------------------------------Figure (D-1)
plt.axis([-75,75,-50,50]) #--------------------------+Y goes up
plt.axis('on')
plt.grid(True)

xc=0
yc=0

xp=20
yp=0

Rz=60
```

```
Rz=radians(Rz)

plt.arrow(xc,yc,20,0,color='k')

xg=cos(Rz)*xp -sin(Rz)*yp

yg=sin(Rz)*xp +cos(Rz)*yp

xg=xg+xc
yg=yg+yc

plt.arrow(xc,yc,xg,yg,color='k',linestyle=':')

plt.text(-40,-20,'plt.axis([-75,75,-50,50])')

plt.arrow(-60,0,20,0,head_length=4,head_width=2,color='r')
plt.arrow(-60,0,0,20,head_length=4,head_width=2,color='r')
plt.text(-57,15,'+Y',color='r')
plt.text(-45,-5,'X',color='r')

plt.text(-40,-30,'Z axis pointing out of screen')
plt.text(-40,-40,'Rz=+60 degrees')

plt.show()

#--------------------------------------Figure (D-2)
plt.axis([-75,75,50,-50]) #----------------------------+Y goes down
plt.axis('on')
plt.grid(True)

plt.arrow(xc,yc,20,0,color='k')

xg=cos(Rz)*xp -sin(Rz)*yp

yg=sin(Rz)*xp +cos(Rz)*yp

xg=xg+xc
yg=yg+yc

plt.arrow(xc,yc,xg,yg,color='k',linestyle=':')

plt.text(-40,-40,'plt.axis([-75,75,+50,-50])')

plt.arrow(-60,0,0,20,head_length=4,head_width=2,color='r')
```

```
plt.text(-40,-30,'Z axis pointing into the screen')
plt.text(-40,-20,'Rz=+60 degrees')

plt.text(-57,17,'+Y',color='r')
plt.text(-45,-3,'X',color='r')

plt.show()
```

As explained, the appearance of a rotation about the z-axis appears different in the two cases even though everything is the same in the program except the plt.axis() function. This illustrates the importance of being attentive to the directions specified in the plt.axis() function.

Index

A

Aerosols, 395, 396, 400–404, 410, 411
Albedo, 393, 397, 398, 400–402, 410, 420, 421, 424

B

Butterflies
    components, 459
    See also Ecological diversity/butterflies

C

Climate cooling
    aerosols, 396, 400, 401
    albedo, 397, 398
    carbonaceous fuels, 396
    carbonaceous materials, 396
    Earth, 395
    evapotranspiration, 405
    features, 397
    global climate model
        albedos, 421
        atmospheric levels, 420
        components, 422
        constant, 422
        equation, 419, 423
        feedback term, 420
        IR radiation/albedos, 420
        Laplace transforms, 423
        program code, 424, 425
        representation, 420–425

Printed in the United States
by Baker & Taylor Publisher Services